YUGOSLAV GENERAL LINGUISTICS

LINGUISTIC & LITERARY STUDIES IN EASTERN EUROPE (LLSEE)

The emphasis of this scholarly series is on recent developments in
Linguistic and Literary Research in Eastern Europe; it includes analyses,
translations and syntheses of current research as well as studies in
the history of linguistic and literary scholarship.

Founding Editor: John Odmark †

General Editor:

Philip A. Luelsdorff
Institut für Anglistik
Universität Regensburg
D-8400 Regensburg
Federal Republic of Germany

Volume 26

Milorad Radovanović (ed.)

YUGOSLAV GENERAL LINGUISTICS

YUGOSLAV GENERAL LINGUISTICS

edited by

MILORAD RADOVANOVIĆ
University of Novi Sad

JOHN BENJAMINS PUBLISHING COMPANY
AMSTERDAM/PHILADELPHIA

1989

Library of Congress Cataloging-in-Publication Data

Yugoslav general linguistics / edited by Milorad Radovanović.

    p.   cm. -- (Linguistic & literary studies in Eastern Europe (LLSEE), ISSN 0165-7712; v. 26)

Bibliography: p.

1. Linguistics. 2. Linguistics -- Yugoslavia. 3. Yugoslavia -- Languages. I. Radovanović, Milorad, 1947-   . II. Series: Linguistic & literary studies in Eastern Europe; v. 26.

P125.Y84   1989

410 -- dc 19   88-7614

ISBN 90 272 1531 6 (alk. paper)   CIP

Contents

Editor's introduction   1

Dalibor Brozović
Some remarks on distinctive features: especially in Standard Serbo-Croatian   13

Ranko Bugarski
Generative structuralism   33

Rudolf Filipović
Some contributions to the theory of contact linguistics   47

Lajos Göncz
Psychological studies of bilingualism in Vojvodina   73

Milka Ivić
On referentially used nouns and the upgrading/downgrading of their identificatory force   91

Pavle Ivić
Structure and typology of dialectal differentiation   101

Pavle Ivić
Prosodic possibilities in phonology and morphology   111

Vladimir Ivir
Translation and backtranslation   131

Dunja Jutronić-Tihomirović
Language change in an urban setting   145

Damir Kalogjera
Some aspects of prescriptivism in Serbo-Croatian   163

Radoslav Katičić
Linguistic variety and relationship of languages   187

Melanie Mikes
Language contacts in multilingual Vojvodina   203

Janez Orešnik
Modern Icelandic vowel quantity revisited   227

Predrag Piper
Language in space and space in language   241

Milorad Pupovac
Between sign and act   265

Milorad Radovanović
Linguistic theory and sociolinguistics in Yugoslavia   279

Ljubiša Rajić
Language planning: theory and application   301

Svenka Savić
Psycholinguistics: research directions   321

Dubravko Škiljan
On linguistic autonomy   345

Olga Mišeska Tomić
Language contact, language system and language code   361

List of contributors

DALIBOR BROZOVIĆ
Marka Oreškovića 2
57000 Zadar
Yugoslavia

RANKO BUGARSKI
Dalmatinska 11
11000 Beograd
Yugoslavia

RUDOLF FILIPOVIĆ
Moše Pijade 42
41000 Zagreb
Yugoslavia

LAJOS GÖNCZ
Seljačkih buna 89
21000 Novi Sad
Yugoslavia

MILKA IVIĆ
Ohridska 7/IV
11000 Beograd
Yugoslavia

PAVLE IVIĆ
Ohridska 7/IV
11000 Beograd
Yugoslavia

VLADIMIR IVIR
Szabova 21/7
41000 Zagreb
Yugoslavia

DUNJA JUTRONIĆ-TIHOMIROVIĆ
Prilaz VIII korpusa 8
58000 Split
Yugoslavia

DAMIR KALOGJERA
Solovljeva 18
41000 Zagreb
Yugoslavia

RADOSLAV KATIČIĆ
Liebiggasse 5
A-1010 Wien
Österreich

MELANIE MIKES
Boška Buhe 10 B/III
21000 Novi Sad
Yugoslavia

JANEZ OREŠNIK
Janežičeva 21
61101 Ljubljana
Yugoslavia

PREDRAG PIPER
Vučedolska 4
11000 Beograd
Yugoslavia

MILORAD PUPOVAC
Hrgovići 77
41000 Zagreb
Yugoslavia

MILORAD RADOVANOVIĆ
Takovska 8
21000 Novi Sad
Yugoslavia

LJUBIŠA RAJIĆ
Trg Marksa i Engelsa 9
11000 Beograd
Yugoslavia

SVENKA SAVIĆ
Bulevar radničke samouprave 107
21000 Novi Sad
Yugoslavia

OLGA MIŠESKA TOMIĆ
Bulevar Avnoja 109/III st. 16
11070 Beograd
Yugoslavia

DUBRAVKO ŠKILJAN
Vitasovićeva poljana 6
41000 Zagreb
Yugoslavia

Editor's introduction*

Milorad Radovanović
Faculty of Philosophy, University of Novi Sad

The general developmental trends of linguistic studies during the course of the twentieth century could be presented concisely, at least in a theoretical, methodological and thematic sense, in the following way:

The first of half of the century was marked decisively by the dominance of structuralist orientations, theoretical, methodologial and thematic. Consequently, this was also a time of the culmination of the independence of linguistics as a science, implying also a time of its isolation from neighbouring disciplines in the study of man, and also a time of the isolation of language as a subject of research from other aspects of man's existence and expression (from the psyche, society, culture, etc.). Since the fifties the dominance of *structural linguistics* on a world scale began to be neutralized by *generative linguistics* and its theoretical, methodological and thematic orientations, making at least a step toward bringing linguistics back toward the neighbouring disciplines in the study of man (philosophy, logic and cognitive psychology) and also representing a return toward language as a subject of study to other aspects of man's existence and expression (thought, cognition, creation). The result of these processes is the current state of linguistics, in which both structural and generative linguistics are sometimes more or less 'isolationistically' oriented and therefore 'insensitive' to the pragmatic functions of language and to meaning and context, oriented at the present time (in the meantime they have evolved considerably in the cited sense) toward somewhat 'pragmatized', 'semanticized', 'contex-

* This Introduction was originally written in Serbocroatian. I wish to express my gratitude to Vladislava Felbabov (Faculty of Philosophy, University of Novi Sad) who translated it into English.

tualized', and (or) 'functionalized' research (understandably, in a theoretical, methodological, and a thematic sense). As a direct or indirect reaction to structural and (or) generative linguistics, from the sixties, and especially from the seventies up to the present, linguistic studies have become more and more interdisciplinary (understandably, once again, in a theoretical, methodological, and a thematic sense). This is, therefore, a time in which along with the still vital *structural* and *generative linguistics* various *interdisciplinary orientations* in the study of man and his language have produced the interdisciplines of the type *psycholinguistics, sociolinguistics, pragmalinguistics, philosophy of language*, etc., dominant today. In related areas of study linguistics is linking itself more and more directly with the neighbouring sciences of man (with *psychology, sociology, pragmatics, philosophy*, etc.) forming a connection, in this way, between language as its basic subject of study and the other aspects of man's existence and expression (the psyche, society, culture, thought, etc.). Such studies are, therefore, by definition 'pragmatized', 'semanticized', 'contextualized' and (or) 'functionalized', yet by their basic (inter)disciplinary status unstable, resulting not infrequently in a largely ununified and unstable disciplinary terminology (for instance, socio*linguistics, sociology* of language, linguistic *sociology*, psycho*linguistics*, social *psychology* of language, social psycho*linguistics*, pragma*linguistics*, linguistic *pragmatics*, etc.), uncoordinated conceptual and terminological apparatuses, methodologial procedures, demonstration techniques, metalinguistic symbols, theoretical standpoints, research aims, scopes of study and the like. This is, therefore, a time of quite inhomogeneous linguistic studies, disintegrated into many directions, and with very different motivations and hence corresponding results (this is, it would seem, most prominently manifested in the theoretical sense).

The future of linguistics probably does not lie in *structural linguistics, generative linguistics, psycholinguistics, sociolinguistics* or in any of the other mentioned or unmentioned, yet well known and current (inter)disciplinary studies. Its future, if it is at all possible to predict it at this moment, is a future in which by way of studies in the areas of *structural linguistics, generative linguistics, psycholinguistics* and *sociolinguistics* and related alternative (inter)disciplinary activities there will be a recrystallization into *a reintegrated linguistics* by the gradual removal of partitions which have been put up during its still current institutionalized parcellings. This future reintegrated linguistics can, understandably, still not be given a precise name. It seems wisest, considering the present knowledge of man and his language and the insight into the general laws of development of scientific thought, to expect that the form of this future science can rather validly be indicated, employing the terms available to us today, by choosing the least binding phrase in this regard: *contextual linguistics*. The most important task of this future science of man and his language could in fact be to develop and substantiate a more or less generally acceptable and consistent *theory of the organization of language and the functioning of language in the organization of the context*.

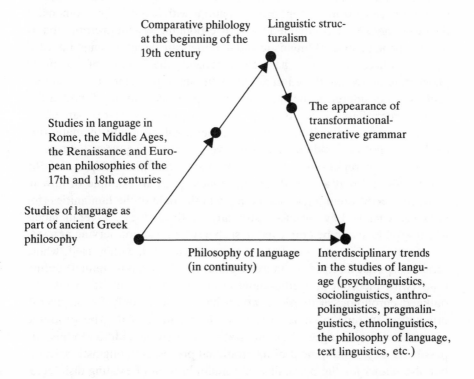

Comparative philology at the beginning of the 19th century

Linguistic structuralism

The appearance of transformational-generative grammar

Studies in language in Rome, the Middle Ages, the Renaissance and European philosophies of the 17th and 18th centuries

Studies of language as part of ancient Greek philosophy

Philosophy of language (in continuity)

Interdisciplinary trends in the studies of language (psycholinguistics, sociolinguistics, anthropolinguistics, pragmalinguistics, ethnolinguistics, the philosophy of language, text linguistics, etc.)

Fig. 1

Considerations of this kind could be represented, on a spatial level, by *Fig. 1*. (To those more informed, this schematization will be clear, but it is necessary to add, for the sake of those less acquainted with the history of linguistic studies, an explanation that the sides of the proposed triangle represent only approximate proportions, directions, durations and degrees of rise, that is to say, decline of the independence of Europocentrically conceived continuous linguistics, while the hypotenuse indicates the continuity of philosophical preoccupations with language — with the belief that the future of linguistics lies in the above-mentioned reintegration of all the disciplines and interdisciplines into a kind of, at the present only imaginary, general, and by definition 'interdisciplinary' science of man and his language.)

It is understandable that the presented historical and discipline-'status' generalizations would not be sufficient of themselves to form an adequate matrix for recognizing current preoccupations with language phenomena, if they were not also accompanied by a corresponding systematization, that is to say schematization of linguistic and nonlinguistic disciplines and interdisciplines whose presence has characterized the study of language phenomena in twentieth century. This is the more true since the twentieth century is considered to be the century of truly scientifically founded linguistics, regardless of its discipline, interdiscipline and status parcellings and unifications, as well as theoretical, methodological and thematic turmoils. It is not by accident that in this very century linguistics held, for a long time, the reputation of being the 'most scientific' discipline of the humanities and that it served, not infrequently, as an example of how to view, from a different angle, phenomena in the field of the humanities (for instance, Claude Lévi-Strauss's structural anthropology). Overall labels which would have to be employed in such a schematization serving as a systematization (cf. *Fig. 2*) would have to condense, each within itself, whole series of special disciplinal, interdisciplinal (or even subdisciplinal) definitions (with theoretical, methodological and thematic content), while the outlined chronological divisions would have to serve only for an overall orientation in time, that is to say, for localization in it. The proposed schematization serving as a systematization *suggests*, in addition to this, the possibility of a development of integrational processes in linguistic science, but also *allows for* the possibility of a multiplication of existing disintegration tendencies in a linguistics which is already overly inhomogeneous. The nineties (the end of this century) are seen here as that new period of possible paradigmatic changes in scientific thought on language as part of the human domain (the informal conclusion of the XIII International Congress of Linguists, Tokyo, Japan, 1982, oriented, generally speaking, toward the

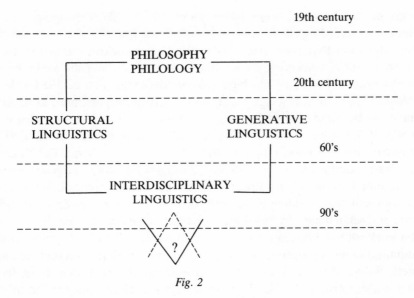

Fig. 2

subject of 'linguistics in the eighties, with an emphasis on differences in theoretical standpoints and methodologies', was quite indicative in this sense, since it held that 'in linguistics there is still mainly a discussion of the events in the sixties, and that, due to this, linguistics is having great difficulties in entering its eighties'). Finally, everything said so far is also supported by the idea that paradigmaticness (in Kuhn's sense) and cyclicness are, in fact, two of several fixed developmental constants of science in general, and so also of linguistics, as one among the sciences.

The fifties found Yugoslav studies of language phenomena still deeply involved in traditional European *philology*, in the 'neogrammarians' or some other version stemming from it, with all of its theoretical, methodological, thematic and conceptual-terminological, status, intentional and other important implications (positivism, historicism, descriptivism, comparativism, traditional conceptual and terminological apparatus, lack of interest in theory, etc.). The late fifties and early sixties, however, marked the gradual, though quite belated, opening of the Yugoslav science of language (that is, languages) toward *structural linguistics* of the descriptive type — mostly toward the 'Prague' version, and to a lesser extent toward the 'Geneva', 'distributionalist', 'Harvard' and other ones, depending, as a rule, on whether the linguistic studies and linguistic education, and connected with them the scholarly, that is, professional orientations of the linguists, were based more on the Slavic languages, the Romance ones, English or some others (cf., for instance, the book which best illustrates that time: Ivić, Pavle. *Die serbokroatischen Dialekte. Ihre Struktur und Entwicklung*. Erster Band. *Allgemeines und die Štokavische Dialektgruppe* [Ivić P. 1958] which was considered 'the first detailed dialectological study of a language based on the structural principle', as it continues to be often termed in current histories of linguistics, but also the works of Milka Ivić, Radoslav Katičić, Dalibor Brozović, Žarko Muljačić, Radivoj Mukuš, Rudolf Filipović, Blaže Koneski, and others). For Yugoslav linguistics the accepting of structural insights into language phenomena represented not merely its 'opening up' to then current trends in world linguistics, but also its siding along with the new and altered positions on science and scholarship. In this sense structural linguistics became, in view of the work yet to be done on describing the complex Yugoslav language situation, quite an appropriate scientific orientation (both in a theoretical and methodological and in a conceptual-terminological sense), due to the fact that it also satisfied, besides its modest explanatory adequacy at the time, fully and in a new way, the requirements of descriptive adequacy. The sixties did not, however, bring with them a possible 'opening' toward the then, in world proportions, already prestigious *generative linguistics* (in any of its more or less syntactically, semantically or even pragmatically founded versions), primarily because of the many (already mentioned) unfinished tasks of a descriptive nature. Namely, in these tasks, the traditional philological approach had already been replaced, during the transition from the fifities to the sixties, by the structural approach to the study of linguistic phenomena (in one of its above-mentioned versions) so that a devotion to the predominantly explanatory and theoretical focuses of generative linguistics lacked in Yugoslav conditions available professionals, time, available research facilities, financial and, naturally, institutional teaching potentials and training and even personal (individual or group) linguistic interest. (The generalizations drawn here, of course, exclude the possibility of devoting attention to episodic events and realities.) On the eve of the seventies, due, probably, to a great extent to the already mentioned unfinished tasks of a descriptive nature and supported by the then already altered notions on the prerequisites for satisfying descriptive (and also explanatory) adequacy in the sciences of man, and so also in the science of languages, that is to say, language, favourable conditions arose in Yugoslavia for accepting the third prominent paradigm in world linguistics following World War II, defined (at the beginning of this introduction) as a series of *interdisciplinary research orientations* in the fields of *psycholinguistics, sociolinguistics, the philosophy of language* and (though quite sporadically) others. Without much delay, this time (not even a decade as compared to the rest of the world), but lacking professional potentials and with undeveloped facilities for professional instructions, in conditions of a very limited circulation of new foreign books and periodicals of a general linguistic relevance, the above mentioned *interdisciplinary research orientations*, along with the still active studies of a traditional *philological* and *structuralist* type, became part of the matrix for organizing most of the current research and studies in Yugoslav linguistics. Just as elsewhere in the world, so in Yugoslavia as well, the interdisciplinary research orientations of a newer date made their appearance parallel with clamorous disciplinary and interdisciplinary divisions and distinctions, concerning, especially, name, status and scope (and in this regard, it seems that the 'psycholinguists' and the 'sociolinguists' are the most vocal). Undoubtedly, the overall Yugoslav language situation (and, of course, all the aspects linked with it, such as the national, religious, political, legal, social, cultural, economic and others) represents, even in European proportions, exceptionally favourable ground for setting up and organizing 'psycholinguistically' and 'sociolinguistically' relevant study projects, that is to say, for orienting a considerable portion of current linguistic studies toward those marked specifically by the labels 'psycholinguistic' and 'sociolinguistic' (all of this holding true for both the *microlinguistic* and for the *macrolinguistic* levels of observations).

To sum up: when the traditional philological approach to the study of language phenomena ceased, from a general scientific standpoint, to meet the demands of descriptive adequacy (in the Yugoslav situation this occurred in the late fifties and early sixties), it was superseded by the structural linguistic approach to the study of language phenomena which was, from a general scientific standpoint, at that time undoubtedly more descriptive (though also more explanatory) and incomparably more adequate. Prompted by the same linguistic and scientific motivations (in the Yugoslav situation this occurred in the seventies), interdisciplinary orientations, predominantly those of a 'psycholinguistic' and 'sociolinguistic' provenience, entered onto the stage. In the Yugoslav language and linguistic situation, therefore, the prerequisite of explanatory adequacy regularly found itself in second place among the possible factors influencing events of this kind, prominently superseded by the prerequisite of descriptive adequacy (because of a proportionally larger amount of work still to be done of a descriptive linguistic nature). Hence, in the Yugoslav situation, there is an only apparently paradoxical, yet proportionally general lack of interest in generative linguistics as a research study alternative.

The outlined development of Yugoslav *philological* and *linguistic* studies includes, also, a relatively long and confirmed lack of interest of Yugoslav scholars of language phenomena for theoretical problems (with rare exceptions such as the late Aleksandar Belić, for instance). This state of affairs lasted into the sixties and up to the time when structural linguistics made its appearance in these parts. The most effective agent for awakening an interest in the *theoretical aspects* of the study of language was Milka Ivić's *Pravci u lingvistici* [Trends in Linguistics], which has, since 1963, had five printings in Serbocroation (cf. Ivić M. 1970 [1965]), as a kind of 'book on call', a reference work on relevant theoretical subject matter stemming from older and newer studies of language phenomena. In the Yugoslav situation, parallel with this awakening of interest in the theoretical aspects of the study of language, there also appeared a growing interest in general linguistic subject matter, or, more precisely, in subject matter *relevant to general linguistics*. Quite understandably, the additional impulse for a growing interest in subject matter relevant to general linguistics in the study of language was also provided by the findings which were, in the specific and relatively complex Yugoslav language situation, given by descriptive studies (of a structural, 'psycholinguistic', 'sociolinguistic' or some other orientation).

This volume has been put together to include the editor's choice of *studies relevant to general linguistics*, both in the sphere of *microlinguistic* and that of *macrolinguistic* phenomena. Of the six previously published studies which are presented here (with minor additions and revisions, or without them), not by accident, four have been taken over from their original editions on the eve of the seventies (Ivić P. [1964]; Brozović [1966]; Ivić P. [1970]; Katičić [1970]). From the standpoint of chronology, they represent, in fact, the time of the culmination of the theoretical and methodological innovativeness of a generation of basically and predominantly structurally oriented Yugoslav linguists. The remaining studies, on the other hand, represent the results, on the part of the editor in agreement with certain selected authors, to treat certain targeted topics (understandably, neither could all the desired authors nor all the desired topics be presented here) and so compile a more or less representative *review of studies relevant to general linguistics*, on the one hand, representative *of the current Yugoslav linguistic situation* and, on the other hand, representative *of current Yugos-lav scientific potentials, researchers and projects in the domain of linguistic studies in general* (most often in correlation with the prior condition of rep-resentativeness). In addition to this, the volume could, at least in regard to the editor's intention, be promoted, from a thematic standpoint, as the first anthology of readings in Yugoslav general linguistics in English or any other language. It contains twenty contributions, mostly original (first pub-lished), by outstanding Yugoslav scholars in such areas as *comparative, typological* and *contact linguistics, sociolinguistics* (including such topics as: bilingualism, multilingualism, diglossia, language stratification, verbal interaction and communication, language planning, language policy, trans-lation theory, etc.), *psycholinguistics, structural/generative linguistics* (pho-nology, morphology, syntax and semantics), *text linguistics, pragmatics, lin-guistic semiotics* and *the philosophy of language and science.* The collection should appeal to linguists of all persuasions and specializations, including Slavicists with a South Slavic emphasis. The studies are given according to the alphabetical order of their authors' surnames. An important factor for final selection and inclusion in the collection, during one part of the work on the projected volume and its final shaping, was whether the studies were or could be presented in an adequate version in English (either by being written or translated into that language). A subsequent review of the collec-tion revealed (though this was not the editor's primary aim) that both the authors and the studies in the volume represent the six important centres of linguistic studies in Yugoslavia (Belgrade, Ljubljana, Novi Sad, Skopje, Zadar and Zagreb). The fact, also, that the authors of the greater number of the studies selected are Slavicists or Anglicists should not be taken as accidental, but, rather, one could say, as representative.

According to thematic circles, the collection contains: a study which offers a modern, interdisciplinary critical discussion of the place and status of linguistics among the neighbouring sciences, and, in this regard, of its (non)autonomy and the (non)autonomy of its subject — language, both throughout the history of linguistics, and at its contemporary moment and with a projection of its possible future (Škiljan); a study which makes an analytical consideration of the linguistic and non-linguistic consequences of the theoretical construct according to which generative linguistics is an elab-oration of the structural linguistic model — taken in the broadest epis-temological sense, but also in regard to terminology, historical develop-ment, socio-psychological heritage, methodological similarities, programmatic links, general logical sequence and conceptual fit (Bugarski); several studies whose general linguistics oriented subject matter is focused on an original attempt to develop the theory of languages in contact, from positions predominantly structurally and sociolinguistically motived (Filipović), and also a developing of the theory of language variations and language relations, from a genetic, typological and contact standpoint and by a modern, structural and post-structural linguistic conceptual and terminological apparatus (Katičić), and as a discussion of the possibility of establishing an adequate, linguistically and non-linguistically supported theory of translation (Ivir). A number of studies included in the volume discuss particular notions of modern linguistic theory and methodology relevant to general linguistics (on the material of Serbocroatian, and the Slavic and other languages): the prosodic possibilities of languages in their relation to the properties and hierarchy of morphological categories (Ivić P.); the functioning of the binary theory of distinctive features in the "Prague" and "Harvard" versions, based on the example of a possible structural description of the Standard Serbocroatian phonological system (Brozović); a possible 'underlying' approach to phonological description of vowel quantity, on the basis of an explication of related rules, and on the material of modern Icelandic (Orešnik); the structural and typological, yet general linguistically relevant features of territorial linguistic differentiation — both from the aspect of linguistic geography and the theory of languages in contact (Ivić P.); the referential usage of nouns with regard to their 'identificatory force' — from a pragmatic and semantic standpoint (Ivić M.); various aspects of the thesis of a space-like organization of non-spatial semantic spheres in languages — from a typological, intralinguistic and extralinguistic standpoint, by way of a discussion of related 'localistic' conceptions (Piper). Three studies present a review of current interdisciplinary linguistic studies in Yugoslavia, of those 'sociolinguistically' oriented (Radovanović), of those 'psycholinguistically' oriented (Savić) and those in the domain of the philosophy of language (Pupovac). Findings relevant to general linguistics derived mostly from special studies of the Yugoslav language situation are offered by several studies whose subjects are basically of a 'sociolinguistic' or 'psycholinguistic' provenience: the psychological aspects of bilingualism in Vojvodina (Göncz); language contacts in Vojvodina (Mikeš); language contacts in the sphere of the Balkan 'Sprachbund' (Tomić); the phenomenon of prescriptivism — primarily in the Serbocroatian situation, but also in relation to some others (Kalogjera); the institution of language planning — from the theoretical and applied aspect (Rajić); and, finally, on the current processes in the establishing of urban dialects — primarily on the basis of speech of the city of Split (Jutronić-Tihomirović).

Novi Sad, January 1986

References**

Bartsch, Renate and Theo Vennemann (eds). 1975. *Linguistics and Neighboring Disciplines*. Amsterdam/Oxford/New York: North-Holland/American Elsevier.

Bugarski, Ranko. 1984. *Jezik i lingvistika* [Language and linguistics]. Rev. ed. Beograd: Nolit.

Calvet, Louis-Jean. 1975. *Pour et contre Saussure. Vers une linguistique sociale*. Paris: Payot.

Cassirer, Ernst. 1955. *The Philosophy of Symbolic Forms*. Vol. I. *Language*. New Haven: Yale University Press.

Dingwall, William Orr (ed.). 1978. *A Survey of Linguistic Science*. Stamford, Connecticut: Greylock Publishers.

Finka, Božidar. 1979. "Hrvatsko jezikoznanstvo u poslijeratnom razdoblju" [Croatian linguistics in the post-war period]. *Suvremena lingvistika* 19-20: 39-58.

Girke, Wolfgang and Helmut Jachnow (eds). 1976. *Theoretische Linguistik in Osteuropa. Originalbeiträge und Erstübersetzungen*. Tübingen: Max Niemeyer.

Harman, Gilbert (ed.). 1974. *On Noam Chomsky. Critical Essays*. Garden City: Anchor Books.

Heinz, Adam. 1983. *Dzieje językoznawstwa w zarysie*. 2nd ed. Warszawa: Państwowe Wydawnictwo Naukowe.

Hymes, Dell. 1974. *Foundations in Sociolinguistics. An Ethnographic Approach*. Philadelphia: University of Pennsylvania Press.

Ivić, Milka. 1970. *Trends in Linguistics*. 2nd ed. The Hague/Paris: Mouton.

** The articles incorporated in this book are not included (except for the original version of the editor's).

Ivić, Milka. 1976. "Linguistic theory in Yugoslavia". In: Girke and Jachnow (eds). 1976: 217-33.

Ivić, Pavle. 1958. *Die serbokroatischen Dialekte. Ihre Struktur und Entwicklung.* Erster Band. *Allgemeines und die Štokavische Dialektgruppe.* 's-Gravenhage: Mouton.

Južnoslovenski filolog. Beograd: Institut za srpskohrvatski jezik.

Kiefer, Ferenc (ed.). 1982. *Hungarian [General] Linguistics.* Amsterdam/Philadelphia: John Benjamins.

Kuhn, Thomas. 1970. *The Structure of Scientific Revolutions.* Rev. ed. Chicago: University of Chicago Press.

Linguistics Abstracts. Oxford: Basil Blackwell.

Lyons, John (ed.). 1970. *New Horizons in Linguistics.* Hardmondsworth, Middlesex: Penguin Books.

Martinet, André (ed.). 1968. *Le langage.* Paris: Gallimard.

Neustupný, J.V. 1978. *Post-structural Approaches to Language. Language Theory in a Japanese Context.* Tokyo: University of Tokyo Press.

Parret, Herman (ed.). 1976. *History of Linguistic Thought and Contemporary Linguistics.* Berlin/New York: Walter de Gruyter.

Percival, W. Keith. 1976. "The applicability of Kuhn's paradigms to the history of linguistics". *Language* 52. 2: 285-94.

Radovanović, Milorad. 1983. "Linguistic theory and sociolinguistics in Yugoslavia." *International Journal of the Sociology of Language* 44.6 (= *Language choice and language control*): 55-69.

Radovanović, Milorad. 1986. *Sociolingvistika* [Sociolinguistics]. Rev. ed. Novi Sad: Theoria.

Sebeok, Thomas A. (ed.). 1974. *Current Trends in Linguistics.* Vol. 12. *Linguistics and Adjacent Arts and Sciences.* The Hague/Paris: Mouton.

Škiljan, Dubravko. 1976. *Dinamika jezičnih struktura* [The dynamics of language structures]. Zagreb: Teka/Studentski centar Sveučilišta u Zagrebu.

Tomić, Olga Mišeska. 1985. "The generative paradigm?". *Folia Linguistica* 19. 1-2: 233-47.

Some remarks on distinctive features: especially in Standard Serbo-Croatian*

Dalibor Brozović
Faculty of Philosophy (Zadar), University of Split

1.1 The binary theory of distinctive features is today the most promising linguistic trend; it is, in fact, the main current of linguistic events in the world, synthesizing the most essential and valuable elements and optimum solutions of the Prague and American phonological schools by means of Roman Jakobson's creative ferment.

1.2 There is no fear today that the binary trend will dry up, but there is the danger that the stream will overflow (since the main current attracts just because it IS the most powerful!) and so lessen its speed. It is now the right moment to reexamine binary theory in its entirety on the one hand and its particular areas on the other. This has two aspects: (a) the discrimination of binary theory from various accompanying pseudo-binary and pseudo-phonological residues which minimize its effectiveness, and (b) a consideration of the core of the theory itself, of its basis tenets, in order to recognize and concentrate our attention on its weak points.

1.3 Within the modest compass of this article, I shall tackle the latter problem only, without attempting more than its formulation and without presuming to exhaust the subject. In addition, I shall pay special attention to some problems of the application of the binary theory of distinctive features

* This article was originally published as a contribution to the *Festschrift To Honor Roman Jakobson. Essays on the Occasion of His Seventieth Birthday. 11 October 1966.* Volume I. The Hague/Paris: Mouton. 412-26. (1967). It is reprinted here in basically the same form, except for the necessary technical adjustments, sporadic author's revisions, and the correction of typographical errors. Permission to reprint was kindly granted by Mouton Publishers (Division of Walter de Gruyter & Co.).

(DF) to Standard Serbo-Croatian (S.-C.).

I must remark that I agree with most of the opinions formulated by the Serbian Slavicist P. Ivić in his "Roman Jakobson and the growth of phonology";[1] therefore, I do not want to repeat what he has stated in that paper, which is composed from the historical point of view and linked only with the central figure in the development of contemporary phonology.

I shall dwell only upon the field of inherent DFs, without discussing the problem of their spectrographic reflections.

2.1 It is generally agreed that the central problem in inherent DF analysis is the nature of the most important sonority feature, compactness/diffuseness, and its relation to the most important tonality feature, gravity/acuteness. Next in importance would rank the nature of the features vocality/non-v. and consonantality/non-c., and I think that the problem of the tenseness/laxness feature is by no means easier.

2.2 What is most lacking is a clear objective and a hierarchy of principles. It is impossible to solve the above-mentioned problems (2.1) unless one decides which to consider of greater importance, the maximum economy of the code (which is, frequently, the most elegant and witty solution of tabulating the code) or the maximum adequacy of stating the phonological functioning of human speech. Both aims are very important, but the former is subordinate to the latter since it is indeed the means of achieving the latter.

2.2.1 Sometimes this dilemma appear outwardly in this shape: is the binary character of DF oppositions to be preserved at all costs and are they to be defined acoustically, again at all costs? I should think that such resoning is harmful to the very roots of the DF theory as it lets in at the back door what has been defeated in main battle and cannot appear openly under its old name.

The binary principle as a procedural, operative principle of knowledge has a wider scope; its functioning has been tried in various disciplines of modern science, linguistics included. Therefore any difficulty in the application of binary solutions should signal the necessity of a different formulation of the question requiring a (±) answer. The suspect character of such solutions is visible at once from the meaning of (±) answers to such questions as formulated in the shape of vocalic/consonantal in the case of the liquids or the question formulated in the shape compact/diffuse in the case of mid vowels. In the first case the meaning is the sum total of the features;

in the other the meaning is their presence to a smaller degree than with phonemes answering with a (+).

Similarly in the instance when the acoustic and the motoric (articulatory, 'genetical') aspects seemingly contradict each other, can the solution under no circumstances be to relinquish the priority of acoustic level — by the conflations of the levels, by a compromising treatment, in the determination of facts or their formulation. Any such instance is simply a signal indicating the need for further work in the attempt to determine the true and full relation of the two levels (giving priority to the acoustic plane) and to find an adequate manner of representing this relation.

2.2.2 With reference to the binary principle, there are two kinds of sins: (a) the departure from the principle of defining DFs as the presence/absence of a feature which automatically implies potential (±) answers, and (b) the determination of oppositions with reference to zero.

2.2.3 The zero (or blank — the selection is a matter of convention) informs us, as is well known, of two kinds of content. In one case it means that the respective phoneme does not enter into the opposition, e.g., the phonemes answering with a (−) to consonantal/non-c. do not occur in the continuous/disc. opposition. In the other case we deal with features which are present redundantly, e.g., tenseness/laxness opposition in Slavic phonemes answering with a (−) to vocalic/non-v. opposition (/v/ most frequently expected).

2.2.4 In neither case is the determination of the code satisfactory if the answer to question A for phoneme X depends on Ø as the answer to question B for phoneme Y. It is not satisfactory because such a code cannot function effectively in reality. E.g., in R. Jakobson's table of S.-C. phonemes we find a blank at /g/ as the answer to continuous/disc., and at /x/ as the answer to voiced/voiceless.[2] Of course, /k/ answers with a (−) to both questions.

In fact, (−) at /k/ but not at /g/ with the first question depends on Ø at /x/ with the second question, that is, it depends on the redundancy of the voicelessness of /x/. Thus it is necessary to replace the blank with the sign (−) either at /g/ or at /x/. The S.-C. system requires it for /g/ (see below (6.2)).

2.2.4.1 If we present together the S.-C. compact grave obstruent phonemes and variants, then continuousness and voicing result as in the table and diagram respectively (cf. Figure 1).

	k	g	x	γ
(I) continuous	−	−	+	+
(II) voiced	−	+	−	+

and

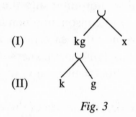

Fig. 1

But since /k/, /g/, and /x/ are phonemes and [γ] is a variant, the table should be re-worked (cf. Figure 2).

(A)

	k	g	x
(I)	−	−	+
(II)	−	+	ø

but not (B)

	k	g	x
(I)	−	ø	+
(II)	−	+	ø

Fig. 2

Table (B) would require the diagram (cf. Figure 3)

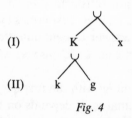

Fig. 3

but it can be realized only in the form of the diagram presented in Figure 4.

(I)	K	x
(II)	k	g

Fig. 4

This is so because /g/, the *phoneme* /g/, cannot move together with /k/ from question (I) to question (II), as is implied if /g/ follows the (−) directive of /k/ and not its own. This could be realized at the level of the so-called archiphoneme which would only mean an unnecessary merging of levels into one and the same procedure. This treatment is hypothetically possible if the complete procedure of binary identification is absolutely and cumulatively synchronic, simultaneous, which it is not, either in the human or electronic brain, nor can it be, by the very nature of the binary theory which implies successivity by definition although with practically minimum expense of time. The realization is simultaneous, but the decoding is not.

2.2.4.2 It is a completely different problem which of the DFs should have precedence; only one thing is important: such tables with three phonemes and two DFs should contain only one zero, not two. The advantage depends on the system of the specific language and on the principles of recapitulation and hierarchy (2.6). We could, also, present the facts as in Figure 5.

	k	g	x
(I) voiced	−	+	−
(II) continuous	−	O	+

Fig. 5

2.2.5 The existence of two kinds of redundant features (RF) is not adequately insisted upon. In one case the RF controls the relation of variants of a phoneme (e.g., continuousness/disc. of the Spanish phonemes /d/, /b/, /g/; in the other case it is linked to a DF, thus having an auxiliary function (the tenseness DF/laxness of the Slavic obstruents is linked to voicelessness/voicing which does not control the relation of the variants under ordinary circumstances). The former case can be termed internal redunancy; the latter, external redundancy. The combination of both is, e.g., the redundant voicelessness of S.-C. /c/: with reference to the variant [ʒ] it is internal, otherwise it is external on the syntagmatic axis and virtual on the paradigmatic one (i.e., with reference to the so-called 'hole in the pattern').

The dual nature of redundancy and the twofold function of the zero result in seemingly identical parts of codes (i.e., the codes of particular classes of phonemes) reflecting totally dissimilar realities in different languages.

2.3 In connection with the DF of compactness/diffuseness we have an instance of the violation of the binary principle (the first sin of 2.2.2). But besides the possibility of bi-polar answers for vowels (not even consonants are, theoretically, excluded!) this DF has another vulnerable spot: we know that the diffuseness of [p] and [t] is less useful than the compactness of [k] and [ć], which potentially allows systems requiring a (−) for both compactness and diffuseness at /t/. Research in this direction could throw light on the opposite instances of a consonantal phoneme doubtlessly non-diffuse in a given system, but doubtfully compact (e.g., Ario-Indian and Dravidian cerebrals).

2.4 The homogeneity of the DF gravity/acuteness is less frequently questioned in the literature than the DF compactness/diffuseness. In principle, however, the situation is the same. The high tonality of [t] and [ć] is more evident and more useful than the low tonality of [p] and [k], which, again, allows for systems requiring a ($-$) at /k/ both for high and low tonalities, or for cases where this would be true of [k_b], while [k_a] would require a ($+$) for low tonality.[3] This involves far-reaching consequences, but it cannot be avoided. It is characteristic that [ŋ] is grave and compact, [n] acute and diffuse, while [m] is grave and diffuse. From the table (cf. Figure 6) one could often expect [ŋ] as an allophone of /m/ because [ŋ] occurs in only one opposition with /m/ and two with /n/.

	n	m	ɲ	ŋ
compact	−	−	+	+
grave	−	+	−	+

Fig. 6

In reality, this is an exception; [ŋ] is often an allophone of /n/.

2.4.1 These facts do not mean that the splitting of the DF of gravity/ acuteness into gravity/non-g. and acuteness/non-a. should be insisted upon in all instances. It is important to allow for this possibility; however, I think that such cases will be rare. I can add some instances illustrating the kinship of grave consonants to those mentioned by Jakobson and Ivić.[4] Thus in Kashubian dialects the shift *ŭ* > *ə* does not occur after the labials and the velars,[5] children usually replace /k/ with /t/, /g/ with /d/, yet in such S.-C. instances as /kupi/ '(he) buys', /kipi/ '(it) is boiling', etc., /k/ is replaced with /p/. Such 'assimilative' change can be shown in the history of certain Indo-European dialects which I shall not discuss now.

Yet, high and low tonalities are different phenomena (in the same manner in which a man who is not tall is not automatically short!) – besides there is no proportion between the unique DF of gravity/acuteness and the split DFs of flatness/non-f. and sharpness/non-s., respectively.

2.5 The splitting of the DF of compactness/diffuseness and gravity/acuteness into four DFs results, in the instance of the former, in an obvious gain to the vocalism; but in both cases gain to consonantism is possible. Let us suppose the oppositions $/k_a/ \sim /k_b/$ and $/t_a/ \sim /t_b/$ which (with the redundancies remaining to make it more obvious) would result as follows (cf. Figure 7), together with /p/ and /ć/.

		p	t_a	t_b	k_a	k_b	ć
(I)	compact	−	−	−	+	+	+
(II)	diffuse	+	+	−	−	−	−
(III)	grave	+	−	−	+	−	−
(IV)	acute	−	+	+	−	−	+

Fig. 7

Adding up the common signs, we have the material, the phonetic basis for the separation from [p] and the approach to [ć], which is one of the strongest universal trends in the consonantism. The figures prove this clearly (cf. Figure 8).

p	t_a 2	k_a 2	t_b 1	k_b 1	ć ∅	6
t_a	t_b 3	p 2	ć 2	k_b 1	k_a ∅	8
t_b	t_a 3	ć 3	k_b 2	p 1	k_a 1	10
k_a	k_b 3	p 2	ć 2	t_b 1	t_a ∅	8
k_b	k_a 3	ć 3	t_b 2	p 1	t_a 1	10
ć	k_b 3	t_b 3	k_a 2	t_a 2	p ∅	10

Fig. 8

2.5.1 The consonants $[k_a]$ and $[t_a]$ are in truth equally removed from [p] and [ć], but $[k_b]$ and $[t_b]$ are nearer to [ć]. In addition, the stops$_a$ have no common features, neither have [p] and [ć], but stops$_b$ do have them. It is clear, in this light, why the cardinal square of consonants cannot be geometrically regular. In addition, we do not know the phonetic repartition of stops$_a$ and stops$_b$ in individual languages, but it would seem that /k/ and /t/ often appear as $/k_b/$ and $/t_b/$. There are three consequences:

1. The difference in the stages of structuring the vocalic and consonantal systems[6] are not exhausted in the sequence in which the specific DFs are introduced. The differences should be reflected in two additional manners: in the structures of the patterns and in the inverted marking of the basic oppositions (2.6).

2. The construction of the basic triangle (cf. Figure 9)

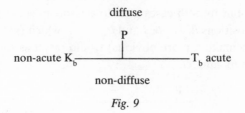

Fig. 9

is more adequate than (cf. Figure 10).

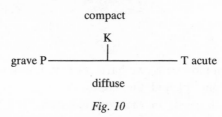

Fig. 10

3. There is no parallel between the vocalism and the consonantism, i.e., although ancient Indians were already aware of the relation of [a] and [k] on the one hand, and [u] and [p] on the other,[7] yet the opposition $a : i, u$ is indeed superior to all others, but with the consonants it is p: K_b, t_b and not $k : p, t$.

2.5.2 Such treatment of the DFs of compactness, diffuseness, gravity, and acuteness seems to require a detailed and consistent reconstruction at first sight only. Namely, this splitting is necessary for operational purposes only when two related oppositions co-exist in the same system, which is frequent with compactness and diffuseness in the case of vowels. In all other instances, one DF can be selected from the two pairs of oppositions to act as a differentor in terms of Šaumjan's two-level theory.[8] In such instances, in Šaumjan's terms, four differentoids are grouped into two differentors. The idea is in the possibility of determining the substance more precisely and, consequently, overcomng contradictions in empirical facts and in diachronic trends. In his comprehensive and shrewd review of *Selected writings* I, P. Ivić found a few such contradictions with reference to spectrographic, phonetic, perceptual, and diachronic facts,[9] but they remain at differentoid level and do not thwart the binary analytic function of the differentors.

It is clear that these facts are of considerable importance in the determination of the RFs where necessary.

2.6 In this connection, some general questions concerning the DFs have special significance. By this I mean the classification of the DFs according to their relationships in substance (i.e., as to the respective differentoid, or differentoids), according to the principle of recapitulation (whether they are primary or secondary or tertiary from the point of view of glottogony, children's speech, aphasia, etc.), according to functions and mutual combinations, and according to specific prosodic DFs. Besides, there is the problem of determining the marked member of an opposition, which is not always simple — in consonantal patterns only, non-diffuseness and non-acuteness should be taken as marked, comparable to compactness and gravity. At the differentoid level, the first opposition

$$\text{diffuse P} \sim \text{A compact}$$

should be split as in Figure 11.

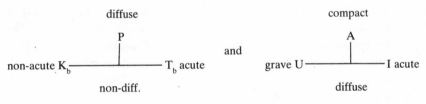

Fig. 11

Hence we have one of the important disharmonies of the development of vocalic and consonantal systems (2.5.1), and all the consequences.

2.6.1 These phenomena are to be seen with special clarity in the opposition tenseness/laxness. As a differentor, it implies the differentoids of tension/laxness, aspiration/non-a., intensity/non-i., and pre-aspiration/non-pre-a.[10] Since in practice none of these differentoids, as far as it is known, requires a promotion to differentor level (which is not required for gravity/acuteness, but frequently for compactness/diffuseness), the single remaining difficulty is the one of determining the marked member of the tenseness/laxness opposition at the differentor level, which obviously depends on the actual differentoid in question. Besides, here we are in any case concerned with a privative opposition, as distinct from both compactness/diffuseness and gravity/acuteness. There is another DF having differentoids which are rather differentiated, i.e. that of flatness/non-f., but there is no problem of marking. A similar case can be seen in the DF of continuousness/discontinuousness.

2.6.2 The specific ties of the oppositions of tenseness/laxness and voicelessness/voicing is a distinct problem in many languages. It is always the question of one DF and one RF, but the problem is not exhausted in the difficulty of determining distinction and redundancy. Here we have the case of distinctive voicing without laxness as a separate differentoid. Such is the case with the S.-C. /v/ ~ /f/, hence the special status of /v/ in the phonological system of S.-C., which is not, however, reflected on the phoneme level (3.2.1.d, e).

3.1 In most languages, the greatest number of difficulties results from unsettled conflicts between the requirements at distinct levels (the phonologies of the sound, of the syllable, of the word) and the different possibilities of interpreting responses from the so-called linguistic consciousness. The consideration of the latter should not, in my opinion, be rejected beforehand but should be taken as a signal indicating the necessity for further endeavours to find an adequate interpretation. Thus, as early as 1929, R. Jakobson put forth, with much esprit, a simple explanation of the conflict between the unquestionable fact that the Russian [y] is a combinatory variant of /i/ and the equally unquestionable fact that Russian linguistic consciousness separates [y] from [i], though it does not distinguish allophones of other phonemes.[11]

3.2 The phonology of the syllable, in my opinion, is not allowed enough importance or independence. Its relation to the phonology of the sound and the phonology of the word is not sufficiently clear and, as a consequence, the problem is on the one hand underrated by a sort of doctrinary art-for-art's-sake attitude, and, on the other, it is overrated by concepts burdened with traditional phonetics. Šaumjan's extreme solution is a specific combination of both: vocality/consonantality is rejected from the inherent DFs to become associated with prosodic DFs in the category of culminators.[12]

3.2.1 R. Jakobson's treatment of these problems is the only correct solution leaving, at the same time, enough space for manoeuvres, capable of far-reaching internal development and improvement.

Let us consider, for instance, the problem of the nasals. Jakobson (1962 [1956]) classifies phonemes as sonorants or sonores (the semi-vowel /j/, the liquids and the nasals, respectively these plus the vowels) and obstruents (stops, affricates, and constrictives, except /v/ and /v'/ in Russian, which is also more or less valid in most other Slavic languages).[13] This concept has not been adequately utilized in componential analysis. There are several reasons for assigning the nasals to the class of phonemes having vocality:

a. Phonemes answering with a (+) to vocalic/non-v. cannot very well avoid the question of nasality/non-n. because of the nasal vowels. With phonemes answering with a (−) to vocalic/non-v., the DF of nasality/non-n. can always be dispensed with if the nasals are associated with the liquids.

b. This implies the reduction of one DF with all obstruents; it does not imply that this DF should be introduced into code systems having no nasal vowels, because in this case oral vowels are opposed to nasal sonorants with the sign (−) for the DF of consonantality/non-consonantality.

c. This reduction is considerable as obstruents are more numerous than liquids. In some tables the (−) sign is absent for the DF of nasality with all obstruents except with voiced (or lax) plosives. This is not correct, as the selection depends on the redundant voicing and redundant discontinuousness of the nasals (2.2.4). If nasals are left among obstruents, the only correct solution is (−) with all obstruents, or the introduction of new DFs with nasals, which both markedly increase the number of bits per phoneme. Besides, it cannot be stated that nasals are redundantly lax; rather, we could say that they are redundantly tense.

d. When obstruents make use of the DF voicing/voicelessness, the voiced member is marked. In those rare instances where the DF is used with the liquids, the voiceless member is marked. Nasals again behave like liquids.

e. Voicing as a DF is very rare with liquids, but it is almost regular as a RF, and marked clearly on the spectrogram. A specific feature of the redundant voicing with the liquids is the absence of laxness, which is almost regular with voiced obstruents (/v/ alone being excepted in some systems, e.g., in most of the Slavic languages, wholly or positionally). Nasals agree with liquids in this respect too.

f. In phonetic terms, the sign (+) for the DF of vocality is equally justified for the nasals and for the liquids, if not more (because of the nasal tract).

3.2.2 The relations of [r]-[ɾ], [l]-[ʎ], [j]-[ɟ]-[i], [w]-[u̯]-[u] create great problems in many systems. Obviously there are trends both to ignore and neglect them, and to give them too much importance.

The problem appears in S.-C. in connection with [r]-[ɾ] and [i]-[ʝ]. The sound [j] is merely the optional variant of [ʎ] but this variant is relatively rarely realized; whereas [ļ] is without any doubt the mere positional variant of [l], occurring in loan-words only in complementary distribution with [l].

3.2.2.1 Traditional phonology tended to regard S.-C. [ŗ] as a phoneme.[14] Modern inventories of S.-C. phonemes (5.1) list /r/ only. In fact we should write /ŗ/ in the same way in which we write /i/: if we accept the concept of the phonemes /[ŗ] + [r]/ and /[i] + [ʲ]/, they ought to be treated identically.

Between two consonants, or word-initially, S.-C. /r/ cannot function both as a syllabic and as a non-syllabic; cf. the Old Czech minimal pair /bŗdu/ (disyllabic, 'to the top of the hill') and /brdu/ (monosyllabic, 'I wander'), which is an argument against the phonemic treatment of the S.-C. [ŗ].[15] In the sequence vowel-r-consonant, [ŗ] can occur only after a prefix (zaŗzati 'to start neighing', poŗvati se 'to come to grips; za- and po- are prefixes); in gŗoce 'little throat', the stress shows that /r/ cannot be non-syllabic, likewise in tŗo 'chafed'. In such instances as ŭmŗo 'he died', etc., the pronunciation [ŗ] is optional in Standard S.-C.; disyllabic ŭmro is more common. Still, with ȋstŗo 'he wiped off', trisyllabic pronunciation is predominant.

On this point I tested 232 speakers of Standard S.-C., coming from different regions of the country. The first question concerned the meaning of the form /istro/. Without a *single* exception, all answered that it was the vocative case of Istra (Istria, a peninsula in Croatia), while only 27 (or 11.64%) remembered afterwards that it "could be the participle of *istrti*" ('to wipe off'), most of them remarking that they would not use the form. Next I took the sentence *Istro mu je nos* (literally: 'He wiped his nose'; idiomatically: 'He scolded him'). Out of 232 informants, 8 (3.45%) chose ȋstro, 81 (34.91%) chose ȋstrō, and 143 (61.64%) chose ȋstŗo. The form with /ō/ is not standard since in the so-called *l*-participle such a form is admitted only in the contraction of *-oo*, plus *-ao* (sometimes *-eo*, *-uo*) in the language of poetry alone; but *-ŗo* > *-rō* can hardly be considered as a contraction. In the next stage I modified the popular saying *Trla baba lan* (literally: 'The old woman crushed flax'; idiomatically: 'to fritter away one's time') into *Tro djed lan* ('The old man crushed flax'). The form *trō* was not selected by a *single* informant (the prefix *tro*-means 'triple'), *trô* was selected by 84 (36.21%), and *tŗo* by 148 (63.79%). In addition, 12 informants tried to use the dialectal form *trâo* but later 5 decided in favour of *trô*, 7 in favour of *tŗo* which is included in the above figures. The form *trô* is not standard since the norm does not allow for monosyllabic *l*-participles ending in /ō/. The form *trŏ* is permissible, yet nobody selected it!

R. Jakobson defines the [r̩]-[r] relation as follows: 'Without an adjacent vowel, *r* is syllabic. Without an adjacent consonant, *r* is non-syllabic. When *r* adjoins both a vowel and a consonant, the phonemic opposition long/short is in force and is implemented as syllabic/non-syllabic. The non-syllabic *r* is prosodically undifferentiated.[16] The Croatian Romanist Ž. Muljačić comments: 'Since shortness is a prosodic feature, this seeming contradiction should, in my opinion, be accounted for relationally: even when carrying the short falling accent, the syllabic /r/ is at the same time longer than the non-syllabic *r* and shorter than /r̄/. This shortness of the non-syllabic *r* is of a phonetic nature, and is phonologically irrelevant. Even when not stressed, this syllabic *r* is longer than the non-syllabic *r* (e.g. in *mrcváriti*)'.[17]

3.2.2.2 This concept cannot be defended, because it posits a non-distinctive feature of quantity side by side with the prosodic DF of quantity; so it is not, and coult not be, clear what determines the fact that *r* in /istro/ (*ístro*, voc. of 'Istra') is 'phonetically' relationally short and, consequently, non-syllabic; while in /istro/ (*ístro*, *l*-participle) it is 'phonetically' relationally long and, consequently, syllabic. Or, if the stress is considered decisive in determining whether /tro/ is [tr̥o] or *[trŏ], whether /groce/ is [gr̥oce] or *[grŏce], the question still remains what determines the position of the stress (on /r/ or on /o/: in S.-C. stress is a redundant prosodic feature while tone and quantity are distinctive features).

There are two ways out of this situation. One possibility is to consider stress as a DF which is not economical since only a few words are concerned (mostly those with optional syllabicity of /r/) and, besides, it does not solve the problem of [ístr̥o]-[ístro]. The other consists in making the RF of tenseness/laxness with obstruents perform the function of an inherent DF determining syllabicity.

3.2.2.3 The situation with [i]-[i̯] is comparable. Standard S.-C. has *kŏkoši* ('hens'), as well as *kokòšī* ('of hens'), *kokòsjī* ('pertaining to hens'), *pròšīj* ('stitch through', imperative), *lòšijī* ('worse'). The personal name *Katja*, taken from Russian and fairly frequent in Croatia (usually Kaća in Serbia) has a dative case *Katji*. We find *Míji* (rising tone, rarely falling, dat. of *Mijo*, a fairly frequent name), *mî* ('we'), *mîj* ('wash', imperative), *Miji* (dat. of Mija), and *mî* (enclitic dat. of 'I'). Thus the difference [i̯]-[i]-[ī] is quite clear in the linguistic consciousness of S.-C. speakers, if difficult (but not impossible) to analyze as phonematic. It is interesting to note that the difference [r]-[ɽ]-[r̄] is not so evident in the linguistic consciousness, although it can more easily assume phonematic status. An analysis of Croatian graphemics and orthography before standardization indicates that writers educated in the European tradition distinguished between [r] and [ɽ] more radily, while others more easily distinguished between [ị] and [i]. Modern S.-C. orthography follows in the wake of linguistic consciousness, and not vice versa.

3.2.2.4 P. Kuznecov assigns phonematic status to S.-C. [ị].[18] He does not do so with /ļ/ and /ɲ/, but he is alone in this opinion. Modern S.-C. knows the sequence *nj* in loan-words (*konjugacija, konjunktura, injekcija,* etc., where /ɲ/ appears as an allegro form only). The Cyrillic alphabet distinguishes нj and н. In standard orthoepy we have *rèļef* and *rèljef, mìļē* and *mìljē* ('milieu' – *mȋļe* 'miles' is a different word), but the pronunciation *-lj-*is affected.

If we accept the phonemic status of /ị/, regardless of relatively uncertain grounds, the componential analysis yields several solutions for this phoneme which otherwise has a very high frequency. The answer (—) to the DFs of vocality/non-v. and consonantality/non-c., respectively, would be foreign to the S.-C. pattern. H.G. Lunt's opposition of grave /l/ and /ļ/ ~ acute /j/ in Macedonian[19] is not very fortunate either, since there is not sufficient evidence for the gravity of /l/ and /ļ/. Besides, there is no justification for the treatment of the S.-C. /ị̣/ as both vocalic and consonantal, with [j] as an optional or positional variant of /ị/. There remains but one answer: the opposition of tense /i/ ~ lax /ị̣/, as in /ɽ/ ~ /r/.

3.3 I shall not discuss the so-called marginal, optional, stylistic, and similar phonemes in S.-C.; yet, I would like to metnion that B. László has supplied a nearly correct minimal pair for the opposition /c/ ~ /ʒ/ in the onomatopoeic verbs /oʒvɽčati/ (orthogr. *odzvrčati*) ~ /ocvɽčati/ (orthogr. *otcvrčati*).[20] I can add /názōrnīk/ ('a bully') ~ /náʒōrnīk/ (orthogr. *nadzornik*, 'controller), but all of these are facts from the very periphery of the language. They illustrate the random character of minimal pairs *ceteris paribus* and the great value of collaboration with distributional analysis. For example, in this instance, distributional analysis would easily prove that the phonemic status of the S.-C. [ʒ] is groundless; the sound [ʒ] is not even registered in S.-C. linguistic consciousness.

3.4 The reflexes of the Old S.-C. long *ě* in the Ijekavian version of Standard S.-C. constitute a specific problem. The sequence /i̯ē/, when etymologically corresponding to Old S.-C. *ě*, can in all cases in the Ijekavian version be realized monosyllabically as a kind of pseudo-diphthong of the [i̯ē] type (the predominant form in Croatian poetry, where there is much less frequent occurrence of /i̯ē/, likewise, in the standard orthoepy, although the official norm usually permits only /i̯e/, occasionally /i̯ē/). This sound, which can temporarily be transcribed as [ě], is in phonological opposition to each possible combination of S.-C. phonemes and to each phoneme. I have discusses the problem in detail in a paper at the Vienna Symposium on the Occasion of the 25th Anniversary of Trubetzkoj's Death,[21] and do not want to pursue it here. In fact, in Standard Ijekavian, [i̯ē] is the phoneme /ě/, and the sequence /i̯ē/ is rather its stylistic variant.

3.4.1 /ě/ is phonologically opposed to /e/, in fact /ē/, for the DF of tenseness/laxness. Kuznecov thought that the reflex of the Old S.-C. *ě* in the Ekavian version of Standard S.-C. was a separate phoneme too, but this was a misunderstanding.[22]

4.0 I do not intend to discuss the question of terminology here. My views were presented in a paper entitled "The terminology of the distinctive features in Slavic languages and its adaptation to the Slavic terminological system", read at the session of the Terminological Commission of the International Committee of Slavicists (Bratislava, 1965).[23]

5.1 Besides R. Jakobson's table of S.-C. phonemes, there is another by Ž. Muljačić. Since it appeared in a publication which is not readily accessible.,[24] I present it here in conjunction with Jakobson's table. Signs appearing in Jakobson's table only are marked [ ], those used by Muljačić only are marked ( ). The vowels are treated identically, so they are omitted (cf. Figure 12.)

	t	d	c	s	z	p	b	f	v	ć	ӡ	č	ӡ̌	š	ž	k	g	x	n	m	ɲ	r	l	ļ
Vocality																						±	±	±
Nasality			−						−					−					+	+	+			
Compactness	−	−	−	−	−	−	−	−	+	+	+[+]	+	+	+	+	−[−]	+						−	+
Gravity	−	−	−	−		+	+	+	+	−	−	−				+	+	+	−	+				
Continuousness	−	−[±]	+	+	−	−	+	+	−	−	[± ±]	+	+	−	+								−	+[+]
Voicing	−	+		−	+	−	+	−	+	−	+	−	+	−	+									
Stridentness	(−)	(+)								(−)	(−)	(+)	(+)											

Fig. 12

5.2 Muljačić has introduced the DF of stridentness/mellowness, after E. Stankiewicz.[25] Otherwise his table does not differ from R. Jakobson's except in that the number of (+) ~ ø *or* (−) ~ ø oppositions is increased in three instances (/ʒ̆/, m, ḷ/), but in accordance with this conception one could even dispense with the sign (+) or (−) for strident/mellow with /ʒ/ and /ʒ̆/. I have explained my reasons for believing why this treatment does not agree with the facts (2.2.2-2.2.4.2). Moreover, the answer to the DF of vocality is not precise, i.e. ø with the obstruents and the nasals, (±) with the liquids and (+) with the vowels.

6.1 Finally, I propose a revised table of the phonemic inventory of Standard S.-C., Ijekavian version.[26] It contains the result of 2.1-3.4.1, but for the purpose of convertibility with the table in 5.1, I have not modified the terminology or marking (cf. Figure 13).

	t	d	c	s	z	p	b	f	v	ć	ʒ́	č	ǯ	š	ž	k	g	x
Vocality	−	−	−	−	−	−	−	−	−	−	−	−	−	−	−	−	−	−
Consonantality	(+	+	+	+	+	+	+	+	+	+	+	+	+	+	+	+	+	+)
Compactness	−	−	−	−	−	−	−	−	−	+	+	+	+	+	+	+	+	+
Gravity	−	−	−	−	−	+	+	+	+	−	−	−	−	−	−	+	+	+
Continuousness	−	−	−	+	+	−	−	+	+	−	−	−	−	+	+	−	−	+
Voicing	−	+		−	+	−	+	−	+	−	+	−	+	−	+	−	+	
Stridentness	−	−	+							−	−	+	+					

	n	m	ɲ	l	ḷ	r	r̥		ı̣	i	ě	e	u	o	a
Vocality	+	+	+	+	+	+	+	Vocality	+	+	+	+	+	+	+
Consonantality	+	+	+	+	+	+	+	Consonantality	−	−	−	−	−	−	−
Nasality	+	+	+	−	−	−	−	Compactness	−	−	−	−	−	−	+
Compactness	−	−	+	−	+			Diffuseness	+	+	−	−	+	−	
Gravity	−	+						Gravity	−	−	−	−	+	+	
Continuousness				+	+	−	−	Tension	−	+	+	−			
Tension						−	+								

Fig. 13

6.2 Some comments are needed on the phonemic characteristics of standard /c/ and /x/, as well as an explanation of the additional signs.

6.2.1 The comparison of the Standard S.-C. consonant system with an ideal Čakavian and an ideal Štokavian dialect pattern will provide a useful illustration (cf. Figure 14).

Čakavian inventory	t	d	c	s	z	p	b	f	v	ć	č	š	ž	k	g	x
Vocality	–	–	–	–	–	–	–	–	–	–	–	–	–	–	–	–
Compactness	–	–	–	–	–	–	–	–	–	+	+	+	+	+	+	+
Gravity	–	–	–	–	–	+	+	+	+	–	–	–	–	+	+	+
Continuousness	–	–	–	+	+	–	–	+	+	–	–	+	+	–	–	+
Voicing	–	+		–	+	–	+	–	+			–	+	–	+	
Stridentness			–	–	+					–	+					

Fig. 14

This corresponds to the following pattern:

```
p   t   c       b   d   -       f   s   v   z
k   ć   č       g   -   -       x   š   -   ž
```

The ideal Štokavian inventory does not differ from Standard S.-C. except in the presence of /ӡ/, but this phoneme is not present in the whole area of the type and, where it does exist, has a low functional load in the code and in the context. Accordingly, the pattern looks like this:

```
p   t   c       b   d   (ӡ)     f   s   v   z
k   ć   č       g   ӡ́   ӡ̌       x   š   -   ž
```

It is not possible to dispense with the DF of voicing/voicelessness with /g/ ~ /k/ and continuousness/disc. with /x/ ~ /k/ in any of the tables. For the /g/ ~ /x/ opposition, one of the DFs should be selected. As to continuousness, the only non-existent opposition is, in both patterns, /g/ : (γ). As to voicing, we have, in both patterns, no opposition /x/ : (γ); in the Štokavian pattern neither do we usually have the opposition /c/ ~ /ӡ/ (or, if it does exist, it is not on equal footing with other pairs), and in the Čakavian pattern there are no oppositions /c/ : (ӡ), /ć/ : (ӡ́) and /č/ : (ӡ̌). Consequently, it is obvious that voicing is the weaker partner.

   6.2.2 The tendency to develop more stable and more symmetrical patterns can be observed in the Čakavian as well as in the Štokavian dialects. The redundant voicelessness is represented more strongly in Čakavian. There is no strident voiced plosive, while /g/ is the only compact voiced plosive. The vulnerable series /g, k, x/ will be dispensed with by the exemption of /g/. The result is the pattern:

```
p   t   c       b   d   -       f   s   v   z
k   ć   č       -   -   -       x   š   γ   ž
```

The pattern contains neither any voiced compact plosive nor any voiced strident plosive, and every constrictive is placed in a solid square. This is a

very simple definition. The change /g/ > /γ/ occurs not because of the insta-
bility of the continuousness/disc. opposition in Čakavian, but simply
because of its solidity; the liquidation of /x/ would result in a much more
disharmonious pattern which would require much longer definition.

The Štokavian pattern develops in quite a different direction: it is /x/
which must go. There are three possible ways that this change can take
place: /x/ > ø, or /x/ > /k/, or /x/ > /γ/ > /g/. The last change rarely stops at
the middle stage since nothing is achieved by it.

$$
\begin{array}{lll\quad lll\quad llll}
p & t & c & b & d & (ʒ) & f & s & v & z \\
k & ć & č & g & ʒ́ & ž & & š & & ž
\end{array}
$$

The new pattern is defined simply: it is symmetrical without compact grave
constrictives.

6.2.2.1 In all the patterns presented, the status and the nature of the
phonemes /f/ and /v/ are simplified, i.e. some of their additional characteristics have here been neglected.

6.2.3 The two extreme dialect types present very useful information
from the point of view of Standard S.-C.[27] In any case, the S.-C. linguistic
consciousness, based upon the standard, identifies the dialect phoneme /γ/
with the standard /x/, which again proves the redundancy of its voicelessness. This is valid both for locally isolated Štokavian types still having the
non-liquidated /γ/ < /x/ and for fairly common Čakavian types having /γ/ <
/g/. The average S.-C. speaker accordingly hears the dialect Štokavian form
/muγa/ as /muxa/ (standard /muxa/, 'a fly') and the Čakavian /noγa/ as
/noxa/ (standard /noga/, 'leg').

Notes

1. Cf. Ivić (1965).

2. Cf. Jakobson (1962: 421).

3. I shall not discuss here what k_a and k_b would stand for.

4. Cf. Jakobson (1962: 59, 272); Ivić (1965: 58) adds the influence of the velars and the
   labials on Lusatian (in fact, Low Lusatian) and Kashubian /o/.

5. Cf. Popowska-Taborska (1961: 36).

6. Cf. Jakobson (1962: 324, 325, 379).

7. Cf. Jakobson (1962: 644).

8. Cf. Šaumjan (1962). In general, I do not accept Šaumjan's concept of DFs. He elaborates it further in: Šaumjan (1965).

9. Cf. Ivić (1965: 57-60, 63, 64, 67). Ivić supplies an interesting exemplification, not only for plosives but also for other obstruents.

10. Cf. Jakobson (1962: 484) and Šaumjan (1962: 128, 135, 136).

11. Cf. Jakobson (1962: 13).

12. Cf. Šaumjan (1962: 154-56; 1965: 102).

13. Cf. Jakobson (1962: 496, 505).

14. Cf. Trubetzkoj (1939: 168) and Kuznecov (1948: 132-33, 135).

15. Cf. Muljačić (1964a: 32). This work, dealing with the problems of general and Italian phonology, contains many new observations and inventive solutions concerning the phonologies of different languages, especially of Latin and S.-C.

16. Cf. Jakobson (1962: 422).

17. Cf. Muljačić (1964b: 84).

18. Cf. Kuznecov (1948: 136, 139). Kuznecov writes /j/ but in S.-C. [j] is a less frequent variant than [i̯].

19. Cf. Lunt (1952: 10).

20. László's contribution in: Babić (1963: 29).

21. Cf. Brozović (1964: 141-47). In Standard Ijekavian, /lěpo/ ('beautiful'), /němo/ ('mute') can be realized as /li̯ēpo, ni̯ēmo/, but /li̯ēmo/ ('we pour'), /mi̯ēmo/ ('we wash') cannot result in */lěmo, měmo/.

22. Cf. Kuznecov (1948: 133, 134).

23. Cf. Brozović (unpublished ms.).

24. Cf. Muljačić (1964b: 84).

25. Cf. Stankiewicz (1958: 9, 10).

26. For his co-operation, my thanks are due to Vjekoslav Suzanić, expert in English and S.-C. phonetics.

27. The literature on the dialects is ample, but generally traditional and in publications which are not readily accessible. The essential data can be found in: Ivić (1957).

References

Babić, Stjepan. 1963. *Jezik* [Language] (= *Školski leksikon*, 12). Zagreb: Privreda.

Brozović, Dalibor. 1964. "Vom Begriff der Richtung bei den phonologischen Oppositionen (Über die phonologische Individualität des Reflexes des langen Jat im Standardijekavischen)." *Wiener slavistisches Jahrbuch* 11: 141-47.

-----. "Terminologija razlikovnih obilježja u slavenskim jezicima i njezino uklapanje u slavenski terminološki sustav" [The terminology of distinctive features in Slavic languages and its part in the Slavic terminological system]. Unpublished ms. (Data later included in: *Slovník Slovanské lingvistické terminologie*. I. Prague: Prague Academia. 1977: 86-103.)

Ivić, Pavle. 1957. "Dva glavna pravca razvoja konsonantizma u srpskohrvatskom jeziku" [Two main directions in the development of consonantism in Serbocroatian]. *Godišnjak Filozofskog fakulteta u Novom Sadu* 2: 169-85.

-----. 1965. "Roman Jakobson and the growth of phonology". *Linguistics* 18: 35-78.

Jakobson, Roman. 1962. *Selected Writings*. Vol. I: *Phonological Studies*. The Hague: Mouton.

Kuznecov, P.S. 1948. "O fonologičeskoj sisteme serbo-xorvatskogo jazyka" [About the phonological system in Serbocroatian]. *Izvestija AN SSSR. OLJa* 7.2.

Lunt, Horace G. 1952. *Grammar of the Macedonian Literary Language*. Skopje.

Muljačić, Žarko. 1964a. *Opća fonologija i fonologija talijanskog jezika* [General phonology and the phonology of Italian]. Zagreb.

-----. 1964b. "Roman Jakobson, *Selected Writings*, Vol. I: *Phonological Studies*". *Živi jezici* 6.

Popowska-Taborska, Hanna. 1961. *Centralne zagadnienie wokalizmu kaszubskiego*. Warsaw.

Stankiewicz, Edward. 1958. "Toward a phonemic typology of the Slavic languages". *American Contributions to the Fourth International Congress of Slavicists*. The Hague: Mouton.

Šaumjan, S.K. 1962. *Problemy teoretičeskoj fonologii* [Problems of theoretical phonology]. Moscow.

-----. 1965. *Strukturnaja lingvistika* [Structural linguistics]. Moscow.

Trubetzkoj, N.S. 1939. *Grundzüge der Phonologie. Travaux du Cercle Linguistique de Prague* 7.

Generative structuralism*

Ranko Bugarski
Faculty of Philology, University of Belgrade

1   Introduction

According to the 'official' transformationalist view, generative grammar represents a radical break with the established tradition of structural
linguistics. This claim, reiterated many times by Chomsky and his followers, persists despite occasional mild disclaimers by Chomsky himself, who
now concedes that his interpretation of 'structural linguistics' may have
been somewhat too narrow (cf. e.g. Chomsky 1968:19 and 1979:76-7).
While there is some truth to the claim, especially on this narrow interpretation, it appears to be vastly exaggerated on the whole. This has not gone
unnoticed, and there are numerous references in the literature — by
authors of diverse interests and persuasions — pointing out that generative
grammar should properly be regarded as an offshoot of, rather than a
departure from, structural linguistics. Some of these references will be
given below; for the moment they may be exemplified by Anttila
(1974:278), who notes that transformationalism, far from being a revolu-
tion, was a natural further development of structuralism, and by Bolinger
(1976:238), who aptly characterizes generative grammar as a 'reluctant but
nevertheless legitimate heir' of structural linguistics.

---

* This article, based on a paper delivered at the 14th Annual Meeting of the Societas Linguistica Europaea in Copenhagen in August 1981, was originally published in *Acta Linguistica Haf-
niensia* 17 (1982), 1: 49-60. It is reprinted here in substantially the same form, except for the
addition of the last paragraph in Section 3.6. (and with it two new references), minor technical
adjustments, and the correction of typographical errors. Permission to reprint was kindly
granted by the Linguistic Circle of Copenhagen.

Remarks like these, however, are typically made in passing; the thesis that generative grammar is really part of structural linguistics, that an informed view of the conceptual and methodological history of modern linguistics would highlight decisive continuities between the two, has not received a full treatment to date (though parts of the background for this are provided in works such as Hermanns 1977). The present paper can obviously lay no claim to being such a treatment, but it can at least try to indicate some of the problems that would have to be worked out in detail in an undertaking of this nature. The main justification for raising the issue at all in this form is our belief that the question is not simply terminological, as it might appear to be at first sight. In our view it has serious intellectual content — particularly, though not exclusively, from the standpoint of the problem of periodization in the recent history of linguistics, i.e. of identifying the major breakthroughs in theory and methodology (for some discussion of this general problem see Hockett 1965, and Hymes and Fought 1975:1141-6).

2 Terminology

Some terminological clarification is evidently necessary before we proceed any further. The term 'structuralism' is notoriously ambiguous, even when limited to the field of linguistics. For the present purpose, following Lyons (1973:5-6), we distinguish between two relevant senses of the term, one broad and the other narrow. The broad sense is that associated with Saussure and European schools in general, and in the United States mainly with the Boas-Sapir tradition. Language is here seen as a hierarchically ordered relational structure, whose units can on no level be defined independently but can only be identified as points in a network of relations; the parts thus acquire their significance only through their interrelations within the whole structure. In attempting to lay bare the structure of language, this version of structuralism is general and theoretical in its orientation. The narrow sense, on the other hand, is primarily associated with American post-Bloomfieldian distributionalist procedures of the 1940s and 1950s, in some ways culminating in Harris (1951). In effect rejecting the *langue/ parole* distinction and concentrating on the superficial structures of the individual languages, this approach is corpus-based and taxonomic; excluding the study of meaning from linguistics proper, it emphasizes inductive discovery procedures and is descriptivist and methodological in its objectives.

Finally, by generative grammar we mean the transformational variety as developed over the years by Chomsky and his associates, for must purposes — though not for all — including such further extensions as generative semantics. This is, then, a theory of language structure which seeks to relate sound and meaning by a system of rules. It distinguishes between competence and performance and between deep structure and surface structure, stresses evaluation procedures, and is universalist and explanatory in basic outlook.

Generative grammar thus appears to be in a point-by-point opposition to structuralism in the narrow sense as a spatio-temporally restricted, though historically and methodologically highly important, variety of structural linguistics, within which Chomsky himself was reared and against which he came to rebel; there is more here, however, than meets the superficial eye. On the other hand, there seems to be little conflict in principle with the broad sense of structuralism.

3 Continuities

Our claim, then, is that generative grammar is a fully legitimate continuation of structuralism in the broad sense, but also — in partially opposing it — of structuralism in the narrow sense. In what follows, the latter link especially, being less evident, will be stressed by pointing out several interrelated aspects of this relationship. We will proceed roughly from external considerations to more strictly internal ones.

3.1 Historical development

The historical developments on the American linguistic scene from Bloomfield to Chomsky, including the formal educational link supplied by the latter's studies under Harris, are well known and need no elaboration here. Many details are now to be found in Hymes and Fought (1975), an unusually rich historical review likely to dispel several current misconceptions, which — be it noted — squarely accommodates Chomsky under the heading of American structuralism; cf. also the points debated by Lyons (1970, 1977) and Hymes (1972) relating to Chomský's early 'Bloomfieldianism'.

3.2 *Socio-psychological heritage*

The sociology, or social psychology, of American linguistics reveals striking similarities between the earlier structuralists and the transformationalists: the same spirit of orthodoxy, in-group solidarity, intolerance of opposition. As regards ways of thinking, it has been argued (notably by Lyons 1970) that especially the early Chomsky was a Bloomfieldian psychological structuralist, though with very different objectives; it is significant that Hockett's critique of chomsky (Hockett 1968) largely bypasses *Syntactic structures*. There is evidence of the same empiricism, coupled with a continuing distrust of meaning, as against a common liking for discrete units and well-defined structures, for orderly data and neat results. The ways of argumentation and the criteria of validity for arguments are likewise psychologically akin in the two seemingly antagonistic camps.

3.3 *Methodological similarities*

Closely related to the preceding point is the shared emphasis on rigorous methods, explicit statement and exhaustive analysis (where the spiritual antecedents can, of course, be relevantly traced further back — notably to the Neogrammarian ideal of exceptionless sound laws). The 'all and only' claim of generative grammar is reminiscent of the distributionalist slogan 'once a phoneme, always a phoneme', just as the careful formulation of transformational rules reminds one of the equally thorough earlier analyses (many of which can profitably be reread, from this point of view, in Joos 1957; cf. also, once again, Hymes and Fought 1975). Idealizations as a methodological necessity were likewise not invented by the author of *Aspects of the Theory of Syntax*, though he has been severely criticized on this score; such insights have characterized linguistic theory at least since Saussure and Bloomfield, and are in fact an essential ingredient of structuralist thought in general.

3.4 *Programmatic links*

By comparison with generative grammar, earlier brands of structuralism are relatively weak on well-defined goals, particularly extralinguistic ones. Yet it is revealing, in visualizing generative grammar as a system of rules relating sound and meaning and leading to a better understanding of man, to recall the following two passages: "To put it briefly, in human speech, different sounds have different meanings. To study this co-ordination of certain sounds with certain meanings is to study language." — "It is only a prospect, but not hopelessly remote, that the study of language may help us toward the understanding and control of human events." What is instructive, of course, is that these words are not Chomsky's but Bloomfield's (1933: 27, 509). More generally, however one may choose to use one's terms, the fact remains that all schools of structuralism have professed to study, and have indeed studied, aspects of language *structure* — and generative grammar, frequently characterized by its proponents as seeking to provide 'a general theory of linguistic structure', is surely no exception here. That 'structure' means different things to different people does not invalidate this obvious and crucial point.

3.5 *Logical sequence*

If phonology and morphology can in principle be handled distributionally, syntax evidently needs transformations of some kind. This was realized by Harris and taken up by Chomsky, who duly added generation to taxonomy (the latter staying on in the form of phrase structure rules beside the new transformational rules). In the methodological — and largely chronological — progression up the scale of linguistic levels, starting with phonology, this was a clear next logical step once syntax was reached. Harris himself notes that "the work of Bloomfield can be looked at as paving the way for the later methods of transformational analysis" (1973:255; similarly Teeter 1969). The whole development is well summarized by Hymes: "In Chomsky's successful introduction of the goal of generating all and only the grammatical sentences of a language we can see the completion, or carrying through to syntax, of structuralist principle... The trajectory from phonology through syntax to semantics is essentially unified and structuralist, Chomsky's conception of linguistics serving in many ways as its ultimate ideological justification (1972:420, 426).

3.6 *Conceptual fit*

The real testing ground for our thesis, however, is in the implications of the basic concepts. On this level of analysis, the crucial question is whether the notion of transformation can be shown to be properly implied by the notion of structure. This is certainly true in mathematics (e.g. in set theory and mathematical logic), where the concept of structure has been adequately studied. Pointers in the same direction can already be found in fields like psychology and anthropology, as will be noted below (for employment of the concept of structure outside linguistics see Bastide 1962, Boudon 1971, and Robey 1973). But in linguistics itself, for all its impact on many of these other fields, issues like these are still far from clear, for the simple reason that during several decades of 'structural' linguistics the central notion of structure as applied to language has undergone little serious investigation as a technical concept. As a result, it has been rather easy to claim that structuralism is inherently static (and therefore ultimately inadequate), since there are insurmountable difficulties with the notion of dynamic structures. But are there really? Are we truly concerned here with inherent weaknesses, or perhaps merely with insufficient knowledge and inadequate theoretical elaboration?

Questions like these are at present not easily answered. However, by way of illustration from outside linguistics, we might cite Piaget's dynamic view of structure as a system of transformations comprising three basic aspects: wholeness, self-regulation, and transformation (Piaget 1971: chs. 1-2). Stated in linguistic terms, these can be specified as follows. (1) Wholeness is an obvious property of linguistic systems, manifested in the fact that languages are structures rather than mere aggregates of individual terms. (2) Self-regulation is shown in the absence of any need for external intervention: structures can generate new elements from within while remaining conserved and closed (cf. numbers). More generally, this feature allows equilibrium to be maintained in the face of disturbance, whereby disruption in a given subsystem automatically triggers off compensatory action in another (for example, the loss of endings and the parallel fixing of word order in English and other languages). (3) The operation of transformational laws never employs elements, nor yields results, external to the system; thus a structure is a system closed under transformation (cf. Chomský's long-held and later abandoned view of transformations as preserving meaning, which was regarded as fully specified in deep structure and held constant through all transformations). A parallel with music is offered by the anthropologist Leach (1973:40-1), who, borrowing an example from Bertrand Russell, enumerates the many transformations a piece of music goes through on the way to becoming a broadcast version of a piano sonata. What is common to all these forms and remains constant is precisely the structure of the piece — 'structure' in this sense being an essentially mathematical concept.

In generative syntax, a surface structure can be regarded as a realization, by transformation, of an underlying deep structure. But this kind of operation is extendable to other levels, where basically the same principles applied earlier in the development of modern linguistics. Thus a phoneme (or morpheme) may be said to have a transformational field defined by the set of its allophones (or allomorphs). In this sense, 'classical' structuralist phonemes and morphemes are also deep, abstract underlying units; cf. e.g. Teeter's argument (1969:3-4) that this was already true for Bloomfield, or Bloch's oft-repeated dictum 'Phonemes do not occur'. Diagrammatically, this idea can be presented as in Figure 1.

$$\begin{array}{lll}
DS & \Rightarrow & SS \\
\hline
 & & [a] \\
/A/ & \Rightarrow & [b] \\
 & & [c] \\
\hdashline
 & & /a/ \\
\{A\} & \Rightarrow & /b/ \\
 & & /c/ \\
\hdashline
S_d & \Rightarrow & S_s
\end{array}$$

where

DS	=	deep structure
SS	=	surface structure
S_d	=	DS of a sentence
S_s	=	SS of a sentence
$\Rightarrow$	=	'is realized as'
		or
		'is transformed into'

Fig. 1. Transformation on different linguistic levels

It would seem to follow, then, that conceptually — if not explicitly — the notion of transformation has been present in structural linguistics from its inception in phonology, to be fully formalized within the framework of generative grammar on the level of syntax. One is reminded here of Haugen's brief remark (1974:620) about the *-etic/-emic* distinction being the first step towards the surface/deep dichotomy. Furthermore, in terms of a simplified comparison with algebra, which makes use of a triple set of units, relations and operations, it may be said that earlier structuralism restricted itself to the first two, defining language as a relational structure — whereas generative grammar added the third key notion, that of operation, highlighting the transformational structure of language. The point to be observed is that this was, as stated, an addition and not a replacement.

In view of all this, it seems proper enough for Piaget (1971:85) to describe Chomsky's devising of a coherent system of transformations as 'a genuinely structuralist procedure'; cf. also the earlier quotations from Hymes (1972). Perhaps it will also be clearer now why mathematicians and social scientists have on the whole been less reluctant than many linguists to recognize generative grammar as an offshoot of, rather than a break with, structural linguistics. Thus Gandy (1973:152), writing about mathematical structures, flatly states that "one of the ideals of structural linguistics is to provide rules of generation for any given language". Similar allusions can be found in the work of major structuralist thinkers such as Lévi-Strauss, in addition to scholars already referred to, like Piaget or Leach. Conversely, this discussion partly shows how the transformationalists, so obviously concerned with structure in language, have on occasion been able to claim that they were really studying something else.

What these contrasts actually reveal is not just accidental terminological variation, but rather differences in intellectual background and disciplinary training. The polysemous term 'structure' has historically, and no doubt legitimately, been used to refer not only to the method and the result of construction but also to the process of constructing (for a succint but revealing discussion see now Williams 1983: q.v. *structural*). This third, processual and dynamic aspect of structures, while taken for granted in some other academic fields, was largely missed in 'structural' linguistics, with its early theoretical focus on static relations. In this way, as noted before, the technical implications of the notion of structure were never really developed within linguistics, for all the discussion of its emergence and use there in the context of earlier preoccupations with language as an organism and as a system (a historical review of these and related issues can be found in Koerner 1975). When this gap is filled, as it probably will be some day, controversies over the relative status of structural and generative linguistics should fall into their proper place.

3.7 *Epistemological status of structures*

An inquiry into epistemological issues lurking in the background is only incidental to the main argument, but the matter is worth noting here, however briefly. In addressing the question of what 'comes first' (as revealed by practice), we may once again try to interpret Piaget's suggestions in the domain of linguistics. Piaget (1971:6-13) sets up an opposition between 'atomist association' (which may be exemplified by empiricist psychology and pre-structural linguistics) and 'pre-formed wholes' (such as are implied by Platonic or Kantian forms, Husserlian essences, or Saussurean structures). He then poses the question of 'structureless genesis' as against 'ungenerated wholes' — in other words, how can there be genesis without a structure being generated, or a structure that has not been generated in the first place? To answer this, he postulates a link in the form of what he calls operational structuralism, or constructivism. What is primary here are neither elements nor wholes but the processes of formation of wholes from elements — i.e. the laws of formation and transformation. In this case the rules of generative grammar provide an obvious linguistic instance, in that language as a static system of signs (à la Saussure) and language as a dynamic system of rules (à la Chomsky) appear to stand in precisely this kind of relationship. The character of the whole depends on the system's laws of composition, and systems are constantly being reconstructed: "The being of structures consists in their coming to be, that is, their being 'under construction'" (Piaget 1971:140).

Linked with this issue are two alternative views of human knowledge, which may be labelled 'traditional' and 'constructivist' respectively (cf. Piaget 1971:34). The former view implies an analysis of the presuppositions of 'foundations', i.e. of the lover strata; the latter, by contrast, dictates the construction of higher strata. The first may be visualized as a stratified pyramid, the second as an expanding upward-moving spiral — as in Figure 2.

Traditional   Constructivist

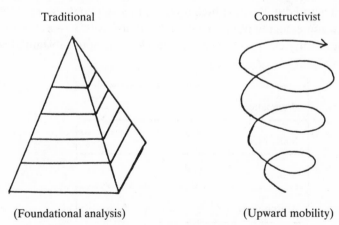

(Foundational analysis)   (Upward mobility)

Fig. 2. Views of human knowledge

The traditional conception has apparently worked better for some fields than for others; cf., for example, the foundations of mathematics as against the foundations of linguistics, where in the latter case even the general meaning of the phrase is not particularly clear. The constructivist conception, on the other hand, is open to the well-known charge of Gödel's theorem, which demonstrates that no formal system rich enough to contain elementary arithmetics is sufficient in itself to establish its own consistency, so that appeal must be made to ever 'higher' theories, ever 'stronger' systems.

The recent history of linguistics supplies telling examples both of the shortcomings of relying on 'foundations' and of the inherent insufficiency of formal systems. On the one hand, orthodox American distributionalists never tired of preaching that there must be no 'mixing of levels', i.e. that work on a given linguistic level may start only after analysis on the next *lower* level has been completed (so that a title such as Pike 1947 was intolerably heretical — for which, among his other sins, its author was duly punished by being excluded from the representative anthology in Joos 1957); the practice, however, was often rather different, and for good reasons. On the other hand, and in line with the practice just noted, in modern linguistics as a whole it proved impossible to stay on a given level looking only down; it rather turned out methodologically inevitable to reach *upwards* for support. Thus the establishment of a phonological level presupposed some reliance on the 'interlevel' of morphophonology, itself perversely anchored in the next higher level of morphology. Morphology in turn implied some degree of syntactic analysis, and syntax — as has by now become abundantly clear — can scarcely be done without substantial refer-

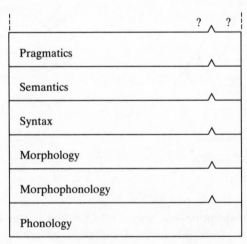

Fig. 3. Linguistic levels and the curse of Gödel

ence to semantics. Soon after serious work in semantics had started, however, there came the new realization that this rather elusive level itself had to hang on something 'higher'. But what? A likely current candidate seems to be pragmatics, a notion at present even more elusive. It remains to be seen what, if anything, pragmatics is going to rely on as the constructivist spiral reaches out into yet more abstract spheres. In any case, 'constructivism' has served linguistics well so far, even if it now appears to have come to the end of its tether. (See Figure 3).

4   Conclusion

The foregoing analysis would weem to suggest that structuralism as a general linguistic orientation can be split up into two branches — one taxonomic (static, distributional and predominantly methodological), the other generative (dynamic, transformational and essentially theoretical). The two branches are complementary rather than mutually exclusive. The contrast between them is clear enough from a formal point of view, though in fact it is only relative. On the one hand, the earlier taxonomic structuralism came close to the notion of transformation, as already indicated (in a less technical sense, of course, the concept had already been present in traditional grammar, in the work of Jespersen, Guillaume, Tesnière and other syntacticians, as well as in glossematics and other European brands of structuralist thinking). On the other hand, rules are taxonomized as well as units, 'deep structures' as well as 'surface structures' (as for example in the identification and labelling of deep-structure cases in case grammar). Further examples could easily be adduced to relativize the distinction made. Yet the dichotomy still seems considerably more appropriate than a sharp split between structural linguistics and generative grammar.

In several of his recent writings, Koerner (see especially 1976) raises but leaves open the question whether Chomsky has — in the terminology of Kuhn (1970) — created a new paradigm, or whether his work represents only a late mopping-up phase within the Saussurean paradigm. The details of this issue can probably not be settled without more historical perspective than is available at present, but the general answer, we would argue, is likely to be along the lines suggested by Lyons (1973:19): "Generative grammar, whether it is conceived more widely as a theory of the nature of language or more narrowly as a formalization of the paradigmatic and syntagmatic relations holding between linguistic units, has enriched, but it has not supplanted or outmoded, Saussurean structuralism".

But there is another and broader sense in which Chomský's work is the logical culmination of the dominant trend in linguistics in this century, including most notably the efforts of both Saussure and Bloomfield; this has to do with the isolation of language — more precisely, the *structure* of language — as a separate object of study. While Chomsky's programme is interdisciplinary, he in effect does tend to cut off language from society, communication and history, attempting to localize it in the human brain and to study it there as a distinct and unique formal system. In the words of Hymes (1977:92): "From a social standpoint, transformational grammar might equally well be seen as the culmination of the leading theme of structural linguistics. To center analysis in a deep structure, one grounded in human nature, is to fulfill an impulse of structural linguistics to treat language as a sphere of wholly autonomous form". To this we would only add that Chomsky's particular interests represent the apex of a trend also in developing, for the first time in history, the goal of fully describing a language, even to the extent of predicting the possible form of its unuttered sentences.

Other current developments within generative grammar do not necessarily follow the same direction; for example, generative semantics, in its abandonment of strict formalization, has introduced alternatives to Chomsky's own approach which in some ways signal a return to more traditional preoccupations. This, however, does not invalidate the main argument of the present paper, which is that generative grammar as a whole is only the most recent branch on the tree of structural linguistics, structuralism in the broad sense still being the dominant linguistic philosophy of our day and age. Rather than being regarded as a finished set of doctrines belonging to the history of ideas, it should still be seen as a living and creative body of thought about human language.

This does not mean, however, that no further relevant distinctions can be made in the area under consideration. There is in fact a larger dichotomy, implied by the preceding paragraphs, which cuts across most of the linguistic work in the twentieth century. It is that between immanent and transcendental linguistics (to make use of Hjelmslev's well-known opposition), or, as some might prefer to put it, between 'microlinguistics' and 'macrolinguistics'. In terms of current theoretical debate, this could also — and perhaps most appropriately — be phrased as a contrast between autonomous linguistics (including, *nota bene*, much of both 'classical' structuralism and generative grammar) and interdisciplinary linguistics (encompassing such hyphenated disciplines as psycholinguistics, sociolinguistics and neurolinguistics, various ethnographic and philological approaches, and the like). Here too the contrast is less sharp than it may appear to be, but a systematic investigation of the two rival views of linguistics as they have emerged over the decades would undoubtedly turn up far more substantial issues than the exaggerated and ultimately unjustified opposition against which this paper has argued.

References

Anttila, Raimo. 1974. "Ist der Strukturalismus in der Sprachwissenschaft schon passé?" *Historiographica Linguistica* 1.2:278-82.

Bastide, Roger (ed.). 1962. *Sense et usage du terme STRUCTURE dans les sciences humaines et sociales*. The Hague: Mouton.

Bloomfield, Leonard. 1933. *Language*. New York: Henry Holt.

Bolinger, Dwight L. 1976. Review of *Idiom Structure in English* by Adam Makkai (The Hague: Mouton, 1972). *Language* 52:238-41.

Boudon, Raymond. 1971. *The Uses of Structuralism*. London: Heinemann.

Chomsky, Noam. 1957. *Syntactic Structures*. The Hague: Mouton.

-----. 1965. *Aspects of the Theory of Syntax*. Cambridge, Mass.: MIT Press.

-----. 1968. *Language and Mind*. New York: Harcourt, Brace and World.

-----. 1979. *Language and Responsibility*. Hassocks: Harvester Press.

Gandy, Robin. 1973. "'Structure' in mathematics". In: Robey 1973:138-53.

Harris, Zellig S. 1951. *Methods in Structural Linguistics*. Chicago: University of Chicago Press.

-----. 1973. Review of *A Leonard Bloomfield Anthology* ed. by Charles F. Hockett (Bloomington: Indiana University Press, 1970). *IJAL* 39: 252-5.

Haugen, Einar. 1974. "Half a century of the Linguistic Society". *Language* 50:619-21.

Hermanns, Fritz. 1977. *Die Kalkülisierung der Grammatik: Philologische Untersuchungen zu Ursprung, Entwicklung und Erfolg der sprachwissenschaftlichen Theorien Noam Chomskys*. Heidelberg: Julius Groos.

Hockett, Charles F. 1965. "Sound change". *Language* 41:185-204.

-----. 1968. *The State of the Art*. The Hague: Mouton.

Hymes, Dell H. 1972. Review of Lyons 1970. *Language* 48:416-27.

-----. 1977. *Foundations in Sociolinguistics: An Ethnographic Approach*. London: Tavistock.

----- and Fought, John. 1975. "American structuralism". In: Sebeok 1975, II:903-1176.

Joos, Martin (ed.). 1957. *Readings in Linguistics*. New York: American Council of Learned Societies.

Koerner, E.F. Konrad. 1975. "European structuralism: Early beginnings". In: Sebeok 1975, II:717-827.

-----. 1976. "Towards a historiography of linguistics: 19th and 20th century paradigms". In: Parret 1976:685-718.

Kuhn, Thomas S. 1970. *The Structure of Scientific Revolutions*. 2nd ed. Chicago: University of Chicago Press.

Leach, Edmund. 1973. "Structuralism in social anthropology". In: Robey 1973:37-56.

Lyons, John. 1970, rev. ed. 1977. *Chomsky*. London: Fontana/Collins.

-----. 1973. "Structuralism in linguistics". In: Robey 1973:5-19.

Parret, Herman (ed.). 1976. *History of Linguistic Thought and Contemporary Linguistics*. Berlin/New York: Walter de Gruyter.

Piaget, Jean. 1971. *Structuralism*. London: Routledge and Kegan Paul.

Pike, Kenneth L. 1947. "Grammatical prerequisites to phonemic analysis". *Word* 3:155-72.

Robey, David (ed.). 1973. *Structuralism*. Oxford: Clarendon Presas.

Sebeok, Thomas A. (ed.). 1975. *Current Trends in Linguistics* 13. I-II. The Hague/Paris: Mouton.

Teeter, Karl V. 1969. "Leonard Bloomfield's linguistics". *Language Sciences* 7:1-6.

Williams, Raymond. 1983. *Key words: A Vocabulary of Culture and Society*. 2nd ed. London: Fontana Paperbacks.

Some contributions to the theory of contact linguistics

Rudolf Filipović
Yugoslav Academy of Sciences and Arts, Zagreb

1 Languages started influencing one another from the very beginning of their history. A systematic examination of language contact began in the 18th century when lexicographers developed their interest in etymology of words. Thus they got in touch with the problem of language borrowing and its basic unit: loanword. The development of linguistic theory in the 19th and the first half of the 20th century did not neglect the questions of language mixture and mixed languages and later the issues of bilingualism and linguistic borrowing (Filipović 1986a). However, a systematic theory based on very precisely defined principles is presented in the works of two linguists who laid foundations for the theory of languages in contact: Einar Haugen (1950, 1953) and Uriel Weinreich (1953).

Therefore, when we had to define the theory and method for our project the *English Element in European Languages* (EEEL) (Filipović 1982a), we began from the theory as it is exemplified in the works of its two founders. We even went so far (Filipović 1986a) as to call the set of principles defined by Haugen and Weinreich *Haugen-Weinreich theory* (H-W theory). Although Haugen and Weinreich do not agree in every respect (each of them has his own terminology and sometimes his own approach), we find the term 'Haugen-Weinreich theory' suitable as their principles put together cover most features we analyse in the field of languages in contact or contact linguistics. If the analysis of a corpus requires a different approach from the one given in the H-W theory, or even an additional principle not found in this theory, then a new research work has to be organized in order to redefine one or more of the already accepted principles, or to add a new principle non-existing in the H-W theory. This process adds new elements to the old theory and we call them contributions to or innovations in the theory of contact linguistics.

The research done for the two projects 'The English Element in European Languages' (EEEL) (Filipović 1966, 1972, 1973, 1974, 1977a, 1977b, 1982a, 1983, 1984a) and 'Croatian Dialects in Contact with American English' (CDAE) (Filipović 1980a, 1982b, 1985a, 1986b) showed that some old principles did not satisfy the needs of these two projects (Filipović 1977a) and therefore several old principles had to be reinterpreted and even some new ones had to be added. Since the basic task of the analysis of the corpus is to investigate the adaptation of the model to the replica, innovations in the theory will be presented through the analysis of our corpus.

2 H-W's division of adaptation into three stages (the model — the compromise replica — the replica) is not sufficient for the analysis of our corpus, since some results of the analysis remain outside of that classification. A thorough analysis of the nature of all changes that appear in this process shows that they can be divided globally into two groups: (1) those that take place from the moment of transfer of the model (an English word) into the receiving language up to the integration of the replica into its system; (2) those changes that take place in the replica, an English loanword — an anglicism, from its integration into the system of the borrowing language. On the basis of this fact we have introduced the conceptual distinction between *primary* and *secondary* in the analysis of anglicisms in European languages (Filipović 1977c).

This new distinction of changes in adaptation of anglicisms includes two elements, a chronological one and a qualitative one, since it does not only define the chronology of changes in the course of adaptation but also analyses the quality of these changes. The chronological element shows that the first period represents the stage of the compromise replica and that it is limited in time; the second period is not fixed in duration, and we know only its beginning. The qualitative element is far more important, for it classifies the changes in the process of adaptation. The changes in these two periods, primary and secondary, are altogether different. Their difference corresponds to the theoretical distinction between bilingualism and monolingualism.

Primary changes are inconsistent and unstable. They give rise to variants which are compromise replicas. They are subject to various influences, which can act in parallel (e.g. the formation of a phonological form on the basis of pronunciation and/or orthography). The influence of both systems – languages is felt, and thus there come about the changeable forms and numerous variants of the compromise replica. All these phenomena are connected with the bilingual speaker, since they are conditioned by linguistic contact which is possible and easily established only in the bilingual speaker.

Secondary changes are entirely different in quality and have scarcely any features of primary changes. They are constant and stable. There is little chance of variants appearing in this period. The replica is rarely subject to change. If some change does occur, it is slow and always in agreement with the development tendency of the receiving language. Changes in this period are typical of the monolingual speaker and his language, which in this case has very little chance of coming into contact.

The value and usefulness of the conceptual distinction between primary and secondary can be seen in the analysis of anglicisms in European languages on three levels: phonological, morphological and semantic. On the phonological level there appear secondary changes in the area of prosody and distribution of phonemes. Secondary changes on the morphological level take place in the three parts of speech that get adapted in the course of linguistic borrowing: in nouns, adjectives and verbs. On the semantic level, in the analysis of the adaptation of meaning in loanwords, secondary changes occur in the forms of semantic extension, i.e. expansion of meaning both in number and in field.

In determining the accent of anglicisms in European languages with an expiratory stress accent, the primary adaptation regulates changes in the place of the stress. The determination of the musicality of accent in anglicisms in European languages having musical accent is carried out during secondary adaptation, and changes taking place then in the accent of anglicisms are classified as secondary (Filipović 1985b).

Adaptation of verbs in most European languages by adding an infinitive ending is done in primary adaptation. The morphological marking of aspect in anglicisms in languages whose verbal system distinguishes the verbal category of aspect, by prefixation, as it is done with native words of the borrowing language, is a part of secondary adaptation and is classified as a secondary change (Filipović 1986a).

On the semantic level, the first semantic change, be it zero adaptation, restriction of meaning in number or in field, belongs to primary adaptation and is called primary change. The changes of meaning that take place after a loan has been integrated into the system of the borrowing language and after it has been in practical use in it for some time, are called secondary changes since they result from secondary adaptation. They are classified as expansion of meaning in number and in field, and pejoration (Filipović 1968).

3 According to the H-W theory the process of linguistic borrowing starts when a model begins to adapt in order to be integrated into the system of the receiving language. The adaptation of the model is governed by two linguistic laws: substitution and importation. Substitution regulates the replacement of the giving language elements by the equivalent elements of the receiving language. Importation takes place if the lending language elements are transferred into the receiving language. In the initial stage of the analysis of our multilingual corpus some results of the analysis remained outside of the classification given by the H-W theory, that is, that substitution can be broad or narrow. Therefore in our theoretical analysis we reexamined the linguistic phenomena called substitution.

Since substitution is a broad concept, not well defined so far, and since it operates at several levels, it needs to be circumscribed and delimited. Therefore we analysed it according to the levels on which it operates and we even tried to find a new, more inclusive and comprehensive classification and systematization on the basis of the results of our investigation. We also tried to find new terms which would more precisely designate the function of substitution on the levels most often examined in the process of linguistic borrowing: the phonological level and the morphological level. We introduced the term *transphonemization* for the substitution of phonemes (Filipović 1981a) and the term *transmorphemization* for the substitution of morphemes (Filipović 1980b). A detailed analysis conducted on our corpus revealed several types of transphonemization and several stages of transmorphemization. This innovation in the theory enabled us to establish a better classification of phenomena connected with the substitution of all phonemic and morphemic elements appearing in the process of adaptation.

While studying the English element in European languages we have encountered a large number of examples of transphonemization during the formation of the phonological shape of the loanword in the borrowing language. The whole process is based on two principles. The first is that the phonological shape of the loanword is formed on the basis of the pronunciation of the model (an English word): the phonemes of the model are replaced by the phonemes of the borrowing language on the basis of pronunciation similarities. According to the second principle the transphonemization is carried out based on the model's orthographic elements which in the loanword may appear in different pronunciation variants.

Investigation of transphonemization in various European languages has shown regularities in replacement of a phoneme of English with borrowing-language phonemes if transphonemization is carried out on the principle of pronunciation (Filipović 1977b). These regularities are based on differences and similarities between the English phoneme and the phonemes of the borrowing languages and can be arranged into three groups. This division into three groups serves as the basis for classification of the transphonemization types.

The classification of phonemes into three groups is carried out according to their description. Those phonemes of the English language whose description corresponds to phonemes in the borrowing language are placed in the first group; this results in *complete transphonemization*. The second group consists of those English phonemes which differ in part from the phonemes of the borrowing language. The difference can be in degree of opening (especially with vowels), or in the place of articulation (with consonants), but without any change in manner of articulation. This is *partial* or *compromise transphonemization*. The third group covers those English phonemes which do not even have partial articulatory equivalents in the borrowing language: transphonemization is not carried out according to phonetic principles (as with the first two types) but is based on orthography or on extralinguistic factors. This is *free transphonemization*.

4 In order to illustrate all three types of transphonemization, we will examine the phenomenon in anglicisms used in Serbo-Croatian which being genetically different offers a lot of structural differences from English. In this analysis we will consider all the elements by which English phonemes differ from phonemes of Serbo-Croatian, so as to establish all variants of the three types of transphonemization.

4.1 *Complete transphonemization* in the area of vowels affects five English vowel phonemes:

E:	S-C:	E:	S-C:
/i:/	/i/	*team* /ti:m/	*tim*
/e/	/e/	*dress* /dres/	*dres*
/ʌ/	/a/	*rugby* /'rʌgbɪ/	*ragbi*
/ɔ:/	/o/	*lord* /lɔ:d/	*lord*
/u:/	/u/	*shoot* /ʃu:t/	*šut*

Transphonemization of consonants is carried out on the basis of three elements: place of articulation, manner of articulation and aspiration. Complete transphonemization of consonants occurs with a large number of English consonant phonemes: /b/ - b, /g/ - g, /m/ - m, /n/ - n, /f/ - f, /v/ - v, /l/ - l, /h/ - h, /s/ - s, /z/ - z, /ʃ/ - š, /tʃ/ - č, /dʒ/ - dž, /j/ - j.

E.g.: E: /b/   S-C: /b/   E: *bar* /ba:/   S-C: *bar*
       /g/   /g/   *golf* /gɒlf/   *golf*
       /m/   /m/   *match* /mætʃ/   *meč*
       /n/   /n/   *nylon* /ˈnaɪlən/   *najlon*

4.2 *Partial transphonemization* occurs with English phonemes which differ from Serbo-Croatian equivalents only in one part of a genetic description, the other elements being the same. This especially refers to differences in place of articulation while the manner of articulation stays the same.

With vowels partial transphonemization is carried out on the basis of shifting the place of articulation and/or changing (narrowing or enlarging) the opening. The shifting of the place of articulation is seen in the S-C phoneme *a* compared to the English phoneme /a:/, the narrowing of the opening occurs in English phonemes /ɪ/, /æ/, /ɒ/, and /ʊ/ when they are transphonemicized into S-C equivalents *i, e, o, u* which are more closed than their English counterparts.

E: /ɪ/   S-C: /i/   E: *lift* /lɪft/   S-C: *lift*
    /æ/   /e/   *jam* /dʒæm/   *džem*
    /a:/   /a/   *start* /sta:t/   *start*
    /ɒ/   /o/   *box* /bɒks/   *boks*
    /ʊ/   /u/   *pudding* /ˈpʊdɪŋ/   *puding*

Both changes (in place of articulation and in degree of opening) occur in the process of transphonemization of the English phonemes /ɪ/ and /ʊ/ into Serbo-Croatian equivalents *i* and *u*. The difference is not only that English phonemes are more open than Serbo-Croatian but that the two English phonemes are centralized.

Some consonants also are good illustrations of partial transphonemization, i.e. the phenomenon that English phonemes are transphonemicized according to the principle of free change of place but maintenance of the same manner of articulation. The presence or absence of aspiration enters into consideration as one of the criteria for partial transphonemization.

E:	/p/	S-C:	/p/	E:	*punch* /pʌntʃ/	S-C:	*punč*
	/t/		/t/		*test* /test/		*test*
	/d/		/d/		*dock* /dɒk/		*dok*
	/k/		/k/		*camp* /kæmp/		*kamp*

While the English phonemes /p/ and /k/ lose their aspiration in the course of transphonemization, /t/ and /d/ change their place of articulation, and /t/ also loses aspiration.

4.3 *Free transphonemization* occurs very frequently and depends basically on the similarities and differences of the phonological systems of the borrowing language and the lending language. If the phonemic inventories of these two systems, for the most part, coincide, especially in the manner of articulation, then the first two types of transphonemization are more broadly represented. If the opposite situation occurs, that is, the borrowing language has a smaller number of phonemes or a different classification according to place and manner of articulation, then a greater number of cases of free transphonemization occurs in adaptation on the phonological level.

This type of transphonemization is especially common when the phonological shape of the replica (loanword) is formed according to the orthography of the model, and not according to its pronunciation. When the two language systems differ so much in the physiological description of their phonemes that there are no conditions for applying the first and second type of transphonemization, then free transphonemization takes place. In this case extralinguistic factors are at work and only these can explain some of the examples of this type of transphonemization.

We find the first example of such transphonemization when the English model contains the vowel phonemes /ɜ:/ and /ə/. Then the replica in S-C is, as a rule, based on the orthography of the model. With the phoneme /ɜ:/ there is also a second possibility for transphonemization, following the pronunciation. This process of substitution is not carried out directly, as in the first two types, but rather with changes which depend on the sociolinguistic condition of the adaptation of English pronunciation in the English teaching in Croatia. At first the pronunciation of the phoneme /ɜ:/ is incorrectly identified with the pronunciation of the German phoneme /œ/, and later, by simplification, rounded /œ/ opens to *e*. Only in this manner can we explain the free transphonemization of the English phoneme /ɜ:/ into S-C phoneme *e* in words of the type *flert* (E flirt /flɜ:t/).

This is how we arrive at variants; a single English word may at one time adapt according to orthography, and at another time according to pronunciation, depending on extralinguistic factors.

E:	/ɜ:/	S-C:	/ir/	E:	*flirt* /flɜ:t/		S-C:	*flirt*
			/er/					*flert*
	/ə/		/ar/		*standard*			
					/'stændəd/			*standard*
			/a/		*pyjamas*			
					/pə'dʒa:məz/			*pidžama*
			/er/		*corner* /'kɔ:nə/			*korner*
			/o/		*canyon* /'kænjən/			*kanjon*
			/or/		*detector*			
					/dɪ'tektə/			*detektor*
			/ir/		*Yorkshire* /'jɔ:kʃə/			*jorkšir(ac)*

Diphthongs make up the largest group of examples in which free transphonemization occurs. Since the Serbo-Croatian phonological system has no diphthongs, transphonemization of the English diphthongs in Serbo-Croatian is necessarily free transphonemization because the changes are effected in the manner of articulation. In most cases the components of the English diphthong become independent phonemes which are adapted according to their genetic description so that they approach as closely as possible the phonemes of the borrowing language. In other cases, transphonemization follows the orthography, and here variants occur.

The simplest form of free transphonemization of diphthong phonemes occurs in cases where the first element of the English diphthong transphonemicizes according to the principles of complete or partial transphonemization while the second element is replaced by the phoneme /j/.

E:	/eɪ/	S-C:	/e-j/	E:	*grape* /greɪp/	S-C:	*grejp*
	/aɪ/		/a-j/		*nylon* /'naɪlən/		*najlon*
	/ɔɪ/		/o-j/		*boycott* /'bɔɪkɔt/		*bojkot*

Somewhat more complicated is the free transphonemization of the English diphthongs /aʊ/ and /əʊ/. The first possibility is transphonemization based on orthography. Thus /aʊ/ is changed to *ov* and /əʊ/ is reduced to *o*. The second possibility is that the diphthong /aʊ/ is transphonemicized into a two-member group *a-u* keeping the phonetic value of the individual elements.

E: /aʊ/   S-C: /a-u/   E: *cowboy* /'kaʊbɔɪ/   S-C: *kauboj*
                  /ov/   *kovboj*
   /əʊ/   /o/   *goal* /gəʊl/   *gol*

The third group of English dipthong phonemes, in /-ə/, trans-
phonemicize on the basis of their orthography with a reduction of the
diphthong.

E: /ɪə/   S-C: /i(r)/   E: *clearing* /'klɪərɪŋ/   S-C: *kliring*
                  /er/   *terrier* /'terɪə/   *terjer*
   /eə/   /er/   *fair* /feə/   *fer*
   /ʊə/   /u(r)/   *puritan* /'pjʊərɪtən/   *puritanac*

The four English consonant phonemes /θ/, /ð/, /ŋ/ and /w/ show free
transphonemization carried out on the basis of orthography or combined
with pronunciation. The simplest transphonemization is with the phoneme
/ŋ/ which follows orthography and is replaced by *ng*. The English phoneme
/w/ is transphonemicized into *v*, under the influence of German orthography (⟨w⟩ = /v/). The transphonemization of the phonemes /θ/ and /ð/
combines orthography and pronunciation, and variants also occur. The
phoneme /θ/ is transphonemicized into *t* as a result of orthography by the
equating of *th* with *t* due to German influence. If the result of the transphonemization is *s*, this is the influence of pronunciation, because in incorrect pronunciation of English, /θ/ is replaced by *s* (along with the possibility
of *t* and *f*). Transphonemization of the phoneme /ð/ is carried out by analogy with /θ/, with the addition of voicing.

E: /θ/   S-C: /t/   E: *thriller* /'θrɪlə/   S-C: *triler*
                 /s/   *thirty* /'θɜ:ti/   *serti*
   /ð/   /d/   *Galsworthy* /'gɔ:lzwɜ:ðɪ/   *Golzvordi*
   /ŋ/   /ng/   *pudding* /'pʊdɪŋ/   *puding*
   /w/   /v/   *whiskey* /'wɪskɪ/   *viski*

4.4 From the foregoing analysis it is evident that the three types of transphonemization, which we have illustrated with examples from Serbo-Croatian, form a system from which we can determine the substitution of
phonemes in the lending language with phonemes of the borrowing language. At the outset we established that substitution is a broad concept,
and in order to more easily and better classify the changes in the adaptation
of the model into the replica, we introduced a new term, transphonemization. Now, in closing, we will try to integrate the types of transphonemiza-

tion into the area of substitution.

First we limit substitution to the phonological level, and then we connect each type of transphonemization with one degree of substitution. In this way relationships are established in both areas: three types of transphonemization and three degrees of substitution. Their equivalents line up in this way:

Substitution		Transphonemization
a. first degree	=	a) complete
b. second degree	=	b) partial
c. third degree	=	c) free

If we incorporate this system into the Haugen-Weinreich theory it will represent a very useful and applicable innovation which will enable a researcher to carry out a more precise phonological analysis of the adaptation of lending language phonemes.

5 In order to apply the same principle of systematizing various substitution types to morphology we introduced another new term, *transmorphemization*, to cover changes occurring when a morpheme of the giving language, according to the basic principle of morphological adaptation, must conform to the morphological system of the borrowing language. Such adaptation begins with the formation of the citation form of the loan (Filipović 1961), and goes on in the creation of inflected forms, whatever the part of speech may be. Hence, transmorphemization concerns bound morphemes, since free morphemes, being a part of the lexicon, are borrowed without limitations. Nevertheless, we must study free morphemes as well, since their citation form must fit the morphological system of the borrowing language (Filipović 1981b).

Substitution of bound morphemes in the citation form has three types which correspond to three stages of substitution. When a model is taken over by the borrowing language as a free morpheme with a zero bound morpheme and when it also corresponds to a replica from a morphological point of view, then it is *zero transmorphemization*. When a loan keeps a final bound morpheme that does not conform to the borrowing language's morphological system, this is *compromise transmorphemization*, and the loan is then a compromise replica on the morphological level. When a giving-language bound morpheme is replaced by a borrowing-language bound morpheme (a suffix) with the same function, the process is called *complete transmorphemization*.

Zero transmorphemization is represented by the formula: *free morpheme + zero bound morpheme*.

stem + zero suffix   free morpheme + zero bound morpheme
E: *bridge*   S-C: *bridž*
   cup   *kep*

The citation form of a loan adapted according to this first stage of transmorphemization need not entirely satisfy the rules for permissible word finals in the borrowing language. Some loan finals may not conform to existing finals and may even introduce innovations in the system of the borrowing language.

E: *rugby*   S-C: *ragbi*
   interview   *intervju*
   lift   *lift*
   film   *film*

The examples cited show two kinds of noun finals which are not in accordance with the morphological system of Serbo-Croatian: a) the vowels *-i* and *-u*, b) the final consonant clusters *-ft* and *-lm*.

Compromise transmorphemization is represented by the formula: *free morpheme + English bound morpheme*.

stem + E suffix   free morpheme + E bound morpheme
E: *farm-er*   S-C: *farm-er*
   park-ing   *park-ing*

Complete transmorphemization is represented by the formula: *free morpheme + S-C bound morpheme*.

English word =	*foreign word =*	*loanword =*
model	*compromise replica*	*replica*
stem + E suffix	free morpheme + E bound morpheme	free morpheme + S-C bound morpheme
box-er	*boks-er*	*boks-ač*

Sometimes models go from the donor language directly into loan replicas, skipping the second stage of transmorphemization.

stem + E suffix   free morpheme + S-C bound morpheme
E: *strik-er*   S-C: *štrajk-aš* or *štrajk-ač*

A special form of complete transmorphemization involves determination of noun gender through contamination (Filipović 1986a). In the model

we have (a) a zero bound morpheme (since English gender need not be
marked by a bound feminine-gender suffix) or (b) a bound morpheme
which would not indicate feminine gender in the borrowing language (e.g.
E *-ess* > S-C *-es*), so that gender marking must be done through the third
stage of transmorphemization, by the addition of a bound morpheme from
the borrowing-language inventory. In both cases this will be the S-C bound
morpheme *-a* added to English loans.

   (a) *English word*   *English loanword in S-C (fem. gender)*
        stem + Ø   free morpheme + S-C bound morpheme
  E: *jungle*   S-C: *džungl-a*
   (b) *English word*   *English loanword in S-C (fem. gender)*
        stem + -ess   free morpheme + E bound morpheme
                          + S-C bound morpheme
  E: *steward-ess*   S-C: *stjuard-es-a*

During transmorphemization interesting situations can appear which
do not follow the expected order. We can wonder why: a) some examples
remain at the second stage of transmorphemization, b) some skip this stage,
and c) others go through both the second and the third stages. It is hard to
give a definitive answer, but we will analyse some examples and try to show
what factors could have been decisive in the various cases.

Comparing our examples with the pattern that has passed through both
stages we find, for instance, that the English word *striker* is not attested as
a compromise replica *strajker* or *štrajker*, although German as an intermediary language was decisive for the present-day shape of the word, *štraj-
kaš* or *štrajkač*. Both shapes are the result of the third stage of transmorphemization, complete transmorphemization.

The English word *sprinter* has remained at the second or compromise
stage of transmorphemization, i.e. *sprinter*, and has not been accepted in a
third-stage form *sprintaš* although such a form would be possible if only by
analogy. The reason may be that the language already has a very frequent
semantic equivalent *trkač na kratke staze*.

Thus transmorphemization provides a system (part of the system of
substitution on the morphological level) within which we can analyse various types of substitution of bound morphemes of the lending language by
bound morphemes of the borrowing language. Such substitution can have
from one to three stages of transmorphemization, and each stage corresponds to one transmorphemization type:

Substitution		Transmorphemization
a) first stage	=	a) zero
b) second stage	=	b) compromise
c) third stage	=	c) complete

This system included in the theory of languages in contact is also classified as an innovation which can serve as a suitable and efficient way of analysing substitution on the morphological level.

6 When one of the first theoreticians of linguistic borrowing, Haugen (1950), presented the basic principles of languages in contact, he established that linguistic borrowing causes two types of structural changes in the phonology: (a) redistribution of phonemes, and (b) importation of phonemes. We examined them both (Filipović 1959, 1960 a & b) when we were developing the theory and working method for our Projects (EEEL & CDAE). The final results of our investigation of the nature and consequences of importation of phonemes add so much to the H-W theory that they can be classified as an innovation in the old theory.

There were two reasons why we devoted separate studies to the problem of importation of phonemes. The first was that certain principles have been defined too abstractly without enough illustrations; the second was that the majority of principles were derived on the basis of a limited two-language corpus. Our multilingual corpus is a corpus of examples of the contact of several European languages with English some of which are genetically very different from English. In this way our corpus is highly representative and suitable for a possible re-examination and redefinition of the basic principles of linguistic borrowing including the principle of phonemic importation. The system of investigation that we thus put into effect has been changed in several ways from the old approach and has determined the course that must be followed in the development of a new theory and working method.

Our first stimulus was the fact that despite Haugen's assertion that importation is one of the two forms of structural change in phonology under the influence of linguistic borrowing, in the literature this phenomenon has not been analysed on the basis of examples from a large number of languages in contact, nor have the conditions under which it takes place been given. Therefore, it seemed that importation could take place in all situations and in all languages.

In the course of our research on theoretical questions of linguistic borrowing on the phonological level (Filipović 1967), we were particularly interested in the problem of the importation of phonemes and the way in which other linguists approached this problem (Filipović 1960), for in our thinking we had posed three questions for which we found no real answers in the literature:

1. How can it be explained that in the course of the process of adaptation of the model on the phonological level a larger number of phonemes of the lending language are replaced by phonemes of the borrowing language, but a smaller number of phonemes are passed on to the replica, that is, are 'imported' into the borrowing language?
2. Do there exist structural reasons for this transfer of phonemes from one phonological system to another, or is this a result of other external influences?
3. Can importation be explained by phenomena within the phonological system of the borrowing language?

It is on account of all this that we decided to analyse several languages for which the importation of phonemes into the phonological structure had been asserted but not explained further (Filipović 1960). Our intention was to take these cases of 'phoneme importation' from the lending to the borrowing language as a basis and to explain how and why this had come about and under what conditions phonemes are 'imported' into the phonological system of a language.

We analysed the importation of the phoneme /ŋ/ into French, the phoneme /ʒ/ into Italian, the phoneme /ʒ/ into English, the phoneme /w/ into Swedish, and the phonemes /f/, /dʒ/ and /dz/ into S-C. In the analysis we came to conclusions that were in accord with the general assumptions presented in the literature and also answered many questions that had not previously been resolved or even asked. These were: (1) the importation of phonemes is not an uncontrolled and completely free phenomenon; (2) importation is phonetically conditioned; (3) there also exist other specific conditions under which it can take place, and these must be determined individually for each case (Filipović 1960).

The conclusions we arrived at in our first extensive analysis of phoneme importation suggested that it is not an altogether clear phenomenon, because it requires that certain 'external' and 'internal' conditions be fulfilled. It is these conditions that we sought and found. Some of these have remained a problem to which we returned in our work on the Project whenever we explored the adaptation of the English model and its transition into the replica in one of the more than twenty borrowing languages we are studying (Filipović 1977b). One of our main reasons for doubting the existence of any importation of phonemes from a lending language into a borrowing language which would introduce a structural change in the borrowing language's phonological system was the basic assumption of structuralism that a phonological system is closed and therefore cannot take in elements from outside. This would mean that the appearance of 'new' phonemes in the borrowing language cannot be explained by importation, by the introduction of these phonemes into the phonological system, but must be explained in some other way (Filipović 1982c).

The phenomenon that we have been calling 'phoneme importation' must, therefore, be studied only within the phonological system of the borrowing language, in the framework of its development and under only external pressure from linguistic borrowing. We have not found support for this assumption of ours in the linguistic literature, since the linguists who have worked on the theory of languages in contact have proceeded from importation in the sense of the introduction of some element of the lending language and even have asserted that any aspect of the model may be transferred to the replica. True, there were minor reservations and limitations and even attempts to formulate general principles that would regulate the process of importation in general and the importation of phonemes in particular, but the basic idea of importation with foreign elements being introduced into the system of the borrowing language remained the same and unchanged.

Vogt (1954) emphasizes that a linguistic system is capable of *accepting* only a number of structural innovations. Haugen (1953: 388) concluded, on the basis of his investigation of Norwegian dialects in the United States, that the first generation *replaces* (this is substitution), but the second generation *imports* (this is importation). Deroy (1956) admits the possibility of the *importation* of morphemes without limitation, but of phonemes only occasionally. As an example he mentions the importation of the phoneme /f/ in the Slavonic languages. Jakobson (1949) expounds a general law according to which languages *accept* only those elements of foreign structures that are in accord with their developmental tendencies. Martinet (1959) formulates his view on this question somewhat differently; he says that foreign forms are more easily *adopted* by a borrowing language if they can be integrated into its structure without difficulty, and that little resistance against a new element is observed if it fits an empty space in the system. Martinet's student Weinreich (1953) expressed this thought even more concretely; he holds that the existence of holes, that is, empty places, in the system allows the *introduction* of phonemes from the secondary system into the primary one.

Are these opinions of several outstanding theoretical linguists in agreement with our position that one must approach 'phoneme importation' with the assumption of a closed phonological system in the borrowing language into which nothing from the outside penetrates, and in which all changes that take place must be explained by the internal development of the system? They are not, for they all talk about the conditions for the acceptance and introduction of elements of the lending language into the system of the borrowing language. We will try to prove that this is not a matter of the introduction and adoption of phonemes from other systems but rather that under certain conditions and in case of need, that is, under external pressure, some (and only some!) phonemes can develop in the phonological system of the borrowing language. Thus, it is our position that phonemes, which we have up to now treated as a part of importation on the phonological level, develop within a closed phonological system and so do not represent phoneme importation nor the introduction of phonemes into the borrowing language. There are, to be sure, elements in the opinions of the linguists cited above which we too will use in our interpretation of this phenomenon.

We do not agree with the theoretical linguists when they talk about 'the *acceptance* of structural innovations' (Vogt), about 'the *possibility* of the *importation* of phonemes only occasionally' (Deroy), about 'the *acceptance* of those elements of foreign structures that are in agreement with their developmental tendencies' (Jakobson), about the '*adoption* of foreign forms ... and a new element ...' (Martinet), or about the '*possibility* of *introducing* phonemes ...' (Weinreich) since all this presupposes an open phonological system that can accept foreign elements from the lending language. On the other hand we agree with them when they say that in the phonological systems of many borrowing languages there are empty places (Martinet and Weinreich) which must be brought into the discussion, and we agree that the developmental tendencies of the borrowing language can and must be taken into consideration (Jakobson), which we will do in our analysis of this problem.

7 The starting point for our analysis is our position that filling an empty place in the phonological system of the borrowing language is not the importation of that phoneme from some lending language; it is a new developmental stage that has begun under specific conditions and under pressure of need during linguistic borrowing. To show and describe this, we will analyse these conditions and these internal and external pressures in several languages in contact. The introduction of this new element into our theory sets it further apart from the old theory giving it a new character which can be also classified as an innovation.

To confirm our hypothesis, we will analyse those languages in which 'phoneme importation' has been mentioned and see whether there is really importation, introduction of a phoneme from the lending language into the phonological system of the borrowing language, or whether this phenomenon can be explained differently and reinterpreted according to our initial position.

In his description of consonantism in the French phonological system, the French phonetician Fouché (1956: xix) says that one new phoneme /ŋ/, a velar nasal, has been added to the list of consonants from the English suffix -*ing*, and that it 'penetrated' the French phonological system by way of borrowing. Did this English phoneme 'penetrate' the French phonological system? According to our theory, which is based on a closed phonological system, this is not a matter of a phoneme of the lending language penetrating the phonological system of the borrowing language, but rather of a change within the phonological system of the borrowing language.

Jakobson (1962), in his insistence on systematizing sound changes according to their phonological significance, has asserted that some changes relate only to the subphonemic level, while others affect the inventory of phonemes. Changes that affect the phoneme inventory can be: 1) dephonologization — when two phonemes merge and one disappears; 2) phonologization — the creation of a new phoneme; 3) rephonologization — a change in certain relevant features of a phoneme. Phonologization also includes the change of an allophone into a phoneme. We will apply this principle to show that in the French phonological system the phoneme /ŋ/ developed from an already existing allophone [ŋ], which appears in the French system when certain conditions are fulfilled internally, that is, within the system, and externally under the influence of need and linguistic borrowing, that is of foreign words that enter the language and must be integrated into it.

In the French system the allophone [ŋ] appears when a nasal sound follows the phoneme /g/; here assimilation takes place. This can be illustrated by the pronunciation of the phrase *les langues modernes*. Instead of pronunciation /le lã:gmɔdɛrn/ we hear /le lã:ŋmɔdɛrn/ (Jones 1956: 227, note 19). We find another example of the occurrence of the allophone [ŋ] in those French dialects in which nasalized vowels are denasalized, and after an oral vowel the nasal /n/ occurs. If a velar /k/ or /g/ comes after this /n/ then the latter is assimilated to become a velar nasal [ŋ]. This can be observed in the word *brancard* (Gilliéron and Edmont 1910: fasc. 25, c. 1772).

The only conclusion that comes out of this analysis is the following. In the French phonological system by the principle of phonologization there arose out of the allophone [ŋ] a phoneme, which occurs in English loanwords in -*ing*. This change took place when the need for it arose under the pressure of foreign words and when conditions existed in the system, that is, an allophone that could develop into a phoneme.

The S-C language too offers confirmation for this explanation of a change in the system. The appearance of the phoneme /dʒ/ in the S-C phonological system can be explained in the same way. In the dictionary (*RHSJ*) we find /dʒ/ in loanwords from Turkish (*džamija, hodža, dželat, hadžija*), from Italian (*dženerao, madž*), from Hungarian (*Madžar, Madžarska*) and from English (*džem, džungla, pidžama, bridž*). In the course of its history the S-C phonological system did not have a phoneme /dʒ/, the voiced counterpart to the voiceless affricate (RHSJ: 527). An allophone [dʒ] appears in certain native words in the phonetic context in which a voiced consonant comes after /tʃ/. If a noun in -*ba* (*svjedoč-ba*) is derived from *svjedočiti*, according to the principle of assimilation for voicing the /tʃ/ is changed into /dʒ/: *svjedodžba*. Thus the allophone [dʒ] in the S-C phonological system made possible the development of the phoneme /dʒ/ in the system on the basis of phonologization; the allophone developed into a phoneme when under the pressure of linguistic borrowing a need for this phoneme was created.

Everything that has been said about the development of the phoneme [dʒ] appears in certain native words in the phonetic context in which a voiced consonant comes after /tʃ/. If a noun in -*ba* (*svjedoč-ba*) is derived from *svjedočiti*, according to the principle of assimilation for voicing the /tʃ/ is changed into /dʒ/: *svjedodžba*. Thus the allophone [dʒ] in the S-C phonological system made possible the development of the phoneme /dʒ/ in

The development of the phoneme /f/ is very interesting. Since this phoneme did not exist in the old phonological system of Serbo-Croatian (since in classical words it was replaced by /p/ in the west and by /v/ in the east), it is often mentioned as a phoneme introduced into the Slavonic languages with foreign words (Vaillant 1950: 27) or as a result of onomatopoeia (Ivić 1957: 162-5; Vaillant 1950: 26). In this case too there exist conditions for phonologization, that is, for the development of a phoneme /f/, since it appears in onomatopoeic expressions such as *fijukati* and *frknuti* (which Vaillant thinks is based on an onomatopoeic *frr*), and could also have developed from the cluster *hv* (e.g. *hvala* > *fala*) (Ivšić and Kravar 1955: 25).

Aside from the possibility of the development of a phoneme on the principle of phonologization under the condition that a corresponding allophone exists in the system, we also find another possibility in which a phoneme develops in the phonological system of the borrowing language as a result of the activation of a latent phoneme. In this case too we have the development of a new phoneme within a closed system without the addition of any sort of element from the lending language.

This principle is based on the existence of empty places in the system and of asymmetrical or incomplete parts of the system of one group of phonemes. Most often these are the groups of fricatives and affricates. In some languages that we are studying in the Project (EEEL) just these parts of the phonological system are very incomplete. All the empty places represent latent phonemes which are activated under certain favourable conditions. These conditions can be the influence of linguistic borrowing and the need for taking over foreign words. Thus phonemes that occur in adopted foreign words 'develop', that is, are activated in the system and become a part of this system. In some cases the activation of a phoneme concurs with phonologization, which, it seems to us, confirms the theory of the development of new phonemes in the phonological system of the borrowing language under the influence of linguistic borrowing even more strongly.

In the Italian phonological system the fricative group has one empty place in its system (Camilli 1947: 15-37):

| /f/ | /s/ | /ʃ/ |
| /v/ | /z/ | |

When the pressure of linguistic borrowing began, that is, when French loanwords were taken over, the voiced fricative /ʒ/ was activated and filled the empty place in the system. Until the moment of borrowing, /ʒ/ was only a latent phoneme and was not actively expressed in the system, so its place remained empty. When the pressure of linguistic borrowing began, that is, the adoption of French words containing the phoneme /ʒ/, it was activated, and this made it possible to form an Italian pronunciation for French loanwords:

F	*le garage*	–	I	*il garage*	/ga'raʒ/
	le reportage	–		*il reportage*	/repor'taʒ
	le maquillage	–		*il machillage*	/maki'jaʒ/ or /maki'laʒ/

The development of the phoneme /ʒ/ in the Italian phonological system can also be explained by phonologization, that is, on the condition of the existence of an allophone [ʒ] in a certain phonetic context. The allophone [ʒ] can appear in Italian in the Tuscan and Rome pronunciation of the affricate /dʒ/ when it occurs in intervocalic position and then loses its dental part (Camilli 1947: 39):

agile   /a:dʒile/   > /a:ʒile/
la gente /la dʒɛnte/ > /la ʒɛnte/

An allophone [ʒ] can likewise appear in southern Italian dialects where preconsonantal *s* appears as /ʃ/, and thus as /ʒ/ before a voiced consonant (Camilli 1947: 46):

scala   /ska:la/   /ʃka:la/
sdegno /zdeɲo/   /ʒdeɲo/

Thus the development of the phoneme /ʒ/ in Italian can be confirmed in both ways presented, but always under external influence, that is, pressure from linguistic borrowing and the need for taking loanwords into the borrowing language.

In Serbo-Croatian we have similar examples of empty places in the system. The affricate group shows a particularly asymmetrical system, with as many as two empty places:

ć /tɕ/   č /tʃ/   c /ts/
đ /dʒ̢/

Thus these empty places represented latent phonemes which could be activated if external conditions were right, that is, if there came to be a need for them under the pressure of linguistic borrowing.

Above we explained the development of the affricate /dʒ/ in the Croatian phonological system on the basis of phonologization, since it was the existence of the allophone [dʒ] that made possible the development of the phoneme /dʒ/ when the need for it appeared. The development of the phoneme /dʒ/ can also be acknowledged as the activation of a latent phoneme. As a latent member of the system of affricates, where historically that place was empty, this phoneme was activated under the same conditions as the others and filled the empty place in the system.

The principle of the activation of a latent phoneme can also be applied to the development of the velar nasal /ŋ/ since there is an empty place in the system of nasals (labial /m/, dental /n/, palatal /ɲ/, no velar). Thus the development of the velar nasal /ŋ/ in French can also be interpreted as the activation of a latent phoneme /ŋ/ in an empty place in the nasal system. This fact leads us to conclude that the existence of an allophone and of an empty place in the system can combine, since it has already been shown that new phonemes can develop in the system of a borrowing language in both these ways in almost all cases.

8 The above analysis of the development of phonemes under the pressure of linguistic borrowing shows that: (a) If the phonological system is closed, then it is impossible to explain how phonemes from the lending language can be imported into the system of the borrowing language. (b) If the supposition under (a) is accurate, then the only possible explanation for new phonemes in the borrowing language is that they developed in the system itself. This does not contradict any theory of the historical development of the phonological system of a language. Quite the opposite! (c) Jakobson's phonologization provides for the creation of new phonemes in the system; they can develop from allophones. (d) Thus if these allophones exist in the system, they can develop into phonemes. (e) Empty places that appear in some groups of phonemes within the phonological system have led us to the conclusion that they hide latent phonemes that are not active in the system. Thus each empty place represents the temporary absence of some phoneme in the series of a given type of phonemes (for example velar /ŋ/ in the series of French nasals) or the non-existence of the voiced or voiceless counterpart in some group of phonemes (e.g. the voiced affricate /dʒ/ next to existing voiceless /tʃ/). (f) Latent phonemes can be activated under certain conditions. Then the empty place is filled and the system is completed or else its asymmetry is reduced. (g) We have applied all these principles to linguistic borrowing. The conditions for the development of a phoneme within the system are the same: pressure to take foreign words into the system and the need for these phonemes. (h) Thus we have explained one phenomenon in linguistic borrowing (which had previously been interpreted as importation) in a new way, which seems to us the only acceptable one.

By way of conclusion we can state that the crucial change in the theory was reached when we found out that phoneme importation must be studied only within the phonological system of the borrowing language and not as an importation from the lending language. Thus, it is our position that phonemes, which were treated as a part of importation on the phonological level, develop within a closed phonological system. This theory is supported by the fact that in the phonological systems of many borrowing languages there are empty places that can be filled. Filling an empty space is not the importation of that phoneme from some lending language but a new developmental stage that begins under specific conditions and under pressure of need during linguistic borrowing. The analysis of these conditions and the internal and external pressures in several languages in contact helps with a reinterpretation of one of the basic laws of linguistic borrowing – phoneme importation.

References

Camilli, Amerindo. 1947. *Pronuncia e grafia dell'Italiano*. Firenze: Sansoni.

Deroy, Louis. 1956. *L'emprunt linguistique*. Paris: Les Belles Lettres.

Filipović, Rudolf. 1959. "Consonantal innovations in the phonological system as a consequence of linguistic borrowing". *Studia Romanica et Anglica Zagrabiensia* 7: 39-62.

-----. 1960a. "Phonemic importation". *Studia Romanica et Anglica Zagrabiensia* 9-10: 177-189.

-----. 1960b. *The Phonemic Analysis of English Loan-Words in Croatian*. (= *Acta Instituti Phonetici*, 8.) Zagreb: University of Zagreb.

-----. 1961. "The morphological adaptation of English loan-words in Serbo-Croatian". *Studia Romanica et Anglica Zagrabiensia* 11: 91-103.

-----. 1966. "The English element in the main European languages". *Studia Romanica et Anglica Zagrabiensia* 21-22: 103-112.

-----. 1967. "Compromise replica and phonemic importation". *To Honor Roman Jakobson: Essays on the Occasion of his Seventieth Birthday*. Vol. I, 626-666. The Hague-Paris: Mouton.

-----. 1968. "Semantic extension changes in adaptation of English loanwords in Serbo-Croatian". *Studia Romanica et Anglica Zabrabiensia* 25-26: 109-119.

-----. 1972. "Some problems in studying the English element in European languages". *Studia Anglica Poznaniensia* 4: 141-158.

-----. 1973. "Some problems in studying the English element in European languages". *English Studies Today* 5: 25-52.

-----. 1974. "A contribution to the method of studying anglicisms in European languages". *Studia Romanica et Anglica Zagrabiensia* 37: 135-148.

-----. 1977a. "Some basic principles of languages in contact reinterpreted". *Studia Romanica et Anglica Zagrabiensia* 43-44: 157-166.

-----. 1977b. "English words in European mouths and minds". *Folia Linguistica* X (3-4): 195-206.

-----. 1977c. "Primary and secondary adaptation of loan-words". *Wiener slavistisches Jahrbuch* XXIII: 116-125.

-----. 1980a. "Croatian dialects as markers of croatian ethnicity in the United States". In: *The Role of Ethnicity in American Society*, 99-108. University of Zagreb and Commission for Educational Exchanges between the USA and Yugoslavia.

-----. 1980b. "Transmorphemization: substitution on the morphological level reinterpreted". *Studia Romanica et Anglica Zagrabiensia* XXV: 1-8.

-----. 1981a. "Transphonemization: substitution on the phonological level reinterpreted". In: Pöckl 1981: 125-133.

-----. 1981b. "Morphological categories in linguistic borrowing". *Studia Romanica et Anglica Zagrabiensia* XXVI: 197-207.

-----. 1982a. *The English Element in European Languages*. Zagreb: Institute of Linguistics.

-----. 1982b. "Serbo-Croatian in the United States: Croatian dialects in contact with American English". In: Sussex 1982: 23-31.

-----. 1982c. "Phonologization and activation of latent phonemes in linguistic borrowing". *Journal of the International Phonetic Association* 12: 36-47.

-----. 1983. "An etymological dictionary of anglicisms in European languages". In: Nelde 1983: 59-68.

-----. 1984. "Can a dictionary of -ISMS be an etymological dictionary". In: Hartmann 1984: 73-79.

-----. 1985a. "Croatian dialects in the United States: sociolinguistic aspects". *Folia Slavica* 6: 278-292.

-----. 1985b. "Accentuation of English loanwords in Serbo-Croatian". *International Journal of Slavic Linguistics and Poetics* XXXII-XXXIII: 143-149.

-----. 1986a. *Teorija jezika u kontaktu. Uvod u lingvistiku jezičnih dodira* [The theory of languages in contact. An introduction to contact linguistics.] Zagreb: Jugoslavenska akademija znanosti i umjetnosti.

-----. 1986b. "Croatian surnames in the process of dialect-shift and dialect-maintenance". *Spracherwerb und Mehrsprachigkeit. Language Acquisition and Multilingualism.* Tübingen: Gunter Narr.161-171.

Fouché, Pierre. 1956. *Traité de la prononciation française.* Paris: Librairie C. Klincksieck.

Gilliéron, J. and E. Edmont, 1910. *Atlas linguistique de la France.* Paris: Honoré Champion.

Hartmann, R.R.K. (ed.) 1984. *Lexeter '83 PROCEEDINGS.* Tübingen: Niemeyer.

Haugen, Einar. 1950. "The analysis of linguistic borrowing". *Language* 20: 210-231.

Haugen, Einar. 1953. *The Norwegian Language in America: A Study in Bilingual Behavior.* Philadelphia: University of Pennsylvania Press.

Ivić, Pavle. 1957. "Dva glavna pravca razvoja konsonantizma u srpskohrvatskom jeziku" [The two main trends in the development of consonantism in Serbo-Croatian.] *Godišnjak Filozofskog fakulteta u Novom Sadu* 2: 159-184.

Ivšić, Stj. and M. Kravar. 1955. *Srpsko-hrvatski jezik* [The Serbo-Croatian language] (= *Acta Instituti Phonetici*, 4.) Zagreb: University of Zagreb.

Jakobson, Roman. 1962. "Principes de phonologie historique". In: *Selected Writings. I Phonological Studies.* 202-220. The Hague: Mouton.

Jones, Daniel. 1956. *An Outline of English Phonetics.* Cambridge: Heffer.

Martinet, André. 1959. "Affinité linguistique". *Bollettino dell'Atlante Linguistico Mediterraneo* 1: 151.

Nelde, P.H. 1983. *Theory, Methods and Models of Contact Linguistics.* Berlin: Dümmler.

Pöckl, W. 1981. *Europäische Mehrsprachigkeit.* Tübingen: Niemeyer.

Popović, Ivan. 1955. *Istorija srpskohrvatskog jezika* [History of the Serbo-Croatian language.] Novi Sad: Matica srpska.

RHSJ = *Rječnik hrvatskog ili srpskoga jezika* [Dictionary of the Croatian or Serbian language.] Zagreb: Jugoslavenska akademija znanosti i umjetnosti.

Sussex, Roland. 1982. *The Slavic Languages in Émigré Communities*. Carbondale & Edmonton: Linguistic Research.

Vaillant, André. 1950. *Grammaire comparée des langues slaves*. Paris.

Vogt, Hans. 1954. "Language Contacts". *Word* 10: 365-374.

Weinreich, Uriel. 1953. *Languages in Contact: Findings and Problems*. New York: Linguistic Circle of New York.

Psychological studies of bilingualism in Vojvodina*

Lajos Göncz
Faculty of Philosophy, University of Novi Sad

1   Introduction

Throughout the world, the phenomenon of bilingualism has attracted the attention of scholars and scientists from a variety of disciplines. The interest shown in bilingualism by neurophysiologists, sociologists, linguists, teachers, psychologists, sociolinguists and psycholinguists may be attributed to the increasingly evident social demand for the results of scientific research to be incorporated in the solution of problems arising from the phenomenon of bilingualism. It may be said that, if one accepts the definition of bilingualism which is currently most often referred to, i.e. that one may consider as bi- or multilingual all those who know and use two (or more) languages, it will emerge that more than half the world's population is daily confronted with at least some of the problems associated with the bilingual situation. Such problems are encountered by all who live in an ethnically or linguistically heterogeneous environment, by all pupils and students receiving their education in a language other than the mother-tongue, by 'guest-workers' and their families living abroad, and to some extent even by those who learn a second language at school or who are self-taught.

Let us note, for the present, just some of the issues relating to bilingualism for which solutions have been sought — though more rarely offered — by the various disciplines. These include questions such as: What is the optimal period in the learner's development for the aquisition of a second

---

* The research project was financed by the Self-managing Scientific Research Unit of Vojvodina in conjunction with the Institute of Education and the Department of Psychology of the Novi Sad Faculty of Philosophy.

language? What methods are best suited for instruction in a second language at the early stage of learning? What organizational forms of bilingual instruction are possible at school? What role do the learner's attitude, motivation and aptitude play in the acquisition of a second language? What effects does bilingualism have on the development of the personality, and particularly on general cognitive, language, social and emotional development? Do different forms or types of bilingualism produce different effects? What is the relation between the two language systems in the mind of a bilingual person? What are the factors which may, on the one hand, enable the bilingual person to attain functional independence in the two languages, or, on the other hand, cause him or her to confuse the two language systems? Can bilingualism, in spite of any negative sociocultural consequences it may entail, prove to be an enriching experiencing?

It will be already apparent, even from this brief outline of the questions, that bilingualism is a complex phenomenon, governed by a multitude of variables, in which it is by no means easy to identify prevailing rules or laws. An important connection exists between bilingualism and the psychological variables, such as sex, age, and the nature and degree of language learning motivation; but there also exists an equally vital link with certain sociological and linguistic variables, such as the relative status of the languages and the degree of interference between their respective structures. It remains the task of psychology, sociology, and linguistics, i.e. of the interdisciplinary sciences, to endeavour by variation of these key variables to determine more precisely their relationship with the phenomenon of bilingualism. For this purpose, the interdisciplinary approach proves to be most desirable, since it is only by using the conceptual apparatus and methodological synthesis of two or more disciplines that it becomes possible to examine comprehensively such a complex segment of reality as bilingualism.

In this paper, we shall be presenting a review of a series of research studies carried out in Vovjodina on various psychological aspects of bilingualism.[1] The studies were made on groups of pupils and students ranging in age from pre-school to university level, who spoke either Hungarian only or both Hungarian and Serbo-Croatian, though not at the same level. There were several objectives to this research. Firstly, to enable us to establish the laws or rules determining the phenomenon of Hungarian/Serbo-Croatian bilingualism in Vojvodina, and hence bilingualism in general; secondly, to provide us with a suitable means of testing, in addition, certain hypotheses of more general importance in psychology, psycholinguistics, linguistics and didactics (e.g. the hypotheses concerning the relation between language and thought, in connection with the problems of glotto-didactics — the theories of language instruction — or with the problems of language 'switching').

The various problems associated with Hungarian/Serbo-Croatian bilingualism in Vojvodina are approached in our research from the standpoint not only of developmental psychology and developmental psycholinguistics, but also of experimental psycholinguistics; some of the results may, in addition, be referred to the fields of educational psychology and applied psycholinguistics. A short survey is given of the results obtained from this series of studies, though the technical details have not been entered into.

2 The study of bilingualism from the standpoint of developmental psychology

In our research into bilingualism from the standpoint of developmental psychology and developmental psycholinguistics we have attempted to cast light upon the relation between early Hungarian/Serbo-Croatian bilingualism (acquired at pre-school age) and certain of the mental functions in the learner's development. The results of these studies have been published in the following works by the present author: Göncz 1973, 1979a, b, c, 1981a, b, forthcoming a.

The aim of the research was to determine whether there exists a regular relation between early bilingualism and linguistic and general cognitive development, and, if so, what its essence is.

Bilingualism may be said to be a distinctly variable phenomenon associated with those segments of reality for which it is not easy to determine and generally applicable laws or rules and which do not readily lend themselves to valid generalizations based on individual research studies. This statement would appear to be borne out by the highly contradictory results obtained by foreign researchers into bilingualism. Reviews of such studies have been given, for instance, by Darcy (1953, 1963) Peal and Lambert (1962), MacNamara, Ben-Zeev (1977), Göncz (1981a), and others. This disparity in research findings may primarily be explained by the fact that bilingualism is not a single phenomenon, and that there exist many substantially different forms of bilingualism (e.g. 'linguism' and 'glottism', 'balanced' and 'dominant', 'subtractive' and 'additive') which may have quite different effects on mental development. The task of scientists in this field, therefore, should be specifically to detect the factors which stimulate the development of those forms of bilingualism which are likely to exclude any possibly negative influences on the learner's development and which will at the same time enable the learner to make fullest use of his or her potential.

In our studies, we have used the method of parallel groups in conjunction with a cross-section approach. Our subjects were monolingual children (who knew only Hungarian) and bilingual children (who knew both Hungarian and Serbo-Croatian). The monolingual groups were compared, at the average ages of 6 and 10, with the dominant bilingual group (which had a significantly better knowledge of Hungarian than of Serbo-Croatian) and with the balanced bilingual group (which spoke both languages equally well – or badly) in relation to 20 indicators of oral and general cognitive development. Amongst other things, we measured the extent of the passive vocabulary and the knowledge of language structures in the mother tongue, the ability to discover and apply rules, analytical skill, the presence or absence of the concept of nominal realism (the strength of the relation established between the object and its verbal indicator, the ability to remember concrete and abstract concepts, etc.). In order to enable us to ascribe any difference that might arise between the groups to the influence of only one language or of both languages, the groups were first equalized according to the factors of age, sex, socio-economic status, socio-emotional maturity, and, in certain instances, according to the results obtained in a general intelligence test. The above indicators were chosen as we anticipated that certain of the differences between the monolingual and the bilingual situation, which might influence the relation between bilingualism and language and general cognitive development, might be revealed by these indicators. The basic difference between these situations is primarily of a *linguistic* nature: the bilingual child must discover and master the rules of functioning of two languages. Amongst the *non-linguistic* differences, special mention should be made of the additional linguistic and socio-cultural stimulation in the bilingual situation and of the process of 'switching', i.e. transferring from one language system to the other. These differences point to the fact that, in addition to the problem of the relation between language and thought in the process of mental ontogenesis, the problem of additional socio-cultural stimulation also provides a relevant framework within which the results of empirical research into the effects of bilingualism on cognitive development must be interpreted.

From these differences between the monolingual and the bilingual situation, further hypotheses — more restricted in scope — were established concerning the possible relations between early bilingualism and language and general cognitive development. These hypotheses were then subjected to empirical verification. Our expectations were that complicated relations would result and that the associations between early bilingualism and the indicators of language and general cognitive development would emerge according to the task by which the groups were compared and depending upon the age of the individuals and their degree of bilingualism. These expectations proved correct.

The results obtained indicate that early bilingualism has a significant association with the extent of the passive vocabulary and with the knowledge of language structures, but that it is also linked to the early ability to separate language indicators from the objects they denote and with the ability to establish relations. Associations are of differing order: they can be negative in connection with the extent of the passive vocabulary and the abilility to establish relations at pre-school age, and in connection with the knowledge of language structures in the first language at primary school age; and they can be positive in connection with the early ability to separate the language indicator from the object it denotes at pre-school age, and, at primary school age, with the ability to establish relations. The associations observed between early bilingualism and the indicators of general intellectual development cannot be interpreted with complete certainty as causal connections, although they undoubtedly exist. With regard to the relation between early bilingualism and the appearance of nominal realism and speech development in the first language, one may speak with more justification of a cause-and-effect link since it is possible to indicate the psychological mechanisms by which one factor operates upon another, correlated, factor. It is also essential to stress that, apart from the differences already established between mono- and bilingual groups, an equally important finding is that in the majority of comparisons no significant differences were detected. The results of this research also to some extent confirm the conjecture (Cummins 1976) that it is necessary to advance beyond the initial stage of bilingualism and adjust oneself to its increasing demands in order for the negative effects of bilingualism to cease and for its positive effects, or advantages, finally to emerge at a higher degree of bilingualism. It would be well worth studying this hypothesis in greater detail and confirming it through longitudinal research, as it might provide a highly suitable framework for interpreting the results. The bilingual situation within which our subjects were functioning (kindergarten and school lessons being given in the first language, with the second language being taught either at play or in class — the first language, therefore, was neither neglected, nor replaced by the second) meant that no lasting setbacks occurred in the development of those aspects of language and general cognitive progress which were the subject of our research, and that at the same time their situation could also have a positive effect on certain aspects of their cognitive development.

If we are to bring out the full significance of these results, and those of similar research studies into the relation between early bilingualism and cognitive development, they must be considered within the wider context of the relation between language and thought in mental ontogenesis. There are, basically, two approaches which may be adopted in relation to this issue. The first approach emphasises the dominant role of general cognitive structures in this relation, with the understanding that language may accelerate, but cannot of its own produce new cognitive structures (Piaget 1972, 1978). The second approach maintains that language plays a determinant role in this relation (Vygotsky 1962; Ivić, and the concept of the circular effect on linguistic and cognitive development, 1976; the Sapir-Whorf hypothesis of relativistic determinism, Whorf 1956). As these approaches would suggest, it seems hardly likely that the linguistic aspect of the bilingual situation (knowing the structures of two languages as opposed to one) could result in a lasting negative effect on general cognitive development. Of the two approaches, the more acceptable is that the acquisition of two languages instead of one can stimulate that role of speech which is already present in monolingual development. However, although the proponents of the various different concepts attribute different significance to language in the generation of new cognitive structures, they all agree that speech directs thought towards the essential aspects of the environment and that the mastery of speech also requires the ability to overcome the difficulties which arise during the process of learning to control linguistic mechanisms. It is precisely these functions of language which are strengthened in bilingual development.

Naturally, this general approach towards the effect of the linguistic aspect of the bilingual situation on general cognitive development in each particular instance will be modified by the influence of extra-linguistic factors associated with the bilingual situation (a more varied socio-cultural experience and the process of language 'switching' may occasionally lend added force to the language factor, or alternatively obscure this factor, if they are operating in opposing directions) and subjected to the influence of other variables (sex, age, individual character, language status, interference between language system) which together, and in interaction with early bilingualism, establish the factors for development.

3   The study of bilingualism from the standpoint of experimental psycholinguistics

This group comprises research studies of a more fundamental nature, in which the prime concern is with questions relating to the interaction between the language systems of bi- and multilingual persons. In addition, however, such studies also help to provide a more precise definition of the concept of bilingualism, and to determine the various types and forms of bilingualism while at the same time developing the instruments of measurement required to determine the various aspects of bilingualism. The survey has been drawn up on the basis of results elaborated in greater detail in the following works by the present author: Göncz 1975a, b, 1976, 1977, 1984, Göncz and Varga 1985.

In these studies, the starting-point was taken to be the fact that the manifest forms of interaction between the language systems of bi- and multilingual speakers are linguistic independence (a form of behaviour which manifests itself in such persons through the ability to maintain a separation between their language and to use them successfully) and linguistic interference (when the phonological, syntactic and semantic systems of one language 'interfere' with the system of another). Psychologists have shown particular interest in the semantic aspects of interaction. In accordance with the 'theory' of co-ordinate and compound (complex) bilingualism (Ervin and Osgood 1954), it may be stated that the language systems of coordinated bilingual persons are more independent at the semantic level, because the languages have been learnt from separate sources. The languages of compound bilingual persons are less easily separated at the semantic level since they derive from the same sources. Experimental verification of this hypothesis has revealed in our results, as elsewhere, that the connotative or affective meaning of the same words in Hungarian and Serbo-Croatian, measured by the semantic differential, is more different in the coordinated than in the complex bilingual speaker. Likewise, the associative meaning, determined by the matching of continuous associations given on the same words in the two languages, showed a greater degree of difference for the coordinated than for the complex bilingual person, though in this instance the difference did not exceed 5%, the level customarily accepted as statisticaly significant.

In this 'theory', psychological findings relating to interference are in fact applied to the bilingual situation. That is to say that the bilingual person has learned to associate the same object or situation with language indicators from two languages and to respond to the same stimulus with two different reactions. The consequence of this is interference, which may be manifested in prolonged reaction time, in the absence of reaction or in errors of language. In order for interference to be reduced, the languages should be learnt from separate sources and thoroughly consolidated. In the concepts of coordinate and complex bilingualism, the first condition for the reduction of interference was taken into consideration. By further introducing the second condition, through the variables which we have denoted as the degree of bilingualism, it proved possible to draw finer distinctions within this dichotomy. The degree of bilingualism indicates either balanced bilingualism (equal knowledge of the two languages) or dominant bilingualism (notably better knowledge of one of the languages).

By crossing the dimensions of *coordination – complexity* and *balance – dominance* we obtained four types of bilingualism. In *type A*, the languages are in coordinate relation and are equally well known; in *type B*, coordination becomes crossed with dominance; in *type C*, compoundness and balance are taken into consideration; and in *type D*, a relation of compoundness arises between language systems which are not equally well known.

In conformity with our findings on interference, it may be posited that independence between language systems at the semantic level decreases progressively A > B > C > D. Our research study investigated Hungarian mother-tongue secondary school pupils who also had a knowledge of Serbo-Croatian, and who were distributed into the above groups according to the nature of their language instruction and their degree of bilingualism. The results of this study indicated that the similarity between equivalent words in the two languages did indeed decrease in conformity with the foreseen pattern, i.e. the extent of interference between the language systems at the semantic level was smallest in type A, greatest in type D.

Amongst the members of these bilingual groups, certain differences also emerged in their associative behaviour. This behaviour was studied through a number of continuous associations on the same words in two languages and through certain characteristic in the production of free associations. Consideration was given to the number of associations by completion and prediction (it is known that these tend to be more numerous amongst children) and by categorization and opposition (characteristic of the more 'mature' associations formed by adults), also to the number of syntagmatic and paradigmatic associations (syntagmatic associations being more frequent at an earlier age) and to the frequency of associations between adjective and verb rather than noun (which may indicate a 'nuancing' of language knowledge, as may the number of continuous associations). Using these analyses as a basis, one may also summarize certain characteristics of individual types of bilingualism, taking into account the semantic aspects.

In *type A*, the language systems attain maximal separation at the semantic level. Bilingual persons of this type produce an average number of associations in relation to other persons with a knowledge of the same two languages, which may be an indication of the size of their vocabulary. In the first language, the associations are more 'mature' than in the other types of bilingualism.

In *type B* there is somewhat less semantic independence between the languages than in type A. In this group, the greatest number of continuous associations is given for the first language, while the vocabulary in the second language is poorer. The manner of associating is 'mature'.

In *type C* there is still less semantic independence between the language systems. There is only a small number of continuous associations in the first language, and the manner of associating is less 'mature'.

In *type D* the language systems are least separate. Apart from the wealth of continuous associations in the first language, in all other aspects studied this type of bilingualism is the least desirable.

To the question of which type of bilingualism should be developed, taking as indicators the aspects studied, there exists no categorical answer. The answer will depend on which aspect of linguistic behaviour is considered most essential and on which language is given priority.

From the neurological point of view, the independence between the language systems of bilingual persons can be explained by the theory that the neurological systems at the basis of the two languages are functionally separate in such a way as to ensure that when one language is functioning the other is completely excluded. This 'model of bilingual functioing with a single switch' (Penfield and Roberts 1959) has in our research — in which both languages of the bilingual person are simultaneously activated — proved to be less justified than the somewhat more complex more complex 'two switch model of bilingual functioning' (Macnamara 1967). According to this latter model, the bilingual person decides independently of the environment which languages he wishes to speak, and behaves as though he had a language switch which controls his encoding system. Decoding, however, is automatically carried out in the language to whose influence he is exposed, and which he knows. That is, if a bilingual person is requested to react in one language and at the same time is exposed to the other, both his languages will be activated with the result that decoding in the second language interferes with encoding in the first.

In an experiment in which we simultaneously activated the process of encoding in one language and the process of decoding in the other, it was observed that the distractor from the second, 'non-active' language inhibited encoding in the active language. Thus, in a test using the bilingual variant of Stroop's colour naming test (Stroop 1935), in which the names of the colours were written in an incongruous manner (e.g. the word RED written in blue) and the subjects were asked to name the colour of the letters in the second language and ignore what was actually written in the first, it was discovered that bilingual persons were unable to preclude the influence of the distractor from the ostensibly 'non-active' language, for it was observed that the time required for the task in situations where the reaction and the distractor were in either the same or in different languages was considerably greater than in the control situation in which there was no verbal distractor and the subjects had only to name the colour of the surface.

These findings, obtained from studies on 14-year-old pupils, bilingual in Hungarian and Serbo-Croatian, and on multilingual adults with a university background (who spoke, amongst other languages, Hungarian and Serbo-Croatian) indicate that a bilingual is unable to shut out one of his languages if the other one is in function. This does not support the single switch model of bilingual functioning proposed by Penfield and Roberts, (1959) who suggest that 'if one language is on, the other must be off'. The results are more in line with Macnamara's (1967) two switch model of bilingual functioning, and support his hypothesis that a type of neurological mechanism activates both the languages, if the bilingual person is required to react in one language and is, at the same time, verbally distracted by stimuli from the other language. We find that the amount of interference depends on the kind of distractor and on the type of bilingualism. In the case of our research, it must also be taken into account that we were dealing with a specific experimental situation in which the bilingual person, working from a primarily visual stimulus, had to encode the stimulus into a verbal system (i.e. to recognize the colour and name it in one language, while disregarding the word written in the second language which in fact denoted a different colour). The fact that the bilingual person in this experimental situation was not able to exclude the 'non-active' language does not necessarily entail the conclusion that he would never be able to do so; it is recognized that there exist factors which reduce interaction between the languages, and this is substantiated by our results too.

4 The study of bilingualism relevant to educational psychology and applied psycholinguistics

In our research into those aspects of bilingualism which are relevant to educational psychology and applied psycholinguistics we studied the role of motivation and aptitude in language learning which led to the formulation of certain rules relating to the influence of these factors on pupils learning Serbo-Croatian or Hungarian as the language of the social environment. The author of this paper has reported on these studies in the following works: Göncz 1983, 1984. Groups of students from the Novi Sad Faculty of Philosophy, who in addition to foreign languages had also studied Hungarian or Serbo-Croatian at school, were given aptitude and personality tests and questionnaires to establish those aspects of motivation known by the concept of integrative motive. Integrative motive consists of a complex of motivational variables determined by the intensity of motivation for language learning (the amount of effort expended in learning), by the attitude towards the members of the language group whose language is being studied, and by the orientation index. The orientation index represents the reasons for learning: instrumental orientation is understood to be the learning of a language in order to enhance one's reputation or social standing, while integrative orientation refers to the learning of a language in order to acquire a better understanding of another language group. According to results obtained by American and Canadian researchers, greater success in the acquisition of a second language is achieved by a higher degree of motivation, by a positive attitude towards members of the second language group, and by integrative orientation (Gardner and Lambert 1972). In addition, successful pupils manifest a general interest in language learning, a lower anxiety level in language classes at school, and a lower degree of authoritarianism and ethnocentrism; they receive encouragement from their parents in language learning, and in certain social environments they are dissatisfied with their status within their own language group (Gardner and Smythe 1974). In our research, we wished to verify whether these findings would be modified in our own surroundings with regard to learning the language of the social environment and foreign languages.

With regard to the role of aptitude in language learning, we were interested in which of the two models for describing the role of aptitude in language learning — the *G-factor* or the *S-factor* model — would be most acceptable for the situation in Vojvodina. The G-factor model posits the existence of a particular aptitude for language which is relatively stable and within which individual differences in development are conditioned by differences in the succes achieved in the study of any language, while the S-factor model stresses the need for different aptitudes or abilities in the study of different languages.

According to the results of our research, the significant link with success in the acquisition of Serbo-Croatian by native speakers of Hungarian is revealed through the variables: strength of motivation, divergence of skills (particularly fluency), and favourable attitude to the teacher. Correlations with other variables were not statistically significant, but they reflected a tendency towards somewhat greater success in the acquisition of Serbo-Croatian as the language of the social environment among learners who exhibited either integrative or instrumental orientation, whose parents considered it important to learn the language of the social environment, and who adopted a positive approach towards members of the language group whose language they were studying. It should be stressed that those of our subjects who spoke Hungarian as their mother tongue were all equally positive in their assessment of both those who spoke their own language and those who spoke Serbo-Croatian, and that — by contrast with the results obtained by Canadian and American researchers — they exhibited no tendency to devalue members of their own language group, which is often a characteristic reaction of representatives of minority groups. It is probable that our results reflect the internationalist orientation of our subjects, an orientation which has its origins in a divided national interdependence.

Amongst those subjects whose mother tongue was Serbo-Croatian and who were learning Hungarian as the language of the social environment none of the correlations between knowledge of the language and the independent variables proved to be statistically significant. A slightly higher degree of success was recorded by students who adopted a positive approach towards Hungarian as a curricular subject and to the teacher.

The results obtained incline us towards the conclusion that in Vojvodina success in acquiring the language of the social environment (at least, with regard to the students under study) is not determined by that complex of motivational variables known as integrative motive, since many of the variables which constitute this complex do not correlate significantly with success in language acquisition. At the same time, it would appear that in Vojvodina foreign language learning is in fact subject to the influence of integrative motivation because it is determined by integrative orientation, the strength of motivation, the student's attitude towards the subject and the teacher, and the parents' attitude towards language learning. It is likely that these findings may be explained by the more favourable status accorded to the language of the social environment in Vojvodina than in the situations mentioned by the foreign researchers cited above. This is further confirmed by our finding that our subjects who spoke Hungarian as their mother tongue experienced the bilingual situation in which they were living in additive rather than subtractive terms. The additive bilingual situation is characteristic of social situations in which the languages enjoy roughly the same status.

If the G- or S-factor model is not limited only to the role of aptitude, but is extended to include all factors which determine success in language learning, then, according to the results of our research, the G-factor model is better suited to explain a similar result in the mother tongue and in the language of the social environment, conditioned by the influence of the same factors on success in these languages, while success in the mother tongue or in a foreign language, i.e. the language of the social environment and a foreign language less influenced by similar factors, is relatively independent and can be better explained by the S-factor model as understood above.

Finally, it should be mentioned that the results relating to the role of motivation and aptitude in language acquisition have been obtained from a very homogeneous sample of subjects whose general intellectual capacity is high. The study of a less homogeneous sample, with greater variation among the agegroups, would no doubt lead to some modification of these results.

Note

1. Vojvodina is a province in the north-east corner of Yugoslavia with an ethnically and lin-
    guistically heterogeneous population of 2 million and with five official languages (Serbo-
    Croatian, Hungarian, Slovak, Romanian and Ruthenian) all of which enjoy equal status.
    Pupils may attend schools in which instruction is given in the mother tongue, but they also
    learn the other languages which are used in their environment, together with the history
    and culture of the various peoples who form their community. In this way, conditions are
    created for an additive bilingual situation, in which the first language is not replaced by
    another and in which it is ultimately necessary to develop bilingual and multicultural per-
    sons. Language instruction in schools takes various organizational forms, the most com-
    mon of which entails the study of the language of the social environment. This means the
    study of a second language as a curricular subject, beginning (optionally) at the preschool
    stage. In addition, communal extra-curricular activities are organized for pupils in schools
    with two or more languages of instruction. The subjects we studied had acquired their
    second language (Serbo-Croatian) partly in the controlled environment described above
    and partly in the non-controlled conditions of the wider environment, i.e. through contact
    with Serbo-Croatian speakers, through the mass media, the family, etc.

References

Been-Zeev, Sandra. 1977. "The effect of bilingualism in children from Spanish-English low economic neighbourhoods on cognitive develop-ment and cognitive strategy". *Working Papers on Bilingualism* 4: 83-122.

Cummins, James. 1976. "The influence of bilingualism on cognitive growth: A synthesis of research findings and explanatory hypothesis". *Working Papers on Bilingualism* 9: 1-43.

Darcy, Nathalie T. 1953. "A review of the literature on the effects of bilin-gualism upon measurement of intelligence". *Journal of Genetic Psychol-ogy* 82: 21-57.

-----. 1963. "Bilingualism and the measurement of intelligence: A review of a decade of research". *Journal of Genetic Psychology* 103: 259-282.

Ervin, Susan M. and Charles E. Osgood. 1954. "Second language learning and bilingualism". In *Psycholinguistics: A survey of Theory and Research Problems*, ed. by C.E. Osgood and T. Sebeok. Baltimore: Waverly Press. 139-146.

Gardner, Robert C. and Wallace E. Lambert. 1972. *Attitudes and Motivation in Second-Language Learning*. Massachusetts: Newbury House.

Gardner, Robert C. and P.C. Smythe. "The integrative motive in second-language acquisition". In: Carey, Stephen T. (ed.). *Bilingualism, Biculturalism and Education*, 31-45. Edmonton: University of Alberta.

Göncz, Lajos. 1973. "Dvojezičnost kao faktor u objektivizaciji nekih aspekata mišljenja kod dece" [Bilingualism as a factor in the objectivisation of some aspects of thought in children]. In *Dečji govor. Zbornik 6 Instituta za pedagoška istraživanja*, 201-206. Beograd: Naučna knjiga.

-----. 1975a. *Dvojezičnost i govorno ponašanje* [Bilingualism and speech behaviour]. Master's Thesis. Beograd: Filozofski fakultet.

-----. 1975b. "Jedna provera teorije dvojezičnosti o koordiniranim i složenim jezičkim sistemima" [A test of the theory of bilingualism on coordinated and complex language systems]. In: *Materijali sa V Kongresa psihologa Jugoslavije*, 192-197. Skopje.

-----. 1976. "Stepen dvojezičnosti i učestalost upotrebe različitih vrsta reči u maternjem i nematernjem jeziku" [The level of bilingualism and the usage frequency of various words in the mother and non-mother tongue]. *Pedagoška stvarnost* 5: 310-319.

-----. 1977. "Kontinuirane asocijacije kao tehnika za merenje jezičke ravnoteže i jezičke dominacije kod dvojezičnih osoba" [Continued associations as a technique for measuring language equilibrium and language dominance in biinguals]. *Psihologija* 3-4: 107-115.

-----. 1979a. "O mogućnostima uticaja rane dvojezičnosti na kognitivni razvoj" [On the possible influence of early bilingualism on cognitive development]. *Godišnjak Saveza društava za primenjenu lingvistiku Jugoslavije* 3: 161-167.

-----. 1979b. "Rana dvojezičnost i kognitivni razvoj" [Early bilingualism and cognitive development]. Ph.D. dissertation. Beograd: Filozofski fakultet.

-----. 1979c. "Uticaj rane dvojezičnosti na kognitivni razvoj" [The influence of early bilingualism on cognitive development]. *Psihologija*. 3-4: 81-92.

-----. 1981a. *Rana dvojezičnost i kognitivni razvoj* [Early bilingualism and cognitive development]. Novi Sad: Filozofski fakultet – Institut za pedagogiju/Zavod za izdavanje udžbenika.

-----. 1981b. "Rana dvojezičnost i kognitivni razvoj". [Early bilingualism and cognitive development]. *Psihologija* 1-2: 25-39.

-----. 1982. "A korai kétnyelvűség hatása a besédfejlődésre" [The influence of early bilingualism on speech development]. *Hungarológiai Közlemények* 51: 141-174.

-----. ["Vrednovanje osobina ličnosti na osnovu glasa i uspeh u usvajanju drugog jezika" [Evaluation of character traits on the basis of voice and achievement in second language acquisition]. *Paper presented at the III Congress of Yugoslav Applied Linguistics*, Sarajevo, 1983.

-----. 1984. "Uloga motivacije i sposobnosti u učenju jezika društvene sredine" [The role of motivation and capability in learning the language of the social environment]. Filozoski fakultet Novi Sad. Institut za pedagogiju. Unpublished paper.

-----. 1985. *A kétnyelvűség pszichológiája*. A magyar – szerbhorvát kétnyelvüség lélektani kutatása [Psychology of bilingualism. A psychological study of Hungarian-Serbocroatian bilingualism]. Novi Sad: Forum.

-----. Forthcoming a. "A research study of the relationship between early bilingualism and cognitive development". To appear in: *Psychologische Beiträge*.

Göncz, Lajos and Eva Varga. Forthcoming. "Interakcija medju jezičkim sistemima dvojezičnih osoba" [Interaction between language systems in bilingual persons]. To appear in: *Revija za psihologiju*. 1985. 1-2: 13-24.

Ivić, Ivan D. 1978. *Čovek kao animal symbolicum. Razvoj simboličkih sposobnosti* [Man as animal symbolicum. The development of symbolic capacities]. Beograd: Nolit.

Macnamara, John. 1966. *Bilingualism and Primary Education: A Study of Irish Experience*. Edinburgh: Edinburgh University Press.

Macnamara, John. 1967. "The bilingual's linguistic performance: a psychological overview". *Journal of Social Issues* 23(2): 58-77.

-----. 1967. "The bilingual's linguistic performance: a psychological overview". *Journal of Social Issues* 23(2): 58-77.

Peal, Elizabeth and Wallace E. Lambert. 1962. "The relation of bilingualism to intelligence." *Psychological Monographs: General and Applied*. 546 (76): 1-23.

Penfield, W. and L. Roberts. 1959. *Speech and Brain Mechanism*. Princeton: Princeton University Press.

Piaget, Jean. 1972. "Pijažeovo gledište" [Le point de vue de Piaget]. [Piaget's view]. *Psihologija*. 1-2: 85-99.

-----. 1978. "Odnos govora i mišljenja s genetičkog stanovišta" [Le langage et la pensée du point de vue génétique]. [The relation of language and thought from the genetic viewpoint]. In: Pijaže, Ž. and B. Inhelder.

Intelektualni razvoj deteta. Izabrani radovi, 183-190. Beograd: Zavod za udžbenike i nastavna sredstva.

Stroop, J.R. 1935. "Studies of interference in serial verbal reaction". *Journal of Experimental Psychology* 18: 643-661.

Vygotsky, Lev. 1962. *Thought and Language*. Cambridge, Mass.: MIT Press.

Whorf, Benjamin L. 1956. *Language, Thought and Reality*. Cambridge, Mass: MIT Press.

On referentially used nouns and the upgrading/downgrading of their identificatory force

Milka Ivić
Serbian Academy of Sciences and Arts, Belgrade

In the last three decades, the scalar nature of (in)definiteness has been one of the most intensely discussed topics in logic.[1] What we need now is to get more insight on it from linguistics.

Logicians, among others, have called attention to the following fact:

When referring to an individual by means of a general term, the speaker may choose to give more prominence to either the individuative or the descriptive sense of the given noun meaning. Thus, depending on what aspects of its semantic content is being focussed on by the speaker, the expression *a doctor* happens to be interpreted either as (a) 'There is such a particular person who fits the description labelled *a doctor*' or (b) 'It is the property of doctorhood I am speaking of saying that this property is being ascribed to an individual'.[2]

By raising/lowering their discourse-pragmatic importance, the speaker is putting the (a) and (b) senses into perspective and out of it, respectively.

If so, then it seems reasonable to conclude that the occurrence of the foregrounding/backgrounding contrast, which normally concerns sentence constituents, may concern even some particular features of their meaning contents.

This issue is of considerable theoretical bearing and needs to be incorporated in an appropriate way into actual Sentence Perspective Theory.

A question which should be raised at this point is the following: what may influence the speaker's decision to put stronger emphasis on either the individuative or the descriptive meaning feature?

In order to help answer it, I shall point here to some relevant evidence presented by Serbo-Croatian language data. My discussion will be restricted to the referentially used singular nouns.

It is well known that Serbo-Croatian belongs to the group of non-articulated languages in which the raising/lowering of the nound identificatory force interacts with word order and phrasal stress. However, under undefiniteness conditions, the speakers of Serbo-Croatian frequently fill the noun determiner position with the expression *jedan*, which is an individuative word homophonous with the numeric *jedan* 'one'.[3] By doing so, they succeed in calling special attention to the individuation of the referent whose identity[4] the hearer is assumed to ignore. Such a grammatical strategy serves always one and the same purpose; it makes this referent eligible for topichood.

This claim of mine that in Serbo-Croatian the upgrading of the individuation feature is serving topicalization purposes is supported by the following linguistic evidence:[5]

I. When telling about one's personal experiences, the speaker may focus his attention either (a) on a particular individual or (b) on a particular situation. It is only in case (a) that *jedan* is required to occur with the presentational indefinite; in case (b) its occurrence is optional.

Cf. sentences (1) and (2) which exemplify the use of *jedan* under individual-focus telling and situation-focus telling conditions, respectively:

(1)   *Zamisli, **jedan vojnik** je našem učitelju postavio ovakvo pitanje:...*
      'Fancy, a soldier asked our teacher the following question:...'

(2)   *Pogledala sam kroz prozor i videla samo (**jednog**) **vojnika** kako prolazi ulicom, ništa više.*
      'I looked out the window and saw only a soldier passing down the street, nothing else.'

II. The initial sentence position marks the referent of a noun as a topic of the speaker's information; this explains why it is not the sentence subject but the noun occurring in the initial sentence position which gets the individuative determiner. Cf. for example:

(3)   ***Jednom lekaru** umro komšija, pa on pošao kod komšijine familije ...*
      'The neighbour of a doctor died, so the doctor went to see the neighbour's family ...'

III. An indefinite noun occurring in non-initial sentence position must be preceded by *jedan* whenever the speaker wants to instruct the hearer to expect a conversational move toward the referent of this noun as a new topic.[6] Cf. for example:

(4) *Ona je to čula od jednog studenta kome je nekada Irenina majka davala časove klavira. Taj je čak bio svedok na sudu ...*
'She heard it from a student whom Irene's mother used to give piano lessons. This one was even the witness in the court of justice ...'

IV. In cases where the opening sentence contains more than one indefinite, the relevance of the Topic Hierarchy Principle comes to evidence; *jedan* occurs with the most topical noun.[7]

The same observation could be formulated also in this way: in cases where the opening sentence contains more than one indefinite, the function of *jedan* is to elevate one of the given referents to the most prominent position in the Surface Structure Empathy Hierarchy.[8]

The following sentence illustrates this principle in operation:

(5) *Preda mnom je jedan putnik kupio iste takve kruške od seljanke za mnogo manju cenu.*
'I was present when a passer-by bought the same kind of pears from a countrywoman for a much smaller price.'

To sum up and conclude: On the basis of the evidence given by the Serbo-Croatian language data, it seems reasonable to advance the claim that the upgrading of the individuative aspect of the noun meaning is a textual feature functioning as a corollary of topicality.

The next question that interests us is this: What makes the descriptive aspect of the noun meaning especially deserving of focus?

In normal conversational interactions, under noun indefiniteness conditions, the crucial role in this respect is always played by the speaker's understanding of the communication needs. The speaker, namely, foregrounds the descriptive sense of the noun meaning whenever he becomes aware of the fact that, in view of what the conversation is about, it would be of special importance for him to get the hearer informed about the referent's class membership. Cf. sentence (6):

(6) *Ne oseća se dobro, trebalo bi da ode do lekara.*
'He does not feel well, he should see a doctor.'

The relevance of this semantic principle has been pointed to for a long time by logicians in their writings on indefiniteness. Now, I would like to call attention to another, hitherto unnoticed strategy of the speaker. In comparison with the previous one, this strategy serves the opposite purpose: by foregrounding the descriptive meaning feature, the speaker intends to get the identificatory force of the general term increased, not decreased.

This is possible for him to achieve only on very special occasions, namely those which give the necessary clue for the hearer's understanding of his instruction. The hearer, namely, must figure out that he is to identify the referent although the normally required 'previous mention' condition is not being met; he must also understand that, by giving prominence to the descriptive meaning sense, the speaker is, in fact, instructing him as to how to do it. In brief, the hearer must know that, in this case, the identification is intended to be of the 'role-centered' type, not of the 'identity-centered' one.

The 'role-centered' identificational principle comes to evidence, for instance, in story-telling contexts.

In these contexts, the referent may occur presented as identifiable by virtue of his 'typical exponent' role. Namely, the story-teller may suggest to the audience to identify the referent in terms of his fit with a well-known prototype.[9]

Thus, in an opening sentence like

(7)   *Ušao **Škotlandanin** u dragstor da kupi bocu viskija, pa ...*
      'A Scotsman entered a drugstore in order to buy a bottle of whisky and ...'

the omission of *jedan* functions as an overt grammatical mark of the story-teller's intention to inform his audience that the individual he has in mind does not depart from what is generally believed a Scotsman must be.

The 'role-centered' identification comes to evidence also on the occasion of those official events which make it obvious for the hearer that the referent is being presented as identifiable by virtue of the official duty he is performing.

Thus, an opening sentence

(8)   *Molimo **kandidata** da zauzme mesto*
      'We are asking the candidate to take his seat'

sounds quite meaningful to the people gathered in the room where an exam is going to start. Even without any previous knowledge of the referent, everybody is able to understand whom the professor has in mind when saying *kandidat* 'candidate'; he is thinking of the student who is being expected right now to try to pass the exam.

This 'role-centered' identification is less powerful than the normal, i.e. the 'identity-centered' one. Relevant evidence for this is given by Serbo-Croatian language data.

Occurring without determiner in their adnominal syntactic position, the 'possessor' and 'subject' nouns in Serbo-Croatian become either adjectivized or genitivized.[10]

The effect of adjectivization lies in emphasizing the 'identity-centered' perception of the referent and the effect of genitivization in preventing it. The conclusion naturally follows: The adjectivized version of the noun has stronger identificatory force than the genitivized one.

By using, for instance, the adjectival forms *poštarev(u)* and *kapetanov* respectively in sentences

(9)   *Srela sam juče **poštarevu** ženu.*
       'I met yesterday the wife of the postman.'

and

(10)   *Da li si slušao **kapetanov** govor?*
       'Did you listen to the captain's speech?'

the speaker is overtly insisting upon the fact that the 'previous mention' condition for definiteness is being met, i.e. that the referent is being presented as known to the participants in the speech event. On the other hand, in a sentence like

(11)   *Savet **lekara** moraš ozbiljno uzeti.*
       'You must take seriously the doctor's advice.'

the occurrence of the genitive form is meant to signal that the referent is being looked at primarily from the point of view of his class membership, which amounts to the fact that the noun is referring in 'a very weak sense' (Donnellan 1966: 303).

I would like, however, to call special attention here to another example.

Suppose that we are again in a room where an exam is going on. The exam being an official event, its participants are tending to be formal in speech. This is why the professor, after having heard the candidate's answer, expresses his opinion by using a sentence like

(12)   *Nismo zadovoljni odgovorom **kandidata**.*
       'We are not pleased with the candidate's answer.'

instead of a sentence like

(13)   *Nismo zadovoljni **kandidatovim** odgovorom.*
       'We are not pleased with the candidate's answer.'

The professor, namely, knows intuitively that by choosing the genitive form he is giving preference to the 'role-centered' identificatory approach implying *ipso facto* not to pay attention to the identity of the referent. In other words, under the given circumstances, the choice of genitivization is meant to create a sense of distance between speaker and referent.

In this distance-creating function, the genitive case mark is found to occur, although sporadically, even on proper names.[11]

Under the syntactic conditions we have in mind, proper names are normally subjected to adjectivization. The appearance of the genitive mark on a proper name is tolerated only in cases where the referent is being perceived from the side of his professional work, not as a private person, which by itself suggests a rather distant, not close relationship between speaker and referent.

Thinking, for instance, of the linguist Jakobson, the speaker of Serbo-Croatian feels allowed to say not only

(14)   *Oduševljen sam **Jakobsonovim** metodom.*
       'I am enthusiastic about Jakobson's method.'

but also

(15)   *Oduševljen sam metodom **Jakobsona**.*
       'I am enthusiastic about Jakobson's method.'

However, if it is his friend Romka he is speaking of, adjectivization happens to be the only possible choice:

(16)   *Oduševljen sam **Romkinim** metodom.*
       'I am enthusiastic about Romka's method'.

One thing is obvious: In all the cases discussed here, it is by genitivizing the noun that the speaker is weakening its identificatory force; adjectivization is, on the other hand, a grammatical device serving to make it stronger.

I shall conclude this paper with the observation that my discussion of Serbo-Croatian language data has brought to light four theoretically issues, the essence of which could be formulated as follows:

a. It is impossible to dissociate the study of individuation phenomena occurring under indefiniteness and the study of topicalization principles.

b. The distinction between the 'identity-centered' and 'role-centered' identification is one which the linguist must be attentive to. This distinction, namely, happens to be crucial to the description of certain facts about referential markers in natural languages.

c. The distribution of the referential markers may happen to be under the control of a socially-correlated grammatical rule. Therefore it is always necessary to take into account the connection between appropriate language choices and the social settings in which their use comes to evidence.

d. In view of our present knowledge of referential language phenomena, we are required to point to a much more differentiated semantic relationship between referential markers than has hitherto been assumed in the context of linguistic studies of definiteness. Indeed, one of the most important conclusions suggested by the Serbo-Croatian language data is that the downgrading of the noun identificatory force may depend even on such a subjective factor as the speaker's intention to create a sense of distance between himself and the referent.

Notes

1. The easiest access to theoretical issues connected with this problem is provided by Wreen (1984).

2. I am avoiding here to make the usage of current terminological distinctions in view of the lack of consistency in their interpretation. For different definitions of what is referred to by terms such as 'definite', 'specific', etc., cf. Chvany 1983: 71.

3. It is common knowledge that a homophonous relation between the indefinite determiner and the numeric 'one' is found in many genetically and geographically diverse languages. For more details cf. Givón 1981.

4. Following Nunberg and Pan (1975: 421) I shall leave 'identity' as an undefined primitive.

5. In Ivić 1971 and Ivić 1973 my main concern was to call attention to both the frequent occurrence of *jedan* 'one' in standard Serbo-Croatian and the fact that it, nevertheless, fails to meet the most important requirement for article status. The present formulations of the principles underlying its use have not been previously advanced.

6. Birkenmaier (1976: 50) points to the operation of the same principle in Russian where *odin* 'one' is the corresponding individuative word.

7. The same behavior is true of the Russian *odin* 'one'. For more details cf. Nikolaeva 1985: 46.
8. For the notion of 'empathy cf. Kuno and Kaburaki 1977.
9. The operation of this identificational principle is observable in other languages too. For more details cf. Weiss 1983: 236.
10. For more on this point cf. Ivić (Forthcoming).
11. A fuller discussion of this problem is presented in Ivić (Forthcoming).

References

Donnellan, Keith. 1966. "Reference and definite description." *Philosophical Review* 75: 281-304.
Birkenmaier, Willy. 1976. "Die Funktion von *odin* im Russischen". *Zeitschrift für slavische Philologie* 29. 1: 43-59.
Chvany, Catherine V. 1983. "On definiteness in Bulgarian, English and Russian." *American Contributions to the Ninth International Congress of Slavists. Kiev, September 1983*. Vol. I: *Linguistics*: 71-92.
Givón, Talmy. 1981. "On the development of the numeral 'one' as an indefinite marker". *Folia Linguistica Historica* 2: 25-54.
Ivić, Milka. 1971. "Leksema *jedan* i problem neodređenog člana" [The lexeme *jedan* and the problem of the indefinite article]. *Zbornik za filologiju i lingvistiku* 14.1: 103-120.
-----. 1973. "Elementi neodređenog člana u savremenom srpskohrvatskom književnom jeziku" [Elements of the indefinite article in modern standard Serbocroatian]. *Referati za VII međunarodni kongres slavista u Varšavi*. Novi Sad: Filozofski fakultet. 11-14.
-----. Forthcoming. "On referential strategies: Genitivization vs. adjectivization in Serbocroatian". To appear in *Festschrift für Rudolf Růžička*. Leipzig.
Kuno, Susumu and Etsuko Kaburaki. 1977. "Empathy and syntax". *Linguistic Inquiry* 8.4: 627-672.
Nikolaeva, T.M. 1985. *Funkcii častic v vyskazyvanii na materiale slavjanskix jazykov*. Moskva: Nauka (= Akademija nauk SSSR – Institut slavjanovedenija i balkanistiki).
Nunberg, Geoffrey and Chiahua Pan. 1975. "Inferring quantification in generic sentences". *Papers from the Eleventh Regional Meeting of the Chicago Linguistic Society, April 18-20, 1975*: 412-422. Chicago, Illinois: University of Chicago (= Department of Linguistics).

Weiss, Daniel. 1983. "Indefinite, definite and generische Referenz in artikellosen slavischen Sprachen." *Slavistische Linguistik 1982: Referate des VIII. Konstanzer Slavistischen Arbeitstreffens. Kiel 28.9. – 1.10. 1982*: 229-261. (= *Slavistische Beiträge* 172). München.

Wreen, Michael. 1984. "Belief, modality, opacity,and the referential/ attributive distinction". *Linguistics* 22-23: 331-340.

Structure and typology of dialectal differentiation*

Pavle Ivić
Serbian Academy of Sciences and Arts, Belgrade

Dialectology can be structural in three respects:

1. in regarding language patterns in dialects as structures;
2. in examining the social and stylistic structure of the differentiation within particular local dialects;
3. in studying the structure of territorial linguistic differentiation.[1]

In the first case the structural approach differs from the traditional one by the fact that the investigation is not limited to interdialectal relationships concerning the same linguistic element (E_1, E_2, E_3 in dialects 1, 2 and 3 in Figure 1), but includes comparison of relationships between various elements (E ... and F ... in Figure 2) in diverse dialects.

$$E_1 \longleftrightarrow E_2 \longleftrightarrow E_3 \qquad\qquad \begin{array}{ccc} E_1 & E_2 & E_3 \\ \updownarrow & \updownarrow & \updownarrow \\ F_1 & F_2 & F_3 \end{array}$$

Fig. 1   *Fig. 2*

Thus not simply (interdialectal) relationships between elements, but (interdialectal) relationships between (intradialectal) relationships.

In the second case variants coexisting in a local dialect are envisaged as a system of (linguistic) systems each of which belongs to a social layer or generation, or accomplishes a stylistic function.

The purpose of this paper is to draw the attention of dialectologists to

---

* This article was originally published in *Proceedings of the Ninth International Congress of Linguists. Cambridge, Mass., 1962.* The Hague: Mouton. 115-21. It is reprinted here in the same form, except for technical adjustments (*Discussion* omitted). Permission to reprint was kindly granted by Mouton Publishers (Division of Walter de Gruyter & Co.).

the problems of point 3, which have so far been the most neglected ones.

The structure of dialectal differentiation determines the typological physiognomy of a linguistic landscape. By this term we understand here any part of the territory of a language (or of closely related languages).

A necessary prerequisite for the study of differentiation in a linguistic landscape is the knowledge of isoglosses in it, in a number sufficient to be statistically representative. In various language areas this requirement is fulfilled by the existence of linguistic atlases.

By plotting isoglosses from different maps of an atlas on a single map we obtain pictures that in most cases make a chaotic impression, but are as a rule differently patterned in various linguistic landscapes. On closer inspection, the tremendous variegation existing in this respect proves reducible to a limited number of relevant features.. All these features are quantitative indices calculated from the data of linguistic atlases.

1 The *differentiation density* can be determined by counting the isoglosses that cut a straight line of definite length traced on the map. The statistical significance of the index of 'isoglosses per mile' or 'miles per isogloss' should be secured by calculating the average or results obtained in counting intersection points along a sufficient number of lines traced in the same region. Measurements of this kind will, as a rule, give different results in various parts of a single language territory. It is further possible to divide the linguistic landscape into equal squares in order to count, e.g., 'isoglosses per 1000 sq. miles', and also to compute indices of 'inhabitants per isogloss'.[2] In all these case figures have a relative character, depending largely on the number of questions in the atlas, which does not necessarily deprive them of statistical significance. If we establish, basing our analysis on an atlas dealing with 500 features, that region A contains 75 isoglosses per 1000 sq. miles, and region B only 25 such isoglosses, it is highly probable that an augmentation of the number of features included would basically confirm this ratio (in an atlas of 1000 features the corresponding figures would not be very far from 150 and 50, and so on). Moreover, it is possible to remodel the indices and to state, e.g., that the differentiation density in the region A is 15% of features per 1000 sq. miles, and in region B 5%.

2 The *linear distribution of isoglosses* oscillates between two extremes: *a)* even distribution with equal distances between isoglosses, and *b)* concentration of all isoglosses in a bundle. Although these ideal cases never occur, solutions existing in reality often come close to one or the other (Figure 3 and Figure 4). The linear distribution of isoglosses can be determined by tracing a straight line on the map and computing the average distance between the points where isoglosses cut the line and the points where they would cut it in case of ideally even distribution (Figure 5).

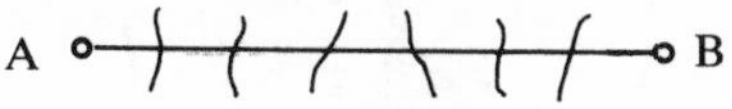

Fig. 3

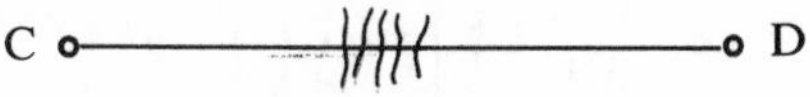

Fig. 4

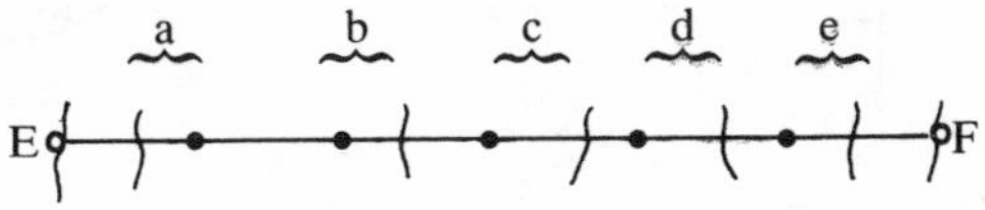

Fig. 5

The index of linear isogloss distribution for the whole landscape can be obtained by calculating the average of indices computed along a statistically representative number of straight lines traced in most different directions. This index will help to answer the question whether territorial dialects do exist in the given landscape (and will help also to realize that the answer to this classical controversial question is usually relative and varies as to landscape). The appropriateness of introducing the notion of territorial dialect in a given landscape is proportional to the closeness of the situation to type *b*. And wherever territorial dialects do exist (in the above sense), it is possible to calculate indices describing the sharpness of their boundaries and their internal uniformity. Numerical indices will also give definitive solutions in controversial cases of dialect classification. The hierarchy of divisions and subdivisions can be expressed in figures.[3]

3 The *distribution of isoglosses as to direction* (= relative density of differentiation as to direction) can be calculated by comparing the numbers of isoglosses that cut straight lines traced in various directions on the map (Figure 6). Thus it can be discovered that in a landscape A the density of differentiation in the north-south direction is about the same as the density measured along east-west lines, and that in a landscape B the two indices differ greatly. The latter case occurs, e.g., in Gallo-Romance, in German and in Russian, where W-E isoglosses prevail over the N-S ones, or in the South Slavic area, where the NNE-SSW isoglosses (shaded area in Figure 7) definitely outnumber those in the remaining three quarters of the semicircle.

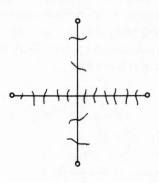

Fig. 6   Fig. 7

4 A statistical survey of the *size of areas* of particular features can classify areas in a number of classes depending on their size, and also determine the average value and standard deviation indices. The feature reflects the degree of evolutive homogeneity of a linguistic landscape. If innovation waves in it have a wide range, the number of ample areas will be high, and if the landscape is divided into several portions innovating more or less independently, small areas will prevail by far. Likewise, when innovation areas are in average large, and areas of archaisms small, it is obvious that the dialects involved have undergone a long-lasting common development, whereas the opposite situation shows that this did not take place.

5 The *shape of isoglosses* varies from almost perfectly straight lines to complete disorder on the map (Figure 8, Figure 9 and Figure 10).

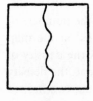   

Fig. 8   Fig. 9   Fig. 10

The curvature of lines is measurable, and the application of statistics can bring a tabulating of isoglosses as to the degree of curvature, as well as indices of average curvature and of dispersion. The shape of isoglosses being correlated with that of areas, we can alternatively study the shape of areas (e.g., the degree of deviation from the circle as the ideally regular geometrical figure).

6 The crucial point concerning the *relationship between areas* is the question whether feature areas covering partly the same territory include one another (Figure 11) or only intersect (Figure 12).[4]

Fig. 11   Fig. 12

In every landscape we shall find instances of both kinds, but their ratio is variable and belongs to the characteristics of the landscape. In fact, this ratio (if we do not take into account areas of archaisms) indicates the relative share of 'Stammbaum' and 'wave' pattern elements in the dialectal differentiation of the given landscape. In the Stammbaum pattern, innovation areas never intersect, but either coincide completely, or include one another. This much-debated problem, too, is to be restated in a quantitative way, and the answer varies depending on the landscape.

Features described above in the points 1-3 can be visualized by observing intersections between isoglosses and lines traced on the map, whereas envisaging of features No. 4-6 requires consideration of isoglosses as wholes (which is tantamount to areas as wholes).

In the first triad, feature No. 1 is a simple quantification, and the remaining two concern relationships between isoglosses – No. 2 in a linear, and No. 3 in a two-dimensional perspective.

In the second triad, only No. 6 pertains to relationships between isoglosses. In the plane, there is but one possibility of such relationship: isoglosses either do or do not intersect. On the other hand, two features are possible here which do not affect relationships between isoglosses: areas have their size and their shape (in the first triad a comparable distinction is precluded). The determination of size is again a simple quantification, and as to the shape, the relevant role is played by ratios obtained in comparing results of measurements in two dimensions.

Relevant features No.: Constitutive elements:	1	2	3	4	5	6
Bearing upon areas as wholes	−	−	−	+	+	+
Relationships between isoglosses	−	+	+	−	−	+
Two-dimensional ratios		−	+	−	+	

Numerical indices concerning five out of the six features described are of such a nature that they make possible direct comparisons of results obtained in various language areas. The only exception is made by indices of differentiation density which are influenced by the number of questions in the atlas (and by the number of phenomena left out because they do not present a noteworthy differentiation within the territory covered). Even the problem itself, just what is meant by the term 'relative density of differentiation' when applied to areas of unrelated languages, involves some vagueness. Nevertheless, a careful adaptation of certain methods proposed by glottochronologists and representatives of cognate trends could provide us with reasonably satisfying criteria. Furthermore, it would be a challenging task to compare circumstances in various sectors of the language system, e.g., to take into account only isoglosses of differences affecting the inventory (or the number) of phonemes, or of inflectional morphemes, or of their allomorphs, and so on.

Theoretically, it is imaginable to cover maps of all continents by isoglosses denoting values of indices of the six relevant features listed (with the only limitation concerning No. 1) and furnishing a typological survey of dialectal differentiation throughout the world. This would open the way for two kinds of conclusions. The study of divergences between various *areas* can illuminate the way and the measure in which particular geographic or historical factors influence differentiation within a language area (this would enable us to verify definitively the existing opinions and to give exact foundations to the theory of dialectal differentiation). Likewise, the different behavior of various categories of *features* can suggest conclusions concerning the very nature of these features.

The development of the studies pertaining to the structure of dialectal differentiation will inspire dialectal maps with new life and give new significance to linguistic geography. For illustration let us look at the peculiarities of two dialectal zones in the Serbo-Croatian language territory. The Torlakian dialect group is characterized by a differentiation density about the Serbo-Croatian average, by a very uneven linear distribution of isoglosses and a fairly uneven distribution as to direction, by the size of areas about the Serbo-Croatian average, by comparatively straight lines of isoglosses, and by the presence of some Stammbaum elements. The characteristic of the Kajkavian dialect group are: very high differentiation density, even distribution of isoglosses (both linear and as to direction), size of areas below the Serbo-Croatian average, comparatively irregular shape of isoglosses, and an almost complete absence of Stammbaum elements. The differences described are at least partly due to the facts that the Torlakian dialects are situated in a region of mountains and valleys, and the Kajkavian ones in a region of hills and plains, and that the former were displaced to a considerable extent by flow-like migratory movements spreading from certain districts, whereas the latter ones had chiefly an organic development without noticeable transplantations.

Besides the six underlying features listed, a number of other phenomena appearing in various linguistic landscapes, and usually evaluated by intuition, can be defined in a more exact way.

A dialectal feature can be labelled *original* if its area is unique, limited and non-diffuse (these characteristics are normally associated with a low degree of probability of a linguistic phenomenon's appearing). Dialectal areas are original when they have a considerable number of original features, and these are, in the sense of the above definition, features occurring nowhere outside of the region (in practice, 5% of such features may be regarded as high). Non-original dialects can be grouped into two major classes. Many of them contain a peculiar combination of features that also exist elsewhere in various dialects (not always the contiguous ones). whereas others are purely transitional, possessing only features present in one or another neighboring area. Dialects of a whole landscape can be surveyed in respect to the percentage of original features contained; computing averages and dispersion indices would also contribute to a more complete characterization of landscapes. Under certain conditions (wave pattern, even linear distribution of isoglosses, ample areas) we will have the impression that every dialect has a transitional nature.

In cases when dialect boundaries do exist, three basic types of *interrelations* between contiguous dialectal territories are conceivable:

1. connection between two *dialects* as wholes (Figure 13; the shaded area represents the diffusion of the common feature/s/);

2. connection between one *dialect* and a *part* of the other one (Figure 14);

3. connection between *parts* of both (Figure 15).

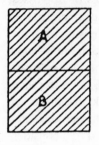
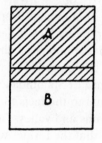
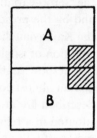

Fig. 13   *Fig. 14*   *Fig. 15*

In the type 2 there is a subdivision: in some cases the relationship is one-sided, but in others it is also possible to adduce some features of dialect B that are present in parts of the area A.

The various types of contacts occur together very often, but not necessarily. All imaginable combinations appear in reality, and one of the future tasks will be to determine the specific factors influencing the typology of interdialectal contacts.

The same distinctions apply to cases of unrelated or distantly related *languages in contact*.

More exact definitions can be given also to other concepts pertaining to the phenomena of linguistic differentiation, such as bundles of isoglosses, degree of concentration of isoglosses in a bundle, kernel and peripheral parts of a territorial dialect, conservatism and progressiveness of dialects, and so one. In all these cases, too, facts are expressible by numerical indices.[5]

Notes

1. This enumeration exhausts the scope of existing possibilities. Dialectology is the discipline dealing with differentiation in linguistic patterns, and the structural approach can be applied either to the study of patterns, or to the study of the differentiation itself. The latter can be vertical (within a local dialect) or horizontal (i.e., territorial).

2. A systematic comparison of indices of differentiation in proportion to the area with those in proportion to the population would illuminate the relative importance of these two factors for dialectal differentiation.

3.   In the author's opinion, methods proposed thus far for dialect classification (traditional historical; synchronically structural, cf. Stankiewicz, in: *Word* 13: 44-59; diachronically structural, cf. Garde, in: *Word* 17: 34-62) are of high value, but more for the description of circumstances in dialects than for the actual classification. The genuine criterion of classification is the statistical one. The taxonomy of dialects should be based on the product of the number and the importance of isoglosses by which they are separated. The importance of differences depends on their material extent, their place in structural hierarchy, the number of words affected, and the frequency of these words. With the increasing quantity of material handled the role of the importance of features diminishes, in accord with the growing chance that the coefficient of importance be approximately equal on both sides and with the decreasing index of standard error for the case of disregarding this coefficient. The problem has been discussed in the author's report to the First International Congress of General Dialectology in Louvain 1960 ("Importance des caractéristiques structurales pour la description et la classification des dialectes", summary in the *Programme* of the Congress: 95-96; full text published in the *Actes* of the Congres: *Orbis* 13.1 (1963): 117-31).

4.   Cases when areas have no contact or when they touch each other from outside, are of much less typological interest.

5.   For a more detailed discussion of some of the questions touched in this paper, see the author's articles "On the structure of dialectal differentiation". *Word* 18 (1962): 33-53, and "Osnovni aspekti strukture dijalekatske diferencijacije" [The basic aspects of the structure of dialect differentiation]. *Makedonski jazik* 11-12 (1960-61): 81-103.

Prosodic possibilities in phonology and morphology*

Pavle Ivić
Serbian Academy of Sciences and Arts, Belgrade

In my paper "The functional yield of prosodic features in the patterns of Serbocroatian dialects" I tried to introduce the concept of the range of prosodic possibilities into the study of phonological typology.[1] The number of those possibilities in an *n*-syllabic word[2] appears to be an index of the role of prosodic phenomena in the pattern of the given language. Of course, we are dealing here with word phonology (rather than with facts pertaining to the levels of phrase or sentence) and with the distinctive function of prosodic phenomena (rather than with their culminative, delimitative or expressive function).

The aim of the present paper is twofold: to elaborate on some aspects of the problem as far as the domain of phonology is concerned, and to investigate the applicability of the concept of prosodic possibilities to morphological description.

The functional load of prosodic phenomena in linguistic patterns without prosodic oppositions can be represented by the formula[3]

$$(1) \qquad P_n = 1.$$

One possibility means of course no selection and no distinctive function. This applies to many languages, varying greatly as to the phonetic realization of the prosodic uniformity of the word. French has an automatic stress on the ultima, Polish on the penultima, Standard Macedonian on the

* This article was originally published in the *Festschrift*: Jakobson, Roman and Shigeo Kawamoto, eds. 1970. *Studies in General and Oriental Linguistics. Presented to Shirô Hattori on the Occasion of His Sixtieth Birthday*. Tokyo: TEC Corporation for Language and Educational Research. 287-301. It is reprinted here in the same form, except for the necessary technical adjustments, additional references, and the correction of typographical errors.

antepenultima, Upper Lusatian on the initial syllable, and so on. A comparable case is that of the Japanese dialects of Fukushima and Kumamoto.[4]

In languages with a distinctive and free place of accent, e.g., in Russian, Rumanian, or Bulgarian, the formula will be:

(2) $P_n = n$.

In Tokyo Japanese the distinctive function is accomplished by the accent kernel which can appear in any syllable ($P'_n = n$), or be absent ($P''_n = 1$), which gives

(3) $P_n = P'_n + P''_n = n+1$.

This amounts to three possibilities in disyllabic words (O˺O, OO˺, and OO),[5] four possibilities in trisyllabic words (O˺OO, OO˺O, OOO˺, and OOO), etc.[6]

In Czech, where only quantity is distinctive, and is independently variable in each syllable, the formula[7] is

(4) $P_n = 2^n$,

which provides two possibilities in monosyllabic words (O and O:), four possibilities in disyllabic words (OO, O:O, OO:, and O:O:), eight in trisyllabic words, and so on. This is also the case in Hungarian (which, however, also has oppositions between short and long consonants, independent from vocalic quantity) and in Classical Latin. An automatic stress falls on the initial syllable in Czech and Hungarian, and on the syllabic containing the last but one mora before the ultima in Latin.

Formula (4) is effective also with quantity in Ancient Greek. However, the place of accent, too, played a distinctive role in that language. In principle, the accent could fall on the ultima (with the additional contrast between circumflex and acute when the ultima is long), on the penultima (with an automatic distribution of the two types of long accents), and on the antepenultima (only if the ultima is short). This provides:

 a. 3 possibilities in monosyllabic words:
  O˺, O˺:, O:˺
 b. 10 possibilities in disyllabic words:
  OO˺, O:O˺, OO˺:, O:O˺:, OO:˺, O:O:˺
  O˺O, O˺O:, O˺:O, O:˺O:
 c. 24 possibilities in trisyllabic words:
  OOO˺, O:OO˺, OO:O˺, O:O:O˺:
  OOO˺:, O:OO˺:, OO:O˺:, O:O:O˺:
  OOO:˺, O:OO:˺, OO:O:˺, O:O:O:˺

OOˀO, O:OˀO, OOˀO:, O:OˀO:
OOˀ:O, O:Oˀ:O, OO:ˀO:, O:O:ˀO:
OˀOO, OˀO:O, O:ˀOO, O:ˀO:O

Words consisting of more than three syllables had in principle the same number of accentuation possibilities as trisyllabic words, since the accent as a rule could not stand on the fourth or further syllables from the end of the word. However, quantity in those syllables was free, so that the addition of each new syllabic meant a new binary choice, i.e., a doubling of the theoretical number of prosodic possibilities. This gives 48 types for tetrasyllabic words, 96 for the pentasyllabic ones, and so on. Thus,

(5) $P_n = 3 \cdot 2^n$

for trisyllabic and longer words ($n \geq 3$).

Monosyllabic and disyllabic words must be treated separately. They can be embraced, together with trisyllabic words, by the formula

(6) $P_n = 3 \cdot 2^n - 4 + 2^{n-1}$.

The incompatability of a long ultima with the antepenultimate accent classifies Ancient Greek among languages with a distributional interdependence of accent and quantity. This is also reflected by the number of prosodic possibilities. Without the limitation mentioned, the number of possibilities in trisyllabic and longer words would not be $3 \cdot 2^n$, which implies three accentual possibilities combined with each quantity type,[8] but $\frac{7}{2} \cdot 2^n$, since words with a long ultima would allow four places of accent. This would provide 28 possibilities in trisyllabic words, i.e., the 24 actually existing ones plus the types OˀOO:, OˀO:O:, O:ˀOO:, and O:ˀO:O: which are excluded by the incompatibility rule. Of course, the analysis of linguistic patterns of this kind must not separate quantity from accentuation; it is justified to treat them together as 'prosodic phenomena'.

In Standard Lithuanian, too, quantity choices are independent in each syllable ($P'_n = 2^n$), but the place of accent is free ($P'' = n$), which gives

(8) $P_n = n \cdot 2^n$.

However, in long accented syllable nuclei we also find (except in the open ultima) an opposition between two 'intonations', which means between the accent on the first and that on the second mora. In words with a long accent (and a closed ultima) this doubles the number of possibilities. Instead of being $\frac{n \cdot 2^n}{2}$, this number is $n \cdot 2^n$. Since words with a short accent have $\frac{n \cdot 2^n}{2}$ types, we get a total of $P_n = \frac{3}{2} n \cdot 2^n$, or

(9) $P_n = 3n \cdot 2^{n-1}$.

This provides:

    a. 3 types in monosyllabic words:
       O⌐, O⌐:, O:⌐

    b. 12 types in disyllabic words:
       O⌐O, O⌐O:, O⌐:O, O⌐:O:, O:⌐O, O:⌐O:
       OO⌐, O:O⌐, OO⌐:, O:O⌐:, OO:⌐, O:O:⌐

    c. 36 types in trisyllabic words:
       O⌐OO, O⌐O:O, O⌐OO:, O⌐O:O:
       O⌐:OO, O⌐:O:O, O⌐:OO:, O⌐:O:O:
       O:⌐OO, O:⌐O:O, O:⌐OO:, O:⌐O:O:
       OO⌐O, O:O⌐O, OO⌐O:, O:O⌐O:
       OO⌐:O, O:O⌐:O, OO⌐:O:, O:O⌐:O:
       OO:⌐O, O:O:⌐O, OO:⌐O:, O:O:⌐O:
       OOO⌐, O:OO⌐, OO:O⌐, O:O:O⌐
       OOO⌐:, O:OO⌐:, OO:O⌐:, O:O:O⌐:
       OOO:⌐, O:OO:⌐, OO:O:⌐, O:O:O:⌐

In words with an open ultima we have to subtract 2^{n-1} possibilities (for the non-existing types with a long falling accent on the ultima, such as O⌐:, OO⌐:, O:O⌐:, OOO⌐:, O:OO⌐:, OO:O⌐:, O:O:O⌐:, etc.), so that $P_n = 3n \cdot 2^{n-1} - 2^{n-1}$, or

(10) $P_n = (3n-1)2^{n-1}$.

However, the Lithuanian situation may be interpreted in another manner: the number of prosodic possibilities can be regarded as a function of the number of morae. Using the symbol O for a mora, we get a very simple picture for words with an open ultima:

       O⌐
       O⌐O, OO⌐
       O⌐OO, OO⌐O, OOO⌐
       O⌐OOO, OO⌐OO, OOO⌐O, OOOO⌐, etc., thus

(11) $P_m = m$.

Formulas based on morae are simpler and more adequate only when the ability of a mora to carry the accent is not conditioned by its position within the syllable or by the position of that syllable in relation to other syllables. In cases such as that of Lithuanian words with an open ultima it would be erroneous to start from morae. A survey of the existing types would provide the formula (11), the same as for words with a closed ultima, because the absence of the types ending in O⌐: (= falling accent on the ultima) would be masked by the existence of combinations ending O⌐O where the last two morae belong to different syllables. On the other hand, in cases where the accentuability of a mora depends on its direct relation to a word boundary, the formula based on morae remains adequate. For example, the situation in a dialect with quantity independently variable in each syllable and with all morae accentuable except for the lack of oxytonesis (= accent on the final mora, i.e., a short or a long rising accent on the ultima) can be described by

(12) $P_m = m-1$.

Thus:

O⌐O
O⌐OO, OO⌐O
O⌐OOO, OO⌐OO, OOO⌐O, etc.

In the Japanese dialect of Kameyama City, Mie Prefecture[9]

(13) $P_m = 2m-1$;

thus:

⌐OOO, ˌOOO, ˌOOO⌐, ˌOO⌐O, ⌐O⌐OO (5 types in three-mora words),
⌐OOOO, ˌOOOO, ˌOOOO⌐, ⌐OOO⌐O, ˌOOO⌐O, ⌐OO⌐OO, ˌOO⌐OO (7 types in four-mora words).

However, in two-mora words, which have to be treated separately, we find 4 types (⌐OO, ˌOO, ˌOO⌐, ⌐O⌐O), i.e., $P_m = 2m$. All this concerns underlying forms of words, in a morphophonemic notation.

The Okinawan dialect of Naha[10] has a prosodic pattern simpler than that of Kameyama City. The accent cannot fall on the last mora, and the distinction between low and high preaccentual tone does not appear unless the accent is at least on the fourth mora from the beginning of the word. There are 3 possible types in three-mora words, 4 in four-mora words, and 6 in five-mora words. This situation can be described by the formula:

(14) $P_m = 2+2^{m-3}$.

However, the two-mora words with three possible types must be treated as a separate case.

The possibility of describing the same realities by formulas in terms of morae or in terms of syllables poses the problem of the commensurability of those formulas. Of course, the number of possibilities is much lower in formulas operating only with morae than in those which also take into account the various ways of combining morae into syllables. The number of these ways is given by Fibonacci's sequence[11]

$$(15) \quad f(m) = \frac{5-\sqrt{5}}{10}\left(\frac{1-\sqrt{5}}{2}\right)^m + \frac{5+\sqrt{5}}{10}\left(\frac{1+\sqrt{5}}{2}\right)^m$$

which yields 1 for $m = 1$, 2 for $m = 2$, 3 for $m = 3$, 5 for $m = 4$, 8 for $m = 5$, 13 for $m = 6$, 21 for $m = 7$, etc. The multiplication of these numbers by numbers of possibilities given by formulas in terms of morae (P_m) gives the total number of possibilities in m-morae words. Thus, if $P_m = m$, in three-mora words we shall have 9 possibilities ($= 3 \cdot 3$), in four-mora words 20 ($= 5 \cdot 4$), in five-mora words 40 ($= 8 \cdot 5$), etc. However, these numbers always embrace word types containing unequal numbers of syllables. For example, among the 20 word types of four morae, 4 are disyllabic words, 12 trisyllabic words, and 4 tetrasyllabic words. Likewise, a word with a given number of syllables may contain different numbers of morae, depending on the share of short and long syllable nuclei. Therefore it is necessary to develop another formula for the conversion of mora-based formulas into syllable-based ones:

$$(17) \quad P_n = P_m \cdot 2^n$$

with the condition[12] that $m : n :: 3 : 2$. This way formula (11) $P_m = m$ becomes (9) $P_n = 3n \cdot 2^{n-1}$.

The conversion in the opposite direction is given by

$$(18) \quad P_m = \frac{P_n}{2^n}.$$

Thus (9) $P_n = 3n \cdot 2^{n-1}$ becomes (11) $P_m = m$.

The existence of a certain number of prosodic possibilities in a language does not imply that all of them are equally utilized in the morphological pattern. Very often only some of the phonologically possible types are represented in a morphological category. This parallels the limitations in the phonemic composition of morphemes (root structure, occurrence of a restricted range of phonemes in inflectional desinences, etc.). Likewise, prosodic alternations, as well as alternations of segmental phonemes, often embrace only some of the possible relations.

In Russian, where the number of prosodic possibilities in principle equals the number of syllables ($P_n = n$), in Instrumental plural forms of first declension nouns only $n-1$ types are represented: in disyllabic forms only O⌢O (e.g., *dnjámi* '[with] days'), in trisyllabic forms O⌢OO and OO⌢O (e.g., *zvúkami* '[with] sounds' and *zubámi* '[with] teeth'), in tetrasyllabic forms O⌢OOO, OO⌢OO, and OOO⌢O, etc. Analogous relations occur in many other inflectional categories, such as the 2nd person plur. of the present tense (with the *-te* ending), the Nominative sing. fem. of adjectives (ending in *-aja*) and in many other adjectival forms. On the other hand, in certain inflectional forms the accent is obligatorily on a given syllable ($P_n = 1$). Thus the Locative sing. of masculine nouns ending in *-u* and the Nominative plur. of masculine nouns ending in *-a* always have a desinential accent (e.g., *béreg* 'shore, Nom. sing.', but Loc. sing. *beregú*, Nom. plur. *beregá*).

In Lithuanian, nominal case forms are hierarchized as to the number of possible prosodic shapes. In disyllabic Nominative sing. forms of feminine nouns ending in *-ė* five types are admitted:

O⌐:O: (e.g., *rýkštė* 'birch rod')
O:⌐O: (e.g., *draũgė* 'female friend')
O⌐O: (e.g., *mùsė* 'fly')
O:O:⌐ (e.g., *giesmė̃* 'song')
OO:⌐ (e.g., *skruzdė̃* 'ant')

Formula (10) provides ten types in disyllabic words, but five of them (O⌐:O, O:⌐O, O⌐O, O:O⌐, and OO⌐) are ruled out by the fact that the ending *-ė* of the Nominative sing. is always long. However, in the Dative sing. the range of possibilities is reduced to three:

O⌐:O (e.g., *rýkštei*)
O:⌐O (e.g., *draũgei*)
O⌐O (e.g., *mùsei*)

It is remarkable that such accents also appear in the Dative sing. of nouns with a final accent in the Nominative sing.: *gíesmei*, *žvaĩgždei* (Nom. sing. *žvaigždė̃* 'star'), *skrùzdei*. Here the opposition between final and initial accentuation is neutralized. However, the phenomenon of neutralization is also present in the Nom. sing. Whereas in the Dative sing. the forms *gíesmei* and *žvaĩgždei* differ in accent, their accents in the Nom. sing. are identical: *giesmė̃*, *žvaigždė̃*.

118 PAVLE IVIĆ

Instrumental sing. forms again show three types, but in a different combination:

O⌐:O (e.g., *rýkšte, gíesme*)
O:O⌐ (e.g., *draugè, žvaigždè*)
OO⌐ (e.g., *musè, skruzdè*)

It is obvious that the morphological characteristics of every declension case in Lithuanian embrace, in addition to the desinence, a specific set of prosodic possibilities. It is possible to classify Lithuanian cases according to their behavior in this connection. The ranges of prosodic possibilities in a given case often vary from one declensional class to another, which again parallels the variation of the desinences.

In the so-called classical variety of Modern Standard Serbo-Croatian, where

(19) $P_n = 3 \cdot 2^n - 4,$

four prosodic types occur in the Genitive sing. of masculine nouns of the first declension:

O⌐O (e.g., *brǎta*[13] 'brother')
O⌐:O (e.g., *sîna* 'son')
OO⌐ (e.g., *pòpa* 'priest')
O:O⌐ (e.g., *stríca* 'uncle')

Again, this is only half of the number of possibilities provided by the general formula (19). The shortness of the desinential vowel *-a* in the Genitive sing. rules out the four the types with a long ultima.

Most other disyllabic case forms of the same nouns agree with the Genitive sing. as to the range of prosodic possibilities. However, in the Vocative sing. only two types occur:

O⌐O (e.g., *brǎte, pǒpe*)
O⌐:O (e.g., *sîne, strîče*)

Likewise, the four possible types in the Nominative sing. (and most other cases) of second declension nouns (*bǎba* 'grandmother', *žèna* 'woman', *lâda* 'ship', *víla* 'fairy') are reduced in the Vocative sing. to two types (*bǎbo = žěno, lâdo = vîlo*). Another neutralization takes place in the Genitive plur.: *bâbā = lâdā* (O⌐:O:) and *žénā = vílā* (O:O⌐:). In the Vocative sing. only initially accented types with a short second syllable nucleus are admitted, and in the Genitive plur. only types with both syllable nuclei long.

Trisyllabic Nominative sing. forms of second declension nouns embrace ten types:

O͡OO, O͡O:O, O˥:OO, O˥:O:O
OO͡O, OO˥:O, O:O͡O, O:O˥:O
OOO˥, OO:O˥

(cf. *úteha* 'consolation', *br̆dānka* 'highlander woman', *cr̂kvica* 'little church', *Vâljēvka* 'woman from the town Valjevo', *bàtina* 'stick', *pèčūrka* 'mushroom', *várnica* 'spark', *Jádrānka* 'woman from the region Jadar', *brzìna* 'speed', *tetíva* 'bow-string').

This is again only half of the existing phonological possibilities. Types with a long ultima are incompatible with the shortness of the desinence vowel. Thus the formula for this situation has to be derived from (19) by dividing all numbers by 2:

(20) $P_n = 3 \cdot 2^{n-1} - 2$.

However, in the Vocative sing. there will be only eight possibilities, since neutralization takes place in two instances: *úteho = br̆zino* and *tḗtîvo = br̆dānko*. Likewise, two different types of neutralization reduce the number of possibilities in the Genitive plur. to eight: *útēhā = bătīnā* and *brzínā = tetívā*. Thus the number of types of disyllabic and trisyllabic words in the Voc. sing. and in the Gen. plur. equals the number in the Nom. sing. given by formula (20) minus two:

(21) $P_n = 3(2^{n-1}) - 4$.

The conclusion is obvious: here too, as well as in the Lithuanian declension patterns, the range of prosodic possibilities belongs to the morphological characteristics of particular cases in the paradigm. The same applies to Serbo-Croatian conjugation; e.g., the number of types admitted is usually higher in thematic infinitives than in the present tense forms of the same verbs. In the *a*-conjugation the following types occur:

Infinitives	2nd pers. plur. forms
O͡OO *glĕdati* 'look'	O͡O:O *glĕdāte*
O˥:OO *prâvdati* 'justify'	O˥:O:O *prâvdāte = pîtāte*
OO͡O *čìtati* 'read'	OO:O˥ *čitáte*
O:O͡O *pítati* 'ask'	(= three types)
(= four types in trisyllabic forms)	
O͡OOO *ŭžinati* 'take a light meal'	O͡OO:O *ŭžināte*
OO͡OO *vèčerati* 'eat dinner'	OO͡O:O *vèčerāte*

120 PAVLE IVIĆ

OO˥:OO *čèpūrkati* 'babble'   OO˥:O:O *čèpūrkāte* = *vènčāvāte*
O:O˥OO *áminati* 'say "amen"'   O:O˥O:O *áminäte*
OOO˥O *orùžati* 'arm'   OO:O˥ *oružáte*
OO:O˥O *venčávati* 'marry'   (= five types)
(= six types in tetrasyllabic words)

The situation is described by (22) for infinitive forms, and by (23) for 2nd pers. plur. pres. forms:

(22) $P_n = 2(n-1)$.

(23) $P_n = 2(n-1)-1 = 2n-3$.

Another hierarchy reflected in the number of prosodic possibilities is that of inflectional classes. In Russian, infinitive forms in the majority of the productive conjugation patterns can be accented on any syllable ($P_n = n$), thus the whole range of phonologically admitted possibilities is covered. Cf. sets of examples such as *závtrakat'* 'breakfast', *obédat'* 'lunch', *golodát'* 'starve', or *gáerničat'* 'play a fool', *razbójničat'* 'plunder', *domovníčat'* 'stay at home and look after the house', *otoždestvlját'* 'identify', or *plésnevet'* 'grow mouldy', *plešívet'* 'get bald', *zdorovét'* 'become strong', or *lákomit'* 'feed with dainty food', *gotóvit'* 'prepare', *tormozít'* 'brake'. But with the verbs in *ova/uje* ('the third productive class', according to the terminology of the Soviet Academy Grammar[14]) the number of accentual types is $n-1$. Examples such as *žértvovat'* 'sacrifice' or *volnovát'* 'agitate' do exist, but there is no type in *-óvat'* (OO˥O). Likewise, among tetrasyllabic infinitives we find *gáerstvovat'* 'play a fool', *skal'pírovat'* 'scalp', and also *publikovát'* 'publish', but no type OOO˥O. The impossibility of a penultimate accent belongs to the features of the suffix *-ovat'*.

In Serbo-Croatian each conjugation class has a different range of prosodic types. The facts concerning the thematic infinitives are presented in the *Figure* 1.[15]

Two hierarchies are apparent in the table: that of conjugational classes, and that of prosodic types, some of them being widespread, and some of them occurring only with one or two paradigmatic classes.

The conjugational classes with the least prosodic types embrace semantically restricted groups of verbs. The verbs in *iva/uje* are all derived, as a rule from other verbs, and with the meaning feature of imperfectivization. Verbs in *e* denote mental processes, with the exception of one, *-speti*, which means overcoming of time, distance or some obstacle, being, again, an abstract process, not a physical action. Verbs in *a/i* are almost all intransi-

PROSODIC TYPE	CONJUGATION CLASS									DIFFUSION of the type
	i	a	a/e	nu/ne	e/i	ova/uje	a/i	e	iva/uje	
O˷O	+	+	+	[+]	+	O	+	+	O	6+[1]
Total disyll. types	1	1	1	[1]	1	–	1	1	–	
O˷OO	+	+	+	+	+	–	–	–	–	5
O˷:OO	+	+	–	–	–	–	–	–	–	2
OO˷O	+	+	+	+	+	+	+	+	–	8
O:O˷O	+	+	+	+	+	–	+	–	–	6
Total trisyll. types	4	4	3	3	3	1	2	1	0	
O˷OOO	+	+	–	–	–	+	–	–	–	3
O˷O:OO	+	–	–	–	–	–	–	–	–	1
O˷:OOO	+	–	–	–	–	+	–	–	–	2
OO˷OO	+	+	+	+	(+)	–	–	–	–	4+(1)
O:O˷OO	+	+	+	–	(+)	–	(+)	–	–	3+(2)
OO˷:OO	+	+	–	–	–	–	–	–	–	2
OOO˷O	+	+	+	+	+	+	(+)	(+)	–	6+(2)
OO:O˷O	+	+	+	+	(+)	–	(+)	–	+	5+(2)
Total tetrasyll. types	8	6	4	3	1+(3)	3	0+(3)	0+(1)	1	
Grand total	13	11	8	6+[1]	5+(3)	4	3+(3)	2+(1)	1	

Figure 1

tive, most of them denote some state or position of the body, or the production of a sound. On the other hand, each of the conjugation classes with a high number of prosodic types includes verbs with a very wide range of meanings and with various derivational backgrounds. Many of them are primary (underived) verbs. Thus the width of the prosodic field of a conjugation class reflects in general lines the width of its semantic field.

As to the hierarchy of prosodic types, a preponderance of penultimate accents (= on the thematic vowel) is noticeable. This is a feature of the infinitive (and of certain other paradigmatic forms agreeing with the infinitive in accent). In a set of other paradigm members, e.g., in the present tense, accents on the thematic vowel are much less common.

In most Russian declension classes, case forms with monosyllabic endings, such as the Genitive, can be accented on any syllable ($P_n = n$):

zvúka 'sound', volá 'ox'; *génija* 'genius', *gerója* 'hero', *rybaká* 'fisher'; *tétereva* 'heath-cock', *učítelja* 'teacher', *inženéra* 'engineer', *bol'ševiká* 'Bolshevik';

mésta 'place', *selá* 'village'; *jábloka* 'apple', *bolóta* 'bog', *veščestvá* 'matter'; *žúlničestva* 'fraudulency', *stremlénija* 'striving', *poloténca* 'towel', *xuligan'já* 'hooliganism';

rýby 'fish', *gorý* 'mountain'; *jágody* 'berry', *refórmy* 'reform', *vysotý* 'height'; *víselicy* 'gallows', *krasávicy* 'beauty', *masterícy* 'nilliner', *skovorodý* 'frying-pan'.

However, in nouns of the third declension the Genitive sing. desinence (and several others) cannot be stressed ($P_n = n-1$):

súti[16] 'essence';

óseni 'autumn', *pečáti* 'press';

zápovedi 'commandment', *obíteli* 'abode', *kolybéli* 'cradle'.

Genitive sing. forms of Serbo-Croatian nouns in most declensional classes have a range of $3(2^{n-1})-2$ possibilities as given by formula (20). This provides 1 possibility in monosyllabic forms, 4 in disyllabic forms, 10 in trisyllabic forms. But, again, the third declension is characterized by a more restricted inventory of types: no monosyllabic forms, two disyllabic types (O⌐O and O⌐:O, e.g., *sŏli* 'salt' and *mâsti* 'grease'), and four trisyllabic ones (O⌐OO, O⌐O:O, OO⌐O and O:O⌐O, e.g., *bŏlesti* 'illness', *vȑlēti* 'crags', *sàmrti* 'agonies of death', and *ljúbavi* 'love'). Thus

(22) $P_n = 2(n-1)$.

As in Russian, forms with a desinential accent are impossible in this declension. This is again a limitation with a twofold bearing: the third declension is inferior to other declensional classes in its richness of prosodic types, and the desinential accent has a more limited distribution than other accentual possibilities.

It is noteworthy that the third declension is subject to a number of other limitations too. Nouns belonging to that declension usually fall within a fairly limited semantic range (as a rule they are abstract nouns or mass nouns or collective formations; only rarely do they denote objects or beings). In contradistinction to the first and the second declension, the third declension is unproductive, except with the suffix *-ost'* serving to derive abstract nouns from adjectives. Finally, the number of different desinences in the paradigm is the lowest in this declension because of the numerous syncretisms. The total number of endings in the third declension (for the seven cases in sing. and plur.) does not exceed five (-ø, -i, -ju, -ī, and -ima), whereas in other declensions there are usually eight different desinences in a paradigm (e.g., with masculine nouns of the first declension: -ø, -a, -u, -e, -om, -i, -ā, and -ima).

As to the desinential accent, its relation to other accentual types is very different from the position of the third declension among declensional classes. It is one of the two accentual types alternating in the cardinal alternation: initial and desinential accent. The Genitive sing., the accentuation of which was discussed above, belongs to the cases with an initial accent.

It is possible to extend the comparison between different paradigms to the relations between different parts of speech. In Serbo-Croatian, the Genitive sing. forms of indefinite adjectives, with the same desinences as corresponding noun forms, show a lesser variety of prosodic types:

1 type in monosyllabic forms (O⌐, e.g., zlă 'bad');

3 types in disyllabic forms (O⌐O, OO⌐, O:O⌐, e.g., zdrăva 'healthy', bòsa 'barefoot', blága 'mild');

7 types in trisyllabic forms (O⌐OO, O⌐O:O, O⌐:OO, OO⌐O, O:O⌐O, OOO⌐, OO:O⌐, e.g., gărava 'sooty', křváva 'bloody', mâjčina 'mother's', gòtova 'ready', blážena 'blessed', zelèna 'green', valjána 'worthy').

The types O⌐:O, O⌐:O:O, OO⌐:, and O:O⌐:O do not occur with indefinite adjectives, although they are common with nouns. The definite adjectives embrace 1 monosyllabic type (O⌐:), 4 disyllabic ones (O⌐O:, O⌐:O:, OO⌐:, O:O⌐:), and 8 trisyllabic ones (O⌐OO:, O⌐O:O:, O⌐:OO:, O⌐:O:O:, OO⌐O:, O:O⌐O:, OO⌐:O:, OOO⌐:)[17] — still less than first and second declension of nouns (cf. formula 20). The comparatives have a uniform pre-desinential accent ($P_n = 1$). Cf. bŏljī 'better', nòvijī 'newer, radòsnijī 'more joyful', prijatèljskijī 'friendlier', komplikovànijī 'more complicated', etc. (O⌐O:, OO⌐O:, OOO⌐O:, OOOO⌐O:, OOOOO⌐O:). This neutralization of the contrasts between all existing prosodic paradigms of adjectives is a formal expression of the semantic markedness of the comparative.

So far we have discussed relations of hierarchy, or at least differences in behavior, among various paradigm members, various paradigm classes (including those of different parts of speech), and various accentual types. Similar relations can also exist among morphemes or syllables within a word (or prosodeme). In many languages there is a distinction between prosodically active and prosodically inactive morphemes (or syllables within morphs). The number of prosodic types occurring in the Russian Instrumental plur. forms with the desinence -ami is $n-1$, whereas in forms with monosyllabic desinences belonging to the same paradigms, the number of possibilities equals the number of syllables. The absolute number of possibilities is, of course, the same in both cases, since the forms in -*ami* are one syllable longer. This means that the added syllable in -*ami* is prosodically inactive: the accent never falls on it, so that its presence fails to broaden the scope of prosodic possibilities. The same property is shared by the second syllable of disyllabic desinences of the Russian adjectival declension. They are not accentuable and do not influence the number of prosodic possibilities. In Russian present tense verbal forms the number of prosodic types is identical when they have the non-syllabic endings (-*š*, -*t*, -*m*) or the (mono)syllabic ending -*te*.

In Serbo-Croatian, too, the first syllable of disyllabic desinences in the nominal and adjectival declensions is prosodically active, and the second syllable inactive. In the present tense the syllabic endings -*mo* and -*te* (in the first and second persons plural) do not yield an increased number of prosodic types in comparison with the forms ending in -*m*, -*š*, and *ø*. However, in one of the two principal varieties of Standard Serbo-Croatian, the endings -*mo* and -*te* are accentuable; cf. *pèčēm* 'I bake' ○○Ꞌ: and *pečémo* 'we bake', *pečéte* 'you [pl.] bake' ○○:○Ꞌ. On the other hand, the type ○○Ꞌ:○ does not occur with those endings. In fact, it is the medial syllable which is inaccentuable in present tense forms with the quantity pattern ○○:○.

In Lithuanian, nominal endings such as -*je* in the Locative sing., -*mis* in the Instrumental plur., and -*se* in the Locative plur. are accentuable, but the preceding (stem-final) syllable is not, although in other forms (with nonsyllabic endings) that syllable can carry the accent. Obviously, the accentuability of an added syllable does not always entail its prosodic activity.

Proclitics and enclitics belong in principle to prosodically inactive morphemes. However, in some languages a possible accent shift in certain types of syntagms makes certain proclitics and/or enclitics prosodically active. Cf. Russian *ná-bereg* 'to the shore', but *na-kámen'* 'to the stone', and of course *na-vostók* 'to the East' (the corresponding forms without a preposition are *béreg, kámen', vostók*). Three prosodic possibilities in prepositional syntagms represent an increase in comparison with the two possible types (○Ꞌ○ and ○○Ꞌ) in forms without a preposition.

A similar situation exists in Serbo-Croatian. The Accusative sing. forms *vȍdu* 'water', *kȕću* 'house' (both ○Ꞌ○) become *nȁ-vodu* (○Ꞌ○○), but *nà-kuću* (○○Ꞌ○) in syntagms with the preposition *na* 'to, onto'. Many other proclitics behave the same way, but there are also inaccentuable and prosodically inactive proclitics, such as the conjunction *a*. As to Serbo-Croatian enclitics, they always remain prosodically inactive. In disyllabic plural forms of past participles three prosodic types occur, illustrated by the examples *šíli* 'sewn' (O˺O), *pèkli* 'baked' (OO˺),and *dáli* 'given' (O:O˺). This range of possibilities remains unchanged when the accentual word also embraces an enclitic, or even a series of enclitics. Thus the types O˺OOOOO (e.g., *šíli-bismo-ti-ga* 'we would sew it for you'), OO˺OOOO (*pèkli-bismo-ti-ga* 'we would bake it for you'), and O:O˺OOOO (*dáli-bismo-ti-ga* 'we would give it to you') exhaust the inventory of possible prosodic shapes of hexasyllabic syntagms consisting of disyllabic past participles and added enclitics, although the theoretical number of phonologically possible types in hexasyllabic words reaches 188, vs. 8 in disyllabic words. On the other hand, the enclitic *-sja* in Russian can be prosodically active. Three possible prosodic solutions in trisyllabic past tense forms with *-sja* (e.g., *pénilsja* 'foamed', *molílsja* 'played', *rodilsjá* 'was born') contrast with two solutions in corresponding forms without *-sja* (*pénil, molíl = rodíl*).

There is a transparent relation between the phenomenon just described and the distinction between constant or variable prosodic characteristics of morphemes in many languages. The versatility of one part of the morphemes as to prosodic shape contributes to lexical distinctions. In Russian, the Locative sing. desinence *-e* can be stressed or unstressed, which makes possible contrasts such as *zámke* 'castle, Loc. sing.' vs. *zamké* 'lock, Loc. sing.'. The consistency of the prosodic behavior of certain other morphemes serves to sharpen the distinction between the given morphological category and other categories. Russian Locative sing. ending *-u* is always stressed; cf. relations such as *beregú* 'shore, Loc. sing.' vs. *béregu* 'shore, Dat. sing.' Of course, the prosodic versatility of a morpheme increases the number of possible prosodic types in the given category, and the constancy of morphemes limits that number. In extreme cases, such as that of the Russian Locatives in *-ú*, having a constant *culminative* characteristic, the number of possibilities is reduced to one.

Prosodic activity differences can accompany other relations in linguistic patterns, serving sometimes as indices of certain hierarchies. In Serbo-Croatian the infinitive ending *-ti* is consistently unaccented and prosodically inactive with thematic verbs. But the same *-ti* is both accentuable and prosodically active in athematic infinitives: *grísti* 'bite' O˺O, but *plèsti* 'knit' OO˺. Athematic infinitives show, in general, more prosodic types than thematic infinitives with the same number of syllables. Disyllabic athematic infinitives appear in three different prosodic shapes (O˺O, OO˺, and O:O˺), and disyllabic thematic infinitives only in one (O˺O). Note that verbs with athematic infinitives are as a rule primary, that their meanings usually belong to the basic set of verbal meanings, and that most of them have a high frequency in texts. Likewise, the enfings -oga/-ega, -ome/-emu and -ima, which have an always unaccented and inactive ultima with adjectives, become, when used with pronouns, accentuable and prosodically active in the ultima as well as in the penultima. Cf. tŏga 'this, Gen. sing.', but kòga 'who, Gen. sing.' (O˺O vs. OO˺), tíma 'to these', but svíma 'to all' (O˺O vs. O:O˺). etc. This makes the number of prosodic types higher with pronominal than adjectival forms of comparable length.

We can conclude that the study of the range of prosodic possibilities provides new tools for the investigation of the properties and hierarchy of various elements and categories in morphology.

Notes

1. Cf. Ivić (1961). The same idea was applied in: Ivić (1961-62); Lehiste (1965); Jacobsson (1972); and Hyman (1978).

2. The term 'word' is used in this paper in the sense of 'accentual word' or 'prosodeme' (in Professor Shirô Hattori's terminology, cf. Hattori 1961a).

3. In the formulas given in this paper, P_n denotes the number of prosodic possibilities in a word consisting of n syllables.

4. Cf. Hattori (1961a:10). In the formulas for Japanese given in the present paper quantity is disregarded. Japanese linguistics strictly separates quantity from accentual (tone) features. This practice, reflecting certain peculiarities of the Japanese language (including its dialects) is as well founded as the treatment of quantity together with accent and tonal features in other languages with different properties, e.g., with a distributional interdependence of quantity and accent. Nevertheless formulas for Japanese which would include quantity could also have a certain typological interest.

5. In the present paper the symbol O denotes a syllable nucleus (except where it is explicitly stated that it denotes a mora), and symbol ˺, the accent (regardless of its physical realization). Of course, the symbol : denotes length, so that O˺: represents a long syllable nucleus with an accent on the first mora, and O:˺ such a nucleus accented on the second mora.

6. It must be stressed that the Japanese material quoted in this paper was always given in the sources in a form making the number of prosodic types explicit, whereas for other languages it was as a rule necessary to determine that number by interpreting descriptive statements and examples given in grammars and dictionaries.

7.   Our formulas, unless stated otherwise, apply to words of any length (measured in syllables). In most cases, in words with a low number of syllables, all possible types actually exist in the language, and 'for longer words, the claim can be made that every existing word will fit into the pattern, but not every possibility provided by the formulas is utilized in the language' (Lehiste 1965: 448).

8.   It is not by chance that formula (5) agrees with R. Jakobson's observations (Jakobson 1962a) to the effect that there were *three* possible types of accent in Greek words with a given syllabic and quantity structure: enklinomena (accent on the final mora), progressive accent (on the first or only mora of the syllable which contains the pre-final mora) and regressive accent (on the second or only mora of the preceding syllable). This corresponds precisely to the formula $P_n = 3 \cdot 2^n$ (where 2^n represents the sum of possible quantity structures in an n-syllabic word). In the Aeolian dialect of Ancient Greek only one out of those three possibilities was utilized, that of the regressive accent. This gives again

(4) $P_n = 2^n$,

a formula effective with all words regardless of their length in syllables. Note that the similarity between the Aeolian and Latin prosodic systems is reflected in identical formulas. The Doric accentuation (in Thumb's interpretation, quoted by Jakobson with a certain reservation, since "the testimonies of the sources, at times, contradict each other") contained two possible accent types: on the final mora, or on the pre-final one. This gives

$P_n = 2 \cdot 2^n = 2^{n+1}$

covering words with $n \geq 2$, whereas monosyllabic words, with three prosodic possibilities, require a separate treatment.

9.   Cf. Hattori (1961a: 2-6). All formulas concerning Japanese dialects given in the present paper are tentative, based on concise data furnished in Professor Hattori's works for other purposes, so that they do not always contain all the information necessary for developing definitive formulas. These provisional formulas were propounded here in order to attract the attention of specialists in Japanese to the typologically relevant tasks of making comparative studies of the range of prosodic possibilities in various Japanese dialects and of comparing Japanese facts with those in other languages.

10.   Cf. Hattori (1961b: 53).

11.   The sequence (15) gives the number of ways in which an m-member string can be devided into one-member or two-member units. It is derived from the recurrent formula

(16) $f(m) = f(m-1) + f(m-2)$

assuming that $f(1) = 1$, and $f(2) = 2$.

12.   This condition reflects the fact that $\frac{3}{2}$ is the average number of morae in a syllable (and the harmonic mean of the numbers of types with various numbers of morae in n-syllabic words).

13.   In Standard Serbo-Croatian two prosodic elements are phonologically distinctive: quantity and the place of the last high pitch in the word. This place can be on any syllable (in long syllable nuclei it is always on the first mora, which especially reminds one of certain phenomena in Japanese). Information about the quantity of vowels and about the place of the last high pitch suffices for predicting the prosodic characteristics of all the syllables of a word. Therefore Serbo-Croatian accents can be adequately marked by using the Japanese sign ⌐ to denote 'the last high pitch in the word'. The traditional signs for Serbo-

128 PAVLE IVIĆ

Croatian accents are synthetic, like those for Lithuanian and partly for Ancient Greek accents. They simultaneously mark quantity and 'kind' of accent ('falling' vs. 'rising'). The term 'falling accent' applies to cases where the last high pitch appears in the first mora, and a 'rising accent' is marked on the vowel in the syllable immediately preceding the syllable with the last high pitch. Thus the word *pòpa = popa*ˀ is considered to have a 'short rising' accent on /o/. This practice reflects the fact that the syllable nucleus tradi- tionally marked by the accent sign is lengthened, so that an 'accent' with a culminative function is perceived on that syllable nucleus. However, in our morphophonemic discus- sion, the term 'accented' will refer to the syllable nucleus with the last high pitch in the word, in conformity with the practice usual in the most recent morphophonemic work on Serbo-Croatian (Stankiewicz, Browne and McCawley, Garde).

14. Cf. *Grammatika russkogo jazyka* (1953: 544-47).

15. The existence of a type is shown in the table by a plus sign, and the non-existence by a minus sign. A zero is used instead of a minus sign in cases where the number of syllables in the suffix precludes the occurrence of the given type with the given suffix. Brackets [ ] indicate that a type occurs only with an added prefix, and parentheses ( ) that it occurs only in forms containing a prefix. The types shown in the table can be illustrated by the following examples:

   snȉti, znȁti, slȁti, [ȕ-gnuti], vrȅti, spȁti, smȅti; gȁziti, glȅdati, gȑtati, gȉnuti, vȉdeti; pȃm- titi, štȃmpati; nòsiti, ìgrati, ìskati, tònuti, žèleti, štòvati, bèžati, ùmeti; brániti, pȉtati, písati, tȑnuti, žíveti, bléjati; brȁtimiti, ȕžinati, vȅrovati; pȁbȋrčiti; dȗndoriti, prȃznovati; bèsediti, vèčerati, gàmizati, gòraknuti, (ùvideti); párložiti, áminati, kákotati, (závideti), (nástojati); dèvòjčiti, ćèpūrkati; govòriti, orùžati, blebètati, jaòknuti, zelèneti, kupòvati, (postòjati), (razùmeti); jednáčiti, venčávati, gonétati, grgútnuti, (dožíveti), (zajéčati), kazívati.

16. Exceptionally, disyllabic Genitive sing. forms of a few nouns can carry a desinential stress: *gluší* 'remote corner', *Permí* 'town Perm', *osí* 'axis' (*Grammatika russkogo jazyka* 1953: 207).

17. The types O:Oˀ:, Oˀ:O:O:, and OOOˀ: occur exclusively with adjectives appearing only in the definite form, e.g., *vrátnī* 'door-', *pȗtnīčkī* 'travellers' ', *ždrebèćī* 'foal-'. Note that some sources of the Classical Serbo-Croatian norm, among them the dictionaries of Vuk Karadžić and of the Yugoslav Academy of Sciences, practically deny the existence of the type Oˀ:O:O:, giving forms such as *pȗtnīčkī* instead of *pȗtnīčkī*.

References

Grammatika russkogo jazyka [A grammar of the Russian language]. Vol. I. 1953. Moscow: Soviet Academy of Sciences.

Hattori, Shirô. 1961a. "Prosodeme, syllable structure and laringeal phonemes". *Studies in Descriptive and Applied Linguistics.* (= *Bulletin of the Summer Institute in Linguistics* 1). Tokyo: International Christian University.

-----. 1961b. "A glottochronological study of three Okinawan dialects". *International Journal of American Linguistics* 27:1.

Hyman, Larry. 1978. "Tone and/or accent". In: Napoli (ed.) 1978: 1-20.

Ivić, Pavle. 1961. "The functional yield of prosodic features in the patterns of Serbocroatian dialects". *Word* 17.3: 293-308.

-----. 1961-62. "Broj prozodijskih mogućnosti u reči kao karakteristika fonoloških sistema slovenskih jezika" [The number of prosodic possibilities in a word as a characteristic of the phonological systems of Slavic languages]. *Južnoslovenski filolog* 25: 75-113.

Jacobsson, Gunnar. 1972. "The prosodic pattern in isolated words in a Slavic and a non-Slavic language. (Comparison of prosodic possibilities in Serbocroatian and Swedish standard languages)". In: Worth (ed.) 1972.

Jakobson, Roman. 1962a. "On Ancient Greek prosody". In: Jakobson 1962b: 262-71.

-----. 1962b. *Selected Writings*. Vol. I: *Phonological Studies*. The Hague: Mouton.

Lehiste, Ilse. 1965. "The function of quantity in Finnish and Estonian". *Language* 41: 447-56.

Napoli, Donna Jo (ed.) 1978. *Elements of Tone, Stress, and Intonation*. Washington, D.C.: Georgetown University Press.

Worth, Dean S. (ed.) 1972. *The Slavic Word. Proceedings of the International Slavistic Colloquium at UCLA, September 11-16, 1970*. The Hague/Paris: Mouton.

Translation and backtranslation

Vladimir Ivir
Faculty of Philosophy, University of Zagreb

1

Translation has been viewed as the replacement of linguistic material (text) of one language by the equivalent linguistic material (text) of another language (Catford 1965: 20). The two texts are in this case said to stand in a relation of equivalence. However, the nature of this process of replacement, and thus also the nature of equivalence, remains unspecified. In particular, insufficient distinction is made between translation as a process and translation as a product, and nothing is said about the translator's strategies in the act of translation. The consequence is that equivalence is viewed statically — as something given in advance, only to be reached by the translator — rather than dynamically, as something that is created in the act of translational communication and that has no existence outside that act. All too often, it is forgotten that equivalence happens rather than is. The analysis of translation focuses on the source and translated texts, seeking to establish how they differ, not how they have come about or how they function in their respective situational contexts of communication.

The present paper will describe a model of translation that is essentially dynamic and will illustrate its application with a very short fragment of Serbo-Croatian to be translated into English. Taking the view that the task of a theory of translation is to account for what actually happens in the act of translation, it will examine the workings of the different components of the proposed model and their amenability to the kind of analysis which linguists or translation theorists are at present capable of. Though it will be seen that proper analytical tools are lacking for some crucial components of an objective, consistent and self-contained theory of translation — which is part of the reason why no such theory is yet available or is likely to emerge in the foreseeable future — there are excellent reasons for trying to unravel what we still do not know about translation and to map these gaps in our knowledge onto a coherent model of translation, so that a systematic study of the process can be made, seeking meaningful generalizations instead of *ad hoc* explanations of individual instances or types of equivalence.

The concept of backtranslation (as proposed in Spalatin 1967 and elaborated in Ivir 1969, 1970) will be used to make what is seen as an important distinction between contrastive correspondence and translation equivalence, or between the *langue* and the *parole* components of the proposed model of translation.

2

The elements of the act of communication involving translation are the following: particular configuration of extralinguistic features, language chosen by the original sender to communicate that configuration of extralinguistic features (L_1), original sender as speaker of L_1, intended receivers of the communicated message as perceived by the original sender, text produced by the original sender (T_1), channel of communication through which T_1 reaches its receivers, translator as speaker of L_1 and receiver of T_1, configuration of extralinguistic features as grasped by the translator, language chosen by the translator as sender to communicate that configuration of extralinguistic features (L_2), translator as speaker of L_2, intended receivers of the translated message as perceived by the translator, text produced by the translator (T_2), channel of communication through which T_2 reaches its receivers, receiver of T_2 as speaker of L_2, and configuration of extralinguistic features as grasped by the receiver of the translated message. These elements are listed here in the order in which they appear in the dynamic model shown diagrammatically in *Figure* 1.

The model functions in the following way: The original sender starts with a particular configuration of extralinguistic features which he intends to communicate and chooses a particular language (L_1) to do so. The language that he chooses is one that he shares with his intended receivers. Being an individual linguistic person and speaker of that language, he uses it as his knowledge of the language at that particular point enables him to use it. At the same time, finding himself in a particular communicative situation, he takes into account the actual or imagined feedback from his

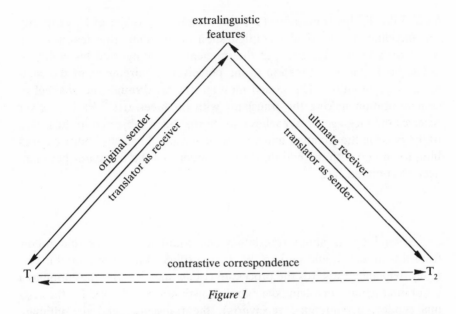

Figure 1

receiver(s). Thus, his text (T_1) is a composite product of L_1's capacity to deal with the extralinguistic content to be communicated, the sender's knowledge of L_1 at the moment of coding, and his ability to assess correctly the nature of his relationship with his receivers and to adjust his linguistic presentation of the extralinguistic content to the perceived requirements of the communicative situation. The extralinguistic content (or information) thus coded in T_1 travels as message through the spatio-temporal channel of communication linking the sender and the receiver. The receiver — who, in this case, is the translator — receives the message as it has managed to reach him given the fact of noise in the channel, and he then decodes it acting as a speaker of L_1. Being an individual linguistic person, he necessarily uses that language as his knowledge of it enables him to use it at that point. The result of his decoding effort is the acquisition of the extralinguistic content or information that the original sender has succeeded in communicating to him. Next, acting as a speaker of L_2, which he knows he shares with the intended receivers of his translation, the translator proceeds to code that information relying on the resources of L_2 as he knows them, being an individual linguistic person of that language. In coding this information, he takes account of the communicative situation in which he finds himself in relation to his receivers and reckons with their (actual or imagined) feedback. Like T_1, his translation (T_2) is a composite product of L_2's capacity for encoding that particular configuration of extralinguistic features, the translator's knowledge of L_2 at the moment of coding, and his ability to adjust his linguistic expression to the perceived requirements of the communicative situation. This coded message travels through the channel of communication linking the translator with his receiver(s). Each receiver receives the message as it reaches him (having been subjected to the action of the noise in the channel) and decodes it as his L_2 linguistic ability enables him, to end up with the extralinguistic content that the translator has managed to communicate.

3

Several points about translation and translation theory that follow from this model should perhaps be made explicit. First, the model is certainly dynamic: it regards the process of communication via translation as a set of interactions, involving the extralinguistic content, L_1 and L_2, the original sender, his intended receiver(s), the translator, and the ultimate receiver(s). There are two places in the model where the process results in a linguistic product: they are T_1 and T_2. Second, the model recognizes the relativity of all communication. including that which relies on translation. Since languages have their preferred ways of linguistic mapping of the extralinguistic content, the choice of L_1 and L_2 for communication will itself determine which extralinguistic features will be coded and how they will be communicated. (Though any configuration of extralinguistic features can, in principle, be coded in any language, particular configurations — those that the speakers of a given language have often felt a need to communicate — are more readily expressed than others and more readily in one language than in another. Speakers, for their part, normally follow the preferred ways of their languages — both because taking what the language offers ready-made requires least effort, and because a radical departure from the usual pattern of expression would present obstacles to communication.) In this respect, the relativity of communication (and of translation) means that the original sender will express those features of the extralinguistic situation that L_1 as a system is equipped to deal with, but these are not necessarily the same features that the translator will have at his disposal in L_2. Hence under- and over-translation is necessitated by the linguistic systems of L_1 and L_2. Relativity results also from the fact that no matter what the extralinguistic configurations and the two languages' capacities to express them, the actual expression will depend on how the original sender and the translator can tap the resources of their respective languages and how they choose (and/or manage) to adjust their expression in the communicative situation, given their different relations to their respective receivers. Hence come different translations of the same text when made by different translators, or by the same translator at different times. Of course, relativity is also due to the noise in the two channels and to the receivers' (including the translator as receiver) ability to decode the coded message.

The third point that needs to be made is that translation does not differ, in principle, from direct communication within one language and that 'intralingual' and 'interlingual' translation (Jakobson 1959: 233) poses the same problems for the theory. The only difference — apart from the fact that the original sender has his own extralinguistic content (ideas, thoughts, perceptions, feelings, wishes, etc.) and the translator that received from the original sender — is quantitative: in intralingual communication the process of translation (coding and decoding) takes place once, while in interlingual communication it takes place two times (or more in the case of translation from a translation).

Finally, this dynamic communicative model of translation presupposes that the theory of translation will have to be conceived of not as a theory of states of affairs but as a theory of events, accounting not for the product but for the process of translation. It will therefore necessarily have different components, with their own methodologies, to account for the different stages of that process. One component will deal with L_1 and L_2 as linguistic systems in relation to each other with respect to their ability to express particular configurations of extralinguistic features. This will be the descriptive linguistic (or *langue*) and contrastive component of the theory of translation. The next component will deal with the linguistic persons: the original sender as producer of T_1, the translator as understander of T_1 and producer of T_2, and the ultimate receiver as understander of T_2. As it is designed to account for what happens when individual speakers of L_1 and L_2 actually use their language, this component is psycholinguistic and it deals with the *parole* aspects of translation. Another component will be needed to account for what happens between the original sender and his receivers in the act of communication (bearing in mind that neither the translator nor the ultimate receiver of the translated message are normally the intended receivers of the original message) and between the translator and the receivers of his translation. This will be the sociolinguistic (again *parole*) component of the theory of translation.

Though such separation of components is justified analytically (it has already been mentioned that each component will require a different methodological approach), an integration of the three components will clearly be needed if a coherent theory of translation is to be formulated. The difficulty is, however, that not all of the components are equally well developed methodologically and that it is not clear how their integration can be achieved. While linguists possess fairly effective analytical tools for the description of linguistic systems, including also their mutual contrastive relationships, they are much less well equipped to deal with the psycholinguistic and sociolinguistic aspects of the translation process. What disciplines such as psycholinguistics, sociolinguistics, pragmatics, text analysis, discourse analysis, stylistics, etc. have to offer at present is partly inadequate and partly irrelevant for translation theory. The best that we can do in this situation is to identify clearly those parts of the process of translation that remain outside the reach of objective analysis and explanation, so that, on the one hand, not everything in connection with translation is lumped together in an amorphous mass of the inexplicable and, on the other hand, that we know where efforts should be concentrated on the way towards a theory of translation. (Computer studies in natural language processing and artificial intelligence are indicative of the progress already made and of the problems that remain. McKeown (1985) and Appelt (1985) try to formalize, respectively, how speakers generate texts, getting from what they want to say to saying it effectively using an organizational schema, and how they pre-judge the effects of illocutionary acts and allow their beliefs about the hearer's knowledge of the world guide them in language production.)

4

In the model of translation described above, T_1 and T_2 are linguistic products independent of each other in the sense that each derives directly from the extralinguistic content and the communicative situation in which it is employed. They are linked only via the extralinguistic content, which holds them together as equivalent expressions of the 'same' configuration of extra-linguistic features in two different communicative situations. No full line connects them in *Figure* 1, indicating that translation is not to be taken to consist in the replacement of L_1 linguistic units (T_1 being an L_1 linguistic unit of a particular rank) by L_2 linguistic units (T_2 being a linguistic unit of L_2), but in the use of linguistic units (texts) that will match the extralinguistic content to be communicated and the requirements of the communicative situation (the language of communication being one of the elements of the situation). This model of translation would thus resolve two dilemmas that translation theory and practice have always faced, namely, whether translation is at all possible and whether — assuming that it is possible — it should be 'literal' or 'free' ('faithful' or 'beautiful', 'sender-oriented' or 'receiver-oriented', etc.) The model says that translation is possible, provided that one accepts the relativity of all communication, as long as there are extralinguistic contents to be communicated and situations in which communication can take place. (It can indeed be shown that translation is impossible if it is to mean the 'copying' of linguistic units, which is why only re-creation, not translation, is possible when language itself is the content of communication — e.g., in word play, rhyme, assonance, alliteration, etc.) The model favours 'free' over 'literal' translation, taking faithfulness to mean faithfulness to the sense rather than the meaning of the original (*Sinn vs. Bedeutung* according to Coseriu 1981: 185-5, where 'meaning' is defined as deriving from the set of oppositions into which units of a linguistic system enter and 'sense' from the communicative functions that linguistically expressed meanings have in particular contexts of situation).

5

The unstated assumption on which this model is built, and on which the possibility of translation also rests, is that separation of form and content is possible. The relationship between them is thus not one-to-one but one-to-many (one configuration of extralinguistic features has more than one possible expression in any given language and in all languages). However, this assumption is fraught with difficulties — both principled and practical. Without involving oneself in the various philosophical implications of this assumption, one notes the practical difficulty of 'getting rid' of the original or translated expression to reach its extralinguistic content. It is not clear in what form that content can be internalized once it has been stripped of its linguistic form. In a realistic translational situation, the translator does not leave the original text behind to create the translated text without reference to it: rather, he works with it, using it as a point of reference for his text. (Of course, this is by no means to say that he uses T_1 as a model to copy in T_2. What it means to work with T_1 and use it as a point of reference for T_2 will be explained further below.) Notice that T_1 and T_2 are connected by an interrupted line in *Figure* 1, with arrows pointing in both directions. The line is interrupted because it is not the line of translation but the line of correspondence — contrastive correspondence between linguistic systems and units of L_1 and L_2 (cf. Ivir 1981) — and it is bidirectional because it involves both the translation of T_1 into T_2 and the backtranslation of T_2 into T_1.

The translator's strategy, now that the model has been completed, can be described as follows: First, he has access to T_1, which he decodes to grasp the communicated content. Next, he tries to replicate T_1 as T_2. This attempt results in a version of T_2 that the translator judges as ungrammatical in L_2 (in the sense in which ungrammaticalness or ungrammaticality is used in transformational grammar, i.e., violating the rules of L_2) or as communicatively inadequate given the requirements of his relation to the ultimate receivers. He tries to repair this result by producing a new, grammatically correct and communicatively adequate, version of T_2, which he then backtranslates into L_1 to see how the meaning of this new version compares with the original T_1. If he finds that the discrepancy is too great, he goes back to T_2 and tries to modify it to reduce the discrepancy, while still preserving both grammaticalness and communicative adequacy. Then he again backtranslates the result into L_1 to compare it with T_1. He repeats the procedure as many times as needed until he is satisfied that he has changed as much as necessary, but as little as possible, in moving from T_1 to T_2.

How much, or how little, he changes will depend on the nature of the contrastive relationship between L_1 and L_2, on his knowledge of L_1 and L_2, and on the nature of his relationship with the original sender and the intended receivers of his translation. However, it is important for him, and for translation theory, to recognise that there are two kinds of changes: those that are dictated by the contrastive differences between the two linguistic systems (over which the translator has no control, unless he decides to expand the L_2 system by borrowing or *calquing* from L_1) and those dictated by the exigencies of what the translator regards as effective communication (over which he exercises considerable control, being an active participant in the communicative situation). The former are changes that are independent of the context or situation in which the communication takes place, and the latter are strictly bound to that context. The difference can be shown experimentally: the former changes are those that will be made each time T_1 is translated, regardless of whether the translator is the same or different or how the communicative situation has changed; the latter changes may be made by one translator but not by another, on one occasion but not on another, and even the same translator on the same occasion may make a change at one moment and delete it at the next (as translators' manuscripts amply testify).

6

The process of translation and backtranslation will now be illustrated, with appropriate comments, on a fairly self-contained extract from a history of Croatian music (Lovro Županović, *Stoljeća hrvatske glazbe*, Školska knjiga, Zagreb, 1980, 182), which has been selected as an example of modern, educated Serbo-Croatian prose free from any literary devices (which would rule out translation and necessitate re-creation) and conveying the extralinguistic content that is not culture-specific.

> Utkavši sve iznesene značajke u djela što nose biljeg njegove umjet-
> ničke i ljudske individualnosti, Lisinki se opravdano nameće kao
> najznačajnija skladateljska ličnost svoga vremena u Hrvatskoj, jer se artis-
> tičkom zaokruženošću i sadržajnošću spomenutih radova visoko uzdigao
> nad svoje suvremenike uključivši i svog učitelja Wisnera v. Morgensterna.
> Ujedno je jedini veliki noviji skladatelj do pojave Ivana Zajca, a u nizu
> kasnijih hrvatskih glazbenih stvaralaca zaslužio je jedno od najistaknutijih
> mjesta.

The attempt to produce a translation close to the interlinear gloss — preserving the structure and semantics of the original text — yields the following result.

> Having woven all the brought forth characteristics into the works
> which bear the stamp of his artistic and human individuality, Lisinski jus-
> tifiedly imposes himself as the most significant composing personality of
> his time in Croatia, because with the artistic roundedness and contentful-
> ness of the mentioned works he rose (himself) high above his contem-
> poraries, including also his teacher Wisner v. Morgenstern. At the same
> time he is the only great newer composer up to the appearance of Ivan
> Zajc, and in the row of later Croatian musical creators he earned one of
> the most prominent places.

This 'translation' reflects the original quite closely, failing only in showing some of its grammatical features (e.g., gender of Serbo-Croatian inanimate nouns, aspectual forms of verbs such as *nametati/nametnuti*, reflexive pronoun *svoj*, clitic position in the sentence) and some properties of the lexical system of Serbo-Croatian (e.g., the fact that in its Croatian variant it offers the speaker a choice in synonymical pairs such as *umjet-nički/artistički, skladatelj/kompozitor, glazbeni/muzički* and that some lexical items are polysemic compared with their English counterparts such as *iznesen* 'brought forth', 'set forth', 'put forward', 'stated', *noviji* 'newer', 'more recent', *niz* 'row', 'line', 'series'). The translated text does show, however, that Serbo-Croatian has lexical items to express meanings for which English has no ready means of expression (e.g., *zaokruženost* 'round-edness', *sadržajnost* 'contentfulness') or which it prefers to express differently (e.g., *opravdano* 'justifiedly' *vs.* 'justly'). Finally, the translation shows a somewhat idiosyncratic combination of present and past tenses which Serbo-Croatian seems to tolerate better than English.

Evaluating this translation as a piece of English, the translator decides that it needs to be normalized in order to be made grammatical. He therefore changes it at those places in the first version where ungrammaticalness is present. This second version incorporates only those changes which are required by the rules of L_2, and not those required by the rules of effective communication.

> Having woven all the stated characteristics into the works which bear the stamp of his artistic and human individuality, Lisinki justly imposes himself as the most significant composing personality of his time in Croatia, because with the artistic completeness and fullness of content of the mentioned works he rose high above his contemporaries, including also his teacher Wisner v. Morgenstern. At the same time he was the only great newer composer up to the appearance of Ivan Zajc, and in the line of later Croatian musical creators he earned one of the most prominent places.

Backtranslation shows that this text is still essentially the same as before, apart from the translation of *iznesen* as *stated* 'izražen, *opravdano* as *justly* 's pravom', *zaokruženost* as *completeness* 'potpunost', *sadržajnost* as *fulness of content* 'punoća sadržaja', and the present tense in the last sentence as the past tense. The translator is satisfied that he has produced a grammatical piece of L_2 and that he has not deviated from the original meaning more than required by the rules of L_2. Judging this text for effectiveness of communication, he may decide that it might be made more effective by removing some of the strangeness that it now has. Notice that the changes that follow are the translator's attempt to meet his receivers' expectations.

> With all of the above characteristics naturally incorporated in the works that bear the mark of his artistic and human individuality, Lisinki is justly regarded as the most important composer of his time in Croatia. Thanks to the artistic completeness and fullness of content of these works, he stands high above his contemporaries, including his teacher Wisner v. Morgenstern, and is the only great composer in the history of modern Croatian music before the appearance of Ivan Zajc. Even compared with later generations of Croatian composers, he occupies a very distinguished and prominent place.

Backtranslation will show how this text differs from the original, but it will not tell us why it differs at all (in addition to the language-produced differences of the earlier versions) or why it differs the way it does and not in some other way(s). The reasons that can be given for the difference will not have to do with grammaticality but with matters such as the speaker's viewpoint, logic of the argument, 'Englishness', smoothness of style, explicitness, etc., the tacit assumption being that these are required for equivalence and that the loss in grammatical and lexical meaning is effectively offset by the gain in communicative sense. The whole passage is now written from the this-is-what-Lisinki-is perspective, not from the what-did-Lisinski-do historical narrative standpoint: Lisinki *is regarded* 'smatra se' (rather than *imposes himself*) as the most important composer; his characteristics *are incorporated* 'uključen' in his works (rather then he *having incorporated* them); he *stands* 'stoji' (rather than *rose*) above his contemporaries; he *occupies* 'zauzima' (rather than *earned*) a distinguished place. The whole is a statement of Lisinki's standing in the history of Croatian music — as the original author is understood by the translator to have intended it to be — and is therefore better expressed in this neutral and static way than in the action-oriented dynamic way that the author preferred. Other changes have to do with the logical organization of this text. The first, complex sentence of the original is here broken into two sentences, and the conjunction *because* is replaced by the conjunct *thanks to*, as the prepositional adjunct *with the artistic completeness*, etc. does not sit very comfortably at the beginning of the *because*-clause. (An alternative, probably less satisfactory in this case, would have been to transpose the adjunct into the subject and change the predicate: *because the artistic completeness, etc., puts him high above his contemporaries*.) The last sentence is again broken into two, the first half being joined to the preceding sentence with *and* 'i', and the last half becoming a sentence in its own right. Nothing important has been lost by replacing *ujedno* by *and*, while replacing *a* by *even compared with* 'čak usporedjen s' only stresses and makes explicit what the original expression implied. Lexical changes, too, while introducing different semantics, help to give a more natural expression to the intended sense: *incorporation* of characteristics instead of their *weaving* into musical works seems a more suitable activity for a composer when an objective and not a metaphorical statement is being made about him; *natural* only serves to stress the organic nature of that incorporation, just as weaving something into a fabric is an 'organic' and not extraneous activity. *Stamp* has been replaced by *mark*, which does not change the meaning but is felt as less metaphorical, more neutral, and therefore more suitable for this type of communication. *Significant* has become *important* 'važan', and the *composing personality* simply *composer* 'skladatelj'. The phrase *in the history of modern Croatian music* 'u povijesti moderne hrvatske glazbe' interprets *noviji*, which was vague but just about acceptable in the original, but hardly acceptable in English, where neither *newer* nor *more recent* would convey the intended meaning of 'post-mediaeval', '19th and 20th century', etc. In the last sentence, *the line of later musical creators* has been replaced by *later generations of Croatian composers* 'kasnije generacije hrvatskih skladatelja', where *niz* becomes *generations* in the interest of explicitness and *glazbeni stvaraoci* becomes *composers*, which is a much more 'English' expression than 'musical creators' or even 'creative musicians'. Similarly, the superlative *one of the most prominent places* becomes *a very distinguished and prominent place* 'vrlo ugledno i istaknuto mjesto'. The adjective *distinguished* merely supports the qualitative against the 'visibility' meaning of *prominent*.

This is just one possible version of the original text in translation. The same translator might produce different versions on different occasions, and a different translator might have produced a different version on the same occasion. The important point is that the considerations by which they would be guided in each case and the justifications which they would offer for their decisions would be of the kind exemplified here. And it is the task of translation theory — for which it must strive to adequately prepare itself — to account for this process both in so far as it concerns two linguistic systems and also in so far as it concerns the behaviour of participants in acts of communication.

References

Appelt, Douglas E. 1985. *Planning English Sentences*. Cambridge: Cambridge University Press.

Brower, Reuben A. 1959. *On Translation*. Cambridge, Mass.: Harvard University Press.

Catford, J.C. 1965. *A Linguistic Theory of Translation*. London: Oxford University Press.

Coseriu, E. 1981. "Kontrastive Linguistik and Übersetzung: ihr Verhältnis zueinander". In: Kühlwein, Thome and Wilss. 1981: 183-99.

Ivir, V. 1969. "Contrasting via translation: Formal correspondence vs. translation equivalence". *Yugoslav Serbo-Croatian — English Project Studies* 1: 13-25.

-----. 1970. "Remarks on contrastive analysis and translation". *Yugoslav Serbo-Croatian — English Contrastive Project Studies* 2: 14-26.

-----. 1981. "Formal correspondence vs. translation equivalence revisited". *Poetics Today* 2.4: 51-59.

Jakobson, R. 1959. "On linguistic aspects of translation". In: Brower. 1959: 232-39.

Kühlwein, W. Thome, and W. Wilss. 1981. *Kontrastive Linguistik und Übersetzungswissenschaft*. München: Wilhelm Fink Verlag.

McKeown, Kathleen R. 1985. *Text Generation*. Cambridge: Cambridge University Press.

Spalatin, L. 1967. "Contrastive methods". *Studia Romanica et Anglica Zagrabiensia* 23: 29-45.

Language change in an urban setting

Dunja Jutronić-Tihomirović
Faculty of Philosophy (Zadar), University of Split

William Labov's linguistic research greatly contributed to the redefinition of the goals, subject matter and epistemology of the scientific study of language. Fundamental problems of linguistic structure and the mechanisms of linguistic changes were given proper stress in the article by Weinreich, Labov and Herzog "Empirical Foundations for a Theory of Language Change" (1968). The authors set up a hypothesis about the heterogeneity of language uses, and they put forth convincing arguments that the association between structure and homogeneity was an illusion. They also stressed that linguistic change could not be identified with random drift and, moreover, that in the development of language change, linguistic and social factors are closely interrelated. If these arguments are correct, they have deep implications beyond the study of language change and the description of such changes mostly in urban centers, extending into the nature of human language and theory of it fundamentally different from the one put forward in the sixties by the adherents of generative grammar and the formal study of language.

Sociolinguistically oriented researchers believe that if the description of grammar does not include the description of linguistic variation, then it does not adequately show what the speakers know about their language. They also point out that a grammar conceived in the Chomskian sense does not account for the total amount of knowledge that native speakers possess. A number of linguists today believe that linguistics should not exclusively deal with language structure but should rather take its place in a wide field of social disciplines which study the relationship between language and society. In a recent article Trudgill (1984:3) states: "...most of its practitioners are primarily concerned with the theoretical questions of how to explain linguistic variation with an important objective in mind, that is, the greater understanding of the nature of language and with it a greater understanding of the nature of society". The three aims that Trudgill mentions are: the improvement of linguistic theory, the better understanding of the nature of language variation and the sources of linguistic change.

Linguists have moved from a narrow to a broader conception of the goals of linguistics description and are trying to integrate the results of the description of linguistic variation into linguistic theory. In this approach, the theory of language is coterminous with the theory of language change. In some of his more recent articles, Labov (see especially 1980) is again stressing the importance of the real problem of how language change is embedded in the social structure. There are other controversies going on as well, such as the changing concept of the speech community (Romaine 1982a) and the primacy of idiolect or sociolect in the description of speech variation. Idiolectal grammar is favoured in British sociolinguistics by Milroy (1980) and Romaine (1982a), while Labov has not abandoned his belief that subgroups in the speech community transmit language change within the community, and that sociolects in this sense are to be favoured over idiolects. There are discussions of the adequacy of the use of the concept of social class and divisions along such lines, with British linguists holding the view that the social network system is more adquate, more real and less abstract.[1] There are also important methodological questions concerning sophisticated quantitative techniques, questions of the forms of variable rule and formalization in sociolinguistic description. There is a need for clarification of the interrelationship between various levels of abstraction from individual to social group to speech community and to language (Romaine 1982a). These are just some of the main issues within the wider context of the sociolinguistic approach to language.[2]

William Labov's book *The Social Stratification of English in New York City* (1966) marked, among other things of theoretical importance, some of which we have just stressed, a new approach to the investigation of non-standard language varieties and dialects. This particular vein of research into the vernacular of the cities has been successfully applied outside the United States[3] in Great Britain by Peter Trudgill (1974), Macaully (1977), as well as a number of other scholars in Europe. Labov's methodology in the examination of non-standard dialects has gone through a certain amount of criticism and reconsideration, with the emphasis on some post-Labovian readjustments as mostly practiced in Great Britain (Romaine

1982a).

Almost two decades of investigation of non-standard language varieties, vernaculars and dialects in everyday social contexts, seen as the central task in social or urban dialectology, have not been properly reflected in Yugoslav linguistic. This has been stated a number of times, especially in recent years.[4] Looking at the arguments that different authors offer, the reasons for such neglect can be summarized as follows: (1) There is a prejudice, belonging to folk linguistics attitudes (Bugarski 1982), that the urban idiom is a corrupted type of speech and, as such, not worthy of scientific study. (2) Although urban dialects play an important role in creating some specific features in the manifestation of standard language in urban communities, Serbo-Croatian dialectology has been concerned with rural dialects (Radovanović 1983; Kalogjera 1985). This kind of dialectology is historically oriented and its primary concern is the pure dialect, one which has not been affected by the corrupting speech of the cities. One of the reasons given for the concern with rural dialects is that not so long ago, the majority of the Yugoslav population lived in villages.[5] There is certainly a broader justification for the interest in rural dialects and those are the reasons demanded by geographical linguistics regarding the genetic relationship of dialects and languages. This is still one of the important studies in linguistics, although somewhat criticized for its non-theoretical orientation.[6] (3) I would add another reason for the neglect of social dialectology in Yugoslavia, which is that the social background of the informants was never taken into consideration and thus the possibility of dialect stratification along these lines was never considered. The need for such urban dialect studies has been stressed, especially recently (Ivić, P. 1983; Bugarski 1983a). (4) There is an additional reason why dialectological studies have not progressed: The Slavists who do most of the dialectological work are not very well acquainted with the most recent advances in Anglo-American (socio) linguistics.[7] On the other hand, general linguists, most of whom are Anglicists, do not feel they should intrude on the territory of the Slavists. However, some of them are beginning to make a contribution to this much neglected area of sociolinguistics in Yugoslavia (Kalogjera 1985).

The primary aim of the study of urban dialectology on the theoretical level should be the discovery of new knowledge about the language and the improvement of some specific theoretical problems such as the theory of language change (Trudgill 1974). On the descriptive level this approach enables the linguist to obtain new descriptive data about the vernacular speech in urban centers. This paper will attempt to give some new descriptive data and to present a preliminary sketch, in the beginning stages, of a more systematic study now in progress of the urban vernacular as spoken in the city of Split. The discussion will center on the loss of dialect and its replacement by urban vernacular and the idea of vernacular norm, a possible sociolinguistic universal, as well as some specific methodological problems in the study of urban dialects in Yugoslavia.

The pioneering work and the first description of speech in a Yugoslav city was done by the American linguist Thomas F. Magner (Magner 1966), in which he described the language spoken in the capital of Croatia, Zagreb. Yugoslav linguist Dalibor Brozović (1976) offered a description of the language in Zadar in which he stressed some points about conversational language in the city (*razgovorni jezik*), which differs in some specific features from the general Dalmatian conversational style. Brozović stressed that his description (see also Brozović 1973) is far from complete, since there is very little knowledge of how and which social groups use different conversational styles. Magner continued his research on the language in Yugoslav cities and gave further descriptions of the language in Split and Niš (Magner 1978, 1984). Dušan Jović (1979) described the speech of the younger generation of Župa, noting the changes in this dialects under the influence of the standard language. Antun Šojat (1979) has some partial comments on the relationship of the standard language and dialects in urban centers in Croatia. Some preliminary consideration of the dialect of 20-year old informations in Split can be found in Jutronić-Tihomirović (1983, 1985). Kalogjera (1985) has interesting remarks on the speech of Zagreb and Korčula in connection with the values and attitudes that the speakers of the vernacular hold towards the dialects they speak.

All the studies mentioned are partial descriptions of language in the cities without consistent consideration of correlations with social variables such as generation, social class or social group and language styles. Jović (1979) stresses that his description is particular to the younger generation of Župa's inhabitants, but the correlations are impressionistic. Magner comes closest to something called urban dialectological study, although he does not attempt any sociolinguistic correlations along the Labovian line.

Since there is a lack of empirical work, we remain unaware of the concrete nature and course of the changes. The simplest evidence which can be offered of the existence of a linguistic change is differing behaviour between the two successive stages of a language with regard to a particular feature or several features. Such evidence would be indicative of a change in real time as opposed to a change in apparent time (Labov 1972). Here we shall offer a description of change in apparent time, that is, differing linguistic behaviour of two age groups at a single point in time. This contemporary variation is viewed as a stage in long-term linguistic change.

There are three main dialect groups in Yugoslavia, named after the interrogative-relative word for 'what' which is realized as *što* (thus štokavian dialect, also the base for standard language), *ča* (čakavian dialect) and *kaj* (kajkavian dialect). This is an ideal division since there are many areas where mixed types occur. Štokavian, or more precisely neo-štokavian, was selected in the 19th century as the basis for standard Serbo-Croatian.

Split is a city on the Adriatic coast of Yugoslavia. Once a small town (18,500 inhabitants in 1900), it has grown rapidly since World War II so that today, according to official estimation, it numbers 350,000 inhabitants.[8]

Although there are a number of descriptions of the čakavian-speaking areas,[9] there is not complete description of the Split dialect. Split was traditionally a čakavian and ikavian-speaking[10] town, and čakavian features were much more prominent than they are today. Some useful comments on the phonological and morphological features of the language spoken by inhabitants of 65 years or older in Split are found in Gačić (1979), and some observations of contemporary speech in Split, in connection with the loss of certain features in comparison with the old Split dialect, can be found in Vidović (1973).[11] The most complete data so far can be found in Magner (1978), in which he discusses the idea of diglossia in Split and the prestigious Split variety.

In this paper we will try to describe some of the phonological, morphological and syntactic features found in the speech of 20-to-25-year-old informants from Split and to relate these findings to the features found among the 60-year-olds.

Older generation	*Younger generation*

Phonology

1. Ikavian forms:
   lipo 'nice', *cili* 'whole',
   čovik 'man'
	1. Ikavian is predominant with
	   occasional use of ijekavian:
	   lijepo 'nice', *čovjek* 'man'

2. *m > n*
   in paradigms: *prijatejen*
   'with a friend', *radin*
   'I work'

2. Still very characteristic with
   occasional mixture in longer
   syntagms: *prid ovon curom*
   'before this girl'

3. *h > Ø*

3. Still a characteristic feature
   with the young

a. In most Croatian conversational
   styles there is no /h/ initially
   and finally: *ajduk* 'highwayman',
   ladno 'cold', *odma* 'immediately'

b. After back vowels *h > v*
   kuvat 'to cook', *kruv* 'bread',
   uvo 'ear'

b. Not as commonly used

c. After front vowels *h > j*
   grijota 'pity', *ij* 'them'

c. Very rarely used

d. *hv > f*
   fala 'thanks', *fatat* 'to catch'

d. Much and commonly used

4. There is no distinction between the affricates /č/) and /ć/ in many Croatian dialects. This is characteristic of the old and young in Split. The
phoneme /č/ is realized close to the standard /ć/.

5. *lj > j*
   judi 'men', *jubav* 'love',
   poje 'field'

5. Standard forms are used:
   ljudi 'men', *ljubav* 'love',
   polje 'field'.

6. *đ > j*
   gospoja 'lady', *meja* 'border',
   rojen 'born'

6. Standard forms with *đ*
   gospo đa 'lady', *ro đen* 'born'

7. Initial reduction of vowels:
   vako 'like this', *nako*
   'like that'

7. Standard forms without reduction are used with the young.

8. Prothetic *j*
   justa 'mouth', *joko* 'eye',
   Jamerika 'America'

8. Not with the young. Standard
   forms are used: *usta* 'mouth',
   oko 'eye', *Amerika* 'America'.

Morphology

1. Genitive plural Ø for
   fem. and neut.:
   kuć 'of houses', *boc*
   'of bottles';
   -i for masculine:
   profešuri 'of professors',
   but also without the ending:
   deset misec 'ten months', *kilo*
   čaval 'kilo of nails'

   1. Only standard forms: *sela*
      'villages', *kuća* 'houses',
      profesora 'professors' with
      occasional lapses into the
      dialect

2. D/L/I plural:
   ženaman/ženan/ženami(n)
   'women', *profešuriman*
   'professors'

   2. Only standard forms: *ženama,*
      profešurima

3. 3rd pl. ending present tense
   -u/-du
   govoru/govoridu 'they speak',
   jemadu 'they have', *radu/ra-*
   didu 'they work'

   3. Standard forms used: *govore,*
      imaju, rade or the dialectal
      form in *-u*: *radu* 'they work'

4. Past participle sing.:
   standard *ao* > *a reka* 'he said'
   standard *io* > *ja radija* 'he
   worked'

   4. Still very common among the
      young

5. Infinitive in *-t*
   stavit 'to put', *radit*
   'to work'

   5. Prominent feature with the
      young

6. Short plural forms *-i* instead
   of *-ovi* or *-evi*:
   bori 'pine-trees', *zidi* 'walls',
   posli 'jobs', *kraji* 'ends'

   6. Still very commonly used with
      the young generation

7. Adjective paradigms
   ludoga/ludega 'crazy',
   tega 'that', *žutega* 'yellow'

   7. Standard forms with the
      young: *ludoga, toga, žutoga*

Syntax

1. Locative and accusative cases mixed up:
   Bija san u Split 'I was in Split',
   Gleda curu na ponistru 'He is watching the girl in the window',
   Sidija u kantun 'He was sitting in the corner'.

1. Much avoided by the young:
   Bija san u Splitu,
   Gleda curu na ponistri,
   Sidija u kantunu

2. *za* + infinitive construction:
   To je dobro za čitat 'It is good for reading'.

2. Very much used with the younger generation[12]

3. *od* reduced to *o* in genitive constructions:
   pismo o sestre 'letter from my sister'

3. Non-reduced form used more: *pismo od sestre*

4. Impersonal constructions:
   Udrilo ga 'He was hit',
   Zatvorilo ga 'he was imprisoned'.

4. Common among the young in all of the dialects

5. Reduction of *mi je* > *me*
   Draga me Ravena 'I like Ravena'.

5. Not at all with the young

6. Pluperfect used frequently:
   Bija je uteka 'He had escaped',
   Bija san ti reka 'I had told you'.

6. Still used with the young

7. Interogative pronoun *ča*
   Ča radiš? 'What are you doing?',
   Ča mi jemaš reć? 'What do you have to tell me?'

7. replaced with *šta/što*
   Šta radiš? Šta mi imaš reć?

Prosody

There are only three basic čakavian accents, short falling (\\\\), long falling (∩) and čakavian acute (~). With the young generation the acute is heard occasionally in the genitive, for example: *Daj mi vodē* 'Give me water', and it is being replaced by standard long rising (/). Short rising (\ )

is also heard, so that the new generation has five accents with the čakavian acute dying out.

The data presented suggest that great changes are taking place but it is not possible to give a full account of such changes and their social motivation until the language of the other generations or social groups in the city has been studied.

What conclusions can be drawn from the above presentation and analysis and what suggestions can be given?

1. The analysis of the 20 to 25 year-old inhabitants of Split certainly confirms statements made some time ago that the Split urban vernacular, especially that of the 20th century, cannot be called pure čakavian. It best deserves the name of *štokavoid čakavian* speech, a kind of half-čakavian idiom. This is evident from many of the non-čakavian characteristics as presented in the analysis. The Yugoslav dialectologist Mate Hraste, who studied mid-Dalmatian čakavian-speaking islands, held the view that the language spoken in Split was hybrid (Hraste 1948). Vidović (1978: 62) states that Split čakavian features are heard in family circles, among some groups of people, especially middle-aged people. The dominant line of Split dialect today is the štokavian-ikavian type of the Dalmatian hinterland and this tone is prevalent in the spoken language in the city. Thus, the picture given of Split dialect in today's dialectological maps does not correspond to the real picture of the language.

Magner (1978: 433) makes a prediction about the future of the Split dialect in the coming decade, stating that "in 1986 the Split dialect will be, if my prediction is accurate, a form of speech distinguished from textbook Croatian by its ikavian forms, a small core of distinctive words, and a few morphologial peculiarities".

2. It seems rather evident that the speech of the educated inhabitants of Split is not čakavian as traditionally defined. We are of the opinion that this type of speech cannot be referred to as a dialect, but we shall call it urban vernacular. The dismissal of the label 'dialect' in urban settings we support with the same view expressed by M. Ivić (1965: 741) when she said: "Language substrate is not simply a folk dialect, as laymen hold. This is a typically urban construct. Among other things it gives to the city a rather specific language physiognomy in contrast to the village language. Dialect in the city is definitely a non-existing category". Kalogjera (1985:94)

expresses a very similar observation: "What an average speaker refers to as 'dialect' today when he makes comments or expresses his attitudes or beliefs is something closer to the reality of usage, namely, a kind of vernacular, coloured more or less by the features said to belong to the historical dialect of that region."

3. The partial presentation of the urban vernacular of the Split youth was partly inspired by the statements of Bugarski and P. Ivić regarding a possible search among heterogeneous accents found in the urban idiom for some core which could represent the urban idiom of a certain city. Bugarski believes that such speech would be one component of all others that are spoken (in this case Belgrade), but it would also be a central one. This central core, he suggests, would be "the very day conversational, communicative language of an educated urban citizen raised in Belgrade" (Bugarski 1931: 222). P. Ivić also believes that there exists a layer which might be typical for a certain town. In his opinion it is the speech of the youth born and educated in that town. He says (1983: 205): "That is something growing out of the soil, that is, out of the asphalt and which grows firmer and becomes unitary among children, that is, the youth. This is also the speech to which the future belongs."

We thus suggest here that the conversational urban vernacular is not as chaotic, nor of such an unsystematic nature, as is often held by some linguists in Yugoslavia. As Kalogjera (1985: 95) also contends: "This dialect-coloured vernacular should not be looked at as a temporary transition from local dialects to standard štokavian, as some linguists suggest, perhaps despairing at defining and describing this loose language variety within the conceptual framework of traditional dialectology. It is a more stable and lasting phenomenon... which has its own values, often superior to the standard." Magner (1978: 426) speaks of a diglossic situation in Split with the use of textbook Croatian and the Split dialect. But he also, more interestingly, touches on this subject by mentioning that the situation in this town is not only diglossic but polyglossic, in the sense that there are 1 to 5 dialects characteristic of different Split groups.[13] Which one has the highest prestige is a question today. (It is not clear anymore that the authentic Split native vernacular has the highest prestige, since this is a variety which is actually dying out.)

Linguists show interest in the theoretical notion of vernacular core, or vernacular norm. For example, L. Milroy (1982) addresses the question of linguistic norm (as she calls it), especially a non-standard or vernacular norm as opposed to a fully codified standard norm. Her Belfast community is a relatively homogenous urban community, and her opinion is that a closeknit network structure imposes a normative consensus on its members and with it creates a vernacular norm. Does such a sociolinguistic norm exist not only in closeknit social network relationships and communities, but also in open social networks which are actually more characteristic of urban communities? The investigation of the Split urban vernacular indicates that it does.

4. With regard to linguistic change, it is necessary to proceed with this kind of investigation in the following directions: Statistical analysis of the speech of different generations should be done. An additional generation, one between the old and the young, should be studied in order to see in which ways and directions the change in the vernacular is progressing. The study of different social groups, which has never been done in Yugoslav urban centers, might prove more interesting. The third possibility is the certainly by now very common approach of the differences in the language of sexes. Further research will probably show us which groups or generations are innovators, and which are those who are maintaining the older tradition and thus delaying the change which is obviously spreading from above, that is, from the standard language. Which social groups have kept most of the dialectal features? What are the probabilities and tendencies? Which features are most resistant to change and why? From the analysis presented, it seems that ikavian forms, final *n*, reduction of *h* to zero, past particle forms and short plural forms are most preserved in the speech of the young generation. Why these and not the other ones?

Some tendencies in the change of the prosodic features seem to be particularly interesting. For example Vidović (1957: 12 as quoted in Magner 1978) noticed that the old features of the Split dialect are best preserved in the accentuation. Čakavian acute, it is true, is dying out under the pressure of the neoštokavian system, but its influence is felt in the resistance to the štokavian tendency to shift the accent toward the beginning of the word. Thus, Vidović (1957:12) believes that "the sharp and static štokavian accentuation softens a bit, while čakavian accentuation loses its characteristics. But it seems that the štokavian system becomes 'čakavianized' much faster and more noticebly than the čakavian system becomes 'štokavianized'". If this is true, and it seems true at least for the melody of the čakavian sentence pattern, by which a person from Split is recognized even if he/she speaks good standard language, then it supports the observation of M. Ivić

(1965: 744) that the least unpleasant mistakes in the relationship to the norm are the mistakes resulting from dialectal prosody. This might be the reason why they persist so long and change very slowly. This observation is also supported by similar finding of J. Milroy and L. Milroy (in Trudgill 1978:20) during their research on changes in the urban vernacular in Belfast. They present patterns in working-class speech and notice the persistent non-standard nature of urban vernacular phonology, observing that they "have no definite evidence, however, that phonetic realizations of vernacular phonology have moved significantly towards the 'standard'". Persistence of prosodic features might be one of the sociolinguistic universals which would certainly be in agreement with some wider findings in the area of languages in contact, which is that phonology is the least susceptible to borrowing from one language into another.

And, finally, some methodological considerations: Since no study within the Labovian approach to language change has been done on our urban vernaculars, it is necessary to stress that one has to be careful not to directly translate the Labovian model (or, for that matter, any other model) to the Yugoslav urban situation. As has been stated, Labov does not take into account the influence of standard language, since he is concerned with the changes taking place within a vernacular which does not have a superimposed institutional language. In other words, in the United States there is no standard language with its codified norms as we have in Yugoslavia. Furthermore, variation among dialects are not as diverse in the States as they are here.

With the lack of empirical work, we remain unaware of many interesting problems, some of which are: Dialects are dying out, but what is not clear yet is how and in which way they are dying out. Should it be assumed that the standard is the desired target towards which all varieties are tending? Linguistic change is often studied but linguistic stability or resistance to change is also an interesting phenomenon.

It also has to be stressed that distinguishing and delimiting the social class category cannot be done as in the States or Great Britain. There are no clear parameters of how to place people in lower middle or upper middle or upper high class categories. Correspondences are much clearer in the working class category. There is a possibility of trying the concept of social network where the tendency is to approach the individual rather than the social group, which might be more appropriate under these circumstances.

All these attempts whould contribute to the discovery of new insights into the Serbo-Croatian language and its varieties as spoken in urban centers. Since very little work has been done on sociolinguistic variation in Slavic languages in general, specific problems and different evidence might open new possibilities of contributing to the mechanisms of linguistic change and language theory.

Notes

1. 'Social network' refers simply to the informal social relationships made by an individual. These are smaller categories which reflect the fact that there are social units to which people feel they belong, and which are less abstract than social class. For more information on social network see L. Milroy (1980).

2. Interesting issues on the epistemological status of sociolinguistic theory can be found in Romaine (1982b), especially the last chapter.

3. There is no fear of the kind Fishman expressed (1972: 154): "The sociology of language, in our day and age, has been very largely an American discipline, particularly insofar as most of its American participants are concerned. As such it is particularly exposed to the risks of historical shallowness and of comparative innocence".

4. See particularly Bugarski (1982, 1983a), Magner (1978a, 1978b), Škiljan (1980), Radovanović (1983), Jutronić-Tihomirović (1983, 1985) and Kalogjera (1985).

5. Magner, (1978b: 400) for example, says: "Indeed, preoccupation with rural dialects is still a feature of Yugoslav linguistics as it was in the days of Vuk Karadžić (1787-1864). At the present time, however, at least half of the Yugoslav population lives in urban centers or in their satellite communities".

6. See Trudgill (1980), L. Milroy (1982), and Shuy (1974).

7. See P. Ivić's statement (1983: 242) in his discussion of some papers at the conference 'Language in modern communication' held in Belgrade. He says: "Serbo-Croatists mainly preoccupy themselves with concrete language questions while the specialists in other languages, for whom foreign literature is more available, turn their interest to theoretical problems".

8. See Magner (1978b) for more detail. Also Vidović (1978).

9. The most complete bibliographies are Wagner (1973), Šimunović (1976) and some of P. Ivić's comments in P. Ivić (1981).

10. Ikavian, ijekavian and ekavian are used traditionally to categorize dialects according to their reflexes of proto-Slavic *ě* (called *jat* in Serbo-Croatian). Those dialects which have *ě*/ *ē* corresponding to the historical *ě* (short/long) are called ekavian, those with *i*/*ī* ikavian and those with *je*/*ije* ijekavian.

11. Reprinted in Vidović (1978).

12. Some of the syntactical features are found in other dialects.

13. For the most recent reinterpretation of diglossia see Fasold (1984).

References

Barac-Grum, V. and V. Zečevic. 1979. "Arealni i granični dijalekatski kontakt" [Areal and marginal dialect contacts]. *Rasprave Zavoda za jezik* 4-5: 105-109.

Benzon, S. 1971. "Opažanja o čakavštini M. Uvodića Splićanina" [Observations on the Čakavian dialect of M. Uvodić's Splićanin]. *Čakavska rič*. 1: 77-98.

Brozović, D. 1970a. "Dijalektološka slika hrvatskosrpskog jezičnog prostora" [A dialectological picture of the Croato-serbian language area]. *Radovi Filozofskog fakulteta u Zadru* 8: 5-33.

-----. 1970b. *Standardni jezik* [Standard language]. Zagreb: Matica Hrvatska.

-----. 1973. "O tipologiji supstandardnih idioma u slavenskom jezičnom svijetu" [On the typology of substandard idioms in the Slavic language world]. *Govornite formi i slovenskite literaturni jazici*. Skopje.

-----. 1976. "O suvremenoj zadarskoj miksoglotiji i o njezinim društveno-povijesnim i lingvističkim pretpostavkama" [On modern mixoglottia in Zadar and its socio-historical and linguistic assumptions]. *Radovi Filozofskog fakulteta u Zadru* 14-15: 49-63.

Bugarski, R. 1982. "Sociolingvističke teme" [Sociolinguistic topics]. *Treći program Radio Beograda* 55: 159-192.

-----. 1983a. "O urbanom idiomu" [On the urban idiom]. In: *Jezik u savremenoj komunikaciji*. Beograd: Centar za marksizam.

-----. 1983b. *Lingvistika o čoveku* [Linguistics about man]. Beograd: Prosveta (2nd edition).

-----, V. Ivir, and M. Mikeš (eds). 1976. *Jezik u društvenoj sredini* [Language in the social environment]. Novi Sad: Društvo za primenjenu lingvistiku Jugoslavije.

Ćupić, D. 1983. "Urbanizacija i dijalekt" [Urbanisation and dialect]. In: *Jezik u savremenoj komunikaciji*. Beograd: Centar za marksizam.

Dittmar, N. 1976. *Sociolinguistics. A Critical Survey of Theory and Application*. London: Edward Arnold.

Downes, W. 1984. *Language and Society*. London: Fontana Paperbacks.

Fasold, R. 1984. *The Sociolinguistics of Society*. Oxford: Basil Blackwell.

Finka, B. 1979a. "Hrvatsko jezikoznanstvo u poslijeratnom razdoblju" [Croatian linguistics in the post-war period]. *Suvremena lingvistika* 19-20: 39-58.

-----. 1979b. "O novim tendencijama i pojavama u čakavskom narječju" [On new trends and phenomena in the Čakavian dialect]. *Filologija* 9: 145-148.

-----. 1981. "Hrvatska dijalektologija danas" [Croatian dialectology today]. *Hrvatski dijalektološki zbornik* 5: 39-48.

Fishman, J. 1972. "The historical dimension in the sociology of language." In: Shuy 1972: 145-157.

Gačić, J. 1979. "Romanski elementi u splitskom čakavskom govoru" [Romance elements in the Čakavian dialect of Split]. *Čakavska rič*. 1: 3-55.

Haugen, E. 1977. "Norm and deviation in bilingual communities". In: Hornby 1977.

Hornby, A. Pater (ed.). 1977. *Bilingualism: Psychological, Social and Educational Implications*. New York: Academic Press.

Hraste, M. 1948. *"Osobine govora otoka Šolte, Čiova, Drvenika i susjedne obale"* [Characteristics of the speech of the islands of Šolta, Čiovo, Drvenik and the neighbouring mainland]. *Rad JAZU* 272: 123-157.

Ivić, M. 1965. "Jezična individualnost grada" [The speech individuality of the city]. *Izraz*. 8-9: 740-747.

Ivić, P. 1971. *Srpski narod i njegov jezik* [The Serbian nation and its language]. Beograd: SKZ.

-----. 1981. "Prilog kategorizaciji pojedinih grupa čakavskog govora" [A contribution to the categorisation of certain groups of Čakavian dialects]. *Hrvatski dijalektološki zbornik* 5: 67-91.

-----. 1983. "O nekim referatima" [About some papers]. In: *Jezik u savremenoj komunikaciji*. Beograd: Centar za marksizam.

Janson, T. 1984. "Articles and plural formation in creoles." *Lingua* 64: 291-325.

Jezik u savremenoj komunikaciji [Language in modern communication]. 1983. Beograd: Centar za marksizam.

Jović, D. 1976. "Jezik urbanih sredina" [Speech in urban communities]. *Gledišta* 7-8: 732-44.

-----. 1979. "Sociolingvistički faktori jezičnih promjena u župskom govoru" [Sociolinguistic factors of linguistic changes in the speech of the Župa region]. *Književnost i jezik*. 2-3: 243-53.

-----. 1983. "Književni jezik i urbani idiom" [Standard language and the urban idiom]. In: *Jezik u savremenoj komunikaciji*: 34-53.

Jutronić-Tihomirović, D. 1983. "Jezik grada" [The speech of the city]. *Argumenti*. 1-2: 196-217.

-----. 1985. "Aspekti socijalne ili urbane dijalektologija" [Aspects of social or urban dialectology]. *Radovi Filozofskog fakulteta u Zadru* 24: 29-38.

Kalogjera, D. 1985. "Attitudes toward Serbo-Croatian language varieties." *International Journal of the Sociology of Language* 52: 93-111.

Kovačić, I. 1971. *Smij i suze starega Splita* [Laughter and tears of old Split]. Split.

Labov, W. 1966. *The Social Stratification of English in New York City.* Washington: Center for Applied Linguistics (3rd edition, 1982).

-----. 1972. *Sociolinguistic Patterns.* Philadelphia: University of Pennsylvania Press.

----- (ed.). 1980. *Locating Language in Time and Space.* New York: Academic Press.

Lehman, W.P. and Y. Malkiel. 1968. *Directions for Historical Linguistics.* Austin & London: University of Texas Press.

Lunt, H. 1984. "Some sociolinguistic aspects of Macedonian and Bulgarian." In: Stolz, Titunik, and Doležel 1984.

Macaully, R.K.S. 1977. *Language, Social Class and Education: A Glasgow Study.* Edinburgh: Edinburgh University Press.

Magner, T.F. 1966. *A Zagreb Kajkavian Dialect.* Penn State Studies 18.

-----. 1976. "Zapažanja o današnjem splitskom govoru" [Observations on present-day Split speech]. *Čakavska rič.* 2: 83-92.

-----. 1978a. "City dialects in Yugoslavia." *American Contribution to the Eighth International Congress of Slavists.* Vol.I. Columbus: Slavica Publishers.

-----. 1978b. "Diglossia in Split." In: Magner and Schmalstieg 1978: 400-437.

-----. 1984. "A Century of the Niš Dialect." In: Stolz, Titunik, and Doležel 1984.

----- and W. Schmalstieg (eds). 1978. *Sociolinguistic Problems in Czechoslovakia, Hungary, Romania and Yugoslavia.* Columbus: Slavica Publishers.

Milroy, L. 1980. *Language and Social Networks.* Oxford: Basil Blackwell.

-----. 1982. "Social network and linguistic focusing." In: Romaine 1982.

----- and J. Milroy. 1978. "Belfast: change and variation in an urban vernacular." In: Trudgill 1978.

Moguš, M. 1966. "Današnji senjski govor" [The present dialect of Senj]. *Senjski zbornik* 2: 1-152.

Naylor, K. 1980. "Some problems for the study of Balkan sociolinguistics." *Zbornik za filologiju i lingvistiku* 28.2: 7-15.

Radovanović, M. 1982. "Naše glavne jezične teme" [Our main linguistic topics]. *Naše teme*. 5: 813-822.

-----. 1983. "Linguistic theory and sociolinguistics in Yugoslavia." *International Journal of the Sociology of Language* 44: 55-69.

Rajić, Lj. 1980. "Jezik i identitet — položaj korisnika dijalekta u procesu standardizacije govora" [Language and identity — the position of dialect users in the process of speech standardization]. *Godišnjak društava za primijenjenu lingvistiku* 4-5: 373-376.

Romaine, S. (ed.). 1982a. *Sociolinguistic Variation in Speech Communities*. London: Edward Arnold.

Romaine, S. 1982b. *Socio-historical Linguistics: Its Status and Methodology*. Cambridge: Cambridge University Press.

Shuy, R.W. (ed.). 1972. *Sociolinguistics: Current Trends and Prospects. 23rd Annual Round Table*. Washington: Georgetown University Press.

-----. 1974. Review of Hans Kurath (1972). *Language in Society* 3: 296.

Stolz, A.B, I.R. Titunik and L. Doležel. 1984. *Language and Literary Theory*. Ann Arbor: University of Michigan.

Šimunić, P. 1976. "Gradja za čakavsku bibliografiju" [Materials for a Čakavian bibliography]. *Čakavska rič*. 1: 67-99.

Škiljan, D. 1980. "Od horizontalne k vertikalnoj stratifikaciji jezika" [From a horizontal to a vertical stratification of language]. *Naše teme*. 6: 952-963.

-----. *Pogled u lingvistiku* [A view into linguistics]. Zagreb: Školska knjiga.

Šojat, A. 1977. "Interferencija dijalekatskih govornih sustava u SR Hrvatskoj" [The interference of dialect speech systems in the SR of Croatia]. *Rasprave Institut za jezik* 3: 143-152.

-----. 1979. "Standardni jezik i dijalekt u urbanim sredinama SR Hrvatske" [Standard language and dialect in urban environments in the SR of Croatia]. *Rasprave Zavoda za jezik* 4-5: 119-125.

----- and V. Zečević. 1969. "Istraživanja kajkavskog govora u Hrvatskom zagorju" [Studies of the Kajkavian dialect in the Hrvatsko zagorje region]. *Ljetopis JAZU* 73.

Trudgill, P. 1974. *The Social Differentiation of English in Norwich*. Cambridge: Cambridge University Press.

----- (ed.). 1978. *Sociolinguistic Patterns in British English*. London: Edward Arnold.

-----. 1983. *On Dialect*. Oxford: Basil Blackwell.

----- (ed.). 1984. *Applied Sociolinguistics*. New York: Academic Press.

----- and J.K. Chambers. 1980. *Dialectology*. Cambridge: Cambridge University Press.

Vidović, R. 1957. "O elementima govora splitskih učenika" [On elements of the speech of Split school children]. *Školski vjesnik*. 7-9: 11-12.

-----. 1971. "Bilješke o redigiranju i akcentuiranju Kovačićeva teksta" [Notes on the editing and accentuation of Kovačić's text]. In: Kovačić 1971: 265-268.

-----. 1973. "O frekvenciji romanskoga leksika talijanskog (mletačkog) porijekla u splitskom čakavskom govoru" [On the frequency of Romance lexis of Italian (Venetian) origin in Split Čakavian speech]. *Čakavska rič*. 2: 51-123.

-----. 1978. *Čakavske studije* [Čakavian studies]. Split: Čakavski sabor.

Wagner, Z. 1973. "Čakavština u zadnjih petnaest godina" [Čakavian speech in the last fifteen years]. *Čakavska rič*. 1: 39-71.

Weinreich, U., W. Labov, and I.M. Herzog. 1968. "Empirical foundations for a theory of language change". In: W.P. Lehman and Y. Malkiel 1968.

Some aspects of prescriptivism in Serbo-Croatian

Damir Kalogjera
Faculty of Philosophy, University of Zagreb

Some aspects of prescriptivism in Serbo-Croatian will be described in this work and, where relevant, compared with prescriptive attitudes in English. It is hoped that the description, however sketchy, will point up to what extent the case of the Serbo-Croatian norm implementation process, and its 'tools', conform to the generalizations made by sociolinguists with regard to this phenomenon, and what its specific features are.

The term *prescriptivism*, in the sense of normative interference with language usage, has been retained in spite (but also because of) its problematic connotations, following some fifty years of critical attacks on this kind of activity by descriptive linguists with a structuralist background. The attacks have mainly been written in English, in the USA and in some other English-speaking countries, supported by illustrative examples from the English language. It would appear that the now current term *language planning* has been partly introduced as a euphemism in order to salvage the dignity of deliberate intervention in language usage in the face of the linguists' criticism. This is, however, not meant to deny certain advances in the theory of normative activity under the new label. Some universal features of language standardization have been noted (Ferguson 1979:51); and the approach to the norm has become more rational, so that cost-benefit analysis for certain precepts is considered (Macay 1980). In spite of these useful developments, normative recommendations and evaluations remain ultimately subjective and 'value-laden' in their goals (Rubin 1985:140). One prefers, then, to keep the old term and thus avoid the implications that its substitution signals an essential change in the process, at least as far as Serbo-Croatian is concerned. The best present-day normativists are certainly better informed than were their predecessors fifty or sixty years ago;

their knowledge of sociolinguistics makes their discourse more sophisticated, but their goals remain subjective and they will always overrule, e.g., efficiency.[1]

Before presenting some features and motives in Serbo-Croatian prescriptivism, a look at attitudes towards prescriptivism in English, both in the USA and in Britain, may give us a useful start.

In America and, to a certain extent, in Britain there is a sharp distinction in the views about the state of the language, correctness and language precepts, between the general public on the one hand, and linguists on the other. The general public seems to believe that English is deteriorating in the areas of correctness of grammar, clarity and precision of expression, logic, vividness and originality, which may be gathered from statements and writings by "editorial writers, political leaders, academic figures, columnists and social critics" (Ferguson 1979:53) who complain about the present state of the language and never suggest that it is satisfactory or that it is improving.

Not only does the public take the view that English is deteriorating but its members also voice their demands that something should be done about it. These demands are frequently expressed despite the fact that so many language scholars have insisted on the unacceptibility of the idea that someboy should dictate to an English-speaking person how to speak or write (cf. Hall 1950:202; Ferguson 1979:53; Harris 1983:17; etc.) and hence, according to them, no Academy designed to take care of the English language has ever been created either in Britain or in the USA, as distinguished from Italy, France, Spain, etc.

Now, the question is who is going to take care of the language when those who should be most qualified to intervene deviate from the general public opinion about the state of the language, and for almost half a century now have taken totally opposing views. Briefly, linguists do not believe in the deterioration of the language in the sense that it has become worse than it used to be. They emphasize that all languages change, and that interfering with language change by prescriptive evaluation is neither possible nor desirable (Ferguson 1979:55-56). This view became crystalized in the late 30's and 40's and supported by research in various areas. It was shown by many researchers, among other things, that the actual usage of educated speakers differs from grammatial precepts (cf. Fries 1940, on *shall* and *will*) and that the origin of these precepts are not to be found in actual usage but have been based on the presumed logic of language structure, have been modelled on Latin grammar, which was taken to be universally binding, have been leaning on the language of great writers as models, on older periods of language and, sometimes, on arbitrary decisions by individual grammarians. The prescribed meanings of lexical items were derived exclusively from etymology. All prescriptive actitivty has been presented as if it were following the tastes and prejudices of the ruling class. Hence the well known sayings and titles of works like *Can Native Speakers Make Mistakes?*, *Anything Goes*, *There can never be in grammar an error that's both very bad and very common* and, of course, *Leave Your Language Alone*. All this was supported by emphasizing the secondary character of written language and the suggestion that standard language may be looked at as just a variety of a language on a par with any dialect. All this evidence, and a deeper interest in purely descriptive and theoretical questions, has discouraged linguists from deliberate interventions in language.[2]

If we now turn to attitudes towards prescriptivism in Serbo-Croatian, in both its variants (Eastern-Serbian, and Western-Croatian) and its two 'subvariants' (those used in Bosnia and Herzegovina and in Montenegro), two points will immediately be clear: a) a total absence of the issue whether prescription in language is the linguist's task, since that is taken as self-evident and b) the lack of systematic criticism of normative demands as being arbitrary and subjective. And yet, most of the prescriptive principles that are criticized when applied to English will be found in the tradition of Serbo-Croatian prescriptivism: etymological 'fallacy', 'good authors' as models, arbitrary decisions by grammarians on language issues etc., in an even more drastic manner. Educated middle class usage has for a long time been the implicit or explicit basis for language precepts in English, with a comparatively small number of structures deviating from what the conservative prescriptive norm demands (*shall/will* future, subject complement in the objective case, preposition at the end of the sentence, split infinitive, double negative, etc.). In Serbo-Croatian prescriptivism, educated usage remains a poorly-defined contributor to the norm. Early Serbo-Croatian prescriptivists (Vuk Karadžić, Duro Daničić and later Tomo Maretić in Croatia) started by following the norm found in the Neo-Štokavian rural dialects, a stance that was modified in the process of elaboration of the language for intellectual use. Present-day prescriptivists, however, insist on the fact that standard language has, in the course of time, become partly divorced from its original basis and is developing further, following its own rules (Silić 1983:159; Ivić 1983:73; etc.). Now, presumably, these rules could be captured by investigating the usage of those who have mastered the standard language. This procedure, however, except in analysing the language of 'good authors', is rarely recommended, and one feels that certain features deviating from the rural Neo-Štokavian dialect systems, even if confirmed in educated usage, are going to be censured.[3] On the other hand, the idea of standard language being divorced from its dialectal basis, theoretically speaking, gives the prescriptivists a free hand in recommending or demanding any arbitrary selected structures or lexical items as obligatory. The insecure basis on which to rely for precepts, the resulting prescriptivists' arbitrariness, with a tendency to change their minds from time to time about 'correct' solutions, and the considerable vitality of non-Štokavian dialects (Čakavian, Kajkavian and Torlak) are some of the reasons why there are noticeable deviations between the full canonical form of the standard language, as required by normativists, and actual educated usage. This is especially true in urban centres situated outside the Štokavian area (Zagreb, Split, Niš, etc.). There would be much more deviation from the norm in evidence in the writing of educated speakers if it were not for the *lektors* (language sub-editors) who intervene in practically everything that is published. As a result of the existing deviations, Serbo-Croatists insist that the standard language must be painstakingly learned and energetically taught (Silić 1983:159; Ivić 1983:74).

If, in the literature or debates on Serbo-Croatian, there has been no objection from the scholarly or theoretical points of view to linguists interfering with usage and taking part in prescriptive work, the question still exists, however, as to whether linguists alone should decide on matters of correctness. It has been suggested instead that some kind of national policy should be devised which would take care of the acceptability of some of linguists' precepts (Škiljan 1985:7; Bugarski 1987). Such a national language policy should be worked out at the federal level, as at present language prescription is within the competency of individual republics. Since Serbo-Croatian is used in four of them, it is not possible to control any convergence or divergence of the variants. Here we find another important contrast between the attitudes towards standard Serbo-Croatian and English. In spite of the fact that various social commentators since the seventeenth century have pointed to the alleged deterioration of English, suggesting that something should be done about it, such as founding a language Academy, proclaiming a national language policy, reforming the spelling system, etc., all such movements have failed for what must have been the fear that this would bring government interference, endangering personal and social freedoms (Ferguson 1979:53; Harris 1984:17). Contrary to the situation with English, various administrations in the territories where Serbo-Croatian is used became interested early on in the standardization process and in language prescription and became involved in it, although the very beginnings of language standardization (selection and codification) was the work of individuals and non-governmental groups. Ever since, the authorities have been the power behind accepting, rejecting or even banning such innocuous manuals as grammars, desk dictionaries and orthographic handbooks. The reason for such an attitude is that even technical (e.g. orthographic) solutions found in such manuals have become politicised, mainly along national and/or territorial lines *čitat ću* : *čitaću*; *tko* : *ko*) and hence interesting for the authorities. Recent proposals for devising a federal language policy (Škiljan 1985) or for compiling a new joint orthography manual[4] (Ćupić 1984:312) obviously reckon with some kind of government involvement and consider it quite normal.

After the Štokavian dialect had been selected as the model for Standard Serbo-Croatian it required a lot of support and propaganda in the acceptance phase, in both the Croatian and Serbian territories as the community's prestigious variety.

The Croats adopted the Štokavian dialect as the basis for their standard language in 1836 and superimposed it over two existing *vital* dialects, one of which, Kajkavian, was then functioning as the literary language, while the other, Čakavian, had already had a distinguished history as such. There was, of course, a Štokavian literary tradition as well. The task of spreading this very familiar but still different dialect and of using it in a written form and at least in formal talk was, and has remained, considerable. One can apparently follow the improvement in the Štokavian of the leading 'Ilirci', the members of the Croatian revival movement who adopted it, from one issue to the other of their journals and other publications (Jonke 1964:185), since most of them were native speakers of Kajkavian. A lack of versatility in Štokavian could be noticed even later, at the beginning of this century, particularly in certain new registers of written language as in advertising (Anić 1983:112). An outstanding čakavian-speaking poet, Vladimir Nazor, who adopted Standard Štokavian, was looking for a job in the Štokavian region of Bosnia and Herzegovina in order to master Štokavian properly (Anić 1983:112; Kalogjera 1985: 102).

The task of the Serbs was somewhat different, but not much easier.

There, the rural Štokavian dialect was to replace an already established though poorly-normalized literary language known as Slavenoserbski, based on Russian and Serbian elements. Its users, an educated elite, offered 'the herdsmen's language' a strong resistance in the 50's and the 60's of the last century, an echo of which may occasionally be discerned to the present day when estimates are made of what has been lost by the abrupt break with the tradition of Slavenoserbski (Mladenović 1983:250). There has also been the problem of spreading Neo-Štokavian among the speakers of the Torlak dialect in South-Eastern Serbia.

It is probably in this difficult task of implementation and expansion of the Standard language that one should look for the beginning and inspiration of a long prescriptivisit tradition in both variants of Serbo-Croatian. Under such conditions the idea of *laissez-faire* in the matter of Standard language hardly occurred to any Serbian, and certainly not to any Croatian philologist. On the contrary, from time to time some prescriptivists imply an idea of the Standard language where every word, every synonym, every compound or neologism coined out of necessity should undergo a check and obtain the stamp of approval by a prescriptivist bureaucracy (cf. Maretić 1924; Stevanović 1983:10; etc.).

The task of the philologists in expanding and implementing the Standard language appears even harder when we look at it now, with the benefit of the comparative sociolinguistic information at our disposal. Sociolinguists seem to agree that speakers select the variety of language used by the group with which they want to be identified. The territory where the Neo-Štokavian dialect was originally used was mainly an economically underdeveloped rural area (Brozović 1970:113) and its speech could hardly carry glamour, class or any socially attractive features in order to be spontaneously imitated. In addition, the dialect 'reflected a body of material and moral associations which correspond to an almost heroic age' (Brozović 1970:112); it showed lexical deficiences in the spheres which are important for standard language, and it was generally difficult for this type of dialect to be re-adapted and intellectualized (Brozović 1970:113). Thus it became a respectable academic occupation to turn this rural dialect into an instrument of modern civilization and to persuade speakers of other dialect backgrounds to master and use it. In English-speaking cultures prescribing, evaluating and recommending items of usage has never been academically appreciated. Quite contrary to this, the most outstanding Serbian and Croatian philologists and linguists of the past century — after Vuk Karadžić and Ljudevit Gaj — and of the present day have taken part in working out the norm of the standard language, both tackling details and developing the theoretical side of the problems. Being informed by current linguistics and sociolinguistics, they now have a considerable area of common views and agreement, but they can also emphatically disagree, especially on the evaluation of the two traditions — and then some of their writings approach the form of pamphlets. But once the sociolinguist develops the ability to decipher the undercurrent of their writings, he is offered an insight into the range of arguments used in the standardization process of a language containing value-laden variants.

Besides the scholars of established reputation operating with elaborate evidence, there seems to exist a tremendous desire on the part of practically every member of each Serbo-Croatian language department in the country to make his or her voice heard in this major and lengthy debate.[5] The topics vary from general statements on standard language and its variants to detailed consideration of why to adopt this instead of that solution in e.g. orthography, morphology, accentuation and especially in vocabulary. It would certainly be sociologically interesting to uncover the motives which direct important and substantial scholars into what appears to some linguistic schools a peripheral linguistic field. It hardly occurs as peripheral to them since, after all, philologists and linguists in neighbouring countries like Hungary, Rumania, Albania, Bulgaria, etc. take prescriptive work equally seriously. It is often implied in their writings that a well-standardized language is a feature of a civilized nation, and that motive may act as stimulus for some of them. Patriotic zeal with its roots in early cultural nationalism aiming at keeping the two grammatical traditions apart, or vice versa, may attract others.

There is also a social feature which should not be disregarded. The scholars who take part in prescriptive work may eventually become important public figures as distinguished from their colleagues dedicated exclusively to pure philological or linguistic research. Such importance is, of course, obtained partly through a wider readership, but it is also due to the fact that the Government often seeks prescriptivists' advice and they thus come into the limelight. If such scholars succeed in steering clear of the Scylla and Charybdis of changing political assumptions concerning the language, they may become known as contributors to the welfare of the nation. Although many of these scholars in delicate and sensitive matters (in Serbo-Croatian it is the delimitation of the variants, the question of one

or two standard languages, etc.) invoke linguistic and, recently, sociolinguistic principles, they are actually activists in a language policy, something
which they are aware of, as when Katičić (1974:225) says: "Among other
features for which Eastern Europe is interesting, the creation of standard
languages, the deliberate directing of language development and language
policy, are some of them...". A policy normally produces an establishment
with "protected ways of viewing, doing and interpreting" but also with
deciding 'blind spots' "i.e. favourite ways of not doing, not viewing etc."
(Fishman 1973:153). Linguists in a descriptive tradition, as the majority in
English-speaking cultures are, would expect the moot points of the norm to
be settled by appeal to the usage of a defined social group. The solution of
such problems by agreement within, or among, language policy establish-
ment(s) looks rather odd. But that is what often occurs in Serbo-Croatian.

The two principles

An overview of certain aspects of prescriptivism in Serbo-Croatian
must assume this to be a polycentric standard language actualized in two
variants: Western and Eastern (Croatian and Serbian), and two 'subvariants' used in Bosnia and Herzegovina and in Montenegro, within which
prescriptive activities are not necessarily identically orientated (e.g. with
regard to the treatment of loan words, etc.) and equally intensive, though
they have much in common. Two principles seem to have been permanently present in all varieties when precepts are formulated.

The first principle concerns the tendency to preserve all the structural-
semantic contrasts that have been described in rural Neo-Štokavian by Vuk
Karadžić and other grammarians and lexicographers after him. The present
day normativists are very reluctant to admit any emendations to the existing
canon of structural-semantic contrasts (the descriptions of which, incidentally, are scattered through various grammars, dictionaries, periodicals and
not easily accessible as synthetic works are scarce), even if large educated
groups of speakers do not distinguish these contrasts. The most striking
illustration of this principle is the Neo-Štokavian system of tonal accents
which is considered to be an integral part of the standard language and is
supposed to be mastered together with other features of this variety. However, it is common knowledge that this elaborate system is widely ignored,
even by professional people in the media, and the top Serbo-Croatists
themselves are sometimes at a loss with it (Magner and Matejka 1971).

Still, hardly anybody dares ask questions from a realistic prescriptive-pedagogical point of view about their actual communicative importance, as the tonal accentual system is often referred to as a national treasure. If by any chance the accents were to be marked in writing, which, fortunately, they are not, it would be a hard task to be considered literate in Serbo-Croatian!

The second principle concerns the tendency to preserve the remnants of the two different orthographic-grammatical-lexical traditions. Although, at the turn of the century, Broz and Iveković as lexicographers and Maretić as a grammarian were to bring the Croatian standard usage into line with that of Vuk Karadžić as used in Serbia, some differences have remained, which have been kept in official orthographic manuals and have attained a symbolic value for the elite on both sides. Lektors in publishing houses and in the media are the main guardians of the differences, which are often invested with political meaning.

The two principles loom large in all normative work, with some prescriptivists heeding more the first, some the second, but it is the interplay between the two that characterizes the precepts.

Purism is another major issue in Serbo-Croatian prescriptivism, mainly because attitudes to at least some aspects of it (e.g. the treatment of loan words) are not identical in the two variants. Purism is usually defined as "the desire on the part of a language community (or the elite to whome responsibility for language has been delegated) to preserve the language or rid it of supposedly foreign elements" (Thomas 1979:405), but Serbo-Croatian purism has another facet, namely, it is applied between the variants following our second principle. Purist attitudes were strong in Austria-Hungary in normative activity in connection with German, Czech and Hungarian. They were taken over by the Croatian Revival Movement in its language work (Vince 1978:550), and only to some extent by certain Serbian philologists.

Now, purism and purists obtain mainly negative marks from linguists in the American linguistic tradition, reinforced by the experience of the development of English. What follows is probably one of the typical opinions coming from that tradition: "... the guardians of linguistic purity, those true purists who want to expunge loan-words from a language and prevent their entry into it — like the Frenchman Étiamble with his phobia of postwar Franglais, and like his predecessors over the centuries in many languages — are engaged in an enterprise as futile as it is foolish, especially when it is grounded in chauvinism and xenophobia, in the fear that the fatherland and the race will be corrupted by foreign words. They all apparently forget that English has been, since 1066, Frenglish and Englench — and that the English nation has not fared too badly notwithstanding its bastard lexicon" (Pulgram 1967:27). Such an uncompromising view would in our case lead to an *a priori* dismissal of the whole problem without even looking into the special situation of Serbo-Croatian, where purism is taken seriously. However, there are American scholars with wider experience in different languages who react differently. Haugen (1972:292), for instance, looks at purism as one of the possible solutions in the process of "making a rural language capable of meeting the needs of a national society ... For English this was accomplished in the period of the Elizabethans by the deliberate importation and imitation of Latin in the learned prose of the time. For modern Icelandic and Hebrew it has been accomplished by the deliberate manufacture of myriads of terms from native material, or a policy of vigorous purism".

This latter solution was fully adopted in Croatia, and only reluctantly in Serbia, where spontaneous formation of the vocabulary has been preferred (Vince 1978:550; Ivić 1984:329). It is considered that purism "... is a stronger assertion of identity than the mere wholesale adaptation of foreign terms" (Haugen 1966:23) and this line may have come naturally to the speakers of a language that was 'objectively dominated' by the neighbouring languages, German, Hungarian and Italian, and according to contemporary references[6] was felt as 'subjectively inferior' (Weinreich 1963). They may have needed proof of its resourcefulness.

When Bogoslav Šulek, the author of the first Croatian dictionary of scientific terminology (Croatian-German-Italian, 1874) was short of a Croatian term he would coin it from native material or calque it, unless there was an adequate Slavonic item (mainly Czech or Russian) available, as purism in those days was mainly directed against the dominating non-Slavonic languages. Purism in Croatia was also diffused by language advice manuals (cf. below). In Serbia purist attitudes were advocated in books by J. Bošković *O srpskom jeziku* (Belgrade 1887), by J. Živanović under the same title (Novi Sad 1888) and in various articles and periodicals as *Kolo, Stražilovo, Brankovo kolo, Nastavnik*, etc. (Herrity 1978).

However, from the beginning, the very lively purist activity in Croatia, with its numerous neologisms and calques, did not meet with approval among Serbian philologists. Although the latter called for attention to the purity of the language in schools land in scientific usage they at the same time warned against taking this policy too far as "then our language ... will soon resemble Croatian, of which God preserve us" (Lj. Nedić, quoted by Herrity 1978:223). Linguistic objections against neologisms and calques forged in Zagreb were that they did not follow the rules of Štokavian word formation but were modelled mainly on German compounds (*veleposjednik, veleizdaja*) or that some of the adopted Slavonic words (*nužda, uštrb*), 'unnecessary Russianisms', do not conform to the Štokavian phonological rules. A psycho-linguistic motive for the rejection of neologisms in Serbia which is sometimes mentioned is that the degree of tolerance for new models of word formation is lower there (Thomas 1979:410). This evidence, close to our first principle, does not seem to explain the problem fully. One could wonder why such a small number of neologisms of native character — at least linguistically blameless ones — have been accepted in Serbia, when at the same time there has been a persistent line of public support for the substitution of loanwords with native ones. The language advice columns in the influential Belgrade daily *Politika* written by Vukadinović and Lalević kept attacking 'unnecessary foreign words' (Klajn 1985:9). A leading linguist A. Belić thought that loanwords should be used only in exceptional cases (Tanasković 1983:97). Purism has been apparently very much in the mind of letter-writers to the language advice columnists so that Klajn (1985:9) reports: ".., first Kosta Timotijević and then myself have carried out a kind of 'antipurist' campaign arguing that loanwords are almost never either synonymous with or equally applicable as the suggested native replacements".[7] The reason, then, for such restricted adoption of neologisms coming either from the Western variant or forged on the spot should be sought not only in the linguistic incompatibility of some of these items, but also in certain attitudes and beliefs that have been socially diffused. The suggestion from influential linguistic sources that loanwords are acceptable in the Eastern variant, especially for abstract and technical vocabulary, must have been generalized as a precept by lektors and language teachers who have then seen to it that neologisms be avoided. Thus, for a full explanation of the attitudes towards loanwords in the Eastern variant the mentioned interplay of *the first and the second principle* must be considered with more emphasis on *the second principle*.

Purism in Croatia, both with regard to loanwords and to lexical and grammatical items considered to belong to the Eastern variant, has been very active in the last two decades, moving along the lines familiar to the sociology of language when variants or languages press for a certain autonomy. A comparison of usage, e.g. in the press, at various times within this period would support this opinion, although the most radical purism would probably be found in the writings of some literati. The contemporary sources for neologisms in technology and science are the dictionaries and glossaries of technical terminology, for a more general usage the periodical *Jezik*, but individual writers from different fields with a knack for coining new words add their contributions, which are then diffused via the printed word or through the network of interested purists. A certain number of lexical items and structures which had gone out of use, or have been on the way out, either through the Broz-Iveković-Maretić reform at the turn of the century or through the normal linguistic processes, are being revitalized. It must be said, however, that critical voices against such dynamic purism can be heard, particularly on two grounds: a) the reaction of mature speakers who feel uncomfortable about having to change their writing and (formal) speaking habits so often; b) the reaction of those speakers who fear the gap thus created between the Croatian variant and usage in other territories where Štokavian is the basis of the standard language. This latter view is often directly connected with political assumptions such as the unity of the country, the problem of internal migrations, etc.

After several generations of speakers of the Western variant have been brought up on purist attitudes, these now seem to have become deeply ingrained, however, in a specific, almost diglossic, manner, with special regard to the written language. In informal styles of speaking the frequency of loanwords of German, Italian, Hungarian, Turkish, and English origin, often hastily adapted, as well as items considered by prescriptivists to belong to the Eastern variant, tends to be high, but in writing a person with an average education goes out of his way to replace the loan word with the native one or to keep within the variant. This seems to have become an automatic process and no longer a result of the fear of the lektor's red pencil.

Sources of normative advice

One would expect that owing to such an active public interest in the standard language Serbo-Croatian linguists and philologists would have produced a substantial number of reference works such as grammars and dictionaries. It may come as a surprise, however, that one could quote only three grammars of any degree of originality and comprehensiveness in a period of eighty or more years: Maretić's *Gramatika i stilistika hrvatskoga ili srpskog jezika* (Zagreb 1899), Stevanović's *Gramatika srpskohrvatskog jezika* (Belgrade 1964, 1969) and Barić et al. *Priručna gramatika hrvatskoga književnog jezika* (Zagreb 1979), if shorter compilations for use in secondary schools are left out. The situation with comprehensive monolingual desk dictionaries is similar. The latest desk dictionary published in Croatia is that by Iveković and Broz of 1901 in 2 volumes.[8]

Although one would be tempted to lay the blame for this state of affairs on the volatile nature of our philologists and linguists, who prefer witty repartee to Johnsonian "harmless drudge's" toil, there are also convincing sociolinguistic reasons for that deficiency, not least their preoccupation with the problem of the variants of Serbo-Croatian (Brozović 1970:35) that complicate the agreement on the corpus on which to base the lexicographical work and the presentation of the entries.

The latest common venture, the dictionary which was to be published by the Matica hrvatska in Latin script and Matica srpska in Cyrilic, partly failed. The group of Croatian linguists taking part gave up, and the Latin script version ceased publication after the second volume. The reason for their dissent was complex, but it boiled down to the claim that the Croatian variant was not adequately represented through the lexicographical principles. The episode illustrates the emotional component involved in such ventures. But even if it had been published in the Latin script the six-volume dictionary would have hardly covered the kind of use intended for a desk dictionary. The lack of such dictionaries points to probably the widest gap that divides English language literacy and culture from literacy and culture in Serbo-Croatian. Since Dr Johnson, the dictionary has been the basis of literacy and the norm in Britain and America. On the other hand, generations of educated speakers of Serbo-Croatian have gone through the education process up to the University level without ever having opened a monolingual dictionary of their mother tongue — or even having seen one, for that matter! "We have a literary language culture practically without a dictionary" (Anić 1983:112). This is probably a disadvantage that no other norm implementation tool can make up for. The insight into a large amount of language material that a solid, usage-based dictionary offers to the speaker or writer with a problem to solve, stimulating him at the same time to seek his own solutions, cannot be compared with a handful of orthographic rules plus an incomplete and rather arbitrary list of troublesome words with authoritative right vs. wrong pronouncements which a Serbo-Croatian speaker has had to rely on. Owing to this situation the technique of making concise monolingual dictionaries is lagging behind, as confirmed, for example, by the criticisms of the entries' definitions in the only two volumes of the Matica hrvatska dictionary that have been published (Brozović 1968:25ff).

Since dictionaries have no function in norm implementation, normative advice and recommendations have been spreading through the following channels: orthographic manuals (*Pravopis*), manuals of linguistic advice (*Jezični savjetnik*), languge culture periodicals (*Jezik* in Zagreb, *Naš jezik* in Belgrade, etc.) and through newspaper and magazine linguistic columns. There are also school manuals with that purpose. A characteristic institution for Serbo-Croatian literacy is the *lektor*, a kind of sub-editor, a language specialist, found nowadays in every publisher's office, every newspaper, and in radio and television stations.

Sociolinguistically the most intriguing of these channels is a special product of Serbo-Croatian literacy, *Pravopis*, essentially an orthographic manual with considerable symbolic meaning. The succession of these manuals, in most cases differing in matters of detail for the Eastern and Western variants in the period from 1892 to 1960, illustrates both how manipulable the standard written language may be (probably while still in its earlier phases) and what an impressive symbolic function certain graphic details, words written separately or jointly (*neću:ne ću*; *pisaću:pisat ću*), punctuation (dr:dr.; VI:VI.) or morphological detail (*starog:staroga*) can be made to play in intergroup relations. Most of these manuals have been accompanied by considerable publicity and sometimes by heated polemics, as their publication has usually been linked with changes in political assumptions and in the atmosphere mainly between the Serbian and Croatian elite, which they noted by introducing more convergence or divergence into the two written usages.[9] The usual content of these manuals consists of a series of spelling principles (on capital letters, the reflexes of the old sound ě, jointly and separately spelt compound words, the spelling of loan words, punctuation, etc.), which are stated as rules. This is followed by a list of troublesome words from the orthographic or prosodic points of view, whose length may vary according to the free estimate of the authors and publishers. These manuals ar extremely fragmentary, put together out of necessity, and they cannot compare with well-produced desk dictionaries as found in English language cultures when one is faced with solving a usage problem. And although this seems to be obvious to some linguists in the field (Ćupić 1984:312), they still plead for new editions of such manuals, ignoring the fact that their energy could be much better invested, with more satisfactory results, if descriptive dictionaries and grammars of the standard language were to be produced instead. These might in turtn educate the literate public in distinguishing between prescriptivists' exaggerations and rational solutions and in so doing render more stability to the orthography. However, for the better part of a century *Pravopis* has become identified by the educated lay public with literacy, with the language and its variants and without it they feel that Serbo-Croatian literacy would break down.

Another influential channel through which the alleged correctness and purity of the language have been propagated is in manuals called *The Language Adviser* (*Jezični savjetnik*), especially characteristic for Croatia, but similar publications have come out in Novi Sad and Belgrade. There have been several since the beginning of this century and the titles are indicative of their subject matter: *Barbarisms in the Croatian language* by V. Rožić (1904, 1908 and 1913), *The Defender of the Croatian language* by Andrić (1911). However, the most important of them has been *The Croatian or Serbian language adviser for all those who wish to speak and write our literary language well* by T. Maretić (1924). The book consists of some 200 pages of mostly lexical but also morphological and syntactic advice in alphabetical order, sometimes explaining the reason for certain precepts and sometimes just authoritatively accepting or rejecting an entry along an idealistic and naïve purist line, most energetically anti-Germanic, somewhat softer but still vigilant towards Slavonic imports (mainly Russian and Czech) and very strict towards Kajkavian and Čakavian dialectisms. The preface to to his *Jezični savjetnik* advocates the idea of the immaculately pure literary language, the image of which has been echoed in Croatian and some Serbian prescriptivists' writings until the present day, in spite of changes in attitudes which have occurred in the meantime. Under the term 'literary language' Maretić obviously had in mind primarily the language of imaginative prose. It would be hard to fit into his design, for example, registers of scientific writings, engineering, etc. His model of the literary language would be recognized by present day sociolinguists as a single-style language (in which, of course, none of them believe), based on the usage of Štokavian-speaking folk, with the minimum of the absolutely indispensable loan words either from foreign languages or Serbo-Croatian dialects, with the minimal number of synonyms, as they appeared to him unnecessary and therefore were to be excluded. The speakers and writers of this language, besides having an excellent *Sprachgefühl* for Štokavian, were to have a solid knowledge of etymology as Maretić suggested that all words of dubious pedigree, i.e. dubious etymology (e.g. *hir* 'whim'; *latica* 'petal'), should be excluded from this chosen language. Many of his recommendations have not lasted and many items that he rejected are now standard forms, but a great deal of his puristic attitude and his idealistic vision of language have remained with us, even with linguists who nowadays criticize his pristine Neo-Štokavian stance. The status of *The Language Adviser* manuals has been characterized as follows: "These have become the most important books in our literacy, in a higher sense of that word, and have marked our thinking to the present day: language purism of changeable mood contradictory in itself (the criterion valid for one word may not be valid for another), with the attention focused on a single mistake instead of on insight into the total language material, trusting judgements regardless of evidence. We may thus speak about a *literary language culture based on The Language Adviser*" (Anić 1983:113).

Another channel for spreading language advice ar the *language columns* in the daily and weekly newspapers. Practically all major dailies and weeklies have at some time run such a column.This means of spreading awareness aboout language problems is known both in Britain and America with the difference that they are written by journalists while in Yugoslavia they are regularly reserved for linguists. However, there have been perhaps half a dozen journalists who have filled such columns in the Zagreb and Belgrade newspapers and they tended to introduce wider topics into their articles than did the linguists, namely, they departed from the usual problems of orthography, grammar and elementary lexis and pointed at tired clichés used to camouflage the lack of content, or for obfuscation (Pavičić 1982). Many authors of such language columns subsequently tend to publish their articles in book form, which, apparently, sell very well (e.g. Ljudevit Jonke: *Književni jezik u teoriji i praksi*, Zagreb 1954; *Naš jezik u praksi* by a group of authors, Sarajevo, etc.) and then function as a permanent source of prescriptive information. Linguists filling such columns have a unique opportunity to determine what section of the public is interested in the problems of usage by looking at the correspondence that they receive. It appears that the prevailing number of correspondents to the language columns are elderly people (Klajn 1985:8). In Britain Burchfield found, going through the correspondence concerning language addressed to BBC, that the age of those interested in language problems was over thirty (Burchfield 1979:8,9). Young people, apparently, show little interest in correctness, which may be sociologically significant.

A service which has considerable power in implementing and spreading prescriptive demands is the institution of the *lektor*, a kind of sub-editor scanning texts before being published or transmitted by radio and TV. The lektors' tasks are not clearly defined but informally diffused, often by word of mouth through their networks. It seems that only recently has the role of the lektor come to the critical attention of linguists partly, perhaps, as the result of the angry voices of authors dissatisfied with the lektors' interventions in their manuscripts. A linguist who had written language columns for the Belgrade press for years says that they are only symbolically present in a newspaper editing: "they care only for the orthography (and even for that superficially) ..." (Klajn 1958:9). In this connection, i.e. owing to their limited interest in wider aspects of texts a suggestion has been put forward that "the lektor's service should be strengthened and revived" (Ivić 1983:74) evidently in the sense of a more comprehensive approach to language. This same linguist finds lektors narrow-minded and guided by two principles: the first, a more general one, consists of a search for words which in their opinion "are more literary or perhaps more elegant" while the second principle consists in rejecting everything that sounds foreign to them (Ivić 1983:74). This is probably what another linguist labels "lektor's mannerisms" (Anić 1983:114). Yet another opinion characterizes the service as follows: "they are the representatives of the small groups of last defenders of basic literacy, but left to their own informal agreements, whose work for various reasons results, not in the development of the communicative functions of language, but in insisting, for example, on the distinctions between variants" (Škiljan 1985:56). And indeed, in the last twenty years their role has been considerable in promoting purist attitudes in the Croatian as well as, according to some indications, rejecting them in the Serbian media. An inevitable conclusion must be drawn from the kind of comments quoted above, and from one's own experience, that a service which ought to be creative has declined into a routine procedure. This may be due partly to the recruitment method and partly to the shortage of contemporary lexicographical and grammatical works of reference based on the analysis of usage to help develop an individual comprehensive approach to texts.[10]

The actual impact of these individual channels on the written usage and then on the formal spoken usage can be established only after a considerable amount of research. There is historical evidence of the dramatic effect on the Croatian variant produced by the prescriptive activity at the turn of the century. Owing to the switch from morphophonemic (known also as etymological) to phonological spelling (*otac*; gen. *otca* > *oca*), to the dropping of archaic forms of the dative, instrumental and locative plural (*ženam* > *ženama, ženami* > *ženama, ženah* > *ženama*) accompanied by a more exclusive leaning on the vocabulary of the Neo-Štokavian dialect, all of which was prescribed by Broz's *Orthography* of 1892, Maretić's *Grammar* of 1899 and Iveković's and Broz's *Dictionary* of 1901, the 'feel' of the standard written language had changed in a comparatively short time. Texts only one hundred years old now appear very archaic and are difficult to read (Brozović 1970:141).

The acceptance of many prescriptivists' demands has often depended, in Serbo-Croatian, on the contemporary social and political assumptions, which are expressed in captivating social, political, national and patriotic slogans. Vuk Karadžić in the past century struggled for the new, rurally-based, literary language by emphasising that his was the language of the common folk — a slogan which went down very well in the Romantic period. The Croatian Revival Movement — the Illyrians — adopted the Štokavian dialect as the basis for the standard language — although most of the members were speakers of Kajkavian — under the slogan that such a literary language will unite all the South Slavs including the Slovenes and the Bulgarians. With that aim in view they retained the archaic case endings and the morphophonemic spelling. When struggling to implement the phonological spelling and the Neo-Štokavian case-endings Maretić accused his opponents of rejecting his reform only because the Serbs use the same systems (Jonke 1964:181). The pattern has continued to the present day. The much discussed *Novi Sad Orthography* of 1960 was also launched with the slogan that it should contribute to brotherhood and unity within this multinational country (Jonke 1964:22). This link between political slogans and language precepts probably helps to make a wider public aware of the changes introduced but also contributes to politicising language problems.

As concerns the impact of newspaper language columns, Klajn (1985:8) considers them to be too learned and difficult for the general public so that they end up being 'read by those to whom they are least necessary' i.e. by other linguists.

The language culture periodicals have a restricted readership among language teachers and occasional enthusiasts so that their impact is indirect. Observations would suggest that one of the areas where the lektors' impact on usage is particularly felt, at least in Croatia, are the neologisms and archaisations in the lexis (directed towards purism) and in the derivational morphology (towards certain regularity presumably closer to the Croatian tradition, e.g. the spreading of the -*elj* suffix as against -*lac* in masc. nouns: *rukovodilac* > *rukovoditelj*, etc.).

In presenting the channels diffusing the norm of the standard language we should not overlook the school, which once was central in this activity, a status it could hardly claim nowadays as the media are probably more important in instilling standard forms in the young people. It should, however, be mentioned that the characteristic fragmentariness in Serbo-Croatian prescriptivism is reflected in the teaching of the standard language in schools. What is vigorously corrected is the list of traditionally stigmatized words and phrases (from the language advice manuals) and, in non-Štokavian regions, the few most prominent or at least well-recorded departures in stress, grammar and lexis from Neo-Štokavian. A lot of others remain undetected by the teacher, himself the speaker of a local dialect, and are freely but unintentionally used.[11]

There have been attempts at grading the treatment of language in different language communities on a kind of universal scale as, roughly, basic and advanced (Neustupny 1978) according to the type of normative problems that obtain the most attention. The prescriptivist activity in Serbo-Croatian reviewed in the previous pages would, according to this gradation, probably be classified as basic, as it tackles primarily problems of literacy, elementary standardization and the language code as a whole (Neustupny quoted by Takahara 1980:377,378). This type of prescriptivism is associated, in the same source, with developing societies. However, a review of Serbo-Croatian prescriptivism would be incomplete without a mention of the emerging *language cultivation* approach which is becoming a part of the Serbo-Croatian Departments' curricula and which concentrates on the problems which Neustupny links with language treatment in developed societies. This approach "is characterized by interest in questions of correctness, efficiency, inner structure of linguistic levels fulfilling various functions" (Takahara 1980:38). This fresh approach may be discerned from the criticism of clichés which have penetrated various styles of language, coming partly from the register of politics, where it is often used to cover up vacuousness. Demands for coherent, economical expression are now frequently voiced by the young generation of Serbo-Croatists. Prescriptivists' efforts in this area are not devoid of problems linked with the subjectivity of judgements as the controversy around Bernstein's *codes* have shown, but more attention paid to the functional side of the standard language does indicate that in the second century of its official existence standard Serbo-Croatian is obtaining the type of care that stabilized standard languages are given.

Notes

1. To take a simple example: the cost-benefit type analysis would certainly result in the suggestion that, of the two reflexes of the old sound *ě* now in the standard usage, *ije/je* and *e*, the use of the latter only would be the most economical solution for both variants, especially in writing. The rules governing the use of long *ije* and short *je* are not completely clear to the normativists themselves (in examples like: *slijedeći:sljedeći*; *neprimjetan:neprimijetan*, etc.). However, the symbolic value that *ije/je* has acquired since it was adopted as the standard form in Croatia (*e* was adopted in Serbia) overrules the spelling problems and even the fact that many Croats in informal talk use the two other reflexes of *ě:e* and *i* (*reka, rika*). Any attempt to adopt that economical solution at present would be doomed to failure. One such attempt in 1914 lasted for some time but failed for this very symbolic reason (Anić 1983:113).

2. By this comparatively recent development in linguists' attitudes towards correctness a situation has been created in America where, owing to the lack of 'licensed practitioners', the general public has to turn to 'shamans' when they have a language problem (Bolinger 1980:1). The 'shamans' here are journalists who have made their names in pointing out errors (and pseudo-errors) in the public use of language. The best known among these are Edwin Newman, John Simon, William Saphire and one or two others. In Britain, the role of language advisers has been held by a number of philologically trained persons (the Fowlers, Gowers, and recently Crystal), but this work is not academically appreciated.

3. One wonders whether they would allow the 'official' obliteration of distinctions between: *kuda, kamo, gdje*; *evo, eto*; the definite and indefinite use of adjectives signalled by tonal stress, etc. just because many educated speakers of the standard language are not aware of these distinctions.

4. The latest undertaking of this king, accomplished in 1960 under the name of *Novosadski pravopis*, was rejected in 1971 by one of the sides, the official Croat cultural and linguistic bodies, for allegedly failing to do justice to the Western (Croatian) variant.

5. "Whenever a topic like the national language becomes a public issue, as it has in Norway, its problems are perforce simplified down to a level where every man becomes his own linguist" (Haugen 1966: 295).

6. Latin was the offical language of the Croatian Assembly until 1847 for various reasons, but the low social status of the Croatian dialects may have been one. Pavao Štoos (1806-1862), in a much-quoted poem says that the Croats are ashamed of their language and are abandoning it.

7. The Serbian public sympathizing with purism has found its champion in the person of Professor Dragiša Vitošević, with his somewhat naïve populist attitude towards the problem. Having launched the slogan "it is better to be a purist than an impurist" he delights in Étiamble's views and takes the French official attitudes towards correctness as his favourite model. (Vitošević 1983: 19-24, 309-312).

8. Here we disregard the three important multivolume dictionaries: the Yugoslav Academy Dictionary (Zagreb), the Serbian Academy Dictionary (Belgrade, not yet completed, 12 volumes published so far) and the Matica Srpska Dictionary (Novi Sad) as they, for obvious reasons, are accessible to a restricted public and cannot fulfil the functions of a solid desk dictionary.

9. Thus there were minor or major changes in orthography in Croatia in 1892, 1915, 1923, 1929, 1941, 1942, 1944, 1945, and 1960 connected with the publications of orthographic manuals respectively by Broz, Broz and Boranić, Boranić, by ministerial decree during the dictatorship, by Boranić again, by decree of the Ustaše regime during the war, by Boranić again, and by a group of philologists and literati from four republics using Serbo-Croatian known as *Novosadski pravopis*.

10. Sub-editors, of course, intervene in texts published in the English speaking countries as well, but from what one gathers the difference between their treatment of texts and the lektor's task in Serbo-Croatian must be considerable. The latter is more concerned with orthography, morphology, certain syntactic structures stigmatized as alien, substitution of loan-words by domestic ones, and with variants. Much of the lektor's intervention seems to be done out of context. Economy and coherence of texts figure rather low on the lektor's list. What may be annoying to data-collecting descriptive linguists is the fact that they can never be sure whether an item represents the author's or the lektor's usage.

11. As long as it is spoken language the departures from the strict Štokavian are socially tolerated even in formal situations in non-Štokavian regions, partly because the public is unaware of the deviations.

References

Anić, Vladimir. 1983. "Poticajnost Mirkovićevih misli i svjedočenja o jeziku" [Inspirational power of Mirković's thoughts and his witnessing about language]. In: D. Crnković (ed.). *Susreti na dragom kamenu*. Vol. II. Pula.

Bolinger, Dwight. 1980. *Language: The Loaded Weapon*. London and New York: Longman.

Brborić, B. et al. (eds). 1983. *Aktuelna pitanja naše jezičke kulture* [Topical questions in our language culture]. Beograd: Prosvetni pregled.

Brozović, Dalibor. 1964. "Vuk i naš standardni jezik" [Vuk and our standard language]. *Mogućnosti* 11: 910-17.

-----. 1968. "Tko čeka — katkada i ne dočeka" [Those who wait may not see]. *Kritika* 1: 25-37.

-----. 1970. *Standardni jezik* [The standard language]. Zagreb: Matica hrvatska.

-----. 1974. "O jeziku hrvatske književnosti 17 stoljeća" [On the language of Croatian literature in the 17th century]. *Zbornik Zagrebačke slavističke škole* 51-58. Zagreb: Medjunarodni slavistički centar SRH.

Bugarski, Ranko. 1987. "Politique et aménagement linguistiques en Yugoslavie". In: Jacques Maurais (ed.). 1987. *Politique et aménagement linguistiques*. Québec: Conseil de la langue française/Paris: Le Robert. 417-452.

Burchfield, R.W., Donoghue Denis, and Timothy Andrew. 1979. *The Quality of Spoken English*. London: BBC.

Ćupić, Drago. 1984. "Srpskohrvatska standardnojezička norma i njen društveni kontekst" [The Standard Serbo-Croatian language norm and its social context]. *Sveske Instituta za proučavanje nacionalnih odnosa* 5-6: 309-14.

Ferguson, Charles. 1979. "National attitudes toward language planning" *Georgetown University Round Table on Languages and Linguistics*, 51-60. Washington: Georgetown University Press.

Fishman, Joshua. 1972. "Historical dimension in the sociology of language." *Monograph Series on Languages and Linguistics* 25: 145-55. Washington, D.C.: Georgetown University Press.

Fries, Charles C. 1940. *American English Grammar*. New York.

Hall, Robert A. Jr. 1950. *Leave Your Language Alone*. Linguistic Press. (2nd revised edition: Linguistics and Your Language. Anchor Books, 1960.)

Harris, Roy. 1984. "The misunderstanding of Newspeak". *The Times Literary Supplement*. 6 Jan.: 17.

Haugen, Einar. 1966. *Language Conflict and Language Planning*. Cambridge: Harvard University Press.

-----. 1972. "Language planning: Theory and practice." In: *The Ecology of Language*. Selected by Anwar S. Dil. Stanford: Stanford University Press. 287-98.

Herrity, Peter. 1978. "Puristic Attitudes in Serbia in the second half of the nineteenth century". *The Slavonic and East European Review* 56. 2: 202-23.

Ivić, Milka. 1965. "Problem norme u književnom jeziku" [The problem of the norm in the literary language]. *Jezik* 13: 1-8.

Ivić, Pavle. 1971. *Srpski narod i njegov jezik* [The Serbian people and their language]. Beograd: Srpska književna zadruga.

-----. 1983. "Normativni zahvati u jeziku" [Normative moves in language]. In: Brborić et al. (eds). 1983: 73-6.

-----. 1984. "L'évolution de la langue littéraire sur le territoire linguistique serbo-croate." *Revue des études slaves* 56(3): 313-44.

Jonke, Ljudevit. 1964. *Književni jezik u teoriji i praksi* [The literary language in theory and in practice]. Zagreb: Znanje.

Kalogjera, Damir. 1978. "On Serbo-Croatian prescriptivism". In: W. R. Schmalstieg and T.F. Magner (eds). *Sociolinguistic problems in Czechoslovakia, Hungary, Romania and Yugoslavia*, 388-99. Columbus, Ohio: Slavica Publishers, Inc.

-----. 1985. "Attitudes toward Serbo-Croatian language varieties." *International Journal of the Sociology of Language* 52: 93-109.

Katičić, Radoslav. 1964. "Normiranje književnog jezika kao lingvistički zadatak" [The normalizing of the literary language as a linguistic task]. *Jezik* 11: 1-9.

-----. 1974. "Nešto napomena o postanku složenog suvremenog jezičnog standarda hrvatskog ili srpskog" [A few notes on the origin of the complex Croatian or Serbian standard language]. *Zbornik Zagrebačke slavističke škole*, 225-48. Zagreb: Medjunarodni slavistički centar SRH.

Klajn, Ivan. 1985. "Kultivisanje jezika i jezične rubrike u štampi" [The cultivation of language and the language columns in the press]. *Odjek* 38(7): 8-9.

Macay, D.G. 1980. "On the goals, principles and procedure for prescriptive grammar: singular *they*". *Language in Society* 9(3): 349-67.

Magner, T.F. and L. Matejka. 1971. *Word Accent in Modern Serbo-Croatian*. University Park, PA: Pennsylvania State University Press.

Maretić, T. 1924. *Hrvatski ili srpski jezični savjetnik* [Croatian or Serbian language adviser]. Zagreb: Jugoslavenska akademija znanosti i umjetnosti.

McDavid, Raven, I. Jr. 1979. "American English: A bibliographic essay." *American studies international* 17(2): 3-45.

Mladenović, Milan. 1983. "Trenutak našeg književnog jezika" [An instant of our literary language]. In: Brborić et al. (eds). 1983: 249-51.

Pavičić, Josip. 1982. *Novogovor* [Newspeak]. Zagreb: Stvarnost.

Pulgram, Ernst. 1976. "Review of *External History of the Romance Languages* by Robert A. Hall, Jr." *General Linguistics* 16: 24-8.

Rajić, Ljubiša. 1983. "Teorijske osnove planiranja jezika" [Theoretical bases for language planning]. In: D. Vulović and Z. Stojiljković (eds). 1983: 174-94.

Rubin, Joan. 1985. "Review of C.M. Eastman *Language Planning: An Introduction.*" *Language in Society* 14(1): 137-41.

Silić, Josip. 1983. "Nekoliko misli o normi" [Some thoughts about the norm]. In: D. Vulović and Z. Stojiljković (eds). 1983: 155-61.

Stevanović, Mihailo. 1983. "O nekim negativnim pojavama u današnjem jeziku" [On some negative phenomena in today's language]. In: D. Vulović and Z. Stojiljković (eds). 1983: 9-17.

Škiljan, Dubravko. 1985. "Društveni aspekti standardizacije jezika" [Social aspects of language standardization]. *Odjek* 38(7): 7-8.

-----. 1985. "Kriza jezika ili jezik krize" [The crisis of the language or the language of the crisis]. *Danas.* Zagreb. 10 Sept.: 55-8.

Takahara, P.O. 1980. "Review of J.V. Neustupny *Post-structural approaches to language: Language theory in a Japanese context.*" *Language in Society* 9(3): 374-9.

Tanasković, Darko. 1983. "Sociolingvistički aspekti ideologizacije pozajmljenica" [Sociolinguistic aspects of loan-word ideologizing]. In: D. Vulović and Z. Stojiljković (eds). 1983: 95-116.

Thomas, George. 1979. "The origin and nature of lexical purism in the Croatian variant of Serbo-Croatian." *Canadian Slavonic Papers* 20: 405-20.

Vince, Zlatko. 1978. *Putovima hrvatskoga književnog jezika* [Following the roads of the Croatian literary language]. Zagreb: Liber.

Vitošević, Dragiša. 1983. "Lepota i čistota jezika" [Beauty and purity of the language]. In: B. Brborić et al. (eds). 1983: 309-13.

Vulović, D., and Z. Stojiljković (eds). 1983. *Jezik u savremenoj komunikaciji* (Language in contemporary communication). Belgrade: Center for Marxism of the University of Belgrade.

Weinreich, Uriel. 1983. *Languages in Contact.* The Hague: Mouton.

Linguistic variety and relationship of languages*

Radoslav Katičić
Institut für Slawistik, Universität Wien

When we say that comparative linguistics tries to find out whether there is a genetic relationship between languages, we imply that other linguistic relationships exist which are not genetic. Therefore, the discussion of the general notion of linguistic relationship is a necessary preliminary for any investigation of the comparative method.

Linguistic relationship implies a variety of languages, because the relationship of a language to itself, though very close, is trivial. It is the relationship of different languages that is worth investigating.

Any inquiry into the nature of linguistic variety presupposes, again, the concept of language itself. Many definitions of this concept have been proposed so far, but this does not relieve us of the obligation to give our own for the purposes of this investigation. From this point of view, it seems most convenient to define language as an organization of texts. By text we understand the physical substance used in speech in order to convey the linguistic message from the performer (speaker) to the addressee (hearer), be it sound, light, electric impulses or any other physical substance. If this concept of language is accepted any particular language can be defined by the statement of its abstract organizational properties as presented in a workable model.[1]

In all essentials this definition of language is in agreement with the well-known Saussurian views based on the distinction between *langue* and

* This article was originally published as Chapter II of the book: Katičić, Radoslav. 1970. *A Contribution to the General Theory of Comparative Linguistics*. The Hague/Paris: Mouton. 12-27. It is reprinted here in the same form, except for technical adjustments. Permission to reprint was kindly granted by Mouton Publishers (Division of Walter de Gruyter & Co.).

parole. It is also in full accordance with information theory. Language, thus conceived, can be said to represent a special case of a code in which messages are given. But speech in our system of linguistic concepts does not correspond to message in information theory. A message is a particular choice among the possibilities provided by the code. It is, therefore, no more material than the code itself. The concept of message in information theory has as its linguistic counterpart the particular choices among the possibilities provided by a language. Such a choice is, in its turn, no more material than language itself is. The particular choices we shall call LINGUISTIC UNITS. This broad and general term already denotes in its accepted meaning all possible choices a language provides on different levels.

A linguistic unit, which may in itself be a string of smaller linguistic units, corresponds to the concept of message in information theory. In fact, a linguistic unit is a special, linguistic case of a message.

According to the terminology of information theory, a channel is the physical substance that every message needs in order to be dispatched from the source to the receiver. In our system of linguistic concepts, speech and its texts correspond to the channel of information theory.

Between linguistic units and texts or segments of texts there is a definite relation. This relation we shall call REALIZATION, and we shall say that linguistic units are realized in texts or in segments of texts.[2]

There is a certain reluctance among some linguists to accept the distinction between linguistic unit and text, but it is easy to show that the distinction is necessary. Nobody will deny that the same linguistic unit may occur in different texts. And as nothing can be simultaneously identical and non-identical, the linguistic unit must be distinguished from the physical substance of the text in which it is realized. In that case one can say that the same linguistic unit is realized in different texts or segments of texts. This is fully in accordance with our intuitive ideas about language and it makes it possible for us to explain the empirical fact that in different instances of speech the same can be said.

In recent times it has become increasingly common to define a language as a set of sentences.[3] But since this set is infinite, no particular language can be defined by enumerating its sentences. It is therefore necessary to state what conditions sentences must fulfil in order to be recognized as belonging to a certain set. In other words, their organization must be described. This shows clearly that both definitions of language, as a set of sentences and as the organization of texts, are in fact equivalent.[4]

It is now necessary to analyze in some detail the implications our definition of language has for the concepts of LINGUISTIC VARIETY and of LINGUISTIC RELATIONSHIP. The concept of linguistic variety is needed in order to account for the empirical fact that a person able to produce and to understand some texts can practically never do so with every existing text. This means that all texts are not organized in the same way or, in other words, that there is more than one language. This again is in full accordance with our intuitive ideas.

Linguistic variety is a set of all languages that can be perceived as different. This means that dialects and even idiolects will appear as members of this set. This is only consistent with our definition of language which implies the annulment of a distinction among dialect, idiolect and language. Dialects and idiolects, being recognizably different organizations of texts, must be accepted as different languages in the linguistic variety set. In fact, it is necessary for our purposes, at least in theory, to disregard this traditional distinction, if any strictness is to be attained in the system of our concepts. For there is no clearcut general criterion by which dialect can be distinguished from language.

The traditional classification is based on a subjective and arbitrary evaluation of differences between organizations of texts are and of their respective social, political and cultural importance. Therefore, it is impossible to prove that two given organizations of texts should be considered as dialects of one language if this happens to be contested. In many cases it is much easier to show that the difference between two given organizations of texts are evidently so far-reaching that it is impossible to consider them as dialects of one language. Until this whole complex is thoroughly investigated and the necessary criteria found, the only solution for linguistic theory is to disregard the distinction.

It is, of course, practically impossible to work with a variety set containing all languages that can be perceived as different. This means that many observable differences will have to be disregarded in practice. This is the only way in which all practical investigations become possible. The investigator is free to state the criteria of identity as they best suit his purpose. But these criteria must be explicit and as general as possible. In our case it would be preferable if it were possible to establish a general unit of language difference. Then it could be stated in a general way and without individual specifications which differences will be disregarded for every investigation.

Unfortunately, the setting of such a unit presupposes again a general objective criterion for the estimation of differences among languages. As our present knowledge does not make it possible for us to set up such criteria,[5] we shall be constrained to introduce in the linguistic variety set the whole subjective traditional language classification, with its arbitrary distinctions between languages and dialects. But we shall do so explicitly, while stressing that no general criterion underlies the inherited classification and that the differences regarded as relevant are to be listed individually because no general statement about them is possible. In doing so, we shall always remember how unsatisfactory this classification is from a stricter theoretical point of view. But no very serious harm should be feared from our using it in our preliminary considerations, since it embodies an intuitive appraoch to language analysis profitably applied through centuries and it would be unwise to underestimate its value.

In working with the linguistic variety set we have thus great freedom. Any language that can be perceived as different from all others may be a member of the set if we choose so. But we are also at liberty to disregard any difference if we think it convenient. So we shall be free to investigate all properties of the language variety set, and we can hope to find at some future time a strict and adequate method for setting identity criteria for its members.

The concept of a linguistic variety set as sketched above implies that a language is a discrete unit and the languages of two sets of texts can be either identical or different and nothing else. According to this theory, there can be no continuum of sameness and non-sameness in the organization of texts. Wherever any difference can be detected, the languages are to be ruled different except for the differences which are to be disregarded by explicit identity criteria. This is a necessary consequence of the assumption, prevailing in the linguistic theory of our days, that the facts of speech are best accounted for by discrete constructs. If language is a set of discrete constructs, it must itself be a construct and discrete.

Once it is accepted that the linguistic unit has to be distinguished from the text in which it is realized, it becomes impossible to state any positive definition of linguistic units as long as we stick to the taxonomic theory of descriptive linguistics.[6] According to it language is most adequately modelled as an inventory of units and a set of rules containing the restrictions in their distribution in strings which, in their turn, form units of a higher rank.

If the units cannot be defined by the properties of the substance in which they are realized, every unit is defined only by its obligatory non-sameness with all the other units in the inventory to which it belongs.[7] This means that every unit in an inventory is defined by all other units. Hence it follows that no same units can be found in different languages. If every item is defined by its non-sameness with the other items in the inventory, there can be no same units in different inventories. This can be shown by a simple example. Suppose two inventories = A $\{a,b\}$ and = B $\{a,c\}$. In this case a, member of A, is different from a, member of B, because the first is defined by $\neq a\ b$ and the second by $\neq a\ c$. The item a in the two inventories is not identical in spite of its identical expression in our symbolic language and whatever closeness in other respects this may mean. Consequently, the languages in the variety set are absolutely different and have no common units.

By this implication taxonomic linguistic theory fails to account for the intuitively well-known empirical fact that all languages are not different to the same degree. So, for instance, High German differs notably from Low German both in the inventory and in the distribution of phonemes and morphemes. According to the taxonomic theory they ought to be two totally different languages. And yet it is evident that they are much less different one from the other than they both are from, say, Hungarian. The same can be said of Slovenian and Serbo-Croatian. They, too, differ in the inventory and in the distribution of phonemes and morphemes and are consequently totally different in terms of taxonomic language theory. And again this difference is in reality much less than the difference between either of them and Basque.

Whereas diversity among languages in the variety set is unrestricted in terms of taxonomic linguistic theory, the empirical fact of mutual understandability of languages which are distinctly different, and the process of language learning, induce us to assume the existence of restrictions on linguistic diversity. In other words, every adequate linguistic theory has to account for the fact that different languages are not always as different as they could be. In order to meet this requirement, taxonomic linguistic theory has to make use of the concept of CORRESPONDENCE.

Units of different languages may correspond, and it is this correspondence that restricts linguistic diversity. The correspondence relation can even be included in the criteria for language identity, and in that case corresponding units are accepted as identical. A unit can thus belong to more than one language. The diversity of languages having common units and distributions is accordingly restricted. In principle it is possible to measure the extent of these restrictions by counting the common units of two or more languages. But this quantitative unity is of little practical value because it is very difficult to survey and to count the corresponding units on all levels. In spite of this difficulty, the classificaiton of different organizations of texts in languages, dialects and idiolects is, in traditional linguistics, theoretically accounted for just by such inexhaustive counting of correspondences.

It is important to point out that, because of these restrictions in linguistic diversity and its resulting graduality, the languages concerned do not cease to be discrete units. Their variety set does not become a continuum, since linguistic diversity is restricted by the correspondence of units which are themselves discrete.

In transformational generative linguistic theory, as often advocated recently,[8] the whole setting of the problem is different. In this approach language is not modelled as a set of classes of units with specified restrictions on their distribution, but as a partly ordered set of rules generating linguistic units which are in their turn strings of smaller units. Such models, too, are organized in levels but in levels of rules and not in levels of units.

In generating the infinite set of grammatical sentences of a given language the transformational generative models start from a universal unit symoblized by S.[9] All languages begin the generation of their grammatical sentences with this symbol, hence it represents every grammatical sentence of all languages in the variety set. These languages differ only in the rules[10] by which actual sentences are generated. It follows that the sets of rules modelling the different languages in the variety set have at least one element in common: the initial symbol S.

Two languages are identical to the extent to which their models provide identical operations by which they generate their strings from S or from any other point which can be defined universally in the process of generation. The generative rules are the units of such a model and their identity depends not only on the sameness of the generative operation for which they contain instructions but also on the sameness of the generative history of the strings to which these operations apply. Whereas the units of taxonomic language models are only negatively defined by their obligatory non-sameness with all other units in the inventory, the rules of a transformational generative grammar can be defined positively by their position with reference to S or to any other universally defined point in the process of generation, and by the identity of the intervening rules in the partly ordered set. From this difference between the models follows another very important one, from our point of view. While it is logically impossible for taxonomic models of different languages to have units in common, it is possible for transformational generative models to have a common subset of rules. Every rule that appears in more than one grammar restricts the diversity of languages.

In order to account for the empirically-given restrictions on linguistic diversity, transformational generative linguistic theory is not obliged to resort to the additional concept of correspondence. Grammars with a common subset of rules necessarily generate sentences which show correspondence relations. The concept of correspondence is thus implicit in the notion of common rules shared by two or more transformational generative models. Moreover, the number or rules appearing as common elements in the models of two languages provides a means to measure objectively the extent to which linguistic variety is restricted. It is much easier to survey and count the identical rules in two generative grammars than to do the same with corresponding units in two taxonomic descriptions. A criterion for the distinction of dialects from genetically-related languages could eventually be found along these lines.

The ease with which linguistic variety is dealt in terms of transformational generative models, and the obvious unit of measurement for the restrictions imposed on linguistic diversity it offers, provide strong additional arguments for the greater explanatory power of transformational generative linguistic theory.

There is one basic difficulty in applying the unit of measurement for linguistic diversity discussed above: alternative transformational generative models for a language are possible, and they may differ substantially as to the subset of rules they have in common with the model of another language. Moreover, this set can always be enlarged at the expense of the simplicity of the model. This serious difficulty can be overcome only by an additional requirement to the effect that the models in which the common rules are counted should be the most adequate of those brought forward for both languages whose relationship is to be measured. Such a requirement is possible since the evaluation of alternative models as a task of linguistic theory is indisputable.[11]

In its present state, linguistic theory is unable to offer even a criterion by which one can decide whether a proposed model is the best for the language of a given corpus. We can only choose the most adequate from a number of alternative models. This means that we can never tell if a more adequate new model may not appear. It is therefore necessary to always have an open mind for a re-evaluation of language relationship as established by counting the common generative rules in models which, at a certain moment, were judged to be the most adequate of all so far proposed for a set of languages. Linguistic relationships are the subject of continuous investigation whose results must be reconsidered in the light of every new idea that may prove significant for the theory of descriptive models.

The genetic relationships of languages, as established and investigated by comparative linguistics, are a special case of restricted linguistic diversity. Not every linguistic relationship can be qualified as genetic, and there are many cases of related languages whose relationship is not genetic. There are two generally recognized types of non-genetic linguistic relationship. One of them is usually labelled typological. For the other there is no generally accepted label. As it is allegedly the result of so-called linguistic loan, whatever this may mean, we shall call it the loan relationship.

It is easy to neatly distinguish the genetic and loan relationships, since the first is a relationship by origin and the second by contact. Although both concepts, on closer examination, raise a host of difficult problems, they form, at least in principle, a clear-cut opposition, the one being primary and the other secondary. Less clear is the distinction between either of them and typological relationship. Even before the notions of the three types of linguistic relationship are subjected to closer scrutiny it is obvious that in this tripartition there is no consistent *principium divisionis*. While genetic and loan relationships are defined by the way they came about, typological relationship is determined by the way it manifests itself. This immediately raises two questions. The first is: how do genetic and loan relationships manifest themselves? And the second: how does typological relationship come about? It is not difficult to conceive of a typological relationship resulting from common origin or from contact. In such a case one and the same restriction on linguistic variety could simultaneously be typological and either a genetic or a loan relationship.

It is quite usual in linguistics to regard languages as related in more than one way. English and French, e.g., are related genetically and also by loan and typologically. This is true only for the languages as a whole but not for the individual restrictions on their diversity, i.e., for their indivdual correspondences. The correspondence between *mother* and *mère* is classified as a genetic relationship and nothing else, while *voice* and *voix* is described only as a loan relationship. The fact that in both languages the difference between the use of a substnative as subject or as object in a sentence is marked by the order of words only and by no change in their phonemic shape is an example of a purely typological relationship. In the case of the individual correspondence *voice* and *voix* it is impossible to ask whether this correspondence, due to a loan relationship (contact), could simultaneously be a consequence of a genetic relationship (common origin). Such a question is logically inadmissible because common origin and contact, as conceived in linguistics, exclude each other. But it is by no means contrary to logic to ask whether the typological correspondence in the marking of the difference between subject and object may perhaps be an instance of genetic or loan relationship.

On the other hand, Hungarian and Turkish correspond in the way they express grammatical categories. By this correspondence a typological relationship of these languages is established. But the question whether it may be due to common origin, and hence be an instance of genetic relationship, is still very heatedly disputed. It follows that genetic and loan relationship, on the one hand, and typological relationship, on the other, do not logically exclude each other.

In order to gain a clearer insight into the true nature of the different kinds of linguistic relationship, it is necessary to subject them to closer scrutiny and to make the underlying principles of division explicit and consistent. Typology is a classification according to some shared features that are for some reason considered characteristic and important, and are therefore selected as relevant for the classification. In this sense, every linguistic relationship is typological because linguistic relationship is nothing else but corresponding features shared by two or more members of the linguistic variety set.

The conclusion that every linguistic relationship is typological is in full accordance with the view commonly held on typological relationship. It is readily explained as common or corresponding features in the organization of languages. But having defined language as the organization of texts, all corresponding features of languages must by logical necessity be features of organization. Genetic and loan relationships hence must be regarded as two special cases to typological relationship. But it is common linguistic knowledge that Serbo-Croatian and Bulgarian are more closely related genetically than either of them is with Russian, whereas Russian and Serbo-Croatian have a higher degree of typological relationship than either of them has with Bulgarian. It follows clearly from this proposition that here a typological relationship is meant that does not include genetic relationship.

In accepting the legacy of the European linguistic tradition, we must distinguish two different meanings of 'typological relationship'. One, broader, includes genetic and loan relationships and the other, narrower, excludes both.[12] In full accordance with tradition, the term can be reserved for the narrower meaning, because the broader meaning is synonymous with plain linguistic relationship, which is necessarily typological in the general sense of the term.

It remains to define the narrower sense of typological relationship as used in linguistics. The mention of it immediately evokes the familiar classification of languages into synthetic, into inflexional, agglutinative, incorporating and isolating types. In the beginnings of comparative linguistics this typological classification was not clearly distinguished from the establishment of genetic relationship.[13] The typology underlying this division is in fact a typology of the rules by which lexical and grammatical morphemes are combined into words. But in spite of the outstanding importance of such a morphological typology, it cannot be accepted as the sole criterion of typology in the narrower sense. There have been also typological studies in phonology and in syntax. All these comparative studies try to establish correspondences of system equivalence.[14] The more equivalent traits can be shown to exist in the languages compared, the closer is their typological relationship.

Genetic and typological relationships differ in the kind of correspondences by which they are established. In comparative linguistics such correspondences are established for which it may be assumed that they are a consequence of a common origin. The corresponding terms may or may not be equivalent in the respective systems of the languages compared. In typology, only equivalent terms are acknowledged as corresponding and they may or may not be of common origin.

The above discussion shows that it is possible to distinguish neatly between linguistic typology in its narrower sense and comparative linguistics by virtue of a clear-cut difference in the correspondence relations they accept as relevant. But it is impossible to find such a criterion in order to distinguish them both from loan relationship. The correspondences resulting from the contact of languages are, by themselves and without additional information, indistinguishable from mere typological or genetic correspondences. There is no difference between the kind of correspondence in *mother* : *mère* and in voice : *voix*. Only additional information, linguistic and extralinguistic, allow us to decide that the former is to be classified as genetic and the second as a loan relationship.

Languages in contact show a marked tendency to increase the number of equivalent units in the system. The comparative with *more* and *most* in English, the rich case system in Ossetic, the lack of grammatical gender in Armenian and of an infinitive in Bulgarian are examples of loan relationships manifesting themselves as typological relationships. Without additional information it is by no mans possible to distinguish such cases from other typologic correspondences occurring among the most remote languages of the world with no contacts whatsoever, such as, for example, Chinese and Ewe in West Africa both having tones. From this it follows that a typological correspondence may be at the same time a loan correspondence by the way it came about whereas a genetic correspondence cannot simultaneously be a loan correspondence.

This tripartition of linguistic relationships provides a variety of seven different ways in which languages may be related (cf. Figure 1).

	I	II	III	IV	V	VI	VII	VIII
typological	+	+	+	+	−	−	−	−
genetic	+	+	−	−	+	+	−	−
by loan	+	−	+	−	+	−	+	−

Figure 1

All the possibilities provided by our theory of linguistic relationship actually occur in the variety set of languages if typological relationship is taken in the narrower sense. In order to prove this, it will suffice to quote an instance for every possibility: I English and French, II Latin and Sanskrit, III Arabic and Serbo-Croatian, IV Chinese and Ewe, V English and Hindi, VI Ancient Greek and Modern Persian, VII Chinese and Japanese, VIII Chinese and Swahili. In this sketch the non-existence of genetic relationship means only that such a relationship has not yet been established, for it is impossible to demonstrate that two languages are not related genetically.

Because of the existence of very important linguistic universals there are no languages which are altogether unrelated typologically.[15] Therefore, in typological classification, such languages are regarded as unrelated which, besides the universals, have no important typological correspondences, i.e., no such correspondences as have been chosen so far as classification criteria in typological research. It is in this sense that the lack of typological relationship in the adduced instances should be understood. It is an important task for linguistic typology to find exact criteria by which languages can be classified as typologically related or unrelated.

In a similar way, the absence of loan relationship in our instances is not to be interpreted as absolute lack of loans. In such a case our example for II could be discarded because Latin and Sanskrit share the loanword *dēnārius dīnāra* and other. Similar objections could be made in the case of other instances cited above. But a few scattered accidental loanwords are not enough to classify two languages as related by loan. Here again it is impossible to give exact criteria, but we can say that loans, whether lexical or typological, must be numerous and important enough for them to be accepted as evidence of a direct and intense cultural contact. Although this formulation is not too satisfactory from a theoretical point of view, it expresses exactly the current procedure as applied in language classification and is in full accordance with the intuitive knowledge we have of linguistic phenomena. The difference between languages sharing some loan words and deep historical loan relationships is, in practice, mostly evident. There remains a small number of border cases which it may be difficult to find a satisfactory criterion to distinguish.

It would be easy to formalize the criteria by classifying as related any two languages having any typological correspondences beyond the universals or any loan correspondence, even if it is a minor typological feature or a single loan word. The result would be a theoretically neat situation. But typological and loan relationship would, so defined, be of little interest. The formal neatness would be paid for by a complete failure to make the distinctions which alone can foster a deeper understanding of language relationship. There is no doubt that further research will clarify many of these concepts. But even as things are now, it is for most practical purposes possible to handle satisfactorily the principal concepts underlying the classification of languages. Less important and scattered typological and loan correspondences must, therefore, be ignored in a general classification of languages.

The fundamental concepts connected with genetic relationship are therefore to be thoroughly investigated, and it must be shown to what extent they can be conceived as discrete units and where a statistic approximation is needed.

According to the theory sketched above, genetic relationship of languages is a special case of restricted linguistic diversity. Generally, it is defined as partial correspondence due to common origin. Therefore it will be necessary to investigate the notions of origin and descent in linguistics and to see how they can be clearly distinguished from borrowing which provides another kind of restriction on linguistic diversity.

On the other hand, common origin of languages can never be established by direct observation. It can only be inferred from a special kind of characteristic correspondences. An inquiry into the fundamental notion of correspondence is essential for any statement of an explicit theory of genetic relationship in linguistics. It is necessary, also, to distinguish genetic correspondences from typological ones and to specify the conditions that must be fulfilled if a set of languages is to be regarded as genetically related.

As genetic relationships of languages occur in time and space, among socially organized speakers, they are to be considered also in this connection. The questions that arise in connection with this subject are twofold. It must be seen whether and how inferences for extralinguistic history can be drawn from established genetic relationships of languages, and if and what extralinguistic data can be relevant for the establishment of genetic relationship between languages.

Notes

1.   Cf. Chao (1962); Hartmann (1965); and Katičić (1966).

2.   Cf. Šaumjan (1962: 36 ff.).

3.   Cf. Chomsky (1957: 13).

4.   Cf. Chomsky (1964: 10) about the Saussurian implications of his linguistic theory.

5.   For some ideas in this direction cf. Greenberg (1955, 1956, 1957a, 1957b, 1960), Kroeber (1960a and 1960b), Voegelin-Ramanujan-Voegelin (1960), Householder (1960), and Lieberson (1964).

6.   For the term cf. Chomsky (1964: 11).

7.   There was an attempt in descriptive linguistics to reduce the relation of obligatory non-sameness to differences in distribution, but it was not fully successful. Cf., e.g., Harris (1951: § 7.3).

8.   Cf. Chomsky (1964: 9 and 11 ff., 1965: 63 ff.).

9.   Cf. Chomsky (1957: 29 and 1961: 121).
10. Cf. Chomsky (1961).
11. Cf. Chomsky (1957: 50 ff.).
12. Cf. Uspenskij (1965: 23 and 30).
13. Cf. Schlegel (1808).
14. Cf. Bazell (1958), Milewski (1963: 5), and Skalička (1963: 32 ff.).
15. Cf. Greenberg (1963) and Chomsky (1965: 35 ff.).

References

Bazell, C.E. 1958. *Linguistic Typology*. London.
Chao, Y.R. 1962. "Models in linguistics and models in general." In: Nagel, Suppes, and Tarski 1962: 558-66.
Chomsky, N. 1957. *Syntactic Structures*. The Hague: Mouton.
-----. 1961. "On the notion 'rule of grammar'." *Proceedings of the Twelfth Symposium in Applied Mathematics* 12: 6-24 (Repr. in *The Structure of Language* by J.A. Fodor and J.J. Katz. Englewood Cliffs, New Jersey. 1964).
-----. 1964. *Current Issues in Linguistic Theory*. The Hague: Mouton.
-----. 1965. *Aspects of the Theory of Syntax*. Cambridge, Mass.: MIT Press.
Greenberg, J.H. 1955. *Studies in African Linguistic Classification*. New Have: Compass Press.
-----. Greenberg, J.H. 1966. "The measure of linguistic diversity." *Language* 32: 109-15.
-----. 1957a. "The nature and uses of linguistic typologies." *International Journal of American Linguistics* 23: 2ff.
-----. 1957b. *Essays in Linguistics*. Chicago: University of Chicago Press.
-----. 1960. "A quantitative approach to the morphological typology of language." *International Journal of American Linguistics* 26: 178-94.
-----. (ed.). 1963. *Universals of Language*. 2nd ed. Cambridge, Mass.: MIT Press.
Harris, Z.S. 1951. *Methods in Structural Linguistics*. Chicago: University of Chicago Press.
Hartmann, P. 1965. "Modellbildungen in der Sprachwissenschaft." *Studium Generale* 18. 6: 364-379.
Householder, F.W. 1960. "First throughs on syntactic indices." *International Journal of American Linguistics* 26: 195-97.

Katičić, R. 1966. "Modellbegriffe in der vergleichenden Sprachwissenschaft." *Kratylos* 11: 49-67.

Kroeber, A.L. 1960a. "Statistics, Indo-European and Taxonomy." *Language* 36: 1-21.

-----. 1960b. "On typological indices, I, 'ranking of languages'." *International Journal of American Linguistics* 26: 171-77.

Lieberson, S. 1964. "An extension of Greenberg's linguistic diversity measures." *Language* 40: 526-31.

Milewski, T. 1963. "Predposylki tipologičeskogo jazykoznanija." In: *Issledovanija po strukturnoj tipologii*. Moskva: Nauka. 3-31.

Nagel, E., P. Suppes, and A. Tarski. (eds). 1962. *Proceedings of the 1960 International Congress on Logic, Methodology, and Philosophy of Science*. Stanford: Stanford University Press.

Šaumjan, S.K. 1962. *Problemy teoretičeskoj fonologii*. Moskva: Nauka.

Schlegel, F. v. 1808. *Ueber die Sprache und Weisheit der Indier: Ein Beitrag zur Begründung der Altertumskunde*. Heidelberg.

Skalička, V. 1963. "Tipologija i toždesvennost' jazykov." *Issledovanija po strukturnoj tipologii*. Moskva: Nauka. 32-34.

Uspenskij, B.A. 1965. *Strukturnaja tipologija jazykov* Moskva: Nauka.

Voegelin, C.F., Ramanujan, A.K. and F.M. Voegelin. 1960. "Typology of density ranges, I, 'Introduction'." *International Journal of American Linguistics* 26: 195-197.

Language contacts in multilingual Vojvodina

Melanie Mikes
Faculty of Philosophy, University of Novi Sad

When treating language contacts in the framework of a paper, one has to decide whether to survey the issues in the whole research field or to focus on one of its segments and treat it in detail. I have decided on the latter, my choice being the use of two languages by secondary school pupils — native speakers of Hungarian, Slovak, Rumanian, Ruthenian and Serbo-Croatian. However, in order to bring the issues closer to potential readers, I have found it necessary to describe the multilingual setting in Vojvodina and the languages involved in this setting.

A European case of language contacts

Vojvodina, an autonomous province (part of the SR Serbia) situated in north-east Yugoslavia (about two million inhabitants), has many of the features of a European multilingual community, especially the following ones:
(1) a centuries-old coexistence of ethno-linguistic communities;
(2) standardized languages used by the members of these ethno-linguistic communities in oral and written communication;
(3) the tradition of an institutional linguistic pluralism.

1 The description of the multilingual and multi-ethnic structure of Vojvodina is based both on sociolinguistic and linguistic criteria. The non-identity of the sociocultural and linguistic community is kept in mind, although a high degree of mutual interpenetration must be admitted. So in Vojvodina there are ethno-linguistic communities — Hungarians, Slovaks, Rumanians, Ruthenians, Germans; ethnic communities — Jews and Romanies; and a complex linguistic community, the Serbo-Croatian pluri-

ethnic community of Serbs, Croats, Montenegrins and Moslems.

In prehistorical and ancient times different peoples and tribes lived in the territory of Vojvodina, Slavs and Hungarians being among them. At the end of the 14th and at the beginning of the 15th century new waves of migrations of Serbs from the Balkan Peninsula took place. Under the domination of the Turks the population of Vojvodina greatly declined in number. It was not before the end of the 17th century that new settlers from Serbia came to Vojvodina, led by the patriarch Čarnojević. In the 18th century the population of Vojvodina increased rapidly due to mass colonization by Germans, Hungarians, Slovaks, Rumanians and Ruthenians. This mass colonization continued into the 19th century, the new settlers being Germans (in the first half of the century) and Hungarians and Slovaks (in the second half of the century). At the end of the 19th century the number of inhabitants became more or less constant, but in the 20th century migrations continued. There were three main migrations: one to America, an economic emigration at the beginning of the century, and two political emigrations after the first and second world wars to Hungary, Germany and Austria. At the same time, two immigrations took place, both originating from the mountainous parts of Yugoslavia which had been devastated by the wars.

Serbs, Hungarians and Croats are the oldest inhabitants of Vojvodina. Serbs immigrated in small and large groups, sometimes spontaneously, but there were also organized and planned immigrations. After the last one (after the second world war) the Serb population in Vojvodina gained much both in number and ethnic compactness. Croats immigrated during Turkish domination. Hungarians were mostly settled there after the Turks had been expelled. They were concentrated in large settlements in the north of Vojvodina near the Hungarian frontier. Rumanians also belong to the old settlers in the part of Vojvodina which borders upon Rumania. The Germans, who represented an important ethno-demographical factor from the middle of the 18th century to 1945, live in diaspora today. That is the consequence of the majority leaving Yugoslavia after the second world war. The Slovaks and Ruthenians are mostly concentrated in settlements situated in the southern part of Vojvodina. The Jews are very longstanding settlers of Vojvodina, from the Ukraine by origin. Their mother tongue is predominantly Hungarian. Today their numbers are very low, because many of them fell victim to the fascist terror, and some of them have emigrated to Israel. The Romanies are, in origin, from Rumania and Turkey, and can be found all over Vojvodina (Bukurov 1954). Their non-ethnic mother tongue is most often Rumanian.

According to the census of 1953, Serbs made up 50,6% of the population of Vojvodina, Hungarians 25,7%, Croats 8,1%, Slovaks 4,3%, Rumanians 3,6%, Germans 1,9%, Montenegrins 1,8%, Ruthenians 1,3%, Romanies and Jews less than 0,5%. According to the census of 1981, Serbs made up 55%, Hungarians 19%, Croats 5%, Slovaks 3%, Rumanians 2%, Montenegrins 2%, Ruthenians 1%, Germans, Jews and Romanies less than 0.5%; 8% of the population of Vojvodina declared themselves Yugoslavs.

The people who declared themselves Yugoslav belong to different linguistic communities in Vojvodina. No general tendency towards making such a declaration can be registered because of the sociolinguistic status of a language. The mother tongue of those who declared themselves Yugoslav (according to the data of the census in 1971) is predominantly Serbo-Croatian (82.8%), followed by Hungarian (9.5%), while German and Slovak are represented by somewhat less than 1%, and the other languages, such as Romany, Rumanian, Macedonian, Slovene, Ruthenian and Albanian, by less than 0.5%.

The effects of the centuries-old coexistence of ethno-linguistic communities in Vojvodina may be seen in the linguistic overlapping of these communities, i.e. in the language shift (when a child's mother tongue differs from the mother tongue of both parents) or in the divergent acquisition of the mother tongue and the nationality by origin (when a child in a mixed ethno-linguistic micro-environment acquires the language of one parent and the nationality of the other parent). However, this process plays a minor role in the interlinguistic and interethnic relations of Vojvodina, because the ethno-linguistic intergroups which have been developing as the result of this process comprise only 1.6% of the total population of Vojvodina (after the census of 1971). The most numerous intergroups are those where the mother tongue of Hungarians, Slovaks, Rumanians or Rutheniana is Serbo-Croatian. However, if the number and size of the ethno-linguistic communities in Vojvodina is taken into consideration, the spread of Serbo-Croatian the mother tongue of Hungarians, Slovaks, Rumanians and Ruthenians is relatively less than the spread of the ethnic languages of each of these nationalities among Serbs, Croats and Montenegrins (together).

The members of the ethno-linguistic intergroups in Vojvodina mainly have their origin in mixed ethno-linguistic marriages. The number of such marriages depends on the ethno-linguistic structure of the population in a mixed region and the tradition of the cultural interpenetration.

2. When taking into consideration the overall genetic linguistic distinctions, language contacts in Vojvodina may be grouped as follows:
(a) language contacts with a high degree of distance — between Hungarian, on the one hand, and the Serbo-Croatian, Slovak, Rumanian or Ruthenian language, on the other;
(b) language contacts of a medium degree of distance — between Rumanian or German, on the one hand, and the Serbo-Croatian, Slovak or Ruthenian language, on the other;
(c) language contacts of a low degree of distance — between Serbo-Croatian, on the one hand, and the Slovak or Ruthenian language, on the other.

Some of these contacts are sporadic; for instance, the contacts between Rumanian and Ruthenian. Other contacts were more prevalent in the past than nowadays; for instance, the contacts between German and Hungarian, or between Hungarian and Slovak, or between German and Serbo-Croatian.

All these languages in contact have their standardized forms and local variants (except Ruthenian) based on dialects brought from the regions the different groups came from. The creation of the standard norm in Serbo-Croatian, Rumanian, Slovak and Hungarian took place in the last century as part of the cultural and linguistic movements of peoples living in the Habsburg Monarchy. In history this process is known as the struggle for the creation of a literary language. It sprang up from the needs of the bourgeois society, aiming at quick and successful communication, to which dialects had been a serious obstacle. However, beside this common feature, there were some differences due to the particularities of the historical development of different peoples and their language tradition, as well as to the different conceptions of solving the problems.

Unlike the other languages of Vojvodina, Ruthenian is spoken only in Yugoslavia (Kočiš 1978). It is a relatively young language. The first school grammar was published in 1923, the first spelling dictionary in 1971, and the first dictionary in 1972. The norms for Ruthenian are set up in Yugoslavia, while the norms for Hungarian, Rumanian and Slovak are in the care of the academies in Hungary, Rumania and Slovakia. Therefore no separate standard variants of these languages have been developed in Vojvodina.

3. Institutional forms of multilingualism have a long tradition in Voj-vodina. The period from 1784 to 1918, i.e. from the first decree on language (isued by the Austrian emperor Joseph II) until the breakdown of the Austro-Hungarian Monarchy, is very important for the history of multilin-gualism. During that time the greater part of Vojvodina was under the administration of the Hungarian part of the Dual Monarchy, and the smal-ler one belonged to Croatia, which was attached to the Hungarian Crown.

In the first half of the 19th century, on the territory under Hungarian administration the use of Hungarian was introduced by language laws in many fields of public life where Latin or German had been used before. Other languages were neglected. The first law on the equality of nationalities was enacted in 1868. One of the principles of this law was the liberal concept of moral and natural legal protection based on the indi-vidual liberty of citizens. It is by this law that the question of state language was regulated. The language was Hungarian, and that was the language of the legislation, too. The laws were enacted in Hungarian, but they were published in verified translations in all the nationality languages. Language use was regulated by the same law. According to it, every citizen had the right to ask for legal protection in his mother tongue. Some legal provisions were made to promote individual bilingualism, by given possibilities to all students to be educated in their mother tongue. However, only public schools were obliged by these provisions.

In the part of Vojvodina which belonged to Croatia the language of administration and legislation was Croatian, according to a law enacted in 1868. Another law, enacted in 1874, declared Croatian the language of instruction in public schools. In schools founded and supported by members of nationalities whose mother tongue was not Croatian the instruction was given in the mother tongue of the respective nationality, but Croatian had to be taught as a school subject. In such schools the language of instruction might have been Croatian, but in this case the mother tongue as a subject was obligatory (Hok 1972).

These, from the historical point of view, progressive tendencies towards institutional language pluralism were interrupted in the period between the two world wars (1918-1941), when the use of Serbo-Croatian was obligatory in all the spheres of public life.

Vojvodina and the Yugoslav model of multilingualism

The Yugoslav model of multilingualism is a heuristic construct, the theoretical basis of which is cultural pluralism, and the institutional forms of multilingualism its operational elements in practice. This model of multilinguals envisages several ways to realize the equal linguistic and cultural rights of nations and nationalities ('minorities'), in conformity with the orientation to cultural pluralism and depending on the cultural heritage, historical conditions, demographical factors, socioeconomical development of the multilingual region, and the linguistic and cultural distance of languages and cultures in contact. The role of language in the realization of equal rights is not limited to the cultural domain, but has been extending to all domains of like (Mikes 1978).

When viewing it from the standpoint of the four paradigms (discontinuity, choice, adaptation and assimilation) of a global typology of interethnic communication, postulated by Bugarski (1986), the Yugoslav model of multilingualism is favourable to the transformation of the adaptation paradigm, which dominated in the period between the two wars, into the choice paradigm, where none of the autochthonous languages is an officially stated language of broader communication. Nevertheless, Serbo-Croatian has practically maintained the role of an unofficial *lingua franca*, but with other socio-political correlates than those it had in pre-war Yugoslavia.

Vojvodina is a socio-political community which bears all the relevant features of the Yugoslav model of multilingualism, and is its most representative example.

The provisions of the constitutional law envisage that the use of Serbo-Croatian, Hungarian, Slovak, Rumanian and Ruthenian enjoy equal rights in public administration, enterprise, jurisdiction, mass media, culture and education. In order to meet the claims of these legal provisions the following facilities have been set up: special services for translation, newspapers and periodicals in five languages, television and radio transmissions in five languages, an institute for editing textbooks in five languages, primary and secondary schools where pupils can choose to be taught in one of the five language while learning another language as a school subject, various associations and institutions in the field of culture, science and university education, etc.

For the main topic of this paper, which is the use of two languages by secondary school pupils, it is of prime interest to see how the Yugoslav model of multilingualism is reflected in the typology of bilingualism in the educational system of Vojvodina. This typology of mine (Mikeš 1974) has been based on Mackey's typology of bilingual education (Mackey 1970) but elaborated so as to fit the system and practice in Vojvodina. The patterns I have set up comprise three criteria:

The first criterion is the language of instruction (ED), which may be the pupils' mother tongue (L1) or their second language (L2), or, if the instruction is bilingual, both languages (L1 + L2). Each of the five languages may be the language of instruction L1, while the language of instruction L2 is in practice Serbo-Croatian (with some exceptions). If the instruction is given in two languages, one of them is always Serbo-Croatian.

The second criterion is the language spoken by at least two-thirds of the population of the respective locality (LOC). With regard to a group of pupils, this language may be L1 or L2. If none of the languages are spoken by two thirds of the population, the languages spoken by at least one third of the population are the languages of the bilingual locality. In most cases one of the languages is Serbo-Croatian, although the combinations of Hungarian and Ruthenian or Slovak may also be found. There are trilingual localities, too: Hungarian/Serbo-Croatian/Rumanian(Ruthenian)(Slovak) localities.

The third criterion is the language spoken by at least two thirds of the population of the respective municipality (MUN). As in the case of locality, this language may be the pupils' L1 or L2. There are bilingual and trilingual municipalities, too.

The most widespread type in the educational practice of Vojvodina is instruction in L1, and teaching L2 as a school subject. (This type may be realized in the patterns presented in *Table* 1.)

However, it may happen that matter-of-fact reasons do not make it possible to organize the instruction in the mother tongue of pupils, or the parents wish their children to be educated in Serbo-Croatian. In such cases the pupils whose mother tongue is Hungarian, Slovak, Rumanian or Ruthenian are not taught in their mother tongue, but they learn it as a school subject, with the aim of improving knowledge of it and cultivating it.

Instruction in two languages is not usual in Vojvodina, except in some kindergartens where it is a part of the preschool educational system, and in some secondary schools as a temporary device. So the children who acquire early bilingualism in the family (about 10% of pupils in some major educational centers) are not included in this typology.

Table 1

ED : L1 + /L2/	Ex. ED : Serbo-Croatian + /Hungarian/
LOC : L2	LOC: Hungarian
MUN: L2	MUN: Hungarian
ED : L1 + /L2/	Ex. ED : Serbo-Croatian + /Slovak/
LOC : L2	LOC : Slovak
MUN: L1	MUN: Serbo-Croatian
ED : L1 + /L2/	Ex. ED : Serbo-Croatian + /Hungarian/
LOC : L1	LOC : Serbo-Croatian
MUN: L2	MUN: Hungarian
ED : L1 + /L2/	Ex. ED : Slovak + /Serbo-Croatian/
LOC : L1	LOC : Slovak
MUN: L1	MUN: Slovak
ED : L1 + /L2/	Ex. ED : Ruthenian + /Serbo-Croatian/
LOC : L1 + L2	LOC : Ruthenian + Serbo-Croatian
MUN: L2	MUN: Serbo-Croatian
ED : L1 + /L2/	Ex. ED : Serbo-Croatian + /Rumanian/
LOC : L2	LOC : Rumanian
MUN: L1 + L2	MUN: Serbo-Croatian + Rumanian
ED : L1 + /L2/	Ex. ED : Serbo-Croatian + /Rumanian/
LOC : L1 + L2	LOC : Serbo-Croatian + Rumanian
MUN: L1 + L2	MUN: Serbo-Croatian + Rumanian
ED : L1 + /L2/	Ex. ED : Hungarian + /Serbo-Croatian/
LOC : L1 + L2	LOC : Hungarian
MUN: L1	MUN: Hungarian
ED : L1 + /L2/	Ex. ED : Rumanian + /Serbo-Croatian/
LOC : L1	LOC : Rumanian
MUN: L1 + L2	MUN: Rumanian + Serbo-Croatian

Patterns of language use

The typology of bilingualism in the educational system of Vojvodina underlies the grouping of our informants, secondary school pupils, and makes possible the comparison of language use between the groups of pupils who belong to the same typological pattern (TP) but are differentiated by their L1 and L2. They were all presented with the same questionnaire in the period from 1973 to 1975, and the partial analyses of the results obtained by these investigations were presented in several papers.[1] For the purpose of this paper I have constructed patterns of language use (LUP), which represent the speech behaviour of groups of informants in various domains of language use with interlocutors of various ethno-linguistic backgrounds and various linguistic competence in L1 and L2 of the informants.

The components of LUP are the following four domains of language use: AT SCHOOL, AT A PARTY, IN PUBLIC and INTIMATE; the ethno-linguistic feature of the interlocutor: L1 interlocutor and L2 interlocutor; the informant's mother tongue and second language (L1 and L2). The answers to the questions in the questionnaire contain many other elements which are not included in LUPs, as for instance: the degree of the interlocutor's bilingualism, role relationship, etc. These data are also taken into consideration in the analysis of language use.

The analysis comprises five TPs, with a total of 13 LUPs, and they illustrate an aspect of language contact both inside an ethno-linguistic group (communication with L1 interlocutors) and between two different ethno-linguistic groups (communication with L2 interlocutors). Institutional (educational) and environmental factors appear in congruent and incongruous combinations, which represent five different situations where the informants' mother tongue has been developing and existing, individual bilingualism has been acquired and both the mother tongue and the second language have been used.

1   Two groups of informants belonging to TP1 have been investigated. The first comprises secondary school pupils in Senta, an agricultural town in the north of Vojvodina. They are all Hungarians, and their mother tongue is Hungarian. Serbo-Croatian is their second language, which they usually begin to acquire in kindergarten, by language teaching methods suitable their age and the kindergarten pedagogical activities (playing, dancing, singing, etc.) The second group comprises secondary school pupils in Bački Petrovac, a municipality not far from Novi Sad, the capital of Vojvodina. These informants are Slovaks, and their mother tongue is Slovak, a language close to Serbo-Croatian, their second language. (Cf. *Table* 2.)

Table 2

TP 1
ED   : L1 + /L2/
LOC : L1
MUN : L1

LUP of Hungarian native speakers (Senta)

Domain	L1 interlocutor		L2 interlocutor	
	L1%	L2%	L1%	L2%
At school	82	2	6	69
At party	84	2	32	28
In public	90	2	31	43
Intimate	86	2	34	29

LUP of Slovak native speakers (Bački Petrovac)

Domain	L1 interlocutor		L2 interlocutor	
	L1%	L2%	L1%	L2%
At school	87	0.3	12	47
At party	89	0.4	27	44
In public	89	2	29	49
Intimate	80	1	26	36

The informants were not obliged to answer all the questions on the questionnaire. So, a rather large number of them did not answer the questions in the domain INTIMATE (5-13% of Hungarians, 9-24% of Slovaks). This result may be explained by the lack of experience in this domain in general, and particularly with the member of another ethno-linguistic community. Namely, this domain of language use was described to the informants as comprising interactions with persons of the other sex to whom they were emotionally attached.

The questions in the domains AT A PARTY, IN PUBLIC and INTI-MATE were so formulated as to reach a conclusion about the relevance of the interlocutors' ethno-linguistic membership and their bilingual competence in the choice of language. When communicating with members of their ethno-linguistic commmunity, the informants of both groups are not concerned very much with the bilingual competence of their interlocutors.

The difference between the use of the mother tongue with the interlocutors who can speak both languages well and those whose knowledge of Serbo-Croatian is very poor makes up only 4% on an average. However, when communicating with members of another (Serbo-Croatian) ethnolinguistic community the interlocutors' bilingual competence has a great relevance. The difference between the use of mother tongue with the interlocutors who can speak both languages well and those whose knowledge of the informants' mother tongue is very poor amounts to 42% Hungarians, and 46% Slovaks.

The informants belonging to the Hungarian ethno-linguistic community attend a school in which there are sections with instruction in Hungarian and sections with instruction in Serbo-Croatian (which are frequented by some Hungarian pupils, too). So we have been able to make inquiries into the use of the mother tongue with the schoolmates attending the same section as well as with those Hungarian pupils attending the sections with the instruction in Serbo-Croatian. We have concluded that the Hungarian language is used far less in communication with Hungarian pupils frequenting sections with instruction in Serbo-Croatian than with those who attend the sections with instruction in Hungarian, the difference being 37%.

2. Three groups of informants belonging to TP2 have been investigated. The first group comprises secondary school pupils in Novi Sad, the capital of Vojvodina, where 13% of the population belong to the Hungarian ethno-linguistic community. All informants are Hungarians who speak Serbo-Croatian well. The second group comprehends secondary school pupils in Senta. Their mother tongue is Serbo-Croatian. A great deal of them have also acquired Hungarian, mainly those pupils whose parents have lived in Senta for a long time, and do not belong to the immigrant population from the central and southern part of Yugoslavia. They all learn Hungarian as a school subject. The third group comprehends secondary school pupils in Vršac, a town situated near the Rumainan border, with a well developed Rumainain cultural life. All the informants are Rumanians. (Cf. *Table* 3.)

Table 3

TP 2
ED   : L1 + /L2/
LOC : L2
MUN : L2

LUP of Hungarian native speakers (Novi Sad)

Domain	L1 interlocutor		L2 interlocutor	
	L1%	L2%	L1%	L2%
At school	78	0.5	3	88
At party	87	3	27	38
In public	78	16	24	61
Intimate	78	2	26	38

LUP of Serbo-Croatian native speakers (Senta)

Domain	L1 interlocutor		L2 interlocutor	
	L1%	L2%	L1%	L2%
At school	94	4	61	22
At party	84	5	56	23
In public	91	3	65	17
Intimate	87	4	68	13

LUP of Rumanian native speakers (Vršac)

Domain	L1 interlocutor		L2 interlocutor	
	L1%	L2%	L1%	L2%
At school	82	8	2	96
At party	85	3	25	56
In public	81	7	18	66
Intimate	84	4	23	56

Inside the ethno-linguistic groups communication in the mother tongue is dominant. It is most evident in the group of Serbo-Croatian native speakers, where it reaches the highest percentage in the domains AT SCHOOL and IN PUBLIC. Vacillations in the choice of language use are not much greater than in LUPs belonging to TP1, but it should be noticed that in the group of Serbo-Croatian native speakers such vacillations depend on the domain of language use, making only 2% in the domain AT SCHOOL, while in the domain AT A PARTY they reach 11%.

When communicating with interlocutors of another ethno-linguistic community, the use of L2 is expressed more by Hungarians and Rumanians than by the Serbo-Croatian speakers. Vacillations in the choice of language with L2 interlocutors are more present than in the intra-group communication. Most vacillations have been observed in the communication of Hungarians with Serbo-Croatian native speakers, and that in the domains AT A PARTY and INTIMATE, but in the domain AT SCHOOL they are quite negligible when Rumanians are communicating with Serbo-Croatian native speakers, and nearly all of them choose Serbo-Croatian (96%).

Refusal to answer, as in the LUPs belonging to TP1, has been mostly observed in the domain INTIMATE (up to 15%).

When communicating with interlocutors of another ethno-linguistic community, the informants pay attention to the bilingual competence of the interlocutors. The difference between the use of mother tongue with interlocutors who speak both languages well and those who have a poor knowledge of the informants' mother tongue is 35% in Hungarians, 34% in Serbo-Croatian speakers, and 39% in Rumanians, on average. However, in the intra-group communication Rumanians, unlike Hungarians and Serbo-Croatian native speakers, pay attention to the bilingual competence of their L1 interlocutors. The difference between the use of mother tongue with interlocutors who speak both languages well and those whose knowledge of Serbo-Croatian is very poor amounts to 23%.

Hungarian and Rumanian informants communicate much less in their mother tongue with schoolmates of their ethno-linguistic community attending the sections with instruction in Serbo-Croatian than they do when communicating with schoolmates of their section. This difference amounts to 48% in Hungarians and 40% in Rumanians.

3. Three groups of informants belonging to TP3 have been investigated. The first group comprises secondary school pupils in Subotica, a city in north Vojvodina, near the Hungarian border, where half of the population is Hungarian and the other half Serbo-Croatian native speakers. There are many bilinguals among the members of both ethno-linguistic communities. The second group comprises secondary school pupils in Ruski Krstur, a place in the central part of Vojvodina. Ruski Krstur is the cultural center of

Ruthenians and the center of their concentration. All informants are Ruthenians. Their knowledge of Serbo-Croatian, which is very close to their mother tongue, is good. In this school the instruction is not given only in Ruthenian, and some subjects are taught in Serbo-Croatian, because of the lack of teaching staff. The third group comprises secondary school pupils in Alibunar, a municipality in the eastern part of Vojvodina, where most of the Rumanians live. This municipality has a very developed bilingual administration. All informants are Rumanians, and Serbo-Croatian is their second language. (Cf. *Table* 4.)

The dominance of the mother tongue has been observed in intra-group communication in all groups, but is less present in Rumanians than in the informants of the other two groups. This dominance is very evident in Ruthenians, where the polarization between the use of mother tongue as the medium of communication inside the ethno-linguistic community and the use of Serbo-Croatian as the medium of communication in inter-group interactions reaches nearly the absolute values in the domain AT SCHOOL. Vacillations in the choice of language with L1 interlocutors are minimal in Ruthenians (0.4-3%), somewhat more present in Hungarians (10-16%), while in Rumanians these vacillations or the alternative use of the mother tongue and Serbo-Croatian are even greater in some domains than in the communication with L2 interlocutors, ranging from 8 to 25%.

In inter-group communication the dominance of L2 has been observed only in the domain AT SCHOOL. In other domains the use of L2 ranges from 50 to 60%, and in Hungarians it is still lower. They use both languages alternately (or they hesitate in their choice) in 21-39% of the cases. This phenomenon is less present in Rumanians (11.5-17%) and in Ruthenians (0,6-11%). It should be mentioned that this phenomenon might be negligible in Ruthenians in the domain AT SCHOOL; namely, nearly all the informants use Serbo-Croatian.

The refusal to answer, unlike in LUPs belonging to TP1 and TP2, has been mostly observed in the domain IN PUBLIC, and that, in Hungarians (up to 14%) and in Ruthanians (up to 11%), while it is quite negligible in Rumanians.

In inter-group communication (with Serbo-Croatian native speakers), the informants of all groups pay attention to the bilingual competence of their interlocutors. This attitude has mostly been observed in Ruthenians, where the difference between the use of mother tongue with interlocutors who speak both languages well and those whose knowledge of Serbo-Croa-

Table 4

```
TP 3
ED  :  L1 + /L2/
LOC :  L1 or L1 + L2
MUN :  L2 or L1 + L2
```

LUP of Hungarian native speakers (Subotica)

Domain	L1 interlocutor		L2 interlocutor	
	L1%	L2%	L1%	L2%
At school	80	4	5	74
At party	86	4	37	32
In public	83	7	34	44
Intimate	85	3	38	23

LUP of Ruthenian native speakers (Ruski Krstur)

Domain	L1 interlocutor		L2 interlocutor	
	L1%	L2%	L1%	L2%
At school	96	2,5	1,4	98
At party	97	1	38	51
In public	95	2	41	52
Intimate	98	1,6	36	55

LUP of Rumanian native speakers (Alibunar)

Domain	L1 interlocutor		L2 interlocutor	
	L1%	L2%	L1%	L2%
At school	81	11	0,5	88
At party	69	6	25	58
In public	67	19	32	53
Intimate	73	7	26	61

tian is poor makes 69% on an average. In intra-group communication Rumanians, as in the previous TP, pay attention to the bilingual competence of their L1 interlocutors. The difference between the use of mother tongue with intérlocutors who speak both languages well and those whose

knowledge of Serbo-Croatian is poor amounts to 28% on average. It ought
to be mentioned that in the domains AT A PARTY and IN PUBLIC this
difference amounts to 33%, and in the domain INTIMATE only 19%.

The difference between the use of mother tongue with schoolmates of
the same section and that with schoolmates who attend sections with
instruction in Serbo-Croatian totals 37% in Hungarians (as in the informants belonging to TP1), 29% in Rumanians and 11% in Ruthenians.

Role relationship is relevant to the language choice in Rumanians
when they talk about family affairs and their intimate life. The use of
mother tongue in intra-group communication is 16% or 12% higher when
they talk with their schoolmates than when they talk with their teachers.

4. Two groups of informants belonging to TP4 have been investigated. The
first group includes Rumanian secondary school pupils in Alibunar. These
pupils attend the same school as the informants belonging to TP3, but they
are taught in Serbo-Croatian, which is their second language. The second
group comprises secondary school pupils in Stara Pazova, a small town
situated in the south of Vojvodina about thirty kilometers north of Belgrade. All the informants are Slovaks who attend instruction in Serbo-Croatian. (Cf. *Table* 5.)

In both groups, the mother tongue is used less in intra-group communication than in the groups belonging to TP1, TP2 and TP3, but is still used
by the majority of informants — 67% in Rumanians and 77% in Slovaks,
on average. The mother tongue is used less in the domain AT SCHOOL
than in the other domains. Its use is 22% lower in Rumanians, and 28%
lower in Slovaks. In this domain 31% of the Rumanians use Serbo-Croatian, and 18% of them use both languages alternately or they hesitate in
their choice. Only 6% of Slovaks use Serbo-Croatian in this domain and
33% of them hesitate in the choice of language or they use both languages
alternately. In other domains the alternate use of both languages or hesita-
tion in choice are less frequent — 11-13% in Rumanians and 7-10% in
Slovaks.

In inter-group communication the dominance of Serbo-Croatian is
almost absolute in the domain AT SCHOOL. In other domains its dominance is 26% lower in Rumanians and 33% in Slovaks. Vacillations in language choice or the alternate use of both languages are approximately as
frequent as in intra-group interactions in Rumanians (14-16%), while this
phenomenon is more frequent in Slovaks (23-34%), except in the domain

Table 5

TP 4
ED   :   L2 + /L1/
LOC :   L1 + L2
MUN :   L2 or L1 + L2

LUP of Rumanian native speakers (Alibunar)

Domain	L1 interlocutor		L2 interlocutor	
	L1%	L2%	L1%	L2%
At school	51	31	0,8	99
At party	73	14	12	72
In public	73	16	12	74
Intimate	73	14	13	73

LUP of Slovak native speakers (Stara Pazova)

Domain	L1 interlocutor		L2 interlocutor	
	L1%	L2%	L1%	L2%
At school	61	6	-	97
At party	88	2	17	60
In public	87	3	13	67
Intimate	91	2	2	64

AT SCHOOL, where this phenomenon has not been observed at all in Rumanians and represented by only 3% of the Slovaks.

Rumanians, as in the previous TPs, pay attention to the bilingual competence of their L1 interlocutors, while this is less relevant in Slovaks. The difference between the use of mother tongue with interlocutors who speak both languages well and those who have a poor knowledge of Serbo-Croatian is 36% in Rumanians, and only 9% in Slovaks. However, in intra-group interactions the informants of both groups pay attention to the bilingual competence of their interlocutors. So the difference between the use of mother tongue with the L2 interlocutors who speak both languages well and that with those who have a poor knowledge of the informants' mother tongue amounts to 21% in Rumanians, and 28% in Slovaks, on average.

It has already been noticed that the Rumanians who are taught in their mother tongue at school distinguish between the use of mother tongue and

Serbo-Croatian when communicating with the schoolmates of their section
and when communicating with Rumanian schoolmates attending sections
with instruction in Serbo-Croatian. This difference amounts to 29%, as has
already been noted. The data obtained from the answers of Rumanian
pupils attending instruction in Serbo-Croatian is in accordance with the
above mentioned difference. These informants use their mother tongue
28% more when communicating with schoolmates who are taught in Rumanian.

In this group of Rumanians, role relationship is only relevant when
they are talking about intimate affairs. The use of mother tongue in intra-
group interactions is higher by 24% when the informants are talking to their
schoolmates than when they are talking to their teachers.

5 Three groups of informants belonging to TP5 have been investigated.
All groups are made up of secondary school pupils in Novi Sad, the capital
of Vojvodina. The mother tongues of these informants are used in
administration and public services in the territory of this city. At school
they attend instruction in Serbo-Croatian as their second language. (Cf.
Table 6.)

Serbo-Croatian is greatly used in intra-group communication in all
groups, and is dominant in the domain AT SCHOOL in Hungarians and
Ruthenians. The Hungarian group shows the dominance of Serbo-Croatian
in the domain IN PUBLIC, too, and represents the group with the lowest
rate of mother tongue use, which amounts to 43% on an average. This is
the only group we have investigated in which the use of the mother tongue
falls below 50%. Vacillations in language choice or the alternate use of both
languages have been noticed in a relatively small number of informants.
They are minimal in Ruthenians (0-4%), somewhat greater in Hungarians
(1-11%), and reach 16% in Slovaks in the domain AT SCHOOL.

In inter-group interactions the dominance of Serbo-Croatian is evident
in all groups, especially in the domain AT SCHOOL. Vacillations in language use or the alternate use of both languages are even less frequent than
in intra-group interactions, the least in the domain AT SCHOOL, and
somewhat more in the domain AT A PARTY.

As to their concern for the bilingual competence of their interlocutors,
the informants of these three groups are very different. This may be seen in
the following survey of the average difference between the L1 use with

Table 6

TP 5
ED : L2
LOC : L2
MUN : L2

LUP of Hungarian native speakers (Novi Sad)

Domain	L1 interlocutor		L2 interlocutor	
	L1%	L2%	L1%	L2%
At school	22	75	2	97
At party	53	36	9	82
In public	44	54	7	89
Intimate	54	37	9	87

LUP of Slovak native speakers (Novi Sad)[2]

Domain	L1 interlocutor		L2 interlocutor	
	L1%	L2%	L1%	L2%
At school	44	40	-	96
At party	84	7	23	64
In public	74	17	21	69
Intimate	84	5	24	64

LUP of Ruthenian native speakers (Novi Sad)

Domain	L1 interlocutor		L2 interlocutor	
	L1%	L2%	L1%	L2%
At school	26	70	-	100
At party	79	21	20	70
In public	79	17	23	73
Intimate	80	18	14	74

interlocutors who speak both languages well and that with those who do not speak one of the languages well:

	Hungarians	Slovaks	Ruthenians
L1 interlocutor	49%	11%	21%
L2 interlocutor	15%	45%	38%

A great difference has been noticed in intra-group communication among Hungarians, while with Slovaks and Ruthenians this difference is minor. Among Hungarians, unlike the other two groups, the difference in inter-group communication is relatively little. This may be due to the infrequent use of L1 in inter-group communication.

In all groups the role relationship is a relevant factor in the domain AT SCHOOL. Hungarians use their mother tongue in interactions with Hungarian schoolmates 18% more than in interactions with Hungarian teachers. This percentage is even greater among Slovaks (42%) and Ruthenians (44%).

Although there has been no instruction in their mother tongue in the school these informants frequented, the possibility of language choice in case they were in a school where such instruction is given was submitted to the Hungarian and Ruthenian informants. The differences in language choice are significant in both groups: 39% of the Hungarians and 45% of the Ruthenians would rather use their mother tongue in interactions with schoolmates of their nationality frequenting the sections where the instruction is given in their mother tongue as compared to the interactions with the schoolmates of their nationality who, like them, are attending the sections where the instruction is given in Serbo-Croatian.

6 Summing up the results of our analysis, we have found it possible to distinguish five groups of informants with respect to *intra-group communication*. The first group comprises the informants of Ruthenian nationality belonging to TP3, where 97% of the informants. on average, use their mother tongue in interactions with L1 interlocutors. The second group comprises informants in which the use of the mother tongue with L1 interlocutors ranges from 86% to 89%, on average. These are the native speakers of Serbo-Croatian belonging to TP2 and the informants of Slovak and Hungarian nationality belonging to TP1. The third group comprises informants in which the use of mother tongue with L1 interlocutors ranges from 80% to 84%, on average. These are the informants of Rumanian nationality belonging to TP2 and those of Slovak nationality belonging to TP4, as well as the informants of Hungarian nationality belonging to TP2 and TP3.

The fourth group comprises the informants in which the use of mother tongue with L1 interlocutors ranges from 66% to 73%, on average. These are the informants of Rumanian nationality belonging to TP3 and TP4, as well as the informants of Slovak and Ruthenian nationality belonging to TP5. The fifth group comprises informants of Hungarian nationality belonging to TP5. Only 43% of these informants, on average, use their mother tongue in intra-group communication.

These data permit us to conclude that such a classification does not coincide with the grouping in TP categories, and that the use of mother tongue inside the same ethno-linguistic community does not depend only on the factors included in the TPs, although they may be very relevant. The use of mother tongue in intra-group communication may also depend on factors such as: language prestige, urban or rural environment, the concentration of the members of an ethno-linguistic community, their number and percentage compared to the rest of the population, etc.

As to *inter-group communication*, the informants have also been divided into five groups. The first group includes informants of Hungarian nationality belonging to TP5, where 89% of the informants, on average, use Serbo-Croatian in interactions with L2 interlocutors. The second group comprises informants in which the use of second language with L2 interlocutors ranges from 73% to 80%, on average. These are the informants of Slovak and Rumanian nationality belonging to TP4, as well as the informants of Ruthenian and Slovak nationality belonging to TP5. The third group comprises informants in which the use of second language with L2 interlocutors ranges from 53% to 69%, on average. These are the informants of Rumanian and Hungarian nationality belonging to TP2, as well as the informants of Ruthenian and Rumanian nationality belonging to TP3. The fourth group comprises informants whose use of second language with L2 interlocutors ranges from 42% to 44%, on average. These are the informants of Hungarian nationality belonging to TP1 and TP3, as well as the informants of Slovak nationality belonging to TP1. The fifth group comprises the native speakers of Serbo-Croatian belonging to TP2. Only 19% of these informants, on average, use Hungarian in interactions with L2 interlocutors.

As in the case of the intra-group communication, in the inter-group communication, too, there are other sociolinguistic factors, besides those included in TPs, which are relevant; for instance: the bilingual competence of L2 interlocutors, the linguistic and cultural distance between the two languages, etc.

In general, the data show that in language choice the informants always pay more or less attention to *the bilingual competence of their interlocutors*. In interactions with L2 interlocutors this criterion is always relevant, while in interactions with L1 interlocutors this criterion is relevant only to all informants of Rumanian nationality and to the informants of Hungarian and Ruthenian nationality belonging to the LUP of TP5.

The analysis of the data also shows that in language choice the informants depend on the criterion relating to *differentiation inside their own ethno-linguistic community*, i.e. they take into consideration whether the interlocutor-pupils are attending the sections where the instruction is given in their mother tongue or not. This criterion is relevant to the informants of Hungarian nationality, and, to a lesser degree, to the informants of Rumanian nationality.

The role relationship in the domain *at school* (where a distinction is made between the pupil and the teacher when deciding upon the language choice) is a relevant factor for the informants of Rumanian nationality belonging to TP3 and TP4, as well as for all the informants belonging to TP5.

Notes

1. The results of these investigations have been presented and discussed in the following papers: Junger (1979); Međeši, and Besermenji (1979); Međeši (1980-81); Mikeš and Bulik (1977); Mikes, Lük, and Junger (1979); Turčan (1976).

2. The great majority of these pupils belongs to the families which live in predominantly Slovak localities not far from Novi Sad.

References

Bugarski, R. 1986. *Jezik u društvu* [Language in society]. Beograd: Prosveta.

-----, V. Ivir and M. Mikeš (eds). 1976. *Jezik u društvenoj sredini* [Language in its social setting]. Novi Sad: Društvo za primenjenu lingvistiku Jugoslavije.

Bukurov, B. 1954. "Fizičkogeografske i antropogeografske prilike Vojvodine" [Physico-geographical and anthropo-geographical conditions of Vojvodina]. *Almanah Vojvodine 1944-1954*. Novi Sad: Matica srpska.

Hok, R. 1972. "Prilog istoriji pravnog regulisanja upotrebe jezika naroda i narodnosti u Vojvodini" [A contribution to the history of the use of the language of the nations and nationalities in Vojvodina]. *Zbornik radova Pravnog fakulteta u Novom Sadu.* Novi Sad: Pravni fakultet.

Junger, F. 1979. "Prilog proučavanju mađarskog kao jezika društvene sredine" [An investigation of Hungarian as a second language]. *Godišnjak Saveza društava za primenjenu lingvistiku Jugoslavije* 3: 81-87.

Kočiš, N. 1978. *Lingvistički roboti* [Linguistic papers]. Novi Sad.

Mackey, W.F. 1970. "A typology of bilingual education." *Foreign Language Annals* 3.4.

Međeši, H. 1980-81. "Prožimanje makro- i mikrosredinskih faktora u upotrebi jezika kod rusinske narodnosti u Vojvodini" [Interaction of macro- and microenvironmental factors in the language use of Ruthenians in Vojvodina]. *Godišnjak Saveza društava za primenjenu lingvistiku Jugoslavije* 4-5: 353-55.

----- and V. Besermenji. 1979. "Upotreba maternjeg i nematernjeg jezika kod srednjoškolske omladine rusinske narodnosti u SAP Vojvodini" [The use of native and non-native language by Ruthenian pupils in Vojvodina]. *Godišnjak Saveza društava za primenjenu lingvitiku Jugoslavije* 3: 95-99.

Mikes, M. 1974. "Tipologija dvojezičnosti u vaspitno-obrazovnom sistemu Vojvodine" [The typology of bilingualism in the educational system of Vojvodina]. *Kultura* 25: 147-67.

-----. 1978. "Jugoslovenski model višejezičnosti" [The Yugoslav model of multilingualism]. *Jezik i rasizam.* Sarajevo.

----- and I.-D. Bulik. 1977. "Obrasci upoptrebe maternjeg i nematernjeg jezika kod srednjoškolske omladine rumunske narodnosti u SAP Vojvodini" [Patterns in the use of native and non-native language by Rumanian pupils in Vojvodina]. *Radovi Simpozijuma o jugoslovensko-rumunskim jezičko-dijalektalnim interferencijama i filološkim paralelizmima.* Pančevo/Zrenjanin: 282-92.

-----, A. Lük, and F. Junger. 1979. "Upotreba maternjeg jezika i jezika društvene sredine kod školske omladine" [The use of the first and the second language among school youth]. *Razprave in gradivo* 9-10: 33-39.

Turčan, J. 1976. "Obrasci upotrebe maternjeg i nematernjeg jezika kod srednjoškolske omladine slovačke narodnosti u SAP Vojvodini" [Patterns in the use of native and non-native language by Slovak pupils in Vojvodina]. In: Bugarski, Ivir, and Mikeš (eds). 1976: 67-76.

Modern Icelandic vowel quantity revisited

Janez Orešnik
Faculty of Philosophy, University of Ljubljana

Introduction

The present paper deals with modern Icelandic vowel quantity descriptively, from the phonological point of view.

Recent phonological studies of modern Icelandic vowel quantity seem to have assumed that adequacy of description has already been achieved, and that it is time to proceed to an explanation of the phenomenon. Endeavours in this direction have brought modern Icelandic vowel quantity into the orbit of general linguistics, this in turn being the reason that the subject matter is deemed worthy of inclusion in the present volume. However, here the discussion of modern Icelandic vowel quantity will not be continued in the same vein, but returned almost to its starting point: it will be argued that the quantity rule has not yet been formulated correctly; whereupon I will try to remedy it.

Section 1 presents briefly the traditional approach to modern Icelandic vowel quantity, and enumerates some of the weaknesses of that approach. Section 2 attempts to remedy those weaknesses, first of all by proposing a modified description. Section 3 contains the concluding remarks.

1

In the present section, the traditional formulation of the modern Icelandic vowel quantity rule is briefly presented (1.1) and criticised (1.2).

1.1 Modern Icelandic vowel quantity has traditionally been described as follows (Ófeigsson 1920-24:XVIII-IX):

(a) Unaccented vowels are usually short (but see 2.1 ad finem).

(b) Accented vowels can be long or short. They are long before what is written as at most one consonant: *bú búa búðu* three forms of *búa* 'live, farm', *búð* 'booth', all containing accented [u:]. Otherwise accented vowels are short: *býrð* [i] form of *búa* 'live, farm', *húss* [u] 'house (gen. sg.)'.

This primary rule has a dark spot, for this purpose called *the irregularity*:

(c) Against (b) above, accented vowels are long even before the clusters, *p t k s + j r v*, although the vowel is followed by more than one consonant in such cases: *vitja* [ɪ:] 'visit', *Esra* [ɛ:] given name.

The above remarks are valid for non-compound words. The situation is partly different in compounds, see 1.2.2.

1.2 The traditional approach to modern Icelandic vowel quantity (1.1) displays at least the following weaknesses:

(a) Its formulation depends in part on the spelling, see 1.2.1.

(b) There is an unnecessary lack of fit between the description of the vowel quantity in non-compounds and the description of the vowel quantity in a certain type of compounds, see 1.2.2.

(c) The explanations of the behaviour of modern Icelandic vowel quantity presented so far (all are in terms of syllable structure) have failed, see 1.2.3.

1.2.1 The traditional account of modern Icelandic vowel quantity relies in part on the spelling of the words whose vowel quantity is considered. This can be illustrated with the word pair *höggva* 'hew' vs. *skrökva* 'tell untruth', with their linmæli pronunciations [hœkva] and [skrœ:kva]. (Only linmæli pronunciation is discussed in the present paper.) In the pronunciation, these two words contain the same [kv] after their accented vowel [œ], which vowel is nevertheless short in one word, and long in the other.

The half-length once postulated by some scholars for the stop in *höggva* (by Ófeigsson 1920-24 and notably by Einarsson 1927:75) is in reality just an automatic accompaniment to the immediately preceding short vowel's correct pronunciation, according to communis opinio (Pétursson 1978:61; Árnason 1980:36-7).

An argument in favour of viewing the half-length as just an automatic consequence of the pronunciation of the preceding short accented vowel can be construed if the half-length is viewed as a consequence of *Silbenschnitt*, the latter being of course a manner of pronouncing VOWELS. Now, accented vowels in modern Icelandic are, of course, pronounced with *Silbenschnitt* before consonants of full length also, e.g. in *húss(ins)* '(the) house (gen. sg.)'. Consequently, if *Silbenschnitt* is made responsible for the shortness of the accented vowels before half-length, *Silbenschnitt* must also be made responsible for the shortness of the accented vowels before consonantal full length. *Silbenschnitt* would thus be responsible for the shortness of all accented short vowels. Moreover, as *Silbenschnitt* is a property of vowels, it follows that VOWEL quantity would be distinctive. This consequence, however, would clash dramatically with the indisputable fact that most quantity values of accented vowels can be determined with the help of the consonants that immediately follow such vowels.

Going back to the beginning of the section, the traditional quantity rule (1.1) cannot account for the difference in the quantity of the accented vowels in *höggva* and *skrökva* unless the spelling of the two words is taken into consideration, in which case there is no problem: the *ö* of *höggva* is followed by more than one consonant, therefore the *ö* is short; the *ö* of *skrökva* is likewise followed by more than one consonant, to be sure, yet the two consonants pertain to the "irregularity", thus the vowel before them is long.

The quantity difference under discussion can of course be explained historically and the explanation is encoded in the etymology-conditioned spellings of the two words. Appeal to the spelling is no obstacle as long as the quantity rules are limited to use in practical language teaching, for which the traditional formulation of the quantity rules may have been prepared in the first place anyway. However, the drawback must be eliminated before there is any attempt at *explaining* the behaviour of modern Icelandic vowel quantity.

1.2.2 It is well known that there is a lack of fit, in the traditional account of modern Icelandic vowel quantity, between the behaviour of the vowel quantity in non-compound words and in a certain type of compounds.

The situation with respect to vowel quantity in Icelandic compounds is described in Jón Ófeigsson's phonetic introduction to Blöndal 1920-24 (later descriptions of the same matter add little or nothing) and my argumentation is based on it.

As is well known, the vowel quantity of compounds behaves, on the whole, as in non-compounds. For instance, in the compound *bókasafn* 'library', the vowel quantity is in principle as in the non-compounds *bóka* 'book (gen. pl.)' and *safn* 'collection', respectively.

As is also well known, special effects on vowel quantity can be observed almost exclusively in those compounds whose initial constituent is both monosyllabic and ends in one short consonant at most, e.g. *húsbóndi* 'master of the house'. Such compounds will here be called *flat-nosed compounds*. Thus the lexeme *húsbóndi* is a flat-nosed compound, *hús-* being its *flat nose*. There is also need for a term covering all the consonants intervening between the vowel of the flat nose and the next vowel in the compound. Let us coin *the critical consonantism*. Thus, in *húsbóndi*, *sb* is its critical consonantism.

To judge by the situation that obtains in non-compounds containing flat-nosed segment structure (= C_0VC^1), the vowels of flat noses ought to be long. E.g. just as the vowel of the simplex form *hús* is long, the vowel of the flat nose *hús-* ought to be long, and is in fact quite often really pronounced as long: [hu:spountɪ] is a correct ('recommended'), expected Icelandic pronunciation.

A well known speciality of flat noses is, however, that their vowels can be shortened, and this is in fact often the case. For instance, *húsbóndi* is often pronounced with short *ú*. As to the conditions under which shortening takes place, the traditional account (Ófeigsson 1920-24) points out that the vowel of the flat nose usually remains long before *p* (= stop) *t k s* of the flat nose, regardless of what follows at the beginning of the next compound constituent; some vacillation (i.e. shortening of vowel) occurs even in this environment (e.g. in *Mosfellsheiði* name of a *heiði*; the vacillation involving the stops is not exemplified, although it is mentioned).

This description is of course at variance with the situation in non-compounds, where accented vowels are long before consonant clusters beginning with *p t k s* only if *j r v* follow next. It will be shown here that this lack of fit between compounds and non-compounds does not obtain in reality, but is due to the failure of the traditional account to formulate the quantity rule correctly. Incidentally, my criticism should not be construed as implying that such lack of fit is necessarily to be avoided.

1.2.3 The explanations of the behaviour of modern Icelandic vowel quantity based on the traditional approach (1.1) have failed.

All the explanations of the behaviour of modern Icelandic vowel quantity known to me take the traditional account as their starting point, and are thus limited to non-compound words, so that, in the present section, I discuss such words only. The explanations assume that the quantity of accented vowels depends on the position of the first syllable boundary to the right of the vowel in question. This idea was first expressed in Vennemann (1972), then in Garnes (1975), in Árnason (1980), and, as an alternative, in Rögnvaldsson (1984).

According to these works, the first syllable boundary that follows upon a long vowel lies nearer to that vowel than the first syllable boundary that follows upon a short vowel. This is the main rule. As regards the vowel quantity of accented vowels before consonant clusters involved in the "irregularity", the first syllable boundary after the accented vowel is hypothesised to lie (contrary to the main rule) as near that vowel as otherwise is the case after long vowels.

Let me illustrate this with Árnason's (1980) descriptional variant, which can be summarised as follows. The syllable boundary normally lies immediately after the last or only consonant that follows that accented vowel (cf. the syllable division at the end of lines in Icelandic orthography), e.g. *tap.a* 'lose', *bölv.a* 'curse'. If an accented syllable thus delimited contains only one post-vocalic consonant (or even none), the accented vowel is long; otherwise it is short. Thus *tapa* [tʰa:-], *bölva* [œ]. The "irregularity" is exceptional in the sense that the critical syllable boundary does not lie *after p t k s + j r v*, as dictated by the main rule, but more to the left, immediately after *p t k s*. Hence the accented vowel immediately before the "irregularity"'s consonant cluster is long, now in accordance with the main rule. For instance, not *vitj.a* 'visit', but *vit.ja*, therefore [ɪ:], not [ɪ].

It is a hypothesis of this and other descriptions of the same kind that the position of the syllable boundaries suffices to predict the quantity values (long, short) of the Icelandic accented vowels.

It is a weakness of such descriptions that they lead to at least one consequence that empirical verification does not corroborate. Les us look at this matter in detail:

If the quantity of an accented vowel is a function solely of the position of the first syllable boundary to the right of that vowel, then all monosyllabic words ending in the same number of consonantal segments have to display the same quantity value of their vowel: length only or shortness only. This prediction follows from the circumstance (1) that syllable boundaries invariably coincide with word boundaries in monosyllabic words, and

(2) that syllable boundaries cannot be moved in monosyllabic words. Regardless of whether the word is *ás* (name of heathen deity) or *ást* 'love', its right syllable boundary lies at the end: *ás., ást..* The difference in vowel quantity that can be observed between *ás* and *ást* can be accounted for by an appeal to the distance between the vowel and the right syllable boundary: in *ás* only one consonant, *s*, intervenes between the vowel and the right syllable boundary; in *ást*, two consonants, *s* and *t*, intervene between the vowel and the right syllable boundary. Hence vowel length in *ás*, vowel shortness in *ást*. A long consonant would count as two short consonants.

Such solutions are impossible where conflicting quantity values obtain before the same number of post-vocalic short consonants, e.g. *skips* [scɪːps] and [scɪfs], both genitive singular of *skip* 'ship'; similarly in numerous other examples. Such word pairs make it impossible to describe modern Icelandic vowel quantity exclusively by an appeal to (the distance of the vowel from) the syllable boundary, for it is not possible to syllabify, say, [scɪːp.s] vs. [scɪfs.], for it cannot be maintained that [scɪːps] contains two syllables. Also, it is not possible to discard genitives such as [scɪːps] as marginal, as they are the normally used genitives of the lexemes in question. Rather, what should be mentioned in such cases is the *kind* of postvocalic consonants. However, if this is done, the appeal to syllable boundaries becomes redundant. It must be therefore that syllable boundaries are not at all mentioned in the traditional formulation of the quantity rule (1.1).

My conclusion is that all attempts made so far at describing modern Icelandic vowel quantity exclusively by aid of syllable structure have failed. Notice that, in asserting this, I am not referring to the *historical explanations* of the origin of modern Icelandic quantity. It is well known that words of the type [scɪːps] (and of another relevant type, *klifr* 'climbing') are probably of such recent origin that the modern vowel quantity may have pre-dated those types, and at that early stage — theoretically speaking — may have been conditioned by syllable structure. Cf. Árnasaon (1980) and Murray & Vennemann (1983) for such historical accounts of modern Icelandic vowel quantity.

2

In the present section, a partly modified description of modern Icelandic vowel quantity will be presented (2.1), aimed at obtaining a unified account of the vowel quantity in compound and non-compound words

(2.2); the consequences of the elimination of the appeal to spelling from that account are discussed in 2.3. As regards the remaining aspect of the traditional approach criticised here, the explanation (cf. 1.2.3), see 3.

2.1 The present section presents a partly modified description of modern Icelandic vowel quantity.

The adequacy of the traditional formulation of the modern Icelandic vowel quantity rule (1.1) has been questioned by Orešnik & Pétursson (1977). Orešnik & Pétursson called attention to the circumstance that accented vowels are long if immediately followed by ungeminated *p t k* pronounced as unaspirated stops + *s* (e.g. *leiks* 'play (gen. sg.)') or + *k* (e.g. *notkun* 'use' (noun)). Against this background, Orešnik & Pétursson proposed the hypothesis that accented vowels are long if they are immediately followed by ungeminated *p t k* pronounced as unaspirated stops, without regard to the nature of the next sound segment, if any. Examples such as gen. sg. *sötrs* [œ:] or *sötr* 'sucking liquid through teeth' show, in addition, that accented vowels can be long even before more than two consonants.

In this way, that part of the "irregularity"'s traditional formulation concerning the ungeminated unpreaspirated stops has been substituted for by a more general statement. What has remained is the vowel length before *s* + *j r v*. In the present paper, an attempt will be made at the reformulation of this last crux, by incorporating it into a partly modified description of modern Icelandic vowel quantity.

As its point of departure the new description has the behaviour of the accented vowels in those inflected non-compound lexemes whose accented vowels alternate between long and short in the sundry inflected forms of the respective lexemes (e.g. *svalur* [a:] 'cool' vs. *svals* [a] 'cool (gen. sg.)'). The basic quantity of such accented vowels is here hypothesised to be length; the long vowels are then shortened in certain phonological environments by a shortening rule. (The accented vowels of the remaining, i.e. uninflected, non-compound lexemes will be discussed in 2.3.)

This view of modern Icelandic vowel quantity has a forerunner in Bergsveinsson (1941). It is also mentioned (briefly, as an alternative to another description, and in a different framework) in Orešnik & Pétursson (1977), in Orešnik (1978:159-61), and recently (again briefly and as a possibility) in Rögnvaldsson (1984:90).

The Shortening Rule. Accented vowels are shortened:
(a) before long consonants: *húss(ins)* '(the) house (gen. sg.)'

(b) before more than one consonant: *himnar* 'heaven, sky (nom. pl.)', *teknir* 'taken (nom. pl. m.)', *hratt* 'fast (nom./acc. sg. n.)', *heims* 'world (gen. sg.)'. The preaspiration counts as a segment. Point (b) has two restrictions attached to it:

(I) If the leftmost consonant in a consonant cluster is an unpreaspirated short stop, point (b) shortens the immediately preceding vowel only if that consonant is synchronically derived from a non-stop, or inserted.

Examples: (i) stop from non-stop *ofnir* [ɔpn-] 'woven (nom. pl. m.),' *sagði* [-ak-], Northern pronunciation, 'say (1st and 3rd p. sg. pret. ind.)', *sagt* [sakt], young speakers' pronunciation, 'say (past part. nom./acc. sg. n.)' (my attention has been called to [sakt] by Stefán Karlsson viva voce, 1981); (ii) stop insertion: *sæll* [saitḷ] 'happy, blessed', *sæll* [saitḷ] 'happy, blessed', *steinn* [steitn̩] 'stone'.

Comment on (I): Since derivation of a stop from non-stop, or insertion of stop, is only evident synchronically in inflected words, the shortness of accented vowels before stops in uninflected words must be assumed to be lexicalised, e.g. *vaxa* [vaksa] 'grow' (Böðvarsson 1979:67), *biblía* 'Bible', *magma* 'magma', *höggva* 'hew', cf. 2.3.

(II) If the leftmost consonant in a consonant cluster is short *s*, point (b) shortens the immediately preceding vowel only if the *s* is immediately followed by a voiceless consonant: *laust* [löist] 'free (nom./acc. sg. n.)' vs. *lausra* [löi:sra] 'free (gen. pl.). *Hvassra* [kʰvasra] 'sharp (gen. pl.)' must be assumed to contain lexicalised shortness, see 2.3.

Comment on (II): This restriction regulates vowel quantity before *s*-initial consonant clusters. The clusters *s* + *j r v*, before which accented vowels are long, are here by implication generalised to the less idiosyncratic clusters *s* + voiced consonant. At first blush, the generalisation is false, seeing that it includes the clusters, *s* + *m n l*, in front of which accented vowels are of course short: *hismi* 'chaff', *gosnir* 'gush' (past part. nom. pl. m.), *vesla* 'wretched' (acc. pl. m.). However, *s* + *m n l* are a special case, seeing that they allow the epenthetic *p* or *t* to be pronounced after *s*: [hɪspmɪ, kɔstnɪr, vɛstla]. In these strengthened pronunciation variants, the *s* is immediately followed by a voiceless (epenthetic) consonant, any immediately preceding accented vowel is therefore short, as predicted by restriction (II). To profit from this situation, I partly reformulate (II) as follows:

(II') If the leftmost consonant in a consonant cluster is a short *s*, point

(b) shortens the immediately preceding vowel only if the *s* is at least optionally followed by a voiceless consonant.

Perhaps (II') can be made even more precise, in that the pronunciation variants containing the epenthetic consonant can be promoted to the basic pronunciation variants, and correspondingly, the pronunciation variants lacking the epenthetic consonant can be relegated to the status of subsidiary variants. (However, I know much too little about the actual use of those variants to be able to elaborate the matter.)

Since unaccented vowels behave as accented vowels if they are accented for some exceptional reason (Benediktsson 1963), it must be postulated here that unaccented vowels are underlyingly long. (The same idea was entertained by Bergsveinsson 1941). The shortening rule must be formulated so that it shortens such vowels under lack of accent.

2.2 In the present section, it will be shown that the description of 2.1 can be extended to flat-nosed compound words. To this end, a first attempt will be made to classify the vowel shortenings obtaining in flat noses (cf. 1.2.2).

With respect to the possibilities for shortening, the following three cases can be distinguished: (i) shortening impossible, (ii) shortening obligatory, (iii) shortening possible, but optional. Let us consider each of these three cases in turn.

Concerning (i), shortening impossible. This case obtains whenever the critical consonantism forms a constellation before which vowel shortening fails to occur even in non-compounds.

This goes without saying whenever the critical consonantism consists just of the flat nose's final consonant, so that the second constituent of the compound begins with a vowel, or with *h* + vowel (in which case the *h* is often silent). E.g. *Hvítá* [i:] 'White River', *alhæfa* [a:l-] 'generalise'.

Further, the vowel of the flat nose cannot be shortened if the flat nose's final consonant is an unpreaspirated short stop that is also historically a stop: *atkvæði* [a:] 'syllable', *sakbær* [a:] 'accountable', *djúpsettur* [u:] 'profound', *matmál* [a:] 'meal-time', *kaupmaður* [öi:] 'merchant', *slaklega* [a:] 'laxly'.

Moreover, the vowel of the flat nose cannot be shortened if both the flat nose's final consonant is a short *s* and the next compound constituent begins with a voiced consonant (excepting, of course, *m n l*, see 2.1 above): *misjafn* [ɪ:] 'unequal'. Recall that accented vowels are long before such consonant clusters even in non-compounds.

Concerning (ii), shortening obligatory. The shortening is obligatory in the cases in which the critical consonantism, especially the flat nose's final consonant, changes in certain ways, the change being due to the interaction (internal sandhi) of the segments within the critical consonantism.

So far, I have succeeded in registering the following pertinent changes:

Accretion of consonant
- introduction of preaspiration (especially frequent in East Iceland, Ófeigsson 1920-24):
  - *róttækur* [rouh-] 'radical'; *hluttaka* [-ɣh-] 'participation'
  - *líklega* [-ihk-] probably'; *kaupmaður* [-öihp-] 'merchant'; *vitlaus* [-ɪht-] 'crazy'
  - the following pronunciations are from Blöndal (1920-24), and are now probably obsolete or obsolescent: *baðstofa* [-ah-] 'living-room'; *bréfpeningur* [-ɛh-] 'paper money'; *mágkona* [-auh-] 'sister-in-law'
- introduction of epenthetic consonant: *Ísland* [istlant] 'Iceland'.

Consonant change
- opening of consonant
  - *reiptagl* [-f-] 'rope'; *strákskapur* [-x-] 'roguery'
  - dialectal and obsolete: *farðagar* 'removing days'; *Herðís* female given name.
- closing of consonant: *aflægi* [-ap-] 'abnormity'; *Hafliði* [-ap-] male given name
- assimilation of consonant
  - devoicing: *forseti* [-ɾ̥-] 'president', *lafhræddur* [-f-] 'scared to death'; *máltið* [-l̥-] 'meal';
  - complete assimilation: *afbæjar-* [-p:-] 'from another farm'; *afmæli* [-m:-] 'anniversary'; *Breiðdalur* [-t:-] place name

Consonant loss: tafllaus [tʰaplöis] 'without *tafl*'

(The flat noses' vowels in the above items may of course have other quantity values when the phonetic phenomena enumerated above do not obtain. For instance, *róttækur* can also be pronounced as if its spelling were *rótækur*, with a long *ó*.)

Recall that the above kinds of changes are accompanied by obligatory vowel shortness even in non-compounds. It seems obvious that the changes and the concomitant shortenings in flat noses are modelled upon corresponding changes in non-compounds.

Concerning (iii): The shortening is possible, but optional, in all remaining cases, in the following sense. In some words of this kind the shortening never takes place, in some seldom, in some often, in some (many) almost always. This category of flat-nosed compounds remains to be studied in detail. Examples : *Ásdís* [au(:)s-] female given name; *Ásgeir* [au(:)s-] male given name; *Dalvík* [ta(:)l-] place name; *holskefla* [hɔ(:)l-] 'heavy sea'.

The situation in flat noses shows that some shortening rule or other must be available in the language anyway, seeing that a means is needed to shorten those vowels of flat noses that can or even must be shortened. If we turn this circumstance to account, formulate the shortening rule as we have done in 2.1, and presuppose that accented vowels are also long in the phonological representations of at least some non-compounds, then we can utilise the same shortening rule as in flat noses to generate all the short accented vowels in the appropriate forms of those non-compounds. (It does not matter, in this context, that the shortening rule sometimes applies just optionally in compounds, whereas in non-compounds its application is normally obligatory.) In this sense, flat noses can be used in the argumentation in favour of the length being the basic (underlying) quantity of (at least some) accented vowels.

As can be seen from the above, we have now succeeded, for the first time since the phonological aspect of Icelandic vowel quantity has been discussed, to formulate the modern Icelandic quantity rule in such a way that the same wording is valid for both compounds and non-compounds. I evaluate the new formulation as progress for exactly this reason, among other things.

There is some indication that the shortening of originally long vowels of flat noses may have progressed beyond the stage described by Ófeigsson (1920-24), seeing that Bérkov & Böðvarsson (1962) adduce pronunciations such as *húsráðandi* [-u-] 'landlord', *vísvitandi* [-i-] 'knowingly', *ósjálfbjarga* [ou-] 'helpless'. Moreover, the spoken language also uses pronunciation variants — not at all exemplified in the existing literature, to the best of my knowledge — such as *brúgglegur* for *brúklegur* 'useful', and *klagglaust* for *klaklaust* 'unhurt' (confirmed by Magnús Pétursson 1985, per litteras), in which the vowel of the flat nose is normally long, as expected on the basis of the shortening rule. Is the complicated situation described in Ófeigsson (1920-24) being regularised with the aid of a novel (and simpler) generalisation (namely, that all vowels are short in flat noses before consonant clusters)?

238 JANEZ OREŠNIK

2.3 The present section discusses the consequences that obtain if the formulation of the modern Icelandic vowel quantity rule avoids mentioning the spelling of the words whose vowel quantity is being determined.

We will continue to use the words *höggva* and *skrökva* as examples, cf. 1.2.1 above. The basic (underlying) quantity of the accented vowel obviously can not be the same in the two words: if underlying shortness is postulated in both words, or underlying length, or absence of quantity, or neutral quantity, under all circumstances we lack means to produce that quantity difference actually observed in the two vowels under discussion. There does not seem to be any way out of the obvious conclusion, that there is already a quantity difference in the underlying forms, in the phonological representations. If so, it is common sense to postulate short underlying quantity in the accented vowel of *höggva*, and long underlying quantity in the accented vowel of *skrökva*, not v.v. In other words, quantity rules do not operate in these words at all.

To ensure this result, it does matter whether the vowel quantity is regulated by a shortening rule or by a lengthening rule. The lengthening rule would lead to undesired consequences, seeing that it would lengthen the short *ö* of *höggva* (this because, normally, vowels before [kv] are long, and the quantity rule, of course, must first of all take care of the normal cases). Only the shortening rule is suitable in the respect under consideration: the shortening rule does not shorten the long *ö* of *skrökva*, as vowels, I repeat, are normally long before [kv], and the shortening rule is formulated accordingly; the shortening rule does not apply to *höggva* either, for its *ö* is already short anyway.

Against this background, I conclude that *höggva* and *skrökva* (both representing types of words, of course) speak in favour of the existence of the shortening rule. Furthermore, seeing that the shortening rule is justified only if it is presupposed that the underlying quantity is length in at least some instances, the words *höggva* and *skrökva* speak indirectly in favour of length as underlying quantity (in at least some cases).

Furthermore, the pair *höggva skrökva* proves that it is necessary to postulate short underlying quantity at least in some words, here in *höggva*. (Recall that consonantal quantity is also partly long, partly short, never neutral, in underlying representations.) As far as I can see, the short underlying quantity never alternates with the long quantity. Perhaps the short underlying quantity should be postulated in ALL non-alternating short vowels, also where the short quantity could have been produced by aid of the shortening rule, e.g. in *bölva*. A good side of this extension would be that examples such as *höggva* would cease to be isolated exceptions, and become instances containing lexicalised quantity upon which the quantity rules simply do not operate. In the remaining cases, the length is (redundantly) lexicalised anyway.

As a postscript to the present section, let me point out that we can expect cases of lexicalised short quantity even in phonological contexts that usually require length: if, for some reason, say, because the lending language dictates it, short quantity appears in such context, it cannot be lengthened, there being no lengthening rule in the language. Example: if the loanwords *drosja/drossía* 'passenger car' and *vodka* 'vodka' are pronounced with short *o*, this *o* cannot be lengthened (in spite of the types *Esja* [ɛ:-] name of mountain and *notkun* [nɔ:t-] 'use' (noun)), as there is no lengthening rule in the language. On the other hand, if a loanword is accepted with long quantity, it freely undergoes shortenings under appropriate phonological conditions; e.g. *bítill* [pi:t-] 'Beatle' as against *bítlar* [piht-] 'Beatle' (nom. pl.), underlying representation of the stem /pi:tɪl/. Returning to domestic words, if shortening does not take place where expected, as it sporadically does not, this can be explained as analogically conditioned suppression of the operation of the shortening rule. An example is the occasional gen. pl. *vanra* [-a:-] beside the expected *vanra* [-a-] of *vanur* 'accustomed' (Einarsson 1927: 44).

3

The concluding remark. The search for the explanatory adequacy of my description must be postponed until the description is accepted as descriptively adequate.

Acknowledgement

My thanks are due to Miss Margaret G. Davis, who has corrected my English. All errors are my own.

References

Árnason, Kristján. 1980. *Quantity in Historical Phonology: Icelandic and Related Cases*. Cambridge: Cambridge University Press.

Benediktsson, Hreinn. 1963. "The non-uniqueness of phonemic solutions: quantity and stress in Icelandic." *Phonetica* 10: 133-53.

Bergsveinsson, Sveinn. 1941. *Grundfragen der isländischen Satzphonetik*. Copenhagen: Munksgaard/Berlin: Metten.

Bérkov, Valeríj P. and Árni Böðvarsson. 1962. *Íslenzk-rússnesk orðabók*. Moscow: Gosudarstvennoe izdatel'stvo inostrannyx i nacional'nyx slovarej.

Blöndal, Sigfús. 1920-24. *Íslensk-dönsk orðabók*. Reykjavík: Verslun þórarins B. þorlákssonar/Copenhagen: H. Aschehoug (W. Nygaard).

Böðvarsson, Árni. 1979. *Hljóðfræði*. Reykjavík: Ísafoldarprentsmiðja.

Einarsson, Stefán. 1927. *Beiträge zur Phonetik der isländischen Sprache*. Oslo: A.W. Brøggers Boktrykkeri.

Garnes, Sara. 1975. "Perception, Production and Language Change". *Papers from the parasession on functionalism*. Chicago: Chicago Linguistic Society.

Murray, Robert W., and Theo Venneman. 1983. "Sound change and syllable structure in Germanic phonology." *Language* 59: 514-28.

Ófeigsson, Jón. 1920-24. "Træk af moderne islandsk lydlære." In: Blöndal 1920-24.

Orešnik, Janez. 1978. "Modern Icelandic preaspiration from the phonological point of view". *Linguistica* 18: 141-66.

Orešnik, Janez, and Magnús Pétursson. 1977. "Quantity in modern Icelandic." *Arkiv för nordisk filologi* 92: 155-71.

Pétursson, Magnús. 1978. *Isländisch*. Hamburg: Helmut Buske.

Rögnvaldsson, Eiríkur. 1984. *Íslensk málfræði. Hljóðkerfisfræði og beygingafræði*. Reykjavík: duplicated as manuscript.

Vennemann, Theo. 1972. "On the theory of syllabic phonology." *Linguistische Berichte* 18: 1-18.

Language in space and space in language*

Predrag Piper
Faculty of Philology, University of Belgrade

1

Like many others, the title of this paper can be read in two ways: a narrower, more literal way and a broader one which considers the relations between language and space more abstractly. In the first case, the paper could be expected to deal with the problem of an environment's various spatial configurations and how they reflect themselves in a languages's specific structural features developing in given spatial conditions. The thesis that language structure type is conditioned by its speaker living space is not a new one. It is developed quite explicitly, for instance, by Gunaev (1977), who posits, among other things, the interesting fact that as opposed to many languages in which the opposition between proximity and distance is relevant for the system of pronouns, in the pronoun system of some Dagestan languages location according to the vertical is relevant: on the speaker's level, above or below his level, all of which is attributed to the fact that from time immemorial the Dagestan people have inhabited steep mountain slopes and that such spatial relations are essential to their daily life.[1] Examples of this type (with a greater or lesser emphasis on this phenomenon) are also found in descriptions of many non-Indo-European languages, particularly when they are observed by Indo-European linguists, within the framework of broader, anthropological study. This does not, of course, mean to imply that examples cannot be found in Indo-European languages as well. For instance, when the Russian philologist A.F. Giljferding travelled through Bosnia, Herzegovina and Serbia in 1857 he made some

---

* This article was translated into English by Vladislava Felbabov.

interesting observations of a linguistic nature. Namely, in all the Slavic languages there are verbs of movement deriving from the common Slavic verbs *iti* and *hoditi* meaning 'to go', 'to walk', and those deriving from the common Slavic verbs *lězti* and *laziti* meaning 'to crawl', 'to clamber' and the like. Giljferding observed that in the speech of the Slavic populations of the regions he visited, an expansion of the second type of verbs had occurred at the expense of the first. He offered the following explanation for this: ". . . in his region, whether on foot or on horseback, a man cannot proceed normally without climbing from hill to hill, clambering from stone to stone" (Giljferding 1972: 47), by which he pointed out that the expansion of one type of verb at the expense of the other included not only their concrete spatial meanings linked to the movement of men and animals, but many of their transposed meanings as well (*do-laziti* 'to come', for instance, can be said of *vetar* 'the wind', *vest* 'the news', *san* 'sleep', etc.), and so Giljferding draws the conclusion: "So greatly does nature influence language".

This influence extends, it would seem, even to purely phonological phenomena. According to experimental research carried out by Obrenović (1983), altitude above sea-level has an effect on the acoustic parameters of vowels of those who have lived since birth at a height of 1600 ms (or more). It is manifested as a partial altering of the spectral structure of vowels, their pitch and duration in comparison with the pronunciation of people who live at an altitude of 400 ms.[2] This is attributed to the difference in atmospheric pressure and the quantity of oxygen in the air, that is to say, it has a neurophysiological explanation.

This paper, however, intends to try to shed some light on the relation between language and space from another angle: it will pass over extensive descriptions and analyses of specific instances of how spatial and other related relations are denoted by specific languages, and will mainly rely on what has already been registered in order to focus on formulating questions for further study of the subject, which deserves more attention than it has hitherto received, and on attempting to offer an outline, at least, of ways of searching for answers, ways which will be the most promising.

Of the many problems covered by the subject of this paper, three basic ones stand out, each encompassing several narrower ones. First of all, there is the problem of determining, conceptually and terminologically, that approach in the science of language or that circle of studies, linked to the subject, to a greater or lesser extent, whose characterstic is a focus of attention on spatial and non-spatial relations on a paradigmatic and syntagmatic level. Secondly, there is the problem of founding, empirically, the idea that spatial criteria are basic to some (or many, or all) non-spatial semantic sub-systems and their functioning. (Besides linguistic ones, one should also bear in mind, though in a narrower sense, neuro-, psycho- and sociolinguistic data). Thirdly, the problem of invariant structures belonging to both the spatial and non-spatial semantic spheres: the inventory of these invariants, an analysis of their nature and the relations between them and between their variant forms as well.

2

The subject of the relation between language and space is part of the subject matter of the relation between man and space. It is well known that the category of space has an important role not only in the categorial systems of natural sciences, but also in those which deal with man and his spiritual universe. The relation between man and space receives, naturally, different interpretations in different sciences, yet, this does not seem to be merely a manifestation of the categorial pluralism of various sciences, but more a result of an insufficient (on the whole) and uncoordinated, and, therefore, inconsistent study of this subject matter.

Data show that in many languages (independent of how close they are genetically and typologically) spatial meanings are very present, both in the various subsystems of units with spatial meanings, and in speech. This conclusion is, of itself, quite a general one, but since even a thick volume would prove insufficient space to document it in detail, we have to satisfy ourselves with referring to the numerous linguistic descriptions that confirm it. In the systems of many languages (and, most probably, of all the natural ones), there are many such subsystems, often quite complex, whose units are used to denote spatial relations. These can be, for instance, prepositions, postpositions, adverbs, adjectives, nouns (for example, *nomina loci*), verbs, pronouns, and, though less often, some of the other traditional parts of speech. Form the standpoint of language levels spatial meanings are encountered in units on various levels: for instance, pure morphemes (for example, prefixes and suffixes), and various types of morphological and syntactic structures as well. Even a superficial comparison of two or more languages reveals that there are many different formal possiblities for expressing spatial relations, and that certain languages prefer certain ones, or that they make less use of certain others or that they do not know of them at all, or that in two or more languages units on the same level can be organized in more or less in different ways. Linguistics has perceived these facts a long time ago, and they have been supported, time and again, by language data, old and new. In addition to many passing observations on the extent, frequency and complexity of language units denoting spatial relations, and, particularly, on a similar organization of spatial and some non-spatial language subsystems, there have been, for quite some time, more and more successful attempts at giving the concept of 'spatialization' or of the spatial nature of non-spatial fields of language a more adequate theoretical form. This refers, primarily, to the localistic theory of case which has had several versions in modern linguistics. One of the most developed ones is offered by Anderson (1971, 1973, 1977 and elsewhere), who has also made a survey of the development of the localistic notion of case (1971), while the present state of localism is briefly reviewed by Lyons (1977: 718-725).[3]

If *localism* is taken as a term to denote all the interpretations of linguistic phenomena which are fundamentally spatial in their nature and/or which are best interpreted as such within the terms of spatial metaphors, then, the ramified nature of the notions denoted by this term should be observed above all else. In its narrowest sense, localism is a case theory which has had, both during its course of develoment and at the present moment, different forms of manifestation, both in the method by which it has been presented and in the direction in which its basic notions have been developed (in this regard see the different versions of localism given by Anderson 1971 and Kempf 1978). In its broader sense, localism touches upon the anthropocentric notion of language. Typical of this are the works of Kuryłowicz (1971, 1972) and Friedrich (1969, 1970). Independently of case theory, in his analysis of the suffix system in the language of the Tarascana (south-west Mexico), Friedrich shows quite strikingly that the shape of the human body, serves as a prototype for conceptualizing many phenomena, both concrete and abstract, and that it is given grammatical expression in the language.[4] In addition to this, there are many anthropocentric interpretations of different language phenomena which cannot be connected directly to localism or in which the connection is concealed by some other aspect which is to the fore (see, for instance, Benveniste 1966: 225-289).

Another criterion essential for differentiating research within the field of localistic (in a narrower and broader sense) approaches to language is the focus of analysis on the syntagmatic (Anderson 1971; Longacker 1982; Collinge 1980) or on the paradigmatic level (Kuryłowicz 1972; Kempf 1978; Piper 1983). In the latter case, problems are often considered from both a diachronic and a synchronic standpoint.

In this context of considerations, it is finally also necessary to underline the difference between linguistic and metalinguistic localism. In the first case there is the problem of developing the notion of the semantic category of space as the primary one in relation to (some) other semantic categories, while in the second case there is the problem of a theoretically more or less developed conceptual-terminological set of spatial metaphors for use in linguistic modelling.

This is, ultimately, quite a diffuse direction of linguistic study, one which, at present, still lacks a sufficiently clear-cut conceptual-terminological definition. To take over *localism* as an already existing term does not obviate the need to underline that the term refers to all aspects of interpreting language data as primarily spatial, and/or formulated in terms of spatial metaphors, independent of whether it is a question of a specific theory, hypothesis, partial description, which has not pretensions of being a theoretical generalization, or, quite simply, of a casual observation formulated localistically. Though *localism* (by its inner form) is not, perhaps, the most precise of terms (of the two categorial notions of PLACE and SPACE, the latter is, in fact, the key to 'localism'), there seems to be, at the present, no alternative term (such as, for instance, 'spatial linguistics'), which would, by being more precise in a certain sense, also be more applicable according to other criteria. What has been presented here, in brief, as the possible notional nucleus of localism, can be and is being developed in various ways and in various directions, and in order for metalinguistic inconsistency not to hamper the identification of linguistic reality, one of the first tasks of localism is a more thorough study of its own categorial notions and the creation, as much as this is possible, of a more compact conceptual-terminological system for its corresponding theory. Still, before anything is said about this matter, some consideration has to be given to a localistic view of language.

3

Various localistic approaches to language are, naturally, accompanied by various arguments on which particular aspects of localism are founded and which are, in one form or another, its mainstay, and this is the thesis that spatial meanings and their forms of expression are reflected onto other spheres of the semantics and syntax of a natural language, that is to say, that their essence can most adequately be explained in terms of spatial metaphors. Depending on the meaning attributed to the phrase 'other spheres', that is to say, depending on whether a stronger or weaker version of localism is in question, in the sense that Lyons (1977: 718) makes the distinction, there is a difference in both the quality and quantity of argumentation on which such a conception (discussed here only in principle) is founded. Collection of arguments which support it or refute it is the subject of special research. Instead of this, attention is focused here on where to look for appropriate arguments. The most general answer is probably in language data and the conclusions that can be drawn from them. From the standpoint of the autonomy of linguistics among the sciences on man, such an answer could meet with no basic objection other than that it is too much a matter of principle. Yet, there is also another, complementary standpoint: it is, namely, well known that everything in language does not belong to language alone, and in this sense certain laws governing the functioning of language can be taken as manifestations of more general laws of the human universe. To what extent and in what way this could refer to localism has still to be determined by a search for its possible extralinguistic foundations or parallels. Even though their possible existence if not proof in itself that there is something of a similar nature in language, they can lend support to linguistic observations and broaden their sense.

Man's need of localization and, particularly, of autolocalization is revealed by the fact that it has a special physiological expression in the system for maintaining balance (which is one of the basic forms of orientation in space). At present one of the first tests in life for many human beings is that of physical autolocalization. When the blanket a child is lying on is suddenly pulled from under it, the child, if it is healthy, will react by fear caused by a loss of localization and by a grasping gesture, which is instinctive as an effort to hold onto something or to get something back. Loss of spatial-temporal and particularly of spatial localization causes anxiety in the normal adult, while the same phenomenon in the infant reveals its pre-experiential nature. The results of some neuro-physiological and neuro-linguistic studies can, therefore, be of interest to localistically oriented hypotheses and theories. Ivanov (1979), for instance, deals with the binarity related to the asymmetry of the brain and with sign systems which, in departing from the assumption (substantiated quite well by experimental data) that there are two neurological mechanisms, one which governs the external, concrete and spatial world, and another which governs the internal, logical world, thereby links findings in neurology with those in semantics (by way of neurolinguistics and cybernetics). Even further from linguistics, yet not irrelevant to a broader theoretical foundation of localism, is Pribram's (1975) conception of the brain's double process mechanism which corresponds to a topological model of language (Thom 1970) in which syntax and grammar are considered conditional vectors in a topological semantic space (Pribram 1975: 421). Still, it should be said that these observations and conclusions are based on research studies with their own specific aims and methodology and that this is important in regard to their applicability to other planes.

Closer to linguistic, psychology has posited many inspiring observations and notions on man's relation to space. Particularly interesting for a localistic approach to language, are the studies on the structure of thought and the nature of perception, which the literature on localism has recognized, through only in passing (Lyons 1977: 718). This should motivate more thorough studies, as should psycholinguistics as well, particularly developmental psycholinguistics, which has often found that concrete spatial means and their forms of expression precede (and structurally condition) more abstract linguistic contents and their forms,[5] and cognitive linguistics, one of whose central topics is an analysis of metaphors and space-like configurations in semantics and syntax (see, for instance Collinge 1980, Lakoff and Johnson 1980; Longacker 1982).

In addition to this, it is evident that as a social being man has a perpetual need to localize himself within a specific human community — the family, the religious, ethical, political community, and so on — as a member and representative, that is to say, man feels the need to define his social co-ordinates. A loss or absence of social localization can be compared to a loss of physical balance (so banishment is one of the severest punishments in many cultures). Still, what is being dealt with here is evidently not a concretely, but, rather, an abstractly conceived (social) space, which illustrates the often used possibility (both outside of language and outside of linguistic metalanguage) of a spacelike interpretation of non-spatial phenomena. From this standpoint, an extensive analysis of the conceptual-terminological apparatus of various orientations, schools and special theories is needed, not only within linguistics but also within other sciences.

The social dimension of the man-space relationship has, in addition, a semiotic significance as well, and its importance, principal forms in various cultures and the possible directions for its further study have been pointed out by Hall (1969). Just as Hall considers, justifiably, that for a study of a given aspect of the man-space relationship (for which he suggests the term *proxemics*) the category of space in language should be borne in mind (though Hall limits himself to reviewing lexemes with spatial meanings in English), so localism, as a direction of linguistic studies can also find in proxemics much that is complementary to it (see § 7).

Despite the fact that the results of sciences more or less related to linguistics have shed indirect light on the foundedness or unfoundedness of localistic notions, they can also lead to a focusing of attention on other, still untreated linguistic data. Since this is always connected with their explanation, it should be assumed that possible extralinguistic supports to localism can be found not only on an empirical but also on a theoretical level. No less attention, however, should be devoted to the possibility of looking *from* linguistics out toward other sciences and the applicability of localistic hypotheses and theories to explaining extralinguistic data which will be considered in the final paragraph of this paper.

4

Returning from the outer limits of localism closer to its center, a consideration should be made of those notions which are basic to most localistic hypotheses and theories. These are, primarily, the semantic cases of place, direction and path which are believed, according to the localistic theory of cases, to function on different levels of abstraction. In connection with this, it is also necessary to consider the nature of the no less important, though less studied, constitutive elements of spatial relations denoted by language, which are supposed to project themselves onto the non-spatial spheres of the semantics and syntax of a natural language. Since the nature of semantic case is determined by these elementary notions, it seems natural to focus attention on them first of all.

To put it briefly, there are three obligatory elements to a situation denoted by a sentence with a spatial localization and three primary elements to each such meaning: (1) *the object of localization*, (2) *the localizer* (the means of localization) and (3) the actualizer of the relationship between (1) and (2), for which the term *orientation point* seems suitable.

So, for instance, in the sentence *The letter is in the box*, the word *letter* denotes the object of localization, *box* the localizer, and the preposition *in* denotes the orientation point which is, in this case, the interior of the box.[6] The orientation point can also be another part of the localizer, its outer surface usually (such as *The letter is on the box*) or a space outside the localizer, defined by some part of it, such as *The letter is in front of the box*, where the orientation point is a space defined by the front of the localizer, denoted, in this specific example, by the prepositional phrase *in front of*. These examples show the two most general types of orientation points: the *inner* orientation point (an inherent part of the localizer) and the *outer* one (an 'extended' localizer, that is to say, a space defined by some part of the localizer, by which some third portion of space is localized), and these have a large number of forms, most frequently as the systems of prepositions, prefixes, post-positions and adverbs with spatial meanings.

The three constitutive elements of localization do not have to be explicitly expressed by the surface structures of sentences with corresponding meanings, such as, for instance, for the object of localization, *Dawn is rising now in China*, for the localizer, *The letter is inside*, or, for the orientation point, the Serbocroatian dialect sentence *Ona dolazi subota veče* 'She comes Saturday night' where the orientation point is the temporal 'interior' of the localizer, denoted by the noun phrase *subota veče* 'Saturday night', which is not stated explicitly, and not by the period preceding or following the given localizer.[7] The last example shows, likewise, that one and the same constitutive elements of localization can also be treated outside of spatial meanings in the narrowest sense, such as also, for instance, *This trip is beyond his means*, with a modal meaning, where *trip* denotes the object of localization, *beyond* the orientation point, and *his means* the localizer (which should also be compared with the 'inner' orientation point of *This trip is within his means*).The same also holds true for many other meanings, for instance, cause and effect, such as in the Serbocroatian sentence *Oženio se iz ljubavi* 'He married out of love' (inner causal orientation point) as opposed to *Oženio se zbog para* 'He married for money' (outer causal orientation point), or for possession ones, such as in *On je autor prepoznatljivog rukopisa* 'He is an author with a distinctive handwriting' (with an obligatory determination (cf. Ivić 1973) signifying an inner, inalienable possession) as opposed to *On je autor (ovog) rukopisa* 'He is the author of (this) handwriting' (with an optional determination and with a meaning of outer, inalienable possession), and the like.

As localistically oreinted studies have shown, sentences which have a meaning of spatial localization, and, particularly those which have a meaning of non-spatial localization, can be made in very different ways, both in the same language and in different ones, which is in keeping with the notion of semantic cases (Noreen 1925; Fillmore 1968, 1971; Kempf 1978 and others). What holds true for semantic cases on the level of expression also holds true for their constitutive elements, that is to say, the object of localization, the localizer and the orientation point are the elementary *semantic* entities which determine cases as the elementary semantic relationships. In the localistic theory of cases, the primary focus is always on those meanings which reflect a kind of dynamic relationship between the object of localization and the orientation point, represented, typically, by the question words *gde?* 'where?', *kamo?* 'where to?', *kuda?* 'which way?', *odakle?* 'where from?'. In this connection, it should be kept in mind that the orientation point, always in a middle position, in between the object of localization and the localizer, is two-fold in nature: besides being oriented toward the object of localization, it is not less important for us that it is in a relationship with the localizer. It has already been mentioned that the orientation point is a contituent or 'additional' part of the localizer, and that this is reflected by the fact that there are inner (direct) and outer (indirect) orientation points, yet, one other fact is also characteristic of the relationship between the orientation point and the localizer (as opposed to the orientation point-object of localization relationship) and it is directly connected with the former: the given relationship is considered to be a fixed one, leaving no possibility for treating the orientation point as an object (part of space) which can alter its position in relation to the localizer. For this reason it seems best to speak of the *static* aspect of localization here, as oposed to its *dynamic* aspect (the object of localization – the orientation point), which is determined by the fact that the object of localization is considered an object which can alter its position in relation to the orientation point and the localizer, that it can be not only an object which is localized as in, for instance, *The man is on the bridge* (*locativity*), but also one which is *beginning* to be localized, as in, for instance, *The man is coming onto the bridge* (*adlativity*) or which is *ending* to be localized, as in, for instance, *The man is going off the bridge* (*ablativity*).[8] And, finally, the object of localization can be localized by the orientation point of a certain localizer, so that its altered relationship to the outer portion of this orientation point is relevant as, for instance, in *The man is going across the bridge* (*perlativity*). In this case, in addition to the basic orientation point, there are also narrower ones: orientation point$_1$ and orientation point$_2$ — the outer portions of the orientation point in relation to which the localization of the given object is not considered to be a stable one, but, rather, one which is in the process of being changed.

The hierarchy of orientation points can also be considered from the syntagmatic standpoint, as, for instance, *Devojka je u subotu ujutru ustala u četvrt do osam* (in English literally 'The girl got up on Saturday morning at a quarter to eight') where the temporal localizer is the time of speaking ('now'), outside of which the object of localization — the time when the girl's getting up is situated, that is to say, the basic orientation point is a time outside the localizer (more specifically, anterior to it), superior to a series of narrower orientation points: orientation point$_1$ *subota* 'Saturday', orientation point$_2$ *u* 'on', orientation point$_3$ *ujutru* 'morning', orientation point$_4$ *osam* 'eight', orientation point$_5$ *do* 'to' (anterior to orientation point$_4$), orientation point$_6$ *četvrt* 'quarter', orientation point$_7$ *u* 'at'.

From this same standpoint, a hierarchy of the other constitutive elements of localization can be established: for instance, in one and the same sentence, an object of localization can function as a localizer for another object of localization, such as in *The girl is sitting on a bench in front of the house*, where 'bench' is an object of localization in relation to 'house', but a localizer in relation to the object of localization 'girl', so, therefore, the orientation point denoted by the preposition 'on' is indirectly subordinated to the orientation point denoted by the prepositional phrase 'in front of'.[9]

It is a known fact that opinions are divided about the inventory and nature of semantic cases of place and path (to which the meanings locativity, perlativity, ablativity and adlativity in this paper correspond) and about semantic cases in general. Yet, it is the four, above-mentioned meanings that are discussed, though they are also denoted by different terms.[10] Some authors shorten the list of cases (for instance, Anderson 1971: 119-121, 169-171), while others add to it (for instance, Bennett 1975: 40-44), though, it seems, in some cases, not to be a question of essential differences but rather of viewing the same phenomenon from different levels of abstraction, that is to say, a question of cases and 'hypercases' (Fillmore 1971: 52). This difference reflects the different degrees of generality of corresponding meanings which are organized on a binary principle into a microsystem. Here the basic criterion is the *dynamicity* of the object of localization, according to which locativity is neutral (for instance *The man is standing/jumping on the bridge*), while the other three meanings marked by the given criterion are opposed to one another according to the narrower criterion of *direction* of movement where perlativity is neutral, since it refers to the path, but not also to the direction of movement of the object of localization in relation to the orientation point. Finally, adlativity and ablativity come under the narrowest, equipollent opposition since they refer to *the process of localization in* a certain orientation point or to *the delocalization from* a certain orientation point.

These categorial meanings of localization do not, however, reflect only the variable relationship between the object of localization and the orientation point, but, in a generalized way, what is permanent in this relationship as well, and this is revealed by the fact that the object of localization is found, in two cases (ablativity and adlativity), of necessity, along the line of its movement *also outside the orientation point* (see, for instance, *He is pouring water into a glass/He is pouring water out of a glass*), while the other two meanings (locativity, perlativity) are netural according to this same criterion. The relevant point is that the object of localization is *within* the orientation point, while the possibility of its partial extralocalization is secondary (as, for instance, locativity in *The water is in the glass* and *The flowers are in the glass*, or perlativity in *The fly is going across the table* and *The fly has flown over the table*, and the like).

When one attempts, in the space of an article, to review the most important questions of localism, one has, understandably, to be very selective, both in regard to the problems and the examples chosen. For this reason the examples that predominate are of sentences with concrete spatial meanings. Examples of non-spatial localizations within the semantic categories of modality, possession and cause have been briefly discussed in the first part of this section. In connection with this, it seems important to stress that various semantic types of localization are realized not only within the scope of certain semantic categories, but on a level between the categories as well: certain semantic categories are easily included under a specific categorial type of localization, as, for instance, cause and ablativity, aim and adlativity, manner and perlativity, etc. (which is, on the level of expression, often manifested by a polysemy of corresponding linguistic means). For example, within the meaning of *manner* as a qualification of a certain action, there is a certain element of process indicative of the quality *through* which the given action is realized, that is to say, manner is the more abstract notion of its path of realization, though the difference between a concrete and a more abstract path may be irrelevent: assume, for instance, in Serbocroatian, that the answer to the questions *Kako je ova mačka ušla?* 'How did this cat get in?' and *Kuda je ova mačka ušla?* 'Which way did this cat get in?' can be the same — *Kroz prozor* 'Through the window'. So also in Latin *quā?* can mean 'which way' and 'how' and 'when' (which also reveals a connection between a linear notion of time and perlativity); in Greek *tēde* means both 'this way' and 'in this manner', and the like (see Piper 1983: 95-107).

5

Even though the localistic theory of cases went, a long time ago, beyond the formal scope of the category of case, it should be stressed that its possibilities of explanation are not limited by the sentences, nor even the exclusively linguistic aspects of communication. If we consider the structure of a *text* from these positions, we will come across the well known fact that a basic feature of a text as a specific kind of linguistic unit is its limitedness, its closedness (Lotman 1976: 90, 277-278) revealed primarily by the clearly marked beginnings and endings of certain types of texts (for instance, of a letter, a telephone conversation, a fairy tale and the like) which are shaped, in fact, as specific kinds of 'journeys' from the beginning (ablativity) toward the ending (adlativity). There are, sometimes, special features of perlativity as well, such as, for instance, the repeating of the adverbs *then* or *after-wards* in narratives, though not in the initial or final positions. In the structure of a text, locativity as an absence of direction can be represented by the title, the static, presice sub-text, which is, at one and the same time, its own beginning, middle and end. The three-part (ablative-perlative-adlative) model can also be found in the compositional structure of some types of text, as, for instance, in the case of myths, where there is often a special emphasis on journey, on change, that is to say, on the middle, perlative position.

The same syntagmatic model can also be found on a purely formal plane: in writing, as, for instance, in Arabic where one and the same grapheme has four forms in which it appears depending on whether it is in an initial, medial or isolated position; in spelling, as, for instance, the use of capital letters, indentation, commas, hyphens, full stops, spacing, etc., to mark the beginning, middle or end of a word, sentence or passage.

6

Though the notion of localistic invariants has been given here in broad strokes, the conclusion that localism reduces to a kind of 'hunt' on given invariants through the forest of their variant forms would be just as superficial as incorrect. Despite the fact that within the framework of localistically oriented research the question of localistic invariants appears as a basic one, it is just one among many more or less closely related ones. They cannot all be given equal attention here, though some can at least be mentioned.

One such question is the principle of spatial metaphorization and the stratification of localizations of various degrees of abstraction.[11] Though there are several linguistic models of stratification, some of which are more closely related to localism (for instance, Pottier 1974; Bennet 1975), within the growing number of studies on the nature and form of metaphor in everyday speech there seems to be a greater interest in solutions considered to be new, rather than in revaluating existent ones and an attempt at creating a synthetic theory of metaphor in grammar and semantics. In these efforts the conclusions of localistic studies should probably not be ignored.[12]

In a language, the question of the primacy of spatial localizations in relation to non-spatial ones has a historical dimension to it as well. Though it has been evidenced many a time and for several languages, this primacy is always shown by the more recent history of a language as recorded in written documents, though the assumed process of 'spatialization' must have begun in the most distant history of the language. Assumptions about this process can thus be made only on the basis of indirect evidence, or by mere speculation, and they would not lead to conclusions in favour of the above mentioned thesis. Namely, it seems quite probable that in natural languages the formation of the system of semantic categories did not proceed in a straight line and in succession from spatial to non-spatial meanings, but in a *simultaneous* manner as well — from a syncretic language model of the extralinguistic universe toward a differentiation and specialization of language means and contents, both on the paradigmatic and on the syntagmatic level, wherein the linguistic conception of space, due to its extralinguistic relevance for man, could serve as a model for structuring certain non-spatial meanings without hindering, at the same time, a parallel development of the categories of space and of certain 'spatially' conceived aspects of certain other categories. The cause of such homologies, unconditioned by one another, lies, probably, in the very foundations of the system, or, perhaps, still deeper — in the structure of the human mind, something that should certainly be the subject of interdisciplinary research and not guesswork.

7

Studying the specific features of language compared to other sign systems, along with the attempt to establish, as precisely as possible, the dividing line between linguistics and the sciences closely related to it, does not end, as is well known, the need to discover everything that connects them, above all the common categorial features of system closely related on a functional plane. If the assumption should prove true, that many language phenomena are structured on principles best formulated in spatial terms, and that the phenomenal diversity of the linguistic universe only varies the same invariants, then, since such a notion assumes an extralinguistic conditioning of the nature of man by spatial factors, it could be supposed that the localistic image of language is just part of a localistic image of man in the larger portion or even totality of homologous forms which manifest his essence. The consequences of this assumption could be very far-reaching indeed, though equally far-reaching and difficult would be its confirmation by facts, at the present moment, and within the framework of linguistics alone even quite impossible. Instead, this assumption can be illustrated by two examples.

The first example is closer to a natural language and it concerns the *language of space*. It is well known that over the past decades research studies have revealed strong and complex connections between man's activities and their spatial frameworks. In short, the way in which personal and social space is organized and the way it is used by the representatives of a culture forms a special code and a knowledge of it is an assumption for communication. In this code the oppositions *inner/outer, central/peripheral, near/far* and the like are very evident and relevant, though, understandably, the notions of 'central', 'inner' or 'near' do not have the same content in various cultures. Still, worthy of attention is how this pair (these pairs) of opposite notions are varied in forms of spatial organization related to movement. This has been studied explicitly by H. Osmand (see Hall 1968: 91) who suggests a division of this space into *sociopetal* (places where people go intending to stay for a while in the company of others, as for instance, various clubs, cafés and the like) and *sociofugal* (places whence people depart in various directions, that is to say, where they come in order to leave, as for instance, railway stations, airports and the like). From the standpoint of the notions discussed in the preceding paragraphs, the first type of sociospatial form is, evidently, *socioadlative* in nature, while the second type is *socioablative*. The idea of there being a *socioperlative* space comes to mind here inevitably and such a space is not difficult to identify: various forms of 'ways' (roads, streets, stairs, hallways and the like) or, in another form, various means of transportation; and, also of there being *sociolocative* space: spaces where people stay (a city, house, room, desk and the like). Of course, there is also the possibility of a syncretism of functions for one and the same space. A street, for instance, in addition to a basic, socioperlative function, can also have a socioadlative one, as for instance, a promenade, which is a specific feature of the language of space of a certain culture. Does this description of the basic elements of the functional paradigm of social space cover its most relevant features? There are, of course, other features of social space (quantitative, ethnic, configurational, etc.), but none of them seem to be as general, relevant and evidently homologous to some other aspects of man's universe as the ones just presented.

The second example is from psychology. It is further from a natural language since it does not illustrate, as the previous example does, a *specific* form of behaviour which is essentially homologous to some linguistic categories, but, rather, that it is possible to treat localistic postulates in linguistics as a function of corresponding localistic postulates on human nature. As in linguistics, in psychology, too, an analysis of the conceptual-terminological apparatus would reveal many possible common points between a localistic image of language and an interpretation of various psychological phenomena. Let us consider one case briefly: Fromm's typology of personality.

It would seem, at first, that K.G. Jung's distinction between introvert and extrovert personality types is closer to what we would like to demonstrate, yet, this similarity with linguistic intra- and extralocalizations, except on a terminological level, would be too general to serve as an illustration of broader connections between a localistic image of language and its projection on psychology, that is to say, on the typology of personality. The typology offered by E. Fromm shows this in fact. Though it is not formulated in terms of spatial metaphors, it can easily be translated into them. For Fromm, personality is "the relatively permanent form in which human energy is canalized in the process of assimilation and socialization" (Fromm 1971: 59). He distinguishes five basic personality types, of which four are of an unproductive orientation from the standpoint of assimilation: a) Receiving (Accepting), b) Exploiting (Taking), c) Hoarding (Preserving), d) Marketing (Exchanging); and from the standpoint of socialization, a) Masochistic (Loyalty), b) Sadistic (Authority), c) Destructive (Assertiveness), d) Indifferent (Fairness). The fifth type is of a productive orientation which Fromm characterizes as activity ('Working') from the standpoint of assimilation, and love and reason ('Loving, Reasoning') from the standpoint of socialization. Without making any essential changes, the distinctive features of these types can also be expressed by terms indicating a subordination of personality types to more general categories:

	Intralocalization	Extralocalization
Locativity	'Hoarding' type, preserving, conservative	'Marketing'
Ablativity	losing	'Exploiting'
Adlativity	'Receiving', receptive	'Giving', 'productive'
Perlativity	?	innovative

Fromm's terms are given in quotation marks. The table shows that such an interpretation of a well known typology of personality makes it possible not only to establish a conceptual and terminological connection between quite distant, apparently unrelated phenomena (as was suggested by the Serbian mathematician M. Petrović, who, in his day (1940), sought homologies of types among apparently quite disparate phenomena, see Petrović 1962), but also to reveal more distinctly the very subject of typology.[12]

In concluding this consideration of some importation problems of localism, it should be stressed that it did not aim nor could it aim at giving a final answer to how far the possibilities of localism extend for explanations in linguistics, or even less outside of linguistics. Until our knowledge about this matter becomes more precise, we cannot exclude the possibility that it may seem that localism tends to place the infinite variety of empiricism onto the Procrustean bed of its own strict model. Still, in the belief that the variety of the universe, or, at least, of man's universe is not a chaotic one, and that everything created by man, including man himself, should function according to some common fundamental principles, this paper has attempted, relying on the notion of localistic invariants, to illustrate by two examples at least that the possibilities of localism should not be exhausted on explaining (some) linguistic phenomena alone. This would open up the perspective for localism to develop from a linguistic theory into a broader epistemological one. If this could have been considered in greater detail, and more fully documented, the present paper could have been more appropriately entitled 'Localism in Linguistics and Linguistics in Localism'. This may remain the title for a study yet to be written.

Notes

1. Leontjev (1974: 73) finds relevance of the same criterion of locating according to the vertical in the pronoun systems of the Papuan Veri and Keva languages, but he does not connect this with any extralinguistic factors.

2. Both groups were taken from the same dialect region (mountain Golija in Serbia) and were of similar age and sex. Subjects living at an altitude of 400 meters formed the control group.

3. The emphasis in the literature of today is on the works of authors in English, and more rarely, in French. The modern localistic or paralocalistic approach to language has gained diverse (in subject, though in methodology less uniform) and, on the whole, less formalized forms also in the studies of Civjan 1973; Mihailović 1977; Kempf 1978; Fleischmann 1983; Piper 1983; Toporov 1983, and others.

4. Though Friedrich does not express an attitude toward localism, he is mentioned here because it is considered that form meanings should be treated as aspects of spatial meanings — as meanings of inner space as opposed to localization, connected with outer space (Piper 1983: 131). The use of the form of the human body as a prototype for a conception of various non-spatial relations is also characteristic of other languages (see Cassirer 1953: 207). Tarascana stands out by the pronounced grammatization of corresponding meanings which are either less present (for instance, the systems of post-positions in Nganasanese is similar, on a semantic plane, to the Tarascana suffix system, see Tereščenko 1979: 304), or quite absent in other languages, that is to say, the corresponding meanings often have a predominantly lexical expression. For Slavic languages, see for Serbocroatian toponyms Mihajlović (1970); for Bulgarian Legurska (1985).

5. For a more detailed consideration of some psycholinguistic aspects of localism, see Piper 1983-1984.

6. The notions object of localization', 'localizer' and 'orientation point' are not new to linguistics (see Weinsberg 1973: 22-25; Bennet 1975: 15-16; Piper 1977: 5; Longacker 1982: 47; Piper 1983: 34), but what has been written about them so far is the result of initial,

and as yet still quite uncoordinated, studies which are accompanied by significant terminological differences.

7. The localizer and the orientation point can also be expressed syncretically as, for instance, in the case of some pronominal adverbs, such as Serbocroatian *tu* 'here', where the localizer is the person speaking, and the orientation point the place where he/she is or a place near by; or take also for example the form for the future in Serbocroatian such as *pisaću* 'I'll write', where the morpheme *-ću* denotes both the localizer — the time of speech — and the orientation point — posteriority — within which the action denoted by the root *pisa-* is situated.

8. Whether this is a question of localization or (de)localization-in-process also depends on the aspect of meaning. In the given examples imperfectiveness strengthens the other meaning. Since, phasally, the verb *prestati* 'to stop' is semantically derived from *početi*, 'to begin' (*prestati* 'to stop' = 'početi ne. . .' 'to begin not to . . .', see Apresjan 1980: 27; for instance *Prestala je da ga primećuje* 'She stopped noticing him' = *Počela je da ga ne primećuje* ('she began not to notice him') this simplifies the conceptual apparatus for interpreting the semantics of localization, approaching the model Wierzbicka (1973) suggested for spatial and temporal meanings, and which can be reduced to two semantic parameters: *biti deo* 'to be a part of' and *početi* 'to begin'. Within the scope of this study, it is revealed that the former is relevant for the orientational (static) and the latter for the dynamic aspect of localization.

9. It is quite clear that the number of such localizations is quite limited in speech, and also that the choice of localizer for an object of localization is not completely arbitrary, yet a consideration of limitations of this kind exceeds the framework of this paper.

10. For instance, what is here termed perlativity (after Weinsberg 1973: 77-78) is also called *Path case* (see Bennet 1975: 29 *et passim*) and *Itinerative case* (Fillmore 1971:50). As far as the number of formal cases is concerned, which, since they belong to the surface structure of the sentence, can differ considerably from language to language, according to Kempf (1978: 46-68) there are as many as 88 in the Tabarasan language of the Caucasian group.

11. A modest contribution in this direction could be the analysis (presented in the author's book on pronominal adverbs, Piper 1983) of the opposition *intralocalization/extralocalization* as a possible constituent factor of the system of semantic categories and the basis principle in the hierarchy of categorial meanings of space, time, agency, possession and the like, which are also partially reflected in some notions and their interpretations in this paper.

12. The fifth type, according to Fromm, has not been given separately here since it is closest to what the table denotes as a *productive* type. The scheme provides place for three more types. Two of them (termed *losing* for the type of person who is said not to have luck and who is usually the object of someone's exploitation; and *innovative*, that is to say, the type of person who tends to change environments) seem to receive an amount of confirmation in reality. For types with features of perlativity and intra-localization, the author does not at present find satisfactory examples. Perhaps this is an empty spot in the paradigm. For the sake of brevity, the aspect of social orientation, which finds a place in Fromm's typology, has been left out. Just as Fromm concludes, pure types are constructs, and each of them has both positive and negative sides and phenomenal forms.

References

Anderson, John M. 1971. *The Grammar of Case: Towards a Localistic Theory*. Cambridge: University Press.

-----. 1973. *An Essay Concerning Aspect: Some Considerations of a General Character Arising from the Abbé Darrigol's Analysis of the Basque Verb*. The Hague: Mouton.

-----. 1977. *On Case Grammar: Prolegomena to a Theory of Grammatical Relations*. London: Croom Helm.

Apresjan, Jurij D. 1980. *Tipy informacii dlja poverxnostno-semantičeskogo komponenta modeli Smysl* ↔ Tekst [Types of information in the surface semantic component of the model meaning ↔ text]. Wiener Slawistischer Almanach. (= Sonderband 1.)

Bach, Emmon and Robert T. Harms (eds.) 1968. *Universals in Linguistic Theory*. New York: Holt, Rinehart and Winston.

Bennet, David C. 1975. *Spatial and Temporal Uses of English Prepositions: An Essay in Stratificational Semantics*. London: Longman.

Benveniste, Émile. 1966. *Problèmes de linguistique générale*. Paris: Gallimard.

Cassirer, Ernst. 1953. *The Philosophy of Symbolic Forms*. Vol. I. *Language*. New Haven: Yale University Press.

Civ'jan, Tat'jana V. 1973. "O nekotoryx sposobax otraženija v jazyke oppozicii *vnutrennij/vnešnij*" [On some means of the reflection in language of the opposition *internal/external*]. In: Zaliznjak. 1973: 242-261.

-----. (ed.) 1983. *Tekst: semantika i struktura* [Text: Semantics and structure]. Moscow: Nauka.

Collinge, E. 1980. *Case and Space*. Trier: Linguistic Agency University of Trier. (= Series A, Paper No. 76.)

Fillmore, Charles J. 1968. "The Case for Case." In: E. Bach and R.T. Harms (eds.). 1968: 1-88.

-----. 1971. "Some Problems for Case Grammar." In: R.J. O'Brien. 1971: 35-56.

Fleischmann, Eberhard. 1983. "Der semantische Lokativ: Eine Untersuchung an Hand russischer Wortfügungen." *Zeitschrift für Slawistik*. 1: 1-8.

Friedrich, Paul. 1969. *On the Meaning of the Tarascan Suffixes of Space*. Bloomington. (= Memoir of the International Journal of American Linguistics 23.)

-----. 1970. "Shape in grammar." *Language*. 2: 379-408.

Fromm, Erich. 1971. *Man for Himself: An Enquiry into the Psychology of Ethics*. London: Routledge and Kegan Paul.

Giljferding, Aleksandar. 1972. *Putovanje po Hercegovini, Bosni i Staroj Srbiji* [A journey through Herzegovina, Bosnia and old Serbia]. Sarajevo: Veselin Masleša.

Gunaev, Z.S. 1977. "O vyraženii prostranstvennyx otnošenij v nekotoryx dagestanskix jazykax" [On the expression of space relations in several Dagestan languages]. *Voprosy jazykoznanija*. 6: 126-130.

Hall, Edward T. 1968. "Proxemics." *Current Anthropology* 9: 83-95.

Householder, Fred W. (ed.) 1972. *Syntactic Theory* 1. *Structuralist Selected Readings*. Harmondsworth: Penguin Books.

Ivanov, Vjačeslav V. 1979. *Čet i nečet: asimmetrija mozga i znakovyx sistem* [Even and uneven: The asymmetry of the brain and sign systems]. Moscow: Radio.

Ivić, Milka. 1972. "Non-omissible Determiners in Slave Languages." In: Householder. 1972: 135-140.

Kempf, Zdzisław. 1978. *Próba teorii przypadków: Część I* [Attempt at a theory of cases: Part I]. Opole: Opolskie Towarzystwo Przyjaciół Nauk.

Kiefer, Ferenc and Nicolas Ruvet. (eds.) 1973. *Generative Grammar in Europa*. Dordrecht: D. Reidel Publishing Company. (= *Foundations of Language. Supplementary Series*, 13.)

Kuryłowicz, Jerzy. 1971. "Podstawowe kategorie morfologiczne" [Fundamental grammatical categories]. *Biuletyn Polskiego Towarzystwa Językoznawczego* 28: 3-13.

-----. 1972. "The role of deictic elements in linguistic evolution." *Semiotica*. 2: 174-184.

Lakoff, George and Mark Johnson. 1980. *Metaphors We Live By*. Chicago: University of Chicago Press.

Legurska, P. 1985. "Nominativni metafori, izrazeni s nazvanija za časti na tjaloto v b'lgarskija knižoven ezik." *B'lgarski ezik*. 1: 36-42.

Leontjev, Aleksej A. 1974. *Papuasskie jazyki* [Papuan languages]. Moscow: Nauka.

Longacker, Ronald W. 1982. "Space grammar, analysability, and the English passive." *Language*. 1: 22-81.

Lotman, Jurij. 1976. *Struktura umetničkog teksta*. Beograd: Nolit.

Lyons, John. 1977. *Semantics*. Vol. I-II. Cambridge: Cambridge University Press.

Mihailović, Ljiljana. 1977. "Lokalistička teorija padeža i pojam neotuđivog pripadanja" [Localistic case theory and the notion of inalienable possession], *Zbornik radova Filozofskog fakulteta u Nišu* 4: 173-190.

Mihajlović, Velimir. 1970. "Anatomska leksika u srpskohrvatskoj onomastici i geografskoj terminologiji" [Anatomical lexis in Serbocroatian onomastics and geographical terminology]. *Zbornik za filologiju i lingvistiku* 2: 7-49.

Noreen, Adolf. 1925. *Vårt Språk*, t. V: *Betydelselära*. Lund.

Obrenović, Joviša. 1983. *Izgovor vokala u funkciji nadmorske visine* [The pronunciation of vowels in the function of height above sea level]. Beograd. (Unpublished master's thesis.)

O'Brien, Richard J. (ed.) 1971. *Report of the Twenty-Second Annual Round Table Meeting on Linguistics and Language Studies*. Washington, D.C.: Georgetown University Press.

Petrović, Mihajlo. 1962. *Metafore i alegorije* [Metaphors and allegories]. Beograd: Srpska književna zadruga.

Piper, Predrag. 1977-1978. "Obeležavanje prostornih odnosa predloško-padežnim konstrukcijama u savremenom ruskom i savremenom srpskohrvatskom književnom jeziku." [The denotation of spatial relations by preposition-case construction in modern Russian and the modern Serbocroatian standard language]. *Prilozi proučavanju jezika* 13-14: 1-51.

-----. 1983. *Zamenički prilozi: gramatički status i semantički tipovi* [Pronominal adverbs: grammatical status and semantic types]. Novi Sad: Institut za strane jezike i književnosti.

-----. 1983-1984. "O psiholingvističkim osnovama opozicije 'unutra/spolja' kao mogućeg konstitutivnog faktora sistema semantičkih kategorija" [On the psycholinguistic foundations of the opposition 'inside/outside' as a possible constitutive factor of the system of semantic categories]. *Godišnjak Saveza društava za primenjenu lingvistiku Jugoslavije* 7-8: 283-291.

Pottier, Bernard. 1974. *Linguistique générale*. Paris: Klincksieck.

Pribram, Karl. 1975. *Jazyki mozga* [The languages of the brain]. Moscow: Progress.

Tereščenko, N.M. 1979. *Nganasanskij jazyk* [The Nganasan language]. Leningrad: Nauka.

Thom, René. 1970. "Topologie et linguistique". In: *Essays on Topology and Related Topics: Memoirs dediés a George de Rham*. Berlin: Springer Verlag. 226-248.

Toporov, Vladimir N. 1983. "Prostranstvo i tekst" [Space and text]. In: Civ'jan. 1983: 227-285.

Weinsberg, Adam. 1973. *Przyimki przestrzenne w języku polskim, niemieckim i rumuńskim*. Wrocław: Polska Akademia Nauk.

Wierzbicka, Anna. 1973. "In search of a semantic model of time and space." In: F. Kiefer and N. Ruvet. 1973: 616-629.

Zaliznjak, Andrej A. (ed.) 1973. *Strukturno-tipologičeskie issledovanija v oblasti grammatiki slavjanskix jazykov* [Structural-typological research in the domain of the grammar of the Slavic languages]. Moscow: Nauka.

Between sign and act

Milorad Pupovac
Faculty of Philosophy, University of Zagreb

Even those philosophers whose interests are in different fields would probably agree with the statement that language is one of the central threads in a large part of 20th-century philosophy. For some this is believed to be the result of the very successful development of linguistics, while others think that the stormy development of linguistics and the orientation of philosophy towards language are closely linked with the development of modern means of communication and with the unbelievably complex ways in which people connect not only with each other but with things. Furthermore, it is also often thought that it may be due to the question of language criticism, i.e. criticism caused by a really large discrepancy between the potentials for communication and the existing rather low level of communication among people. Perhaps closest to philosophical truth is the opinion that the question of language in contemporary philosophy is, at the same time, the prime question of philosophy itself, i.e. of the possibility of philosophizing.

In the same way as many other essential issues of our time (science, technology, politics, etc.) have become distinct areas, language has also become the subject of a separate branch of philosophy — the philosophy of language — and moreover, through modern glottocentrism, acquired the status of 'first' philosophy. The ontologization of the subject matter of language and of the status of philosophy of language is also evident through the fact that the study of language is treated as being superior to other areas of investigation. The view that it is possible to explain the essence of the world by means of the being of language (as indeed it was once done using the being of work) is, owing to modern glottocentrism, quite evident, and it is characteristic of other philosophical disciplines, such as the philosophy of science and the philosophy of politics. This and the philosophy of language only indicate that contemporary philosophy operates in the sphere of separate entities, separate kinds of being, so that it can be assumed (as in the case of science) that it represents 'pure' philosophizing. In other words, I am suggesting that such 'behavior' of philosophical disciplines, including the philosophy of language, should be observed in the context of the relationship between philosophy and science, i.e. in the context of efforts to define (critically or not) philosophy in relation to scientific knowledge — the scientific vision of the world.

Due to the emphasis on the importance of the subject matter of language (evident in its ontologization and the leading role of linguistics among the social sciences) the relation between the philosophy of language and linguistics is, to a large extent, paradigmatic for the relation between contemporary philosophy and science. Philosophy, in the same way as linguistics, has been divided into different areas. The aspect of language being treated at any moment may depend on direct linguistic achievements or, more often, on an ideological context. Thus we can say that a structurally oriented philosophy of language is based on the theoretical achievements of structural linguistics, while the philosophy of language in analytic philosophy is being developed in the general atmosphere where philosophy is regarded as metascientific reflection on metascientific presuppositions and scientific knowledge. For this reason I consider the philosophy of language as basically an expression of our scientific (linguistic) knowledge of language. Such a relation between the philosophy of language and linguistics is equally important for both, and for the possibility of philosophic and scientific knowledge about language.

In spite of considerable differences in the thematic and ideological characteristics of contemporary orientations in the philosophy of language, it seems to me that we can, nevertheless, divide them into three predominant groups: structuralist, hermeneutic and analytic (pragmatic). For structuralism the predominant aspect of language is the sign system, for hermeneutics it is comprehension and interpretation of signs, whilst for analytic (pragmatic) philosophy it is the activity aspect of language. Taking into consideration the differences in range, duration and intensity all of these orientations have influenced the development of the philosophy of language in Yugoslavia.

This development is without doubt connected to the development of philosophy and linguistics. Philosophy started its development in this part of the world only at the end of the last century and the beginning of this one. In spite of a relatively rich literary tradition, up to then we cannot talk about the existence of philosophy in the disciplinary and educational sense of the word. The main factor effecting the later development of science and philosophy in what is now called Yugoslavia was the long-lasting deprivation of the political, economic, cultural and linguistic freedom of our peoples and states. For example, the great names of renaissance philosophy and science — Franjo Petrić and Ruđer Bošković (Croats) — wrote in Latin, and it is only comparatively recently that translations of their works have brought them within reach of a Yugoslav philosophical public. For a long time after that it lagged behind the dominant trends of world philosophy. Linguistics was far more developed, but it was still rather difficult to keep pace with quick and up-to-date developments in the rest of the world. Prewar Yugoslav philosophy deals with topics from the sphere of cognitive theory, logic, ethics and aesthetics without explicitly touching the subject matter of language. As far as linguistics is concerned, even its more developed areas, covering comparative linguistics, stood apart from linguistic modernism, i.e. the Geneva, Moscow and Prague schools.

After World War II Yugoslav philosophy had to face a twofold task: to become active in the revolutionary changes, i.e. to exist in the context of the growth of the socialist system, and to continue its development and integration into European and world trends, in short to establish a theoretical basis for its existence. The former considerably determined its direction and thematic development, so that the greatest part of Yugoslav philosophy was and still is Marxian and principally oriented towards social and political aspects of world Being. Such an orientation (it is common knowledge that Marxism did not take language much into consideration) explains the fact that up to the 60's language was not an explicit topic of Yugoslav philosophy.

Marković (1961) made the first significant study of language used in Yugoslav philosophy in his book *Dijalektička teorija značenja* [The dialectic theory of meaning]. The value of his work can be judged through a rather elaborate survey of various (mainly analytic, i.e. Anglo-Saxon) theories of meaning, such as functional, formalistic, conceptualist and realistic. Marković's contribution becomes even greater if we bear in mind the fact that, at that time in Yugoslavia, analytic (Anglo-Saxon) philosophy gave rise to a number of negative prejudices. However, the way he interpreted these theories, and the concept of his dialectic theory of meaning itself, only contributed to reducing interest in the above mentioned theories, which might otherwise have become widespread. He takes as a starting point the hypothesis that these theories, together with their aspects of meaning, can be put together by means of dialectics into a unique theory of meaning which presupposes their unity. According to him, meaning is a complex of meaningful structures which are built on the following relations: the relation between the sign and the mental state it expresses, the relation between the sign and the subject it denotes, the relation between the sign and other signs within a particular sign system, and the relations between the sign and the utterances of the speaker. All of these imply the existence of the relation between two speaking subjects one of whom uses while the other interprets these signs. Each of the relations mentioned has a relevant aspect of meaning: mental, topical, linguistic and practical. Besides their basic meanings, signs also have an intersubjective character. In other words they should be observed as a social product and within a social context. Neglecting the specific aspect of the theories of meaning which was taken as a springboard, and because of the insufficient theoretical and practical use made of his concept of meaning, Marković's study of language is confined to this book and makes very little contribution to the orientation of our philosophy towards the subject matter of language.

At the end of the 60s many Yugoslav periodicals published the first translations of texts about well-developed structuralist and hermeneutics orientations in the philosophy of language (e.g. *Delo* (Belgrade), *Pitanja* (Zagreb), *Problemi* (Ljubljana)). Strong links between many social sciences, particularly linguistics and the theory of literature, and leading orientations of the time helped philosophical interest in language in Yugoslavia, thus at least partly encouraging the glottocentric experience of contemporary philosophy. The period from the 60s to the middle of the 70s might be characterized as one of getting to know these two orientations, while that from the 70s up to the present could be called the period of arbitrary interpretations, during which efforts to establish the subject matter of the philosophy of language and an individual approach to language were made.

Throughout the 70s there were several attempts to establish the hermeneutic theory of language (Aćin 1975). Most of them, regardless of whether their subject matter was literary criticism or philosophy, remained whithin the pages of periodicals and had no considerable effects. Of all of these, the greatest attention should be paid to a rather small text by **Pejović** (1976): *Language as an experience of the world*. His work is characterized by an attempt to trace the hermeneutic (especially the concept of the philosophic hermeneutics of H.G. Gadamer) and von Humboldt's concepts of language: a reflection of our experiences of the world as a free product, on the basis of which we derive comprehension, i.e. linguistic articulation of the productive experience of the world. Production and comprehension are central notions Pejović uses to explain the phenomenon of language. Pejović says that if we understand the truth of Being as a production of Being in the historic world, it can be articulated in language, and therefore language is an important and inevitable question of philosophizing and philosophy itself. Such an interpretation of language by far exceeds the limits of a discipline like philosophy of language and the individual aspects of language raised by 'the spirit of the age'. It is, therefore, necessary to understand it as a kind of ontology. Even within certain limits of such an approach, Pejović tries to solve all the important issues in the philosophy of language: language and thinking are one; the basis of this unity is comprehension while the world provides the framework; the relationship between language and reality is, in fact, a constant 'putting together' of stable things and changing reality, by means of language itself, and not a reflection, onomatopoeia or anything else; it is this language production that provides this ever present unity of words and things, i.e., the possibility that words always denote the same things; as a structural entity language enables meaningfulness of speech and writing which is directly connected with its own articulating nature, i.e. with the ability of language to produce, using a limited number of language signs, an unlimited number of statements about extra-linguistic reality, thus articulating reality itself; the sign system, as an instrument of speech, presupposes language as speech activity, and not vice versa, as is the case with structuralism. Depending on its expressive characteristics, language can be equally an expression of soul or body. Language as genuine understanding within a community, is the understanding of things, of the speakers themselves, of the meaning present in utterances and of the utterances themselves. Being an experience of the historical production of the world, language has a threefold relationship to history: language in time, time in language and language as time (history); the question of Being — one of the first questions of philosophy — is put forward as a question of language, thus language becomes an inevitable part of philosophy. In the same way as the whole reception of hermeneutics has not moved away from its first efforts, so Pejović's concept of the philosophy of language is still only an outline, probably because it has already answered all the questions. Ontologizing the notion of comprehension, Pejović, like the hermeneutics which he uses as a starting point, neglects the equal importance of other aspects of language. Moreover he forgets that the aspect he uses as a starting point is only an aspect, and not an ontological basis of language. In spite of the thoroughness of his approach I can not help feeling that it falls short in one basic respect; that is, it fails to deal with other approaches to language which also have grounds for their own ontological status.

In contrast to hermeneutics, the structuralist orientation of the philosophy of language in Yugoslavia had more success in influencing the development of the philosophy of language and other sciences such as the theory of literature, art, culture, etc. Without extensive research it is rather difficult to say whether it is due to the fact that structuralism is, in certain aspects, very often associated with Marxism which, as has already been said, is a dominant philosophical orientation in Yugoslavia — perhaps because of the fact that structuralism deals primarily with a wide, and for this part of the world, particularly interesting branch of ideology.

As in the case of hermeneutics, I shall concern myself only with the most outstanding advocates of structuralism. At the beginning of the 70s a group of young philosophers and literary theoreticians in Zagreb, led by **Kolibaš** (Bošnjak and Kolibaš 1970), made an attempt to link Heidegger's concept of language and Lacan's psychoanalysis based on the structuralist approach. Apart from a number of contributors to the periodicials *Delo* (Belgrade) and *Dometi* (Rijeka), structuralism has been most ardently followed by a group of young Ljubljana philosophers, sociologists and theoreticians of the fine arts and literature, headed by **Žižek** (1976, 1980). In 1974 they founded the *Semiotic Section* of the *Sociological Society of Slovenia*, thereby turning structuralism into one of the predominant philosophical orientations in Slovenia. The scope of their interest is rather wide. So, for example, **Rotar** (1972, 1981) deals with the semiotic elaboration of fine arts and architecture; **Močnik** (1981, 1983) with semiotic research in the field of literature; **Skušek-Močnik** (1980) with the semiotics of theatre, while **Dolar** (1982) is carrying out investigation into the nature and types of totalitarian discourse. In short, their treatment of whole regions of culture is semiotic and their approach is primarily on the level of discourse. Žižek, who deals with the philosophical (theoretical) questions of structuralism, is the principal theoretician of the group. A few years ago several members split away from the *Semiotic Section* (now being headed by Močnik and

Rotar) and founded the *Society for Theoretical Psycho-analysis* together with the *School of S. Freud*. As the rest have not been concerned with general theoretical questions but with the analysis of sign systems, and taking Žižek as the most interesting personality of the group, I shall restrict myself to his approach to language.

In the first place it should be said that he is not primarily a philosopher of language. For him, language is an important, even central topic but not because of language itself. He is, namely, a follower of Lacan's school of psychoanalysis and tries to apply philosophical techniques to Lacan's findings. The peculiarity of his approach lies in his efforts to link Lacan with Hegel and Marxism, above all, with their critical theory of society. The language of psychoanalysis is structured in the Unconscious. It cannot be analyzed only as a sign system (imaginary, which is consciously being denoted), but as a system of signifiers. In contrast to a sign having denotation as its basis, a signifier is a mere connotation. It contains nothing psychic, but it is a material instance of unconscious confirmation of the lack of reality, i.e. a material instance of the establishing and coming into existence of another, symbolic order. The subject of speech advocated by Lacan and his followers is to be found in the signifier and in pure differentiation — mediation. The signifier, which shows itself as a discourse about Other, Unconscious, lack of reality, destroys the subject from within, breaks the sign instance by weighing down on it. Only then, what had been pushed aside into the Unconscious comes out and the subject speaks to us from within — thus there are differences in the chain of signifiers. In Saussure's concept the signifier and the signified are connected, whereas in Lacan's there is an impassable barrier caused by the difference between the two. This difference is represented by the difference between the essence of the signifier and what is, in fact, understood by it. Žižek has tried to find the links between Lacan's, Hegel's and Marx's hypotheses, thus distinguishing two kinds of production: production by people and production by things together with their respective processes — the process of work and that of symbolization. In addition he speaks of two types of practice: production and signifying. Liberation from the ideologem of sign, which only has the role of substituting for things, is made possible only by reaching the level of signifying practice which is, in fact, the only practice in this sense of the word. This means that it is not production but signifying practice that indicates the superiority of the symbolizing. In spite of Žižek's claims that it is the question of the signifier which determines the subject of speech, and in

spite of his efforts to prove that signifying practice is the only level at which
we can establish the subject matter of speech, I can not help feeling that
here we are dealing with the problem of the ontologization of the symbolic
and its superiority over the subject. In other words, the problem is one of
contemporary glottocentrism as a means of emancipating the subject. This
might be the origin of his materialistic interpretation of Hegel, where glottocentrism of the signifier takes the place of logocentrism of the notion.

It cannot be said for any of the authors mentioned that the philosophy
of language is their primary discipline. This is not the case with **Miščević**
(1977, 1978, 1980, 1981, 1983). He is not only the writer of the only review
and introduction to the philosophy of language, but he has also contributed
greatly to its introduction into Yugoslav philosophy and its establishment in
Yugoslavia itself. In the course of his development, Miščević has gone
through several stages starting with Marxism, passing through structuralism, and finally reaching analytic philosophy. His structuralist stage
can undoubtedly be considered the most productive, thereby contributing,
together with the Ljubljana semioticians and psychoanalysts, to the expansion of the structuralist philosophical theories of language in Yugoslavia. In
addition to interpretations of various structuralist (and non-structuralist)
authors (Derrida, Lacan, the members of the group *Tel-Quel*, etc.), what
should most certainly be mentioned is his application of all these theories to
the analysis of ideological discourse and historic story-telling. As at the
beginning of this decade he left structuralism and its respective approach to
language, I shall not discuss this period any further. His recent interest in
analytic philosophy and its consequent theory of action is by far more
interesting and important for this paper.

Miščević is the first among Yugoslav philosophers who has tried, starting from Austin and his followers, to observe language as a sort of action.
He began by analyzing Austin's, Searle's, Strawson's and Grice's points of
view. Though criticizing Austin for falling into the trap of generalizing performative analysis of language, he defends him against, in his view, unjust
and inadequate criticism from Searle and Strawson. In comparison to
Austin, Searle's attempt to systematize the speech act could be interpreted
as a sort of triviality, while on the other hand Strawson overemphasizes the
importance of convention in Austin's theory, paying too much attention to
the importance of the speaker and his intentions. This step forward in Miščević's study of language is reflected in his shifting the focus of interest from
the sign aspect of language to its practical aspect. As a matter of fact,

people speak because they want to do something, so that in this way speech can be treated as a part of meaningful practice. Therefore, practical activity itself can be observed from the point of view of speech activity. Central to such an approach are illocutionary acts, the context of utterance, the conventions of communication and the intentions of the speaker. However new, this shift of Miščević has already tried, using the experience of structuralist analysis, to apply Austin's theory of illocutionary acts to the analysis of practical discourse, i.e. to global discourse formations — ideologies. Some more significant results in the reception of the theory of action, of the pragmatic, semantic and linguistic theories might, most probably, still be expected.

Apart from Miščević, we should mention other writers who share his views. **Potrč**, for example, who has adopted an analytic approach and is researching the pragmatic and semantic aspects of language. Furthermore, other authors have undertaken specific studies of language: **Hribar** (1981) (language as a central topic within the framework of the ontologically set problem of Truth); **Prohić** (1970, 1976) (who, in the form of an essay treats the relationship between language and art) and **Čačinović-Puhovski** (1981) (criticism of the limits of structuralist theories of language and their analyses of art).

It would surely be a mistake not to mention the contribution (though indirect) to the development of the philosophy of language, and its theoretical reflection, of Yugoslav contemporary linguists. Of those dealing with theoretical problems of language and linguistics we ought to stress the work done by **Katičić** (1971), **Bugarski** (1972, 1975) and **Škiljan** (1976, 1978, 1980, 1985). All have greatly contributed to the enlargement of the theoretical range of linguistics, and have enriched it with relevant insights into the philosophy of language. This is especially true of Škiljan, one of the rare Yugoslav linguists who has tried to analyze the philosophical basis of his linguistic position. Katičić has contributed to linguistics and similar fields by increasing the awareness of the need for a general linguistic and theoretic approach towards language. The same might be true of Bugarski who advocates the latent equality of status between the philosophy of language and linguistics, approaching both from an anthropological (in the philosophical sense of the word) point of view. Škiljan's concept of linguistics and his interpretations of language represent a constructive combination of basic methodological statements about the structuralist Marxist interpretations of language, which have proved to be particularly productive in the criticism of orthodox structuralism and the analysis of the social aspects of language and communication. Apart from his work in the fields of general linguistics and other linguistic-related disciplines such as sociolinguistics and psycholinguistics, a considerable part of Škiljan's work is aimed at semiology. Taking primarily into account the results of French poststructuralist semiologists and early Soviet theories of language and sign, Škiljan tries to find out the basis for his semiology in the metasignifying dimension of sign, i.e. the common ground existing between sign and things and sign and man. According to Škiljan this is the place where meaning is formed, which is for his concept of semiology the most important dimension of sign. Semiology of this kind envelops various spheres of activity, ranging from symbolic to artistic. Bearing in mind not only their description, Škiljan pays much attention to the ideological nature and ideological function, thus aiming at de-mystifying present ideology and bringing about revolutionary changes in our ideas about the symbolic actions of man; that is to say, about the symbolic order and ideological forms of sign practice. The search for the original, direct and vivid common ground existing between sign, things and man is the basis of semiology.

Even this short paper might show that the study of language in Yugoslav philosophy is still dominated by other world orientations: structuralism, hermeneutics and analytic philosophy (pragmatism) and has not reached the level characteristic of more developed philosophies. The origin of this situation might be sought in the dominant orientation of Yugoslav philosophy towards social and political issues. It is difficult to predict which way further development will go, and whether the interest in language will be lost. In spite of only a very limited number of people dealing with the subject matter of language, glottocentrism and ontologization (characteristic of the principal orientations of the philosophy of language in general) are, nevertheless, predominant themes of their work.

Can we, ultimately, say what is the central topic of the philosophy of language in Yugoslavia? The introduction of the study of language into philosophy started with the analysis of the sign aspect of language — primarily in the countries of the Old Continent — using the positive and critical approach. This analysis is characterized by attempts to interpret fields traditionally belonging to culture, ideology and science by studying the sign, very often by taking into account the whole ontological structure. There is nothing strange in this if we take into consideration a very rich historical tradition, on one hand, and the domination of signs throughout the world, on the other. The sign can be an indication of the absence of things and even speakers, i.e. it can substitute for them and show an infinite number of possible worlds of realities through its ability to 'stand for' or show their structure. Thus, this 'opening' and 'closing' of the world becomes the predominant aspect of language. Language as an act, i.e. as a kind of action, is the second most important aspect of language whose study has been undertaken in different cultural and notional environments in the Anglo-Saxon countries. This aspect of language reveals its non-instrumental dimension — language as a vivid and direct activity, language used by participants in any communicative act, the importance of communicative context, social conventions of communication and the intentions of the speaker. The differences and contrasts between these two approaches to language have been shown in the polemic between their different advocates — a polemic which, nevertheless, shows that in spite of their thematic differences two aspects of language dominate the contemporary philosophy of language: *sign* and *act*. Though not in a sharp and developed form, especially where act is concerned, such a study of language and the aspectual approach to language lie in the basis of the philosophical theory of language in Yugoslavia.

References

Aćin, Jovica. 1975. *Izazov hermeneutike* [The challenge of hermeneutics]. Beograd: DOB.

Bošnjak, Branimir and Darko Kolibaš. 1970. *Slovo razlike: Teorija pisanja.* [On differences: The theory of writing]. Zagreb: Centar za društvenu djelatnost.

Bugarski, Ranko. 1972. *Jezik i lingvistika* [Language and linguistics]. Beograd: Nolit.

-----. 1975. *Lingvistika o čoveku* [Linguistics about man]. Beograd: Beogradski izdavačko-grafički zavod.

Čačinović-Puhovski, Nadežda. 1981. *Pisanje i mišljenje* [Writing and thinking]. Zagreb: Studentski centar.

Dolar, Mladen. 1982. *Struktura fašističneg gospostva* [The structure of fascist governments]. Ljubljana: Univerzum.

Hribar, Tine. 1981. *Resnica o resnici* [The truth about truth]. Maribor: Obzorja.

Katičić, Radoslav. 1971. *Jezikoslovni ogledi* [Essays on linguistics]. Zagreb: Školska knjiga.

Marković, Mihailo. 1961. *Dijalektička teorija značenja* [The dialectic theory of meaning]. Beograd: Nolit.

Miščević, Nenad. 1977. *Govor drugog* [Other's discourse]. Beograd: Ideje.

-----. 1978. *Bijeli šum* [White noise]. Rijeka: Izdavački centar Rijeka.

-----. 1980. "Struktura ideologijske riječi" [The structure of the ideological word]. *Ideje.* 5: 65-74.

-----. 1981. *Filozofija jezika* [The philosophy of language]. Zagreb: Naprijed.

-----. 1983. *Jezik kot dejavnost* [Language as activity]. Ljubljana: Univerzum.

Močnik, Rastko. 1981. *Mesečevo zlato* [The moon's gold]. Ljubljana: Univerzum.

-----. 1983. *Raziskave za sociologijo književnosti* [Research into the sociology of literature]. Ljubljana: Državna založba Slovenije.

Pejović, Danilo. 1976. "Language as an experience of the world: An outline of the philosophy of language." *Forum.* 1-2: 66-109.

Popović, Milko. 1963. *Filozofija značenja* [The philosophy of meaning]. Zagreb: Grafički zavod Hrvatske.

Prohić, Kasim. 1970. *Odvažnost izricanja* [The courage of utterance]. Zagreb: Studentski centar.

-----. 1976. *Figure otvorenih značenja* [Figures of open meanings]. Zagreb: Studentski centar.

Rotar, Braco. 1972. *Likovna govornica* [The speech of fine arts]. Ljubljana/Maribor: Državna založba Slovenije/Obzorja.

-----. 1981. *Pomeni prostora* [The meanings of space]. Ljubljana: Delavska enotnost.

Skušek-Močnik, Zoja. 1980. *Gledališče kot oblika spektakelske funkcije* [The function of theatre as spectacle]. Ljubljana: Univerzum.

Škiljan, Dubravko. 1976. *Dinamika jezičnih struktura* [The dynamics of language structures]. Zagreb: Studentski centar.

-----. 1978. *Govor realnosti i realnost jezika* [The speech of reality and the reality of language]. Zagreb: Školska knjiga.

-----. 1980. *Pogled u lingvistiku* [Insight into linguistics]. Zagreb: Školska knjiga.

-----. 1985. *U pozadini znaka* [Behind the sign]. Zagreb: Školska knjiga.

Žižek, Slavoj. 1976. *Znak, označitelj, pismo* [Sign, signifier, writing]. Beograd: Ideje.
Žižek, Slavoj. 1980. *Hegel in označevalec* [Hegel and the signifier]. Ljubljana: Univerzum.

Linguistic theory and sociolinguistics in Yugoslavia*

Milorad Radovanović
Faculty of Philosophy, University of Novi Sad

1 Linguistic theory: sociolinguistics

In the 1950s linguistic theory, linguistic methodology, and even the practical study of language were marked by a variety of prominent and dominating structuralist 'schools' and trends. Since then, despite the continued vitality of structuralism, transformational-generative grammar has become dominant, and it has affected the shape of linguistic theory, its methods, and the practical study of language. During this series of events in the science of language, the past 30 years, and the last 15 in particular, have also seen the gradual introduction, advancement, proliferation, and popularization of interdisciplinary approaches to language, between linguistics and other, related sciences, deriving frequently from a reaction, whether direct or indirect, to either structuralism or transformational-generative grammar and also from the need to transcend the essentially 'isolationist' positions and methods of structuralist and transformational-generative theory. For language, society and culture, and even for mankind, our time is one when new horizons are opening up for sociolinguistics, psycholinguistics, text linguistics, the ethnography of communication, the philosophy of language, general semantics, semiotics, and many other related disciplines. If some of the latest 'functionalist' and 'contextually

---

* This article was translated into English by Vladislava Felbabov. Originally published in the *International Journal of the Sociology of Language* 44 (1983). (= *Language choice and language control*): 55-69, it is reprinted here in the same form, except for the addition of the last paragraph in Section 2.4., necessary language and technical adjustments, and the correction of typographical errors. As well as this, the *References* are presented in a reconstructed form. Permission to reprint was kindly granted by Mouton Publishers (Division of Walter de Gruyter & Co.).

situated' orientations of the structuralists, and the various semantic and pragmatic orientations of the transformational-generative grammarians, are added to the above list, it becomes a fairly representative outline of most of the present (and even some of the future) notions of linguistic theory and linguistic studies deriving from corresponding notions and definitions of language.

2   (Socio)linguistics in Yugoslavia

In the 1950s language studies in Yugoslavia (particularly Slavic studies and even those of Serbocroatian) were still deeply involved with elements of traditional European philology. The attendant features were a positivist, historicist, and evolutionist approach to language and a pronounced disinterest in linguistic theory (exceptions such as the work of A. Belić were rare). The 1950s also introduced a gradual, though belated, change. Yugoslav linguistics began to turn toward the achievements of the descriptive version of structuralism, mainly the 'Prague' school, but toward some others as well, such as the 'Geneva' school and the distributional version of structuralism, and to a lesser extent toward the achievements of transformational-generative grammar. Despite this, Yugoslav linguistics entered the present-day controversies of linguistic theory and methodology and the practical study of language, already well underway in the world, and an age of an increasing number of interdisciplinary orientations, quite unready for them — though, it must be admitted, with a very interesting language situation to study. The number of experts was small and their professional organization unsatisfactory (cf. Ivić M. 1976 for information on the evolution and the state of linguistic theory in Yugoslavia).

Such a situation requires consideration of what a practicable plan for interdisciplinary linguistic study, particularly for sociolinguistic study, would be in Yugoslavia in the light of the fact that there is as yet no organized form of sociolinguistics in the country. (The first attempts to right this situation were Bugarski 1974; Bugarski et al. 1976; and Radovanović 1979). It seems reasonable and tenable that in the absence of theories of its own, Yugoslav sociolinguistics, no matter how it is envisaged, should set out from a critical selection and comment, generalization, and actualization, from a testing and sythesizing of available general linguistic theories, and of sociolinguistic ones in particular, of their hypotheses, methods, and techniques, definitions and terminology, and also from an analysis of research results already obtained for languages elsewhere in the world. Yugoslav sociolinguistic theories would, however, also have to reflect the specific language, social, cultural, and other situations, conditions, and circumstances (where there are such) of Yugoslavia. They would have to offer an objective conception of language, deriving from contemporary linguistic and sociolinguistic theory, but they would also have to transcend such theory and remain open to other, different kinds of 'linguistics' and 'nonlinguistics' and to the achievements of so-called 'applied linguistics', in the fields of socialization, education, translation, informing and advertising, psychiatry, law, administration, etc. In its present state and in light of the above, the subjects, aims, and concerns which are priorities for Yugoslav linguistics could, selectively and concisely, be defined as the following (without pretending to offer a definitive description, listing, or register of all the problems, or, to phrase it differently, without pretending to offer a definitive program for research):

2.1 *Standardization, language planning, and language policy*

Yugoslavia is a country of many nations and many languages. Serbocroatian, Slovenian, Macedonian, Hungarian, Albanian, Slovak, Czech, Romanian, Ruthenian, Ukrainian, Bulgarian, Italian, Turkish, Romani, and other languages are spoken and written in different population distributions and proportions. That is to say, spoken and written in Yugoslavia are languages which are, from the standpoint of origin, related to a greater or lesser extent, and which are, from the standpoint of typology, similar or different to a greater or lesser extent. The situation is complicated even further by the fact that Yugoslavia is the primary community for some of the languages listed (such is the case with Serbocroatian, Slovenian, Macedonian, and Ruthenian). This means that it is the community in which, according to the nature of things, they can and should be standardized. Some of the other languages listed are, on the other hand, found in two typical kinds of political-geographical-ethnic situations: the first is the border situation, and this is the case with Italian, Hungarian, Romanian, Bulgarian, and Albanian; while the second is the diaspora situation, and this is the case with Slovak, Czech, Ukrainian, Turkish, and Romani. In both these situations, the process of language standardization is not, *a priori*, expected to be carried out in Yugoslavia alone. Yet the theoretical, legislative, and practical aspects of language planning and language policy demand that all these languages be taken into consideration since they are all important elements of the Yugoslav nations and nationalities (whose instruments of communication and creativity they are). Furthermore, Yugoslavia has no 'official' state language to function as a metalanguage for communication between the Yugoslav nations and nationalities nor does it have a language of the *lingua communis* type (for a more detailed discussion, cf. Naylor 1978). The role of Serbocroatian is, generally speaking, that of an 'unofficial' mediator language between the Yugoslav nations and nationalities, yet the role of some other languages (Slovenian and Macedonian) is one of national consolidation within their respective socialist republics (the Socialist Republic of Slovenia and the Socialist Republic of Macedonia), while, on the other hand, certain other languages coexist on an equal basis in both 'official' and 'unofficial' use (as in the case of Serbocroatian, Hungarian, Slovak, Romanian, and Ruthenian in the Autonomous Province of Vojvodina). In addition to this, several Yugoslav nations speak the same language as their primary language (for instance, Serbocroatian is spoken by Serbs, Croatians, Montenegrins, and Muslims), which causes problems in the naming of the language (whether it is Serbocroatian, Croatoserbian, Serbian or Croatian, Croatian or Serbian, Serbian, Croatian, and so on). This complex subject matter requires no further discussion for the purposes of a short survey of sociolinguistics in Yugoslavia, and yet the logic of thought requires us to note some of the practical problems which arise, particularly for sociolinguistics, from the existence and coexistence of many languages in Yugoslavia and the attempt to offer them all optimum conditions and means for effective and appropriate expression in the vital fields of society and culture such as education, mass communication, publishing, politics, administration, law, trade, public transportation, science, the arts, religion, and the like.

Yugoslav sociolinguistics must (primarily for Serbocroatian, Slovenian and Macedonian, but for other languages such as Ruthenian and Romani also) make use of contemporary linguistic experience, scholarship, and theory in order to be able to offer guidelines for passing through the successive stages of achieving a norm in the language standard and from that toward language planning and language policy, as a continuous process. With this goal in mind, one should not neglect the individual stages that have to be passed through, though this has been and still frequently is the case with the chronologically later stages which should not, hierarchically speaking, be considered less important: *selection - description - codification*

- elaboration - acceptation - implementation - expansion - cultivation - evaluation - reconstruction (for further information cf. the detailed schematic representation in Radovanović 1979: 83-89, inspired by the fruitful discussion in Fishman 1974: 15-124). Within this context it is especially important to analyze the linguistic and extralinguistic impetus for the creation, existence, development, recognition, functioning, explanation, and description of variants of standard Serbocroatian (the 'eastern' and 'western' variant) and also to consider their status in relation to particular national identities and characteristic national features (in addition to specific linguistic positions such as that of the Socialist Republic of Bosnia and Herzegovina, which is a community of three nations). Though it is a problem of a different kind, the variant manifestations of Hungarian, Romanian, Slovak, and Albanian, along with some other languages of the border or diaspora type, should also be studied, as should their status in relation to the language standard in the primary national community.

2.2 *The stratification of language*

Generally the *individual* stratification of languages is one of the less interesting aspects of language disintegration and variation for sociolinguistics, since the results are idiolects. Yugoslav sociolinguistics, however, has to regard a broad range of *functional*, i.e. disciplinal and professional, thematic and situational stratifications of language which give rise to disciplinal and professional, thematic and situational styles and registers. It also has to take into consideration *social* stratification which gives rise to sociolects, slang, and various other group speech varieties, such as those according to generation, sex, and the like, as well as *territorial* language stratification which gives rise to rural and urban dialects, or variants of the standard language. This description of the process and result of stratification and the structure of particular language strata should also include an inventory of which repertoires are available to speech representatives, social groups and communities, regions, populations, etc., along with a knowledge of how given language varieties are distributed in domains of usage, with an inventory of their distinctive functions (where such exist), and with specific and corresponding systemic linguistic features. This also requires that the rules for their adequate and appropriate choice, usage, and alternation be found, as well as the psychosocial and cultural causes of incorrect, inadequate, and inappropriate choice, usage, and alternation, i.e. of their application.

Up to now, Serbocroatian dialectology has been almost exclusively a rural dialectology, so that there are, generally speaking, no urban or social dialectologies (rare exceptions are Jović 1976, and the studies of T.F. Magner; cf. Magner 1968; cf. also Jutronić-Tihomirović in this book). In Yugoslavia (and this is true of all societies advancing toward industrialization and urbanization) rural dialects are slowly disappearing under the pressure of literacy, education, mass information, population contacts and mobility, and, finally, the effect of the horizontal and vertical expansion of standard languages. Rural dialects are giving precedence to urban ones. Urban dialects, on the other hand, are often constituted with the significant support of the rural dialect whose background is still productive. This support takes the form of a structural influence since, from the standpoint of linguistics, urban dialects are much affected by population migration, even though they are the result of living and working, the social and cultural circumstances of an urban environment. Urban dialects tend to push their corresponding rural varieties into second place and to set their own specific and functional features in their stead, which is natural and inevitable (cf. the cases of Belgrade, Zagreb, Niš, Split, Novi Sad, Sarajevo, Titograd, and other Yugoslav cities). Urban dialects in this way play a role in creating the specific features by which the standard language manifests itself in a given urban community. They stimulate and foster divergent growth, which gives rise to variants of the standard language, in this case, of Serbocroatian. (T.F. Magner even goes so far as to posit that Zagreb, Split, and Niš, which he takes as representative examples of extreme cases, are characterized by a specific kind of diglossia: Magner 1968.)

This detail alone points out that the results of sociolinguistic studies would be incomplete if they did not consider the influence and interference the variations and varieties in question exert on one another, whether they are of the same type (for instance, the 'eastern' and 'western' variant of Serbocroatian on one another, two or three functional styles on one another, and the like), or whether they are of different types (for instance, the urban and rural dialects on one another, the rural and urban dialects on some of the variants of the standard language or on slang, a functional style on some form of slang, sociolects on functional styles, and the like). Yugoslav sociolinguistics would also be incomplete if it did not consider such types of relations between a standard language and its variations and varieties, which are aspects of the existence and manifestation of the given languages.

For example, the relations between standard Serbocroatian and its standardized and non-standardized variations and varieties, in the form of its variants, dialects, sociolects, functional styles, the idiolects of noted speakers and writers, etc.

Yugoslav sociolinguistic studies, particularly those of sociolects, should make use of available theories and sociolinguistic research being carried out in other countries. Still, these theories and this research should be approached cautiously and critically and without attempting to apply or repeat them mechanically in the specific social, cultural, and language circumstances, problems, and relations in Yugoslavia. This also refers to consistent theoretical systems such as Bernstein's, because a major part of Bernstein's system, in its pure and original form, is applicable only to sharply polarized class societies. In the Yugoslav situation, the search for Bernstein's clearly opposed 'elaborated' and 'restricted' codes (as defined by Bernstein 1971; or by Dittmar 1976), or for speech strategy rules which govern their usage, would be a fruitless one, since these codes and their corresponding rules are the features of the language of specific classes. It would be worthwhile, on the other hand, to apply some of Bernstein's notions in a modified form to Yugoslav circumstances in order to reveal those language variations and speech strategies which are formed and developed, those types and levels of linguistic knowledge which are acquired and reached through membership in a group or through the differentiation of speech representatives, not on the basis of class but on the basis of generation, sex, or education. It would also be valuable to determine how these results could be applied in education, professional orientation, and career choice.

2.3 *Languages in contact, bilingualism, multilingualism, and diglossia*

Specific historical, social, cultural, political, national, and other circumstances and relations have made and continue to make the problematics of language contacts and interference a matter of high priority among those sociolinguistic subjects which demand extensive study in Yugoslavia. The language contacts which will be discussed in this section manifest themselves as several *basic types of contacts*:

The first type is a one-directional influence by one or more of the so-called 'world' languages on the languages spoken and written in Yugoslavia. This influence can be either a direct or an indirect one, and it may vary according to time, territory, culture, history, politics, according to national and even linguistic distribution. The languages in question are German, French, or Russian, and lately the most influential one has been English. These languages partake, generally speaking, of some of the consequences of their society and culture in the areas of economics, trade, politics, diplomacy, the military, culture, science, religion, ideology, engineering, technology, mass communication, and the like. Italian, Turkish, and other languages were also influential at certain times in Yugoslav history. The current importance of English is the result, certainly, of the fact that it is widely taught in schools, spread by the mass media, used in technological, technical, and scientific innovations, introduced by way of the arts, etc. (for further information cf. Filipović 1971; cf. also Filipović in this book).

In the diaspora situation there are also instances of a one-directional influence of the so-called 'world' languages on those of Yugoslavia. Namely, the linguistic competence and speech of representatives of the Yugoslav languages are often affected when they emigrate, temporarily or permanently, for economic or other reasons, to countries such as the Federal Republic of Germany, Austria, Switzerland, France, Belgium, Sweden, the U.S.A., Canada, Australia, etc. This type of interference is described in some recent studies on the subject, which, unfortunately, generally deal with the influence of English on Serbocroatian: Filipović (1971); Jutronić (1972); Albin and Alexander (1972); Lencek and Magner (1976); Surdučki (1978), Jutronić-Tihomirović 1985, etc. In the border situation there are, also, instances of a one-directional influence of the so-called 'environmental' languages on those of Yugoslavia (in Italy, Austria, Hungary, Romania, Bulgaria, Greece, and Albania).

The second type of contact manifests itself as the one-directional influence of Serbocroatian, as a kind of 'unofficial' *lingua communis* (Naylor 1978) on the other languages spoken and written in Yugoslavia. This influence occurs by way of the labor process, education, the mass media, and also in the form of political, self-management, professional, and expert terminologies with their corresponding syntactic calques. In the Socialist Autonomous Province of Vojvodina this is the influence of Serbocroatian on Hungarian, Slovak, Romanian, and Ruthenian, and in the socialist republics the influence of Serbocroatian on Macedonian, Slovenian, and the other Yugoslav languages (for a partial insight into the problem cf. Jocić 1980).

The third type of language contact is a matter of reciprocal influence:

the influence of the Yugoslav languages on one another in bilingual and multilingual communities, in border communities, in diaspora ones, and the like. It takes place on all levels of language, ranging from phonology to syntax and semantics (characteristic again is the situation in the Socialist Autonomous Province of Vojvodina, cf. the study of M. Mikeš in Bugarski *et al.* 1976).

Some additional data will fill out the picture of how complex the Yugoslav situation is. The contacts between the Yugoslav languages manifest themselves differently from a diachronic and synchronic point of view, from the standpoint of political, territorial, national, cultural, religious, and social distribution, and of course from the standpoint of standard language and variant distribution. Substratum and superstratum language situations have been known to affect and alter already established and stabilized language contacts and processes (the case of borrowings from Turkish in some regions, from the Romance languages in other regions, and from German in still other regions, for instance). Some languages are spoken and written by a relatively migratory population, while others are spoken and written by relatively fixed populations (Albanian as compared to Hungarian, Serbocroatian as compared to Slovenian and Macedonian). The contacts between the Yugoslav languages are realized in various ways below the level of the particular language system, on that of the subsystem. For instance, the contacts between a dialect and a variant of the standard language, between variants of the standard languages, between sociolects, between the professional, i.e. the disciplinal functional styles of various languages. Purist tendencies are not equally pronounced, nor the instruments of language standardization and planning equally developed, all over Yugoslavia, for each standard language or its variants. For example, the 'western' variant of Serbocroatian is more purist than the 'eastern' one. It has more developed instruments and more advanced professionals at its service for language standardization and planning. In the case of Macedonian and Slovenian the instruments are more developed and efficient, generally speaking, than in the case of Serbocroatian. Purist tendencies are more pronounced in Macedonian and Slovenian than in Serbocroatian. In language contacts the absence of language standardization and planning instruments is liable to open the road to unexpected, unrestrained, and uncontrollable forces. In addition, popular beliefs on prestige and assessments which set the value of a language or of the relations between a language and some of its varieties and speech representatives (its legitimate speech representatives) orient, in a specific way, the current tendencies, directions, types, and levels of contacts between the languages of the Yugoslav community (cf. the latest theoretical studies, e.g. Bugarski 1980).

The multiplicity of languages spoken and written in Yugoslavia, along with institutionalized and noninstitutionalized bilingual (most frequently) or multilingual (less frequently) situations leads, as a matter of course, to theoretial and practical questions regarding the concepts of bilingualism (or multilingualism) and diglossia, for specific speech communities or individual representatives of specific languages. Not by chance, therefore, though somewhat less dynamically than in similar communities in the world, the first (though limited) efforts are being made to identify and record the existing types of bilingualism (or multilingualism), or, to phrase it differently, to make a typology of bilingualism (or multilingualism) and of bilingual (or multilingual) situations in Yugoslavia, particularly in the Socialist Autonomous Province of Vojvodina (cf. the study by M. Mikeš (this volume) for statistical data; study by L. Göncz; Bugarski and Mikeš 1985; Bugarski et al. 1976). These studies, and some others also, indicate that bilingualism usually manifests itself as a matter of a language of one nation and the language of another nation, or a language of a nation and the language of a nationality (for instance, Serbocroatian-Slovenian, Serbocroatian-Macedonian, Serbocroatian-Hungarian, Serbocroatian-Slovak, Serbocroatian-Romanian, Serbocroatian-Ruthenian, Serbocroatian-Albanian, Serbocroatian-Bulgarian, Macedonian-Albanian, Macedonian-Turkish, Slovenian-Hungarian, Slovenian-Italian, etc.). Other types of situations and contacts are also possible, particularly in the case of multilingualism which may include, for instance, a language of a nation and languages of several nationalities (such as Serbocroatian-Hungarian-Romanian, Serbocroatian-Hungarian-Slovak, Serbocroatian-Hungarian-Ruthenian, Serbocroatian-Albanian-Turkish), or languages of two nations and a language of a nationality (such as Macedonian-Serbocroatian-Albanian, Macedonian-Serbocroatian-Turkish, Slovenian-Serbocroatian-Hungarian, Slovenian-Serbocroatian-Italian).

Bilingualism (or *multilingualism*) is defined as a specific psycholinguistic category, or, to phrase it differently, as the simultaneous, parallel knowledge of two (or more) languages of a particular language community and/or of its speech representatives, implying by this both a systemic and a communicative knowledge (but not implying, often, an equal competence or equal conditions for an active and effective written and spoken language expression, in both the production and interpretation of messages). *Diglossia* (following Fishman 1970; Fishman 1972a) is defined as a specific kind of *functional bilingualism* or a *social bilingualism* in a situation when social, political, and legal, i.e. organizational and legislative documents and actions, have differentiated, both nominally and in practice, between the domains of the individual and the collective, between the private and the public, activity, labor, communication, and creativity, in which specific languages can and may be used. In Yugoslavia, the publicly stated stands on this matter are prompted and defined by political, ideological, ethnic, national, cultural, historical, social, and linguistic initiatives, stands, conditions, and specific features, and are directed at facilitating, stimulating, cultivating, and *expanding bilingualism* (or *multilingualism*) and at a planned and gradual modification, followed by *elimination of diglossia*, wherever possible (in the Socialist Autonomous Province of Vojvodina, for instance, but in other regions as well). Understandably, this problem requires careful and valid sociolinguistic research. Besides this, it also requires a continued observation of the current relations between political and legal codification and linguistic practice, between professional studies and the demands of the 'official' and 'unofficial' use of all the languages, bearing in mind at the same time the important role played by the educational system and the mass media.

The notion of diglossia can be used in a broader sense and applied to include not only distinct languages but also the different varieties of the same language, i.e. all types of language variations (cf. C.A. Ferguson in Giglioli 1972; and the notion of diglossia as elaborated by J.J. Gumperz and J.A. Fishman in Tollefson 1983). In Yugoslavia, diglossia can also be used in the way Magner (1978) uses it to describe and explain the Serbocroatian language situation in a representative sample reduced to the cities of Zagreb, Split, and Niš. According to Magner these cities are typical for their diglossia which derive from a coexistence, i.e. contention, between the urban dialect and standard Serbocroatian, or its variant, the urban dialect itself deriving from the powerful effect of a distinctive rural dialectal background (the Kajkavian, Čakavian, or Torlakian) whose typology and origin are different at all structural levels from the Štokavian basis of standard Serbocroatian. In relation to standard Serbocroatian, the urban dialect of Zagreb is considered to have prestige, the urban dialect of Niš to be provincial, the diglossia situation in Split to be neutral.

No matter how the notion of diglossia is defined, whether in a nar-

rower or a broader sense, for the 'sociolinguist' it represents the problem of
finding and describing the rules of communicative competence, modified by
extralinguistic influences and contexts (psychosocial motivations in particular), of determining the choice and usage of one language variety over
another (for example, of the standard language over slang), the situational
or other motivations for changing from one variety to another, i.e. for *code-
switching*, the causes for prestige valuations in using one variety instead of
another, the possible causes for the choice and application of one variety
instead of another, the reasons for acquiring one variety instaed of another.
(In contrast to the term *code-switching*, applied here, and which refers to
the correct, adequate, and appropriate, i.e. acceptable changing from one
linguistic code to another, the term *code-confusing* is proposed to refer to
the incorrect, inadequate, inappropriate, i.e. unacceptable changing from
one linguistic code to another, which probably results from a speech-com-
petence problem of the speaker.)

2.4 *Verbal interactions*

Besides these subjects and projects, Yugoslav sociolinguistics has yet
to describe and systematize various kinds of verbal interactions, to discover
and study their structure and their organization and performance rules, and
then to reveal the joint operation of linguistic and nonlinguistic means in
personal, social, and cultural interaction — written as well as spoken. Both
monolingual and bilingual (or multilingual) situations have to be considered, and also the stratified structure of a language, its functional polyva-
lence (for both communicative and noncommunicative purposes). The
complexity of social structures must also be taken into account as does the
variety of situations, domains, and fields speech representative live, work,
communicate, and create in. The differences between language and speech
communities (Hymes 1974) have to be researched, the contextual and particularly situational influences on verbal interaction, the need for establishing appropriate typologies of verbal interactions (ranging from person-to-
person interactions to those with many intermediary channels), the differences between traditional cultural types and influences and current language mappings, etc. For all of this, to repeat, a description and systematization of speech acts is needed and their principles of association into
higher units, e.g. speech events, discourses, texts, are to be revealed. As is
an insight into the rules which organize speech events (discourses, texts,

and the like), into how they are chosen and used, and into how these higher communication units are systematized. The appropriate norms of interaction and those of interpretation (Hymes 1974) are to be identified, bearing in mind all the constituents of a communication, particularly the communicators and such pragmatic factors as intention, aim, purpose, strategy, etc.

A typical yet indicative example of all the considerations which must be taken into account is one which is often cited in sociolinguistic literature (cf. R. Brown and A. Gilman in Giglioli 1972, though it contains several outdated and inadequate examples of the current Yugoslav situation; Stone 1977 for the general Slavic situation; Kocher 1967; Vasić 1979; Radovanović 1979; Polovina 1983 for the Serbocroatian situation). The speech role is usually considered to be a more or less changeable role or social function in which the speaker of a language finds himself when realizing or participating in a speech event. It is also considered to be a relative indicator of the interpersonal status of the speech-event participants. In different cultures the relative status of the communicators establishes a relation of *solidarity* or *formality* or one of *status difference* (i.e. superiority, power, supremacy) between them in the form of language and by different manners of expression. Linguistically speaking, the relations are manifested by various means (an indication can even be the use of different languages or of different language varieties, as subsystems of the same language). Yet, most often, it is by grammatical or lexical means within the framework of the given language system. In the case of Serbocroatian and of some other Yugoslav situations the determining factors in expressing such relations are psychosocial motivation and judgement founded on age, acquaintance, kinship, intimacy, formal function, and specific station in life (sometimes domain). In verbal interaction these relations are most often represented (though the situation has not yet been fully stabilized and tends to exhibit significant exceptions, from community to community, from generation to generation) by the alternative use of the second person singular pronoun forms (*ti/vi* 'you'), of forms of greeting (*zdravo/dobar dan* 'hello', and the like) and of forms of address (given name, nickname, surname, title, professional degree, social function, in addition to the relatively less marked forms as *drug* 'comrade', *drugarica* 'comrade' (f.), *gospodin* 'mister', *gospoda* 'madam', *kolega* 'colleague', etc.). The author has analyzed this problem in greater detail elsewhere (cf. Radovanović 1979, particularly the section entitled "The 'grammar' of social status": 33-41). The general

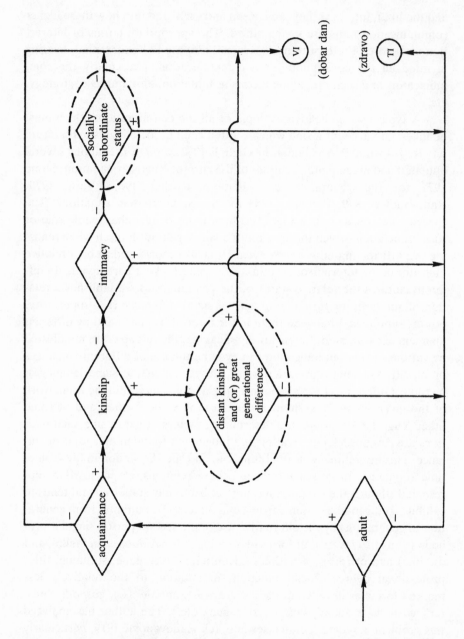

Fig. 1.   Schematic outline of rules and choices according to binary alternatives and a hierarchy of criteria

state of Serbocroatian can perhaps best be represented by a schematic out-line of rules and choices according to binary alternatives and a hierarchy of criteria. In *Figure* 1 the pronouns *ti/ti* indicate a status of solidarity between the communicators, i.e. participants in the interaction, *vi/vi* a status of for-mality, and *ti/vi* or *vi/ti* a difference in status between them. By analogy, in the use of greetings there is *zdravo/zdravo* = solidarity, *dobar dan/dobar dan* = formality, and *zdravo/dobar dan* or *dobar dan/zdravo* = status dif-ference.

From the standpoint of verbal interactions, in the Yugoslav case of possible language communications, there are several possible mic-rosociolinguistic realizations (where the language of communication is given outside of brackets, and the first language of the communicator in italic). In the first instance, communication is realized in the same language and it is the first one for both communicators: $L_1 \rightleftarrows L_1$.

In the second instance, communication is realized in the same lan-guage, but it is the first one for one communicator and the second one for the other communicator: $L_1 \rightleftarrows L_1(L_2)$.

In the third instance, communication is realized in the same language, which, however, is the second one for both communicators, such as: $L_1(L_2)$ $\rightleftarrows L_1(L_3)$, where L_1 (most often Serbocroatian) is a metalanguage mediator (of the *lingua communis* type), since the first languages of the com-municators are not the same, and there is a small degree or no two-way comprehension, that is to say, in the diglossia situation. Another case is $L_1(L_2) \rightleftarrows L_1(L_2)$, where the first language of the communicators is the same, but where L_1 is a prestige language for various psychosociolinguistic reasons (the presence of a third person with competence only in L_1, for instance), that is to say, in those domains of language use which are typical of the diglossia situation.

In the fourth instance, communication is realized in different lan-guages, which are first language for the two communicators, such as: $L_1 \rightleftarrows L_2$, or which are second for both communicators, for example $L_1(L_3) \rightleftarrows L_2(L_4)$, where the metalanguage mediator is translation or where it is absent (depending on the degree of second language competence of the two communicators) or where there is a high degree of two-way comprehension between the languages (independent of the previous condition).

2.5 *Applied sociolinguistics*

The four groups of subjects discussed in this paper which could serve as topics of future projects for sociolinguistic study in Yugoslavia (standardization, language planning, and language policy; the stratification of language; languages in contact, bilingualism, multilingualism, and diglossia; and verbal interactions) all imply the existence of some form of 'applied sociolinguistics' (used in a narrower sense than usual) — in education, in information and the mass media, in psychiatry, in jurisprudence and administration, in publishing and advertising, and in other fields, in addition to all other areas of individual and collective linguistic expression. The priorities are, of course, to find adequate solutions and procedures for dealing with language acquisition, foreign language learning, and socialization, for analyzing their reciprocal functioning, but with respect to all the psychosocial motivations, circumstances, situations, and specific features which have been shown to characterize the Yugoslav milieu; and, with regard to the individual, more narrowly focused cultural, national, social, and linguistic points. Related to these efforts are the general sociolinguistic objectives of cultivating and expanding (both horizontally and vertically) the standard languages through education, publishing, the mass media, and so on, to be accompanied and supported by the continuous advancement of legislation on language as the legal prerequisite, instrument, and regulator for carrying out a formulated language policy, and even to stimulate bilingualism (or multilingualism) and deter diglossia, and, finally, to realize cultural, national, and language equality, for the individual, for culture, for language, and for society.

References

Albin, Alexander and Ronelle Alexander. 1972. *The Speech of Yugoslav Immigrants in San Pedro, California*. The Hague: Martinus Nijhoff.

Bernstein, Basil. 1971. *Class, Codes and Control*. Volume 1: *Theoretical Studies Towards a Sociology of Language*. London: Routledge and Kegan Paul.

Birnbaum, Henrik (ed.). 1978. *American Contributions to the Eight International Congress of Slavists. Zagreb and Ljubljana, September 3-9, 1978*. Volume 1: *Linguistics and poetics*. Columbus, Ohio: Slavica Publishers.

Brang, Peter and Monika Züllig, with assist. of Karin Brang. 1981. *Kommentierte Bibliographie zur slavischen Soziolinguistik*. Band I-III. Bern/ Frankfurt am Main: Peter Lang.

Bright, William (ed.). 1966. *Sociolinguistics. Proceedings of the UCLA Sociolinguistics Conference, 1964*. The Hague/Paris: Mouton.

Brozović, Dalibor. 1970. *Standardni jezik. Teorija, usporedbe, geneza, povijest, suvremena zbilja* [Standard language. Theory, comparisons, genesis, history, modern reality]. Zagreb: Matica hrvatska.

-----. 1978. "Hrvatski jezik, njegovo mjesto unutar južnoslavenskih i drugih slavenskih jezika, njegove povijesne mijene kao jezika hrvatske književnosti" [The Croatian language, its place among the other South Slavic and Slavic languages, its historical phases as the language of Croatian literature]. In: A. Flaker and K. Pranjić (eds). 1978: 9-83.

-----. 1983. "Die soziolinguistische Situation in der jugoslawischen Föderation". *Wiener slavistisches Jahrbuch* 29: 9-23.

Brown, R. and A. Gilman. 1972 [1960]. "The pronouns of power and solidarity". In: Giglioli (ed.). 1972: 252-82.

Bugarski, Ranko (ed.). 1974. *Jezik i društvo* [Language and society]. (= *Kultura* 25). Beograd: Kultura.

-----. 1980. "The interdisciplinary relevance of folk linguistics". In: K. Koerner (ed.). 1980: 381-93.

-----, Vladimir Ivir, and Melanija Mikeš (eds). 1976. *Jezik u društvenoj sredini. Zbornik radova sa konferencije 'Jezik i društvo'* [Language in a social environment. Collected papers from the conference 'Language and society']. Novi Sad: Društvo za primenjenu lingvistiku Jugoslavije.

----- and Melanie Mikes. 1985. "Types and methods of multilingual research in Yugoslavia". In: P.H. Nelde (ed.). 1985: 145-54.

Daneš, František. 1976. "Values and attitudes in language standardization". *Južnoslovenski filolog* 32: 3-27.

Dittmar, Norbert. 1976. *Sociolinguistics. A Critical Survey of Theory and Application*. London: Edward Arnold.

Dunatov, Rasio. 1978. "A sociolinguistic analysis of the recent controversy concerning Croatian/Serbian language(s)". In: H. Birnbaum (ed.). 1978: 256-68.

Ďurovič, L'ubomír (ed.). 1983. *Lingua in Diaspora. Studies in the Language of the Second Generation of Yugoslav Immigrant Children in Sweden*. Lund: Slavica Lundensia.

Ferguson, C.A. 1972 [1959]. "Diglossia". In: P.P. Giglioli (ed.). 1972: 232-51.

Filipović, Rudolf. 1971. *Kontakti jezika u teoriji i praksi. Prinosi metodici nastave živih stranih jezika* [Language contacts in theory and practice. Contributions to teaching methodology of modern languages]. Zagreb: Školska knjiga.

Finka, Božidar. 1979. "Hrvatsko jezikoznanstvo u poslijeratnom razdoblju" [Croatian linguistics in the postwar period]. *Suvremena lingvistika* 19-20: 39-58.

Fishman, Joshua A. 1970. *Sociolinguistics. A Brief Introduction.* Rowley, Massachusetts: Newbury House.

----- (ed.). 1971. *Advances in the Sociology of Language.* Volume 1: *Basic Concepts, Theories and Problems: Alternative Approach.* The Hague/ Paris: Mouton.

-----. 1972a. *The Sociology of Language. An Interdisciplinary Social Science Approach to Language in Society.* Rowley, Massachusetts: Newbury House.

-----. Joshua A. (ed.). 1972b. *Readings in the Sociology of Language.* 3rd ed. The Hague/Paris: Mouton.

----- (ed.). 1974. *Advances in Language Planning.* The Hague/Paris: Mouton.

Flaker, Aleksandar and Krunoslav Pranjić (eds). 1978. *Hrvatska književnost u evropskom kontekstu* [Croatian literature in the European context]. Zagreb: Liber.

Giglioli, Pier Paolo (ed.). 1972. *Language and Social Context. Selected Readings.* Harmondsworth, Middlesex: Penguin Books.

Girke, Wolfgang and Helmut Jachnow (eds). 1976. *Theoretische Linguistik in Osteuropa. Originalbeiträge und Erstübersetzungen.* Tübingen: Max Niemeyer Verlag.

Hymes, Dell. 1974. *Foundations in Sociolinguistics. An Ethnographic Approach.* Philadelphia: University of Pennsylvania Press.

Ivić, Milka. 1970. *Trends in Linguistics.* 2nd ed. The Hague/Paris: Mouton.

-----. 1976. "Linguistic Theory in Yugoslavia". In: W. Girke and H. Jachnow (eds). 1976: 217-33.

Ivić, Pavle. 1971. *Srpski narod i njegov jezik* [The Serbian nation and its language]. Beograd: Srpska književna zadruga.

-----. 1984. "L'evolution de la langue littéraire sur le territoire linguistique serbo-croate." *Revue des études slaves* 56. 3: 313-57.

Janković, Srđan. 1978. "Diglosija — sociolingvistički fenomen savremenog arapskog (s posebnim osvrtom na relaciju diglosija — bilingvizam)"

[Diglossia — a sociolinguistic phenomenon of modern Arabic (with special reference to the diglossia-bilingualism relation)]. *Treći program Radio Sarajeva* 20: 142-77.

Jocić, Mirjana. 1980. "Izučavanje jezika u Vojvodini. Društveno-kulturna sredina kao faktor približavanja i kreativnosti u jeziku" [The study of languages in Vojvodina. The social and cultural environment as a factor of joining and creativity in language]. *RTV teorija i praksa* 18: 188-201.

Jonke, Ljudevit. 1971. *Hrvatski književni jezik 19. i 20. stoljeća* [The Croatian literary language in the 19th and 20th century]. Zagreb: Matica hrvatska.

Jović, Dušan. 1976. "Jezik urbanih sredina" [The language of urban environments]. *Gledišta*. 7-8: 732-44.

Jutronić, Dunja. 1972. "Serbo-Croatian and American English in contact. A sociolinguistic study of the Serbo-Croatian community in Steelton, Pennsylvania". Unpublished dissertation, Pennsylvania State University.

Jutronić-Tihomirović, Dunja (ed.). 1983. "Jezik grada" [The language of the city]. *Argumenti*. 1-2: 169-204.

-----. 1985. *Hrvatski jezik u SAD* [The Croatian language in the USA]. Split: Logos.

Katičić, Radoslav. 1974. "Nešto napomena o postanku složenoga suvremenog jezičnog standarda hrvatskoga ili sprskoga" [Several remarks on the origins of the complex modern language standard of Croatian or Serbian]. *Zbornik Zagrebačke slavističke škole* 2: 225-257.

Kocher, Margaret. 1967. "Second person pronouns in Serbo-Croatian". *Language* 43. 3: 725-41.

Koerner, Konrad (ed.). 1980. *Progress in Linguistic Historiography*. Amsterdam: John Benjamins.

Lencek, Rado L. 1976. "A few remarks on the history of the term 'Serbocroatian' language". *Zbornik za filologiju i lingvistiku* 19. 1: 45-53.

----- and Thomas F. Magner (eds). 1976. *The Dilemma of the Melting Pot: The Case of the South Slavic Languages. Papers Presented at the Michael Pupin Symposium, October 5-6, 1974.* University Park/London: The Pennsylvania State University Press.

Magner, Thomas F. 1978. "City dialects in Yugoslavia". In: H. Birnbaum (ed.). 1976: 465-82.

----- (ed.). 1985. *Yugoslavia in Sociolinguistic Perspective*. (= *International Journal of the Sociology of Language* 52). Amsterdam: Mouton.

Maurais, Jacques (ed.). 1985. *La crise des langues*. Québec: Conseil de la langue française/Paris: Les éditions Robert.

Mikeš, Melanija. 1974. "Tipologija dvojezičnosti u vaspitno-obrazovnom sistemu Vojvodine" [The typology of bilingualism in the educational system in Vojvodina]. In: R. Bugarski (ed.). 1974: 147-67.

-----. 1976. "Prilog proučavanju tipologije višejezičnosti u Vojvodini" [A contribution to the study of the typology of multilingualism in Vojvodina]. In: R. Bugarski, V. Ivir, and M. Mikeš (eds). 1976: 59-66.

-----. 1983. "Dinamika međusobne komunikacije u višejezičnim situacijama" [The dynamics of interpersonal communication in multilingual situations]. *Suvremena lingvistika* 23-24: 23-29.

-----. 1984. "Instruction in the mother tongues in Yugoslavia". *Prospects* 14. 1: 121-31.

-----, Albina Lük and Ferenc Junger. 1978. "O dvojezičnosti u Jugoslaviji" [On bilingualism in Yugoslavia]. *Kultura* 40: 82-99.

Naylor, Kenneth E. 1978. "The Eastern Variant of Serbocroatian as the *lingua communis* of Yugoslavia". In: W. Schmalstieg and T.F. Magner (eds). 1978: 456-68.

-----. 1980a. "Some problems for the study of Balkan sociolinguistics". *Zbornik za filologiju i lingvistiku* 23. 2: 7-14.

-----. 1980b. "Serbo-Croatian". In: A.M. Schenker and E. Stankiewicz (eds). 1980. 65-83.

Nelde, P.H. (ed.). 1985. *Methoden der Kontaktlinguistik/Methods in Contact Linguistic Research*. Bonn: Dümmler.

Okuka, Miloš. 1983. *Jezik i politika* [Language and politics]. Sarajevo: Oslobodenje.

Pešikan, Mitar. 1970. *Naš književni jezik na sto godina poslije Vuka* [Our literary language a hundred years after Vuk]. Beograd: Društvo za srpskohrvatski jezik i književnost SRS.

Platt, J.T. and H.K. Platt. 1975. *The Social Significance of Speech*. Amsterdam: North Holland.

Polovina, Vesna. 1983. "Upotreba jednine i množine ličnih zamenica u obraćanju sagovorniku u srpskohrvatsom jeziku" [The use of the singular and plural of personal pronouns in addressing the interlocutor in Serbocroatian]. *Naučni sastanak slavista u Vukove dane. Referati i saopštenja* 13. 1: 185-95.

Pride, J.B. 1971. *The Social Meaning of Language*. London: Oxford University Press.

----- and Janet Holmes (eds). 1972. *Sociolinguistics. Selected Readings*. Harmondsworth, Middlesex: Penguin Books.

Radovanović, Milorad. 1979. *Sociolingvistika* [Sociolinguistics]. Beograd: Beogradski izdavačko-grafički zavod.

-----. 1986. *Sociolingvistika* [Sociolinguistics]. 2nd ed. Novi Sad: Theoria.

Rašić, Nikola. 1985. "La lingua situacio en Jugoslavio." *Etnismo* 34: 3-12.

Robinson, W.P. 1971. *Language and Social Behaviour*. Harmondsworth, Middlesex: Penguin Books.

Schenker, Alexander M. and Edward Stankiewicz (eds). 1980. *The Slavic Literary Languages: Formation and Development*. New Haven: Yale Concilium on International and Area Studies.

Schmalstieg, William R. and Thomas F. Magner (eds). 1978. *Sociolinguistic Problems in Czechoslovakia, Hungary, Romania and Yugoslavia*. (= *Folia Slavica* 1. 3). Columbus, Ohio: Slavica Publishers.

Stanojčić, Živojin, *et al.* (eds). 1983. *Jezik u savremenoj komunikaciji* [Language in modern communication]. Beograd: Centar za marksizam Univerziteta u Beogradu.

Stone, Gerald. 1977. "Address in the Slavonic languages". *The Slavonic and East European Review* 55. 4: 491-505.

Surdučki, Milan. 1978. *Srpskohrvatski i engleski u kontaktu. Rečnik i morfološka analiza engleskih pozajmljenica u standardnom srpskohrvatskom jeziku i jeziku Srba i Hrvata iseljenika u Kanadi* [Serbocroatian and English in contact. Vocabulary and morphological analysis of English loan words in standard Serbocroatian and the language of Serbian and Croatian immigrants in Canada]. Novi Sad: Matica srpska.

Šipka, Milan (ed.). 1984. *Jezik i nacionalni odnosi* [Language and national relations]. (= *Sveske* 2: 5-6). Sarajevo: Institut za proučavanje nacionalnih odnosa.

Škiljan, Dubravko (ed.). 1982. "Naš jezik danas i sutra" [Our language today and tomorrow]. *Naše teme*. 5: 805-862.

Tollefson, James W. 1981. *The Language Situation and Language Policy in Slovenia*. Washington, D.C.: University Press of America.

-----. 1983. "Language policy and the meaning of diglossia". *Word* 34. 1: 1-9.

Trudgill, Peter. 1983. *Sociolinguistics: An Introduction to Language and Society*. Rev. ed. Harmondsworth, Middlesex: Penguin Books.

Vasić, Ivona. 1979. "Govorno ponašanje predstavnika savremenog srpskohrvatskog jezika u situaciji obraćanja" [The speech behaviour of speakers of modern Serbocroatian in the situation of address]. *Prilozi proučavanju jezika* 15: 57-70.

Vince, Zlatko. 1978. *Putovima hrvatskoga književnog jezika. Lingvističko kulturno-povijesni prikaz filoloških škola i njihovih izvora* [The roads of the Croatian standard language. A linguistic, cultural and historical review of philological schools and their sources]. Zagreb: Liber.

Vuković, Jovan. 1972. *Naš književni jezik danas* [Our literary language today]. Sarajevo: Veselin Masleša.

Weinreich, Uriel. 1963. *Languages in Contact. Findings and Problems*. 2nd ed. The Hague: Mouton.

Language planning: theory and application

Ljubiša Rajić
Faculty of Philology, University of Belgrade

1 Subject, approach and goal

Conscious influence on language system and/or its use consists of three elements: theory, application of theory, and reception of theory and/or its application by the language community. This paper deals with the *theory* of conscious influence on language systems and the *applicative relevance* of particular theoretical interpretations.

The theory of conscious influence on a language system and its use is realized on two different levels, the *general*, e.g. correspondence principles on the grapheme-phoneme level, and the *specific*, e.g. correspondence principles on the grapheme-phoneme level applied when planning a grapheme unit for a specific non-literary language. On the general level, theoretical assumptions are usually explicit in nature, while on the specific level, they are usually implicit. Therefore, it can be assumed that there is no conscious influence on a language system and its use which is atheoretical. Clearly, such a notion exceeds the existing definition of the notion *theory* which is more or less accepted in epistemological literature of different trends. The reason for this is that any conscious influence on language and its use is consciously or subconsciously motivated by specific subjective or objective interests and needs of groups of speakers of the language or the society as a whole. This influence is partly the result of objective needs imposed by the very development of society, politically and economically united in one country, in which, at a certain level of development, a standard language emerges as a means of communication on the societal level without interference of dialects. In addition, this influence is the result of the way those who can influence the language consciously or subconsciously express their interests, which then become a part of theory and practical application. In this sense, the theory and practice of the influence on a language system and its use are of an ideological as well as an axiological nature. Therefore, the title of this paper might have been "Ideological foundations of language planning". This would, however, add new elements to the definition of the notion *ideology*, elements that are more likely of a technical than of an ideological nature. Such an extension would then be as unjustifiable as in the case of the notion of *theory*, mentioned earlier.

There are four groups of principles in language planning: *the ideological and axiological principles* out of which *the legitimacy principles* 'arise', i.e. justification of the need for language planning; furthermore, *the standardization principles* as instruments of realization of language planning; and lastly, *the principles governing the application of the standards*.

Such a division in language planning theory seems necessary since, in the past fifteen years, the focus has been shifted from questions of a *technical* nature to *political* ones (compare e.g. Rubin, Jernudd 1971 and Fishman & Cobarrubias 1981). The tendency to closely link language and politics (see e.g. O'Barr, O'Barr 1976) in the domain of language planning is explained by the fact that "language planning is *nationality* planning as well and, in this respect, it is different from industrial or agricultural planning which, at best, begin as *national* planning" (Fishman 1974b: 89).

In this sense, language planning is also planning of identity, personal and national (see e.g. Koppelmann 1956; Fishman, Ferguson & das Gupta 1968; Fishman 1972b; Baziev & Isaev 1973; Giles 1977; Lamy 1979; Gumperz 1982). The *political nature* of this process is best seen in the so-called ethnic awakening of minorities in Europe in the past decades (see e.g. Krejci & Velinsky 1981) and in certain cases of regrouping into the original social communities, popularly called 'retribalization' (see Khleif 1980). One result of this is the problem of minority languages (see e.g. Haugen, McShure & Thomson 1981).

This paper will discuss the ideological bases for languages planning, the legitimacy principles, the standardization principles. and the principles governing the application of the standards, and their interrelations.

2   Terminology

The literature in the field of language planning has become very extensive, and the terminology used is inconsistent.[1] This inconstistency is mainly the consequence of controversies in the application of terminology (and theory) within general linguistics and sociology, which are direct sources of the theoretical foundations of language planning.

2.1 *Linguistic terminology*

The key term in language planning is always the notion of a language norm. Development of theoretical thought on the notion *norm* began at the turn of the century and was continued by de Saussure, the Prague School, Hjelmslev, Coseriu, and recently by many other linguists and sociologists (see e.g. Guhman 1970; Semenjuk 1970; Hartung 1977; Bédard & Maurais 1983). The norm, however, neither as a term nor as an inherent part of language, can be discussed separately from language as a totality. Therefore, several operational definitions exist. Definitions of other key linguistic terms (*language, speech, system, performance*, etc.) are also subject to discussion and criticism.

This paper, however, will only analyze the notion of norm. The norm consists of three elements. The first element is the oral, phonic realization of the system. It serves as a basis for standardization of phonological, morphological, and syntactic subsystems. A lexical norm has a double function and is significant in the domain of terminology. On the one hand, it is connected to the grammatical norm through rules for derivation of words and formation of constructions which function as equivalents for lexemes. On the other hand, the lexical norm is connected to the semantic norm which regulates meaning, the domain of lexical semantics. A separate issue to discuss is to what extent the phonic realization element includes the semantic norm (at the sentence and contextual levels), which regulates syntax, and the pragmatic norm which regulates the usage of the system and through it the language and its functioning as a means of communication.

Such norms are, for example, conventional language forms used when introducing or greeting someone or when expressing thanks, when delivering a speech, when addressing persons in accordance with their social status, when issuing orders, having discussions, etc.

The second element is realized through the proper relation between speech as *signatum* and written language as *signans*, primarily in the domain of orthography and orthoepy, but also in all other domains of written language connected with segmental and suprasegmental elements of speech. These norms regulate the relations of direct equivalence at the phoneme-grapheme level, as well as the relations of indirect equivalence in which the written language element corresponds to the zero element of spoken language, e.g. spacing between letters corresponds to junctures, indenting a new paragraph most often to a pause in speech, etc.

The third element is realized in the domain of autonomy of written language as an indirect materialization of language. It regulates the type and form of written language; the application of orthographic signs when they are autonomous in relation to speech (e.g., in an interrogative sentence which contains an interrogative word a question mark has no function, it is redundant); the realization of the linear nature of speech in written language (writing from right to left, from left to right, from top to bottom, etc.); writing a title and date; other conventional forms which are partly of a linguistic and partly of a paralinguistic nature; signs for expressing pain, sighs, fear; spacing out to express a specific speech pattern, etc; other conventional forms which are partly of a linguistic and partly of an extralinguistic nature (international, regional and national standards for writing documents, agreements, verdicts, for filling various forms, etc.).

Observed as a whole, these three elements differ qualitatively. A norm which is part of a language system is of a conventional nature and at the same time is necessary. A norm can change some elements of the structure of a given language, but never the whole system. A norm which is part of a correspondence between speech and written language is conventional and arbitrary, and can be changed partly or as a whole at any time (compare the shift from Arabic to Latin script in Turkey), but it cannot be changed in an instant without causing relatively serious consequences to written language communication. A norm which is part of the autonomy of written language is of a conventional and arbitrary nature and can be changed at any time without seriously affecting written communication. The difference, therefore, is in the nature of the norm rules which are necessary on the side of the norm belonging to spoken language but not necessary on the side belonging to written language.

Therefore, it seems justifiable to introduce two terms, the *norm*, which corresponds only to the first element of the series, and *standard language*, which comprises all three elements. The term *norm* would thus have a more specific meaning of a pure, linguistic nature as a set of rules which governs the choice between different structural possibilities of a given language, e.g. the choice between marked and unmarked word order or between different registers. This difference between the norm and the standard can be defined through the terms *implicit* and *explicit norms*. Both types of norm are clearly of a social nature, because language itself is a social phenomenon and because they are norms. The difference is that we are generally not conscious of implicit norms (except when we violate them) but are conscious of explicit norms. It can be concluded that implicit norms are a general feature of language and explicit norms (standards) a specific feature (see e.g. Brozovič 1967). An implicit norm, clearly, can become explicit in the process of formation of standard languages, but then this explicit norm remains a specific case because it never fully corresponds to an implicit norm.

2.2 *Sociological terminology*

A large number of terms, by which conscious human influence on a language system and/or language use is expressed, are used in the sociolinguistic literature: *language planning, language policy, language standardization, normalization of language, language engineering*, etc. These terms differ from each other in intension as well as extension. Their differentiation is possible along a semantic scale on the basis of their intralinguistic or extralinguistic function. In this sense, only two terms exist, one which by its definition 'covers' acting within the language system, and the other which 'covers' acting outside the language system. Therefore, one end of the semantic scale could be defined as influence on language and the other as influence on language use. This understood, the terms *language planning* and *language policy* will be used in what follows.

Language planning: the action which determines the norm in the already suggested narrower sense is the first step, which is then extended to standard language as the second step. Language planning takes into consideration speech (oral manifestation) as a direct manifestation of language and written language as an indirect manifestation of language. Besides, language planning includes the process of making decisions about norms which are of a linguistic nature, i.e. intralinguistic, and which make up the principles of standardization of language.

Language policy: a collection of acts through which institutions, groups and individuals in a society, directly or indirectly, influence the language system, language use, the language situation in one segment of society, in the whole society, or in several synchronic societies. These actions consist of models and implicit and explicit social norms and at the same time involve the whole process of formation and implementation of norms, which means that language planning is included in language policy.

Social norm: social norm implies an implicit norm (expectation) or an explicit norm (statement), which both define social behaviour. These norms can be prohibitive ('must', 'mustn't'), or affirmaive ('doesn't have to', 'may', 'can') or prohibitive-affirmative ('it is recommended', 'it is not recommanded'). Prohibitive norms are often defined according to the principle: everything that is not explicitly forbidden is allowed. Affirmative norms are defined according to the principle: everything that is not explicitly allowed doesn't have to be forbidden, but there is a possibility that it is. Prohibitive-affirmative norms do not have such limitations. Prohibitive, and sometimes affirmative norms, carry certain sanctions when violated, and these sanctions may be legal or ethical. Legal sanctions are, as a rule, explicit and ethical ones are, as a rule, implicit.

This definition requires certain explanations. The problem of the norm in sociology, and in other social sciences which deal with this notion, is a very complex and controversial issue. The same could be said about its implementation in linguistics (see e.g. Gloy 1975, 1979). Therfore, it is necessary to emphasise here the operational character of the given definition. This definition could include many other elements, for example appropriateness and inappropriateness of given norms under certain conditions; however, it is still sufficient to point out the basic problems in determining the way in which a language norm shifts from the descriptive phase to the prescriptive and thus becomes the norm in the narrowest sense.

Another issue is whether and how it is possible to implement the norm. For example, can those who do not have the four-accent system in their native dialect acquire this system, which exists in the standard Serbo-Croatian language? This issue is of extreme importance when determining social norms which further determine language norms. It is necessary to point out that each type of norm can have one or more possibilities of choice, and also that there is a smaller or larger area which is not included in the norm, either because it is unintentionally omitted or because the norm was intended to be simpler. Finally, each norm is legitimate, that is, it has a justification for its existence. But of particular interest are types of norms that involve ideology and politics, thus forming the principles of legitimacy, standardization and norm implementation.

3 Ideology of standardization

Analyzing the historical development of the standardization of language from specialized, mostly Scandinavian literature, the Swedisch linguist Teleman (1979) concluded that there are three basic conceptions of the proper attitude towards language:

(a) The socio-political conception, according to which an individual or a group, classical or modern writers, serve as a model.

(b) The 'laissez-faire' conception, the basic idea of which is that any interference with language is unnecessary and harmful, that language develops by itself and that the best solutions are always crystallized through everyday use.

(c) The communicative-technical conception, the basic idea of which is that language must be standardized in order to serve in the best possible way as a means of communication, and in which the appropriateness of the standard language is extremely important.

Teleman further correlated these three conceptions with the periods in which they were basically formulated. He concluded that the socio-political conception corresponded to feudal society, the 'laissez-faire' to early capitalism (liberalism and free trade), and the communicative-technical to late capitalism. The third conception of Teleman's classification is mostly accepted by East German and Soviet theoreticians of language planning, who only give a somewhat different argumentation and explanation of the legitimacy principles than do Western linguists.

Teleman's classification still has to be revised. Namely, there can be only *two* basic ideologies: *language does not have to be planned* and *language must be planned*. His first and third types are, in fact, subtypes of the conception that language must be planned. Besides, Teleman almost exclusively connected the types of conceptions with the periods in which they occurred. The model conception is typical of the Middle Ages in general (*auctoritates*), but it is accepted nowadays too (e.g. Einar Haugen, many Yugoslav linguists). The conception of 'leave your language alone' is accepted by many older and younger linguists (Otto Jespersen, Paul Diderichsen, Robert A. Hall, and others). Most modern linguists, however, have accepted the communicative-technical type of conception, cf., especially Rubin, Jernudd (1971). Jernudd takes 'planning and business administration' as a model.

Radovanović (1979) sums up modern conceptions of the communicative-technical type and names ten phases in the process of standardization of language: selection, description, codification, elaboration, acceptation, implementation, expansion, cultivation, evaluation and reconstruction. Each phase is defined by a certain framework of circumstances and actions. If these phases are observed along the semantic differentiation scale suggested in the previous section (extralinguistic/intralinguistic), then it can be said that the first four phases (selection, description, codificiation and elaboration) and the last two (evaluation and reconstruction) are intralinguistic, while all the others are extralinguistic. The most important intralinguistic phases in the domain of language planning are, in my opinion, *selection* and *evaluation*, which are the two most comprehensive *value acts* and which require legitimacy. All other phases (description, elaboration, reconstruction, and to a somewhat lesser degree codification) are of a more technical nature and their value aspect is far less evident.

Namely, the only typically axiological element of language planning occurs in selection and evaluation, because they serve for bridging the gap between 'is' and 'ought to be' (in Hume's sense of this dichotomy). How to derive the linguistic *ought to be* from the linguistic *is*, which is the very reason for language planning, is the key question of legitimacy in language planning.

4   From 'is' to 'ought to be'

It has already been mentioned that language planning is interwoven in language policy, and policy and ideology in general. Therefore, before discussing the derivation of *ought to be* from *is* as a preliminary act of codification, it is interesting to see what views certain theorists of language planning hold as regards the relation between language planning and language policy. Generally, these views can be divided into four categories. Some linguists hold that language planning is a relatively independent act which can or must precede language policy (Ray, Tauli, Haugen), while others hold that language policy precedes language planning (Neustupný). The third group of linguists thinks that language planners must be only the administrators of the linguistic aspect of language policy, a kind of executive (Fishman, Jernudd, das Gupta, East German authors), and the fourth group holds the view that between language policy and language planning there exists a dialectic relation in which the language planner must act as a conscious *homo politicus* (Gloy, Vikør).[2] These views are expressed more or less explicitly, especially by Fishman, das Gupta, Jernudd, and East European authors, or implicitly, that is, defined in general terms.

Such an 'external' orientation of authors determines, to a large extent, their choice of criteria for selection and evaluation. Some find these criteria in the intralinguistic domain, defining them as efficiency, rationality, acceptability from the linguistic point of view (Ray, Haugen), and others find them in the extralinguistic domain, primarily in society and social needs (Jernudd, das Gupta). However, the analysis of these criteria and views is complicated because their definitions are not precise. For example, the criteria given by Ray, Haugen, and Tauli (efficiency, rationality, commonality, adequacy, acceptability, clarity and others) are often not precisely defined.

Let us, for example, take the efficiency of a given form in the process of communication. It is not enough to say that the form which is easy to learn and easy to use is efficient. If we speak of use only with the aim of communication, then 'efficiency' must be defined by answering a series of questions: who communicates, with whom, what the communication is about, why one communicates, how, when, and how long one communicates, under what conditions, etc. Without clear answers to these questions, it is difficult to determine precisely the intension and extension of the notion of efficiency of any language form in use. As a result, *a priori* or deductive criteria (Jernudd, das Gupta) are criticized, and explicit demands are being made for empirical and inductive criteria (Hymes).[3] Besides, the imprecision of the definitions of the intension and extension of the notions hides their potential contradictions. For example, economy and clarity as criteria must be defined in relation to certain functional styles. The aesthetic criterion, which according to Tauli coincides with the economy and clarity criteria, can be contradictory to them, which means that what is economic and clear is not necessarily aesthetic, and vice versa. Therefore, when it comes to defining these criteria for specific languages, they become concrete (e.g. Haugen for Norwegian). The same applies to extralinguistic phenomena (Fishman). Therefore, there are two groups of criteria, one connected to more technical procedures of an intralinguistic nature (e.g. procedures of comparison, archaizing and statistical measurement which Haugen gives as possible choices for the selection of elements and their alternatives within the system), and the other connected to extralinguistic factors (e.g. Neustupný's criteria of unity of a country, development of society, democratization and foreign relations).

This dualism of views as regards the relationship between language policy and language planning, and of views concerning the selection of criteria, shows that the critical point of language planning is where the lnguistic *is* becomes the linguistic *ought to be*. In my opinion, this point occurs when we come to the principles of legitimacy which are applied when *is* changes to *ought to be*. Therefore, it seems that the relative confusion which exists when the criteria of selection and evaluation are observed only as technical procedures (as in Byron 1976) can be cleared up through the ideologization of these criteria.

5   Legitimacy principles and normative principles

In the sociolinguistic literature a number of principles are used which belong either to the group of principles of legitimacy or to the group of principles of standardization. All these principles are usually put into the same group, sometimes called *criteria of legitimacy* (Gloy 1975, 1979), and sometimes *principles of standardization* (Vikør 1981), or are given other names. Since the classification that I suggest does not exist in the literature I reviewed, the following are only general ideas on the subject, and are subject to further discussion. As the list of principles is not limited, I have chosen to analyse only two groups of principles which have been directly applied to standardization of some languages. Gloy refers to German and Vikør to Norwegian.

Vikør mentions nine principles: the democratic principle (language of the majority), the principle of identification (the majority should be given the possibility of identification with the written form), the pedagogical principle (choosing the simpler of two given forms), the principle of internal order of the language, the historical and national principle (older and 'more national' forms instead of modern, foreign and common ones), the principle of literary tradition (choosing forms from literary works), the aesthetic principle (avoiding 'vulgar' and 'uneducated' forms), the principle of efficiency (choosing forms which enhance communication), the principle of internationalism (choosing forms that cross national boundaries).

Gloy mentions eleven criteria: the manner in which cultural authorities use the language (language of writers as a cultural elite), the historical background of linguistic phenomena (etymologization), supra-regionality, national unity, comprehensibility, factual use of the language, frequency (of forms), systemic well-formedness, social acceptability (communicative aspect), existence of social standards for interpretation (in the domain of semantic norms), cognitive and emotional consequences of the manner of expression (based on the deficit theory).

These two groups of criteria fall into two domains, the intralinguistic (etymologization, systematicity, factual use, frequency) and the extralinguistic (the remaining criteria). In my opinion, the *principles of legitimacy* are of an extralinguistic nature, and their role is to justify the existence of the norm in language through some extralinguistic phenomena. It seems that the most appropriate division of these principles is into social, political and cultural ones. *Social* principles are the principles of identification, the pedagogical principle, the principle of efficiency, the principle of comprehensibility, the principle of social acceptability, the principle of cognitive and emotional consequences, and partly the principle of cultural authorities. *Political* principles are the democratic principle, the principles of internationalism (supra-regionality), of the national and historical, of national unity, of the existence of social standards for interpretation, and partly of social acceptability. *Cultural* principles are the principle of literary tradition, the aesthetic principle, and partly the principle of cultural authorities. They are all part of language policy.

The *principles of standardization*, which include the principle of internal systematicity, the principle of etymologization and of previous language states, the principles of factual use, and the principle of frequency of forms are derived from these principles of legitimacy.

This kind of classification demands several explanations. First, contradictions between some of the principles within the two groups clearly exist. For example, the national and historical principles, according to which standardization of language should play a specific role in the forming of a nation, the strenghtening of national unity and shaping of national awareness, is, as a rule, in contradiction with supra-regionality and internationalism. Exceptions might be found when supra-regional cultural or political elements take part in the shaping of national awareness; for example, supraregional elements of Islamic civilization are apparent among Yugoslav Moslems (see Tanasković 1983), and the same elements play a considerable role in the development of standard Albanian in Yugoslavia and Albania (see Byron 1976). In the same way, the principle of previous language states contradicts the principle of factual use of language. Exceptions can again be found in Yugoslavia, in the regions where Serbo-Croatian is spoken. In the western variant of Serbo-Croatian there is an insistence on the use of more archaic lexical items, and in the eastern variant on the factual use of words among all Serbs, including those living outside Serbia. In other words, these principles exist and are realized in dialectic pairs which form a hierarchy of principles of legitimacy and principles of standardization. This hierarchy shows which contradictions are of primary and which of secondary importance, i.e. which principles are dominant and which are not. For example, if the principle of national and historical justification of the need for standardization of language is dominant, then the standardization also includes principles of literary tradition, cultural authorities and aesthetics, as well as the principle of internal systematicity and of previous language states. Second, the application of the principles of legitimacy and standardization shows a tendency towards applying principles of a more technical nature, of course with exceptions. For example, in the Soviet Union the theory of language planning starts from the corpus and principles of literature and literary traditions and develops toward principles of accuracy, functionality, appropriateness etc., with due attention to scientific and technical literature. Third, the principles mentioned can be classified according to their relation to changes in language. If we accept Haugen's (1972) definition of language planning as an evaluation of changes in language, then any codification of language becomes either retrospective or prognostic, i.e. takes into account the past or the future of the language. The principle of previous language states and partly the principle of internal systematicity (excluding analogical processes) produce a retrospective codification, while the principles of factual use and frequency, and partly the principle of internal systematicity (including analogical processes) produce prognostic codification. Application of certain principles of codification (standardization) can discourage or encourage changes in language. When selecting the principles of legitimacy, on the one hand we 'standardize' certain social processes by discouraging or encouranging their development, and on the other we determine the choice of principles of standardization in the context of language policy, politics and ideology of a given society, class or group of people. Bugarski (1983:20) defines language planning within language policy as "conscious directing of language development on the basis of extralinguistic evaluation, for the purpose of realizing broader social goals".

Vikør also emphasizes the fact that these principles fit into a given political situation, and he classifies them according to the political view of those who promote them. According to him, leftists most often promote the democratic principle, the principle of identification, and the pedagogical principle, just as do many linguists; conservatives most often apply the principles of literary tradition and aesthetics; national-conservatives apply the national and historical principles and the principle of internal systematicity; technocrats emphasise the principles of efficiency and internationalism.

This classification is not absolute since it is based on pecularities of the development of standard languages in Norway. However, its importance exceeds these limits. This is evident especially when it is correlated with basic principles of standardization: conservatives and national-conservatives most often decide on the feudal type of socio-political standardization as Teleman classifies it, and technocrats most often opt for the communicative-technical conception, or social legitimacy, while leftists opt for both types, excluding conservative or technocratic political elements through the axiologization of the principles and their modification in accordance with the democrative, identification and pedagogical principles. It is characteristic that leftists are the only ones who consistently reject the idea of leaving language alone, because they believe that otherwise language will develop so as to suit the interests of the ruling class.

Such correlation also enables relatively simple classification of principles not mentioned here, for example those given by Jespersen (1925), who also refers to some earlier works of Scandinavian linguists, especially Adolf Noreen. At the same time, this classification helps us to explain why certain principles prevail under particular conditions, for examples, why purist tendencies prevail in Serbo-Croatian, Slovenian and Macedonian at times when nationalistic tendencies in the nations speaking these languages are strongest.[4]

Generally speaking, dominance of certain principles of legitimacy in a given society may be observed as a symptomatic phenomenon which indicates the state the society is in: the dominance of the national principle always indicates that a given nation is not completely formed, or that its ruling class is in conflict with the ruling class of some other nation, or that the ruling class lacks internal cohesion, or that the language of the given nation is endangered; the dominance of the communicative-technical principle indicates that the problem of usefulness of language reforms exists. Since clear-cut cases rarely if ever occur, detailed analyses of the principles of legitimacy and standardization have to be made.

5 Principles of norm implementation

The analyses of language planning and language policy must give a
clear answer to four questions: what is being planned, who is it planned for,
who does the planning and how, and who formulates language policy and
how.

The focus is not on the same elements and procedures in each society.
For example, in the Soviet Union, the focus is on standardization of the
Russian language, the formation of other national standard languages and
the relation between Russian and national languages; in Sweden the focus
is on planning the language of administration; in Norway on problems of
diglossia; in Iceland on puristic problems; in Yugoslavia on the problems of
variants of standard Serbo-Croatian and of language rights, etc.

It is also important for whom language planning is done. In Yugoslavia, for example, the standardization is intended primarily to suit the
needs of schools, and elsewhere it covers the needs of a much greater
number of users of standard languages. Differences also occur in connection with who carries out the standardization: specialized state institutions
(e.g. in Scandinavia), academies or associations (in many European countries), influential linguistic circles, etc.[5] Differences in the ways of solving
the problems of *what, who* and *for whom* essentially influence the way in
which the problem of *how* will be solved.

How to implement a norm? This problem includes three components:
the problem of means, the problem of reception, and the problem of social
norms. The means necessary for the implementation of a norm are determined by the relevant fields that have to be standardized. This problem is
solved by the production of normative grammars, dictionaries, spelling dictionaries, collections of standard forms, collections of standards, etc. The
problem of the reception of the norm, however, is much more complex. It
requires a study of a whole series of elements which influence or might
influence the implementation of a norm: its social, political, psychological,
cultural, linguistic aspects, etc. And finally, depending on what is being
standardized, who does the standardization and for whom, it is necessary to
determine which social norms will be valid for the use of the means necessary for the implementation of the norm, and for fulfilling the demands produced by the analyses made in the domain of the reception of the norm. In
this sense it is necessary to determine in which part of the norm the prohibitive, affirmative and prohibitive-affirmative social norms will be applied

and how they will be treated legally. Obviously, a standard will be in the form of obligation (prohibitive norm), it will be legalized, and its violation will carry a sanction. However, in the domain of terminology (or, in the conception of some linguists, nomenclatures) there will appear certain affirmative or prohibitive-affirmative norms which will not be legalized and whose violation will not carry legal sanctions but will be 'punished' indirectly, by lack of comprehension, or in some other way. As regards the domain of intralinguistic norms, the number of affirmative and prohibitive-affirmative norms rapidly increases in societies where there is more freedom of choice between alternatives and where sanctions are reduced to a minimum. Violation of these norms will not cause disorder in society; it is not a crime. But in societies in which the national principle dominates, violation of these norms may be considered an offence, e.g. the use of foreign, especially English words in France (see *L'Express*, No. 1741, 23.11.84). A similar phenomenon occurs in some parts of Yugoslavia; for example, in connection with the use of the Latin alphabet in Macedonia, or of Serbo-Croatian lexis in Slovenia, or of Serbian lexis in Croatia and vice-versa, or of ekavian dialect in Bosnia and Herzegovina. Solutions to these problems vary from society to society; however, there exists a basic correlation between the principles of legitimacy and the principles of implementation of the norms, as well as between the principles of legitimacy and the principles of standardization.

Among the principles of legitimacy, the principles of democracy and internationalism are most often connected with affirmative norms of implementation of language norms, and national and historical principles with prohibitive norms. As for social principles, the principle of identification, the pedagogical principle and the principle of emotional and cognitive development are most often connected with affirmative norms, and the principle of efficiency and comprehensibility with affirmative and affirmative-prohibitive norms. Cultural principles are mostly connected with prohibitive norms. There are considerable deviations from these trends, but the data that I have analysed (on Scandinavian countries, West and East Germany, USSR, Yugoslavia, Poland, France, Albania, and some other European and non-European countries) show that the degree of correlation is still so high that we can speak of a basic tendency. More precise conclusions would certainly require more detailed investigations.

Notes

1. The basic references are Rubin & Jernudd 1971; Rubin & Shuy 1973; Fishman 1974; Rubin, Jernudd, das Gupta, Fishman & Ferguson 1977; Fishman & Cobarrubias 1981; Sager 1980; and the *Language planning newsletter* (ed. Joan Rubin).

2. See e.g. Ray 1963; Neustupný 1968; Tauli 1968; Haugen 1966 (all of them discussed in Byron 1976); further Fishman 1972a,b; Gloy 1975, 1979; for Soviet and East German authors Girke & Jachnow 1974; Neumann 1976; Normen 1977; Uesseler 1982; Lewis 1972.

3. See also Byron 1976.

4. See Bugarski 1987 for the scope of language policy and language planning in Yugoslavia.

5. See Rubin 1980 and additional lists in later numbers of the *Language planning newsletter*. A very interesting study of language planning institutions and channels in Sweden is Grünbaum 1980.

References

Baziev, A.T. and M.I. Isaev. 1973. *Jazyk i nacija* [Language and nation]. Moscow: Nauka.

Bédard, Édith and Jacques Maurais (eds). 1983. *La norme linguistique.* Québec: Conseil de la langue française/Paris: Le Robert.

Brozovič, Dalibor. "Slavjanskie standartnye jazyki i sravnitel'nyj metod" [Slavic standard languages and the comparative method]. *Voprosy jazykoznanija.* 1: 3-33.

Bugarski, Ranko. 1983. "Jezička nejednakost u savremenom svetu" [Language inequality in the modern world]. In: Stanojčić et al. 1983: 18-23.

-----. 1987. "Politique et aménagement linguistique en Yugoslavie." In: Jacques Maurais (ed.). *Politique et aménagement linguistiques.* Québec: Conseil de la langue française/Paris: Le Robert. 1987: 417-452.

Byron, Janet L. 1976. *Selection among Alternatives in Language Standardization: The Case of Albanian.* The Hague: Mouton.

Fishman, Joshua A. 1972a. *The Sociology of Language. An Interdisciplinary Social Science Approach to Language in Society.* Rowley, Massachusetts: Newbury House Publishers. (First appeared in Joshua A. Fishman (ed.). 1971. *Advances in the Sociology of Language.* Vol. I. *Basic Concepts, Theories and Problems: Alternative Approaches.* The Hague: Mouton. 217-404.

-----. 1972b. *Language and Nationalism: Two Integrative Essays.* Rowley, Massachusetts: Newbury House Publishers.

----- (ed.). 1974a. *Advances in Language Planning.* (= *Contributions to the Sociology of Language* 5.) The Hague: Mouton.

-----. 1974b. "Language modernization and planning in comparison with other types of national modernization and planning". In: Joshua A. Fishman. 1974a: 79-102.

----- and J. Cobarrubias (eds). 1981. *Progress in Language Planning: International Perspectives.* (= *Contributions to the Sociology of Language*, 31.) The Hague: Mouton.

-----, Charles A. Ferguson and Jyotirindra Das Gupta (eds). 1968. *Language Problems of Developing Nations.* New York: Wiley.

Giles, Howard (ed.). 1977. *Language, Ethnicity and Intergroup Relations.* London: Academic Press.

Girke, Wolfgang and Helmut Jachnow. 1974. *Sowjetische Sozio-linguistik. Probleme und Genese.* Kronberg, Ts.: Scriptor.

Gloy, Klaus. 1975. *Sprachnormen 1. Linguistische und soziologische Analysen.* Stuttgart: Fromann.

-----. 1979. "Normer och språknormer. Några grundläggande tankar." *Nydanske studier & Almen kommunikationsteori* 12: 8-24.

Grünbaum, Catharina. 1980. "Språkvårdens kanaler". *Språk i Norden.* 1980: 75-105.

Guhman, M.M. 1970. "Literaturnyj jazyk" [The literary language]. In: Serebrennikov. 1970: 502-548.

Gumperz, John J. (ed.). 1982. *Language and Social Identity.* Cambridge.

Hartung, Wolfdietrich. 1977. "Zum Inhalt des Normbegriffes in der Linguistik." In: *Normen.* 1977: 9-69.

Haugen, Einar. 1966. *Language Conflict and Language Planning: the Case of Modern Norwegian.* Cambridge, Massachusetts: Harvard University Press.

-----. 1972. *The Ecology of Language.* Selected and introduced by Anwar S. Dil. Stanford, California: Stanford University Press.

-----, J.D. McShure and D.S. Thomson (eds). 1981. *Minority Languages Today.* Edinburgh: Edinburgh University Press.

Jespersen, Otto. 1925. *Mankind, Nation and Individual from a Linguistic Point of View.* (= *Serie* A:IV.) Oslo: Institutet for sammenliknende kulturforskning.

Khleif, Bud B. 1980. *Language, Ethnicity, and Education in Wales.* The Hague: Mouton.

Koppelman, H.L. 1956. *Nation, Sprache und Nationalismus.* Leiden: A.W. Sijthoff's Uitgeversmaatschappij.

Krejci, Jaroslav K. and Vitezslav Velinsky. 1981. *Ethnic and Political Nations in Europe*. London: Croom Helm.

Lamy, P. (ed.). 1979. *Language Planning and Identity Planning*. (= *International Journal of the Sociology of Language* 20.) The Hague: Mouton.

Lewis, Glynn E. 1972. *Multilingualism in the Soviet Union: Aspects of Language Policy and its Implementation*. (= *Contributions to the Sociology of Language* 3.) The Hague: Mouton.

Neustupný, Jiri V. 1968. "Some general aspects of 'language' problems and 'language' policy in developing societies". In: J.A. Fishman, C.A. Ferguson, J. Das Gupta (eds). 1968: 285-294.

Neumann, Werner (ed.). 1976. *Theoretische Probleme der Sprachwissenschaft*. 1-2. Berlin: Akademie-Verlag.

Normen in der sprachlichen Kommunikation. 1977. Berlin: Akademie-Verlag.

O'Barr, William M. and Jean F. O'Barr (eds). 1976. *Language and Politics*. (= *Contributions to the Sociology of Language* 10.) The Hague: Mouton.

Ray, Punya Sloka. 1963. *Language Standardization*. The Hague: Mouton.

Radovanović, Milorad. 1979. *Sociolingvistika* [Sociolinguistics]. Beograd: BIGZ.

Rubin, Joan. 1980. *Directory of Language Planning Organizations*. Honolulu: Hawaii University Press.

---- and Björn H. Jernudd (eds). 1971. *Can Language Be Planned? Sociolinguistic Theory and Practice for Developing Nations*. Honolulu: The University Press of Hawaii.

-----, B.H. Jernudd, J. Das Gupta, J. Fishman and C.A. Ferguson (eds). 1977. *Language Planning Processes*. (= *Contributions to the Sociology of Language* 21.) The Hague: Mouton.

----- and R. Shuy (eds). 1973. *Language Planning: Current Issues and Research*. Washington, D.C.: Georgetown University Press.

Sager, J.C. (ed.). 1980. *Standardization of Nomenclature*. (= *International Journal of the Sociology of Language* 23.) The Hague: Mouton.

Semenjuk, N.N. 1970. "Norma" [Norm]. In: Serebrennikov. 1970: 549-596.

Serebrennikov, B.A. (ed.). 1970. *Obščee jazykoznanie*. I. Moskva: Nauka.

Stanojčić, Živojin, et al. (eds). 1983. *Jezik u savremenoj komunikaciji* [Language in modern communication]. Beograd: Centar za marksizam Univerziteta u Beogradu.

Tanasković, Darko. 1983. "Sociolingvistički aspekti ideologizacije pozajmljenica" [Sociolinguistic aspects of the ideologization of loan words]. In: Ž. Stanojčić et al. 1983: 96-115.

Tauli, Valter. 1968. *Introduction to a Theory of Language Planning*. (= *Acta Universitatis Upsaliensis. Studia Philologiae Scandinavicae Upsaliensia* 6.) Uppsala: Almqvist & Wiksell.

Teleman, Ulf. 1979. *Språkrätt. Om skolans språknormer och samhällets*. Lund: LiberLäromedel.

Uesseler, Manfred. 1982. *Soziolinguistik*. Berlin: VEB Deutscher Verlag der Wissenschaften.

Vikør, Lars S. 1981. *Språk*. Pax leksikon. Oslo: Pax.

Psycholinguistics: research directions*

Svenka Savić
Faculty of Philosophy, University of Novi Sad

The state of Yugoslav linguistics and psychology today[1]

Over the past thirty-five years psycholinguistics[2], as an interdisciplinary approach to the study of language, has passed through a stage of establishing its independence in relation to psychology or linguistics (among others, see Carlson and Tannenhaus 1982; Hjelmquist 1978; Linell 1978; Slama-Cazacu 1973). Today, it is passing through a period of intensive influence upon those monodisciplines from which it started. Taking into consideration that the complex relationship between thought and language cannot be isolated from other cultural and social phenomena which have lately been very much in the forefront of attention, we could at the very beginning of this review state that it is extremely difficult to evaluate all that psycholinguistics represents in the world today.

We shall attempt to show the development of psycholinguistics[3] in Yugoslavia during the past thirty-five years in relation to what happened in psycholinguistics in the world during that period, and also in relation to what has been going on in psychology and linguistics in that country.

It should be noted that in the early 60s, which marked the beginning of the development of modern psycholinguistics worldwide, dialectological research dominated Yugoslav linguistics (Lunt 1963). A few years later, descriptive structural linguistics started to coexist with it, and by the end of

---

* This work forms part of a project titled "Psycholinguistic study and acquisition of Serbo-Croatian" carried out at the Institute for South Slavic Languages of the Faculty of Philosophy, University of Novi Sad. I would like to thank my colleagues Milorad Radovanović, Mirjana Jocić and Vera Vasić for their useful advice and Svetlana Berisavljević for her translation of this work into English.

the 1960s structuralism emerged as something new and important. It was emphasized more in Zagreb and Novi Sad but never became the dominant theoretical approach in all the centres where psycholinguistics later appeared.

In contrast to linguistics, in which new structural theoretical influences have very much changed some areas of language studies, primarily phonology and syntax, behaviouristic theories of learning dominated psychology, but in none of the three centres at that time (Zagreb, Belgrade an Ljubljana) was any special attention paid to language research. In the early 60s, when psycholinguistics started to develop worldwide, no need for the interdisciplinary interaction of psychology and linguistics arose in this country. That need usually emerges when the monodisciplines take as their object of research a general problem such as the relation between thought and language in psycholinguistics. A need is felt to creatively change the quality of human knowledge about the problem. It seems that neither psychology nor linguistics had at that time in Yugoslavia outgrown their monodisciplinarity. What is more, although structuralism had planted its roots in different subdisciplines (dialectology, phonology, syntax, etc.), the two leading figures of that early perdiod, Pavlović[4] and Belić[5], were, from the general linguistic point of view, still influenced by mentalistic thoughts on language, characteristics of the European tradition from the end of the last century. Those language theorists speak of it as a unity of structure, function and use, without being aware that with such an approach they were fitting into the new stream of language research. As a result there was no need for any closer cooperation between linguistics and psychology (the latter hardly having any interest in language). So, in view of these facts, at that time the necessary conditions for mutual exchange within the two disciplines did not exist. Therefore there was no impetus toward a change in the monodisciplines in accordance with what was going on in the interdisciplinary area of psycholinguistics.

There was, and still is, a worldwide discussion of whether psycholinguistics is a part of psychology or linguistic research. Different authors classify psycholinguistics depending on their personal views on the study of language, on language itself and on the subject of psycholinguistics as an independent discipline. This general discussion was also reflected in Yugoslavia but without bringing into direct relation the circumstances of the establishment of the psycholinguistic centres. This is illustrated by the fact that in summarising the disciplines some linguists state that psycholinguistics is a part of linguistic studies (Ivić M. 1963, 1970; Bugarski 1976, 1980; Škiljan 1980), while, on the other hand, psychologists (Fulgosi 1976) or psycholinguists (Opačić 1975) take it as a part of psychology. But if the circumstances under which psycholinguistics appeared in each centre are considered in detail, they will show that certain circumstances dictated whether in one centre psycholinguistics would appear as part of linguistics, and in another centre as part of the psychology discipline. This will be shown by two extreme examples.

In the early 60s at the University of Novi Sad as a part of the new Faculty of Philosophy at the Department for South Slavic Languages (1953) (there was no Department of Psychology), Professor Milivoje Pavlović taught general linguistics and the introduction to linguistics. He described (Pavlović 1920) the research done on bilingual learning of Serbo-Croatian and French, which was the basis for developmental psycholinguistics there. Although he did not research child language during his work as a professor at the University of Novi Sad, he always emphasized the importance of this for general linguistics. That inspired several young researchers to work on this problem (Mikeš[6] and, after her, Savić and Jocić and then V. Vasić, see *References*). So, the foundations for developmental psycholinguistics were laid at the Novi Sad centre within Serbo-Croatistics, with special attention being paid to bilingual problems, which remains this centre's main focus of interest.

However, in Zagreb most of the research in the domain of experimental psycholinguistics went on, and continues to go on, in the Department of Psychology, in which experimental psychology has dominated as the core interest in psychology since its foundation in 1920. Therefore, we could conclude that in the Yugoslav situation, and presumably for some other European centres, psycholinguistics appeared at a certain point in time within a predominant monodiscipline. Therefore, a general discussion on where psycholinguistics belongs does not seem adequate. It is more in line with the facts to conclude that, when psycholinguistics started to put down its roots in the world, in Yugoslavia there still did not exist a real reason for psycholinguistics to become a separate discipline. Both disciplines, psychology and linguistics, were working full scale and maintaining their independence; there was no intention among researchers at the language institutes or universities to start any dialogue. If it did happen, it would more likely occur at the newly established institutes and departments of psychology (like the ones in Novi Sad and Skopje) than among those which had a longer research tradition and a more scientifically defined profile (as in the case with the work on the dictionary at the Institute for Serbo-Croatian Language in Belgrade).

Definition of psycholinguistics

For a long time Yugoslav researchers working in psycholinguistics, most often did not identify any need to define the area of their work. It was only necessary for those who taught the courses in general linguistics or psychology where students had been acquiring knowledge of psycholinguistics. Their definition of psycholinguistics depended on the literature which they chose for such courses and their personal interest in the subject. M. Ivić (1970: 170), for example writes:

> "It is concerned with man in the process of communication. Hence the immediate sphere of interest of this science includes: the psychological phenomena of producing and perceiving speech, the intellectual and emotional attitude toward a given communication, and the cultural and social background against which the individual psychology has been formed."

A decade later Škiljan (1980) defined psycholinguistics as a combination of psychological and linguistic methods, the analysis of psychophysiological processes and the conditions under which "*in different situations* the human linguistic act is performed". This author defines psycholinguistics according to the newly developing interest in it in the early 70s, when it turned to the problems of communication, context and the relevance of the situation for interpreting the meaning of a message. This shows that during the history of psycholinguistics and of the study of language in general, language was approached from different points of view: sometimes it was seen as a *process*, sometimes as a *structure*, as (an obvious) *behaviour* or as a *deep structure system*, as *psychological* and/or *sociological* phenomena. Such an attitude was also reflected in our authors' definitions of psycholinguistics.[7]

In contrast to other Yugoslav authors, the attitude that will be expressed here is as follows: between psychology and linguistics there exists a constant dynamic relationship, and consequently psycholinguistics will be defined in the broadest manner as an interdisciplinary area of research concerned with the relationship between thought and languages used by a speaker for successful communication. But there are many difficulties with a definition as broad as the above if it is to be used as a criterion for selecting works in this domain. This would include a broad area of heterogeneous research from phonetics and linguistics, all the way to logic and sociology. The breadth of the domain covered by psycholinguistics is not characteristic of Yugoslav researchers only, but has also been noted by other authors. Kess (1976: xi) says that:

> "Psycholinguistics is many things to many people, depending upon one's specific training and research interests. However, it is certainly safe to say that whatever has to do with the fuller understanding of language behaviour is the proper subject of psycholinguistics."

The subject and the theoretical scopes of Yugoslav psycholinguistics

It has often been remarked that psycholinguistics is heterogeneous with regard to subject, but in respect of theory it has just been nibbled at, i.e. it is methodologically unbalanced, but extremely promising (Bugarski 1976: 266). The same goes for Yugoslav psycholinguistics in addition to its being theoretically dependent. Almost all researchers agree that developmental psycholinguistics, i.e. the acquisition of the first and the second language, is at the base of this discipline.

In the early history of psycholinguistics in the United States it was stated that it "deals directly with the processes of encoding and decoding as they relate states of messages to states of communication" (Osgood and Sebeok 1954: 4). From then on, the object of its interest was to change according to what was happening in psychology and linguistics and to how the relations of thought and language are conceived. So, Miller (1964) writes that the subject of psycholinguistics "is to describe the psychological processes that go on when people *use sentences*". At that time, the focus of interest was on different aspects of sentences (ambiguity, deviant structures, embedding etc.), i.e. perception of linguistic structure by the 'native speaker', whether grammatical or not. The main attention of the research was paid to proving or denying the psychological reality of linguistic structures concerned with describing sentences by the generative procedure. Of all these questions only a few were reflected in the research of Yugoslav authors, with some exceptions from time to time. Yugoslavia had its own line of problems which were in the ambit of psycholinguistics and they were actually 'felt' by those who were trying to find answers to them, without any knowledge of what was going on elsewhere in psycholinguistics. Therefore, in Yugoslavia the discipline followed a specific path of development.

Under 'theoretical work' three kinds of activity are pursued: development of new theories, creative thinking about and modifications of those existing elsewhere, and informative writing about theoretical work from other parts of the world, most often that which is more developed psycholinguistically. There were no independently founded theories. Research in other domains seemed to be more important. There were very successful modifications of Osgood's, Vygotsky's and some other authors' theories, *but most has been achieved* by informing Yugoslav readers about developments elsewhere mainly through creative syntheses and translations of chosen traditional works by known authors in the domain of psycholinguistics.

The reason for this lack of new, independent theorising in Yugoslavia can easily be found when one considers that there were no new theories, either in psychology or linguistics, which would have been relevant to psycholinguistics. Further, there was no essential stimulation for theoretical work or other necessary conditions such as large scale research projects and teams focused on theoretical work. Also, there were no professionally able young researchers.[8] Therefore it can be said that, on the theoretical plane, developments in psycholinguistics took a similar path as in other smaller European linguistic centres; remaining behind and moving at a slower pace then elsewhere; without extending the domain of theoretical thought or forming specific schools, while often closely linked with bigger psycholinguistic centres. That, of course, does not mean that it did not arrive at any remarkable results. It is somewhat paradoxical that, at a time when Osgood's theory is no longer influential in the development of ideas in North American psycholinguistic theory, it remains dominant in Yugoslavia. When Osgood's theory was emerging, in the early stage of development of psycholinguistics in the United States, it insisted on the study of meaning, a domain which neither linguistics nor behaviouristic theories of psychology included. "While the linguistic community felt that Osgood's approach was rather naive, there was nevertheless hope that the most elusive notion of all — the meaning — might be an objective foundation" (Newmeyer 1980: 20). Within the scope of a so-called *mediation theory* for the analysis of meaning, a measuring instrument was constructed which was meant to help in making more definite the meaning measured by the answers to the associative word (the semantic differential). At that time Osgood was of the opinion that the aim of psycholinguistics should be to explain the nature, development and function of language as a psychological phenomenon, and also to develop its own ways of measuring such a phenomenon, mainly from the point of view of the variability in language behaviour of an individual or of a group, as embedded in any particular cultural background.

At the time this theory was developing, it promised advances over existing behaviouristic theories. But it was soon very much criticized in the United States, where it hardly has any influence today, and in other countries as well. Modification of this theory was also made by the author himself and by many others all over the world, including the Yugoslav authors who were working with him on projects or were educated at his centre: Osgood, May and Miron 1975; Pečjak (Ljubljana), Fulgosi (Zagreb), Opačić, A. Kostić and D. Kostić (Belgrade). When this cooperation started, Osgood was just beginning his second phase of research on a big project about the affective meaning of words in different languages and cultures, including Serbo-Croatian. On these problems Yugoslav researchers (most of them psychologists) cooperated for different periods of time, and after they returned to Yugoslavia, they continued to apply this theory in their studies and/or to pass this approach onto their younger colleagues. Mediation theory has passed through different phases in this development, and Yugoslav authors have written about them (A. Kostić, Opačić).[9] In the early 80s, Osgood's interest moved from word to sentence and he advanced a new general performance theory of language called Abstract Performative Grammar in opposition to Chomsky's theory of language competence. From that last phase we have works by Yugoslav authors (Opačić, Pečjak, and Matjan 1979). This explains the fact that Osgood's theory has in the past three decades maintained the most prestigious position in all centres of psycholinguistics. This could be connected with the way the researchers obtained their specialized training in psycholinguistics: linguists and psychologists had postgraduate training in one of the big psycholinguistic centres, or by self-education while working on projects carried out at foreign centres of psycholinguistics.

When we speak of application and modification of or addition to other theories in Yugoslav psycholinguistics, we can see that they are not at all so widespread and here they will be spoken of as parts of certain subdisciplines. A general statement could be made concerning cognitive theories which are rarely used in Yugoslavia, especially in the domain of developmental psycholinguistics. The theories of Piaget and Vygotsky are employed a little more at the Institute of Psychology in Belgrade (by a team of young researchers gathered around I. Ivić). It might seem paradoxical that Vygotsky's theory (apart from some fragments) did not take deeper root in any research until the 80s (in the latter Institute they are using it for analysis of school textbooks and for acquisition for the first language). These facts could be explained by the following. None of the currently active researchers received any specialized professional training in the USSR, or in other countries of Europe where the aforementioned theories appeared.

At the end of this review of theoretical scope, it should be emphasized that the most useful work done for the progress of psycholinguistics is in the domain of popularization of the discipline and information provided about global trends (Bugarski, Filipović, Fulgosi, Opačić, Savić, S. Vasić). Unfortunately, until the present only a few books with authentic research results have been published (Marjanović 1984; Savić 1980; V. Vasić 1984, all in the domain of developmental psycholinguistics, and Vilke 1979 in applied psycholinguistics. The material covered by this research is in Serbo-Croatian (rarely in any of the languages spoken by other nationalities in Yugoslavia).

Methods

It has already been stated that modern psycholinguistics has creatively contributed to discovering new techniques and methods of experimental work, especially those which support (or refute) the psychological reality of syntactic structures or help to show different types of memory processes in the domain of mental lexicon research. In Yugoslav psycholinguistics this progress in methodology has hardly been felt. For this kind of refined experimentation, computer hardware is needed and also a special technology which the Yugoslav psychology and linguistic centres are not yet ready for (with the exception of those which cooperate with other centres elsewhere, as is the case with a group in the Laboratory for Experimental Psychology at the Faculty of Philosophy in Belgrade).

Two traditional methods have been used throughout the development of psycholinguistics; observation (mostly in developmental psycholinguistics) and experiment (in experimental psycholingusitics). Together with these two, there are also methods from discourse or text analysis for spoken language and analysis of narrative text presentation for exploring the narrative abilities of children. Some methods, sporadically used, are the results of microsociolingustics — work with groups — used especially in bilingual research and for the description of child speech, others the results of ethnolingustics. It seems that certain methods are linked with certain centres within Yugoslavia. As is often the case, significant methodological and theoretical differences of approach lead to isolation from each other. The usage of methods is determined by the educational level of researchers and by their interest in psychology or linguistics. There has so far been no cooperation concerning method exchange between different centres. Such a strong division is felt in the use of different terminology; psychologists often introduce their own terminology into psycholinguistics, with which linguists are not acquainted, and vice versa (Savić 1983). This, of course, is not peculiar to the Yugoslav situation of psycholinguistics, but is more evident here than elsewhere since psychologists and linguists still do not communicate enough to lessen such terminological misunderstandings. It is therefore necessary to compile a terminological psycholinguistic dictionary. Finally, it should be emphasized that the researchers strongly believe that the psycholinguistic characteristics of a certain piece of research are not so much in the methods of collecting and analysing the data but in the interpretation of the results.

Developmental psycholinguistics

The study of the development of child language is considered to be the dominant area of psycholinguistic research and in Yugoslavia it is its oldest subdiscipline. It has been developed at the University of Novi Sad, which now has a third generation of researchers working in developmental linguistics. During two decades of intensive and organized research work, the first generation (Pavlović, Mikeš, Vlahović) worked mainly on the problems of bilingual acquisition of language, using structural linguistics combined with the observation method (compiling speech data in natural communicative situations over a longer period of time with a smaller number of children from the earliest age). During that phase, the development of the grammatical system of the individual child was described: the most detailed work was done at the phonological and syntactic levels and less at the morphological, which compares with the research done by others at that time (Brown 1973). The second generation combined the same methods of collecting empirical data, but they moved the focus of the theoretical orientation towards interaction theories, believing that the mechanism directing the development of child language is the interaction between the child and the other person in a conversation (adult, peer, a twin-pair or a nursery teacher) (cf. Savić 1980; V. Vasić 1984; Jocić 1978). This time the focus was not on the development of the language system, but on the participation of a child in the conversation. This theoretical change was in accordance with changes developmental psycholinguistics elsewhere (Ochs and Schieffelin 1979).

The third generation is keeping the focus on the same theoretical basis, but the analysed unit has changed — from an utterance or a sentence to a larger textual unit, a story. The relationship between the recalled story and its narrative organization is being investigated with data collected from children of various ages (kindergarten, primary and secondary schools). This enables detailed interlingual research (the method described by Chafe 1980 is being used by Savić 1985). This kind of research on development psycholinguistics at an early age is being done in detail only in Novi Sad.

At the end of this short review of developmental psycholinguistics, it can be stated that most results are based on the Serbo-Croatian language, occasionally on bilingual children (Hungarian/Serbo-Croatian), but there are no empirical data on other languages spoken in Yugoslavia.

Experimental psycholinguistics

There are three centres for experimental psycholinguistics following a common experimental method, but separated by different theoretical orientations. Representative of one of them is Fulgosi and his colleagues (see *References*) from the first generation of psycholinguistics in Zagreb; he developed through experimental psychology of the traditional behaviouristic type. He tried to describe memory in psycholinguistics by means of a double registered memory: for space and time information. This model, when used on verbal material, tries to prove the hypothesis that verbal information which arrives by way of the visual channel would be admitted better to a long-term memory than is the case with information arriving by way of the auditory channel, due to the dual encoding mechanism. Apart from this contribution, he took part in modifying the Illinois Test of Psycholinguistic Ability (ITPLA) and also in a number of original experiments on semantic research (e.g. synonyms) in which the word is the main research unit.

Representative of the second group are Pečjak and his colleagues at the University of Ljubljana. A social psychologist, he favours an orientation in psycholinguistics which he calls "psychosocial semantics". He is interested in those aspects of word meaning which are connected with the influence of social and cultural factors affecting the development of meaning. In this research, he uses a method of free association, including also the technique of semantic differential. His psycholinguistic education was at Osgood's centre in the United States in the 60s where he worked with Osgood on a project concerned with crosscultural differentiation in the expression of affective meaning. Later, in 1970s, during his stay in Washington, he cooperated on a project which researched the meaning of emotional words in Slovenian and American cultures (Pečjak 1970). Although some interesting results were obtained concerning differences in meaning according to culture, a theoretical question remains unanswered in all crosscultural and crosslinguistic research on meaning, as is the case here. This is the difficulty of conducting objective observations of a culture by means of a static measuring instrument, such as is used in this research.

Within the last twelve years, a group of researchers (Ognjenović, A. Kostić, Todorović, Mandić) from the Experimental Psychololgy Laboratory of the Faculty of Philosophy in Belgrade, and researchers from the Laboratory for High Frequency Signals of the Electrotechnical Faculty in Belgrade (Lukatela, M. Savić, and Urošević) have done research on the so-called cognitive organization of language. The research is within the framework of the methodological hypotheses of the cognitive processing of information. With regard to the properties of the Serbo-Croatian language, and also to the character of orthography (the existence of two systems of writing, the Cyrillic and the Roman one), there are unique possibilities of experimental research into cognitive processes at work in the (so-called) processing of language information.

This group of research workers pays special attention to the examination of the functional and structural aspects of memory, which contain information relevant to the understanding and production of language. In the research so far, special attention has been given to: (a) the cognitive organization of alphabetical spaces; (b) the cognitive organization of the morphology and syntax; and (c) the functional asymmetry of the hemispheres of the brain. Recently, more attention has been paid to the possibility of research into ungrammaticality in aphasiac disorders.

In the course of the past ten years, the Experimental Psychology Laboratory has done a series of research experiments into the initial acquisition of reading, and children's competence in acquiring the vocal structure of the word. Problems of the initial acquisition of reading are of a phonological nature, and they are the result of children's incompetence in acquiring the vocal structure of the word. Therefore, a series of experiments have been carried out, to answer the following questions: (a) whether the child's competence in acquiring the vocal structure is sensitive to external factors; (b) which age group is sensitibe to the external factors; and (c) how to structure exceptional stimulation. From the very beginning of this research work, close cooperation has existed between this Belgrade group of researchers and the research workers from the University of Connecticut (at Storrs), and also Haskin's Laboratories at Yale, New Haven.

A common factor among these three groups is the unit of observation: word, sound/letter, sometimes phrase, very rarely sentence, practically never the whole text. They are more interested in the perception of speech/ writing than its actual use and they are, organizationally, each in its own way, linked with some of the more developed centres for psycholinguistics throughout the world.

Applied psycholinguistics

Bugarski believes that this subdiscipline is simply linguistics applied by means of psycholinguistics to the areas in the general orientation of psychology. This would, therefore, also be the case for sociolinguistics (Bugarski 1976: 266). Although such a point of view can be discussed (cf. Slama-Cazacu 1979), the question of how to choose the domains in which the research character of applied psycholinguistics is seen is crucial. This debate will not be solved here, but only opened for further discussion.

The oldest and most dominant is research on learning foreign languages, and here applied psycholinguistics has a lot in common with applied linguistics. It is the most developed subdiscipline in most centres, especially in Zagreb, where it has very much in common with contrastive linguistics in respect both of subject and method. A little more psycholinguistic orientation can be noticed in work by Vilke on the learning of English by children before puberty, whose native language is Serbo-Croatian. Her results (Vilke 1979) confirm the validity of Lenneberg's theory of learning.

In the Institute for Education at Ljubljana, Kunst-Gnamuš (1979, 1981, 1984) explores the application of different speech act theories (communicative or cognitive of Piaget) on the problem of teaching a mother tongue in elementary and secondary schooling, mostly on Slovenian language data. Differing from this applied research on Slovenian data based on modern language theories, in other centres partial research of pupils' speech is being carried out. It is most often on vocabulary analysis (active or passive) (Lukić 1982) and semantically related items like antonyms, synonyms, etc. (S. Vasić and colleagues).

Within applied psycholinguistics, we could classify research being done at the moment on the narrative ability of migrant children whose native language is Serbo-Croatian, but whose parents live in Western Europe (Savić and colleagues). The development of narrative abilities is being observed in order to test an hypothesis about the existence of two narrative techniques depending on the language used (research based on Chafe's model 1980).

Some outstanding results have been obtained since the early 80s on the language used in schoolbooks (S. Vasić and colleagues).

Some psycholinguistic research on mass communication language has been done in the past couple of years: the language of radio, TV and press has been analysed. In this domain, applied psycholinguistics interacts with sociolinguistics and applied linguistics, illustrating the main mistake made in psycholinguistics when it is defined as a discipline concerned only with the individual, while sociolinguistics treating the problems of language and society. This mistake derives from statements made by certain prestigious psycholinguists who, at a point in psycholinguistic development, claimed that psycholinguistics is not concerned with social issues (Miller 1964). Although such statements are true for some periods in the development of psycholinguistics, and particularly for some authors (especially those working on psycholinguistics during the 60s using Chomsky's theory), expansion has occurred to accommodate the relationship between the individual and the function of language in society within the psycholinguistic framework. This can then lead to results which would indicate the overall social mechanism of language in terms of the function of thought. At that point the language of mass communications and advertisements achieves a central place in psycholinguistic research, as is now the case in the USSR.

From the domain of the language of the mass media, we could classify under applied psycholinguistic research conducted on the attitude of the public towards radio/TV/newspaper language, and also analyses of the speech of speakers, journalists, actors, writer and amateur participants in radio programmes (work by S. Vasić and colleagues). The list of such research work in Yugoslavia is very long, at three research centres (the Zagreb Institute for Phonetics, the Belgrade Institute for Phonetics and

Speech Pathology, and the Novi Sad Institute for South Slavic languages). It is clear why there is so much interest in this language problem, given the language variety in Yugoslavia (detailed explanation can be found in the work of Radovanović in this book). Special research in pscyholinguistics is being done on the contents of TV messages, and their effects on audiences, so as to improve TV programmes. In such an analysis of contents, the focus is again on the vocabulary or on the understanding of the lexicion measured by different methods adapted to the problem of mass communication language.

The second aspect is directed towards gauging of attitudes and/or evaluating systems of audiences, based on language material. In this case, the language material is just a means of acknowledging some socio-psychological phenomena, but the methods and interpretations are based on psycholinguistics. The third part is concerned with the readability of the text in the news and also with the knowledge and use of the two alphabets in the programmes transmitted by the Belgrade and Zagreb TV centres. Most of the research is done on vocabulary and rarely on syntax or discourse.

There are some other areas in applied psycholinguistic research which are not as widespread but which should also be mentioned. There are a few works dealing with problems of translation from one language to another and some with phonetic problems, but from the psycholinguistic point of view. These are by Guberina and his colleagues from Zagreb, and by Đ. Kostić and his colleagues from Belgrade. Most of these have been carried out to improve speech therapy for children of different ages with speech and hearing problems. Most of the researchers are either phoneticians or speech therapists, less commonly psychologists or linguists, which is reflected in a use of theories and methods drawn from their own disciplines. The problems dealt with here could be part of a separate subdiscipline (which Vladisavljević calls *Patholinguistics*) and such research has been intensified during the past decade since the defectology faculties were founded in Belgrade and Zagreb. In Zagreb, work has been done on modifications of the ITPLA for rehabilitation needs, mostly for children from elementary and secondary schools, less so for pre-school children with damaged hearing, sight and speech.

Applied psycholinguistics also touches on some of the latest research in neurolinguistics (aphasic problems in the work of Vidanović, from the University of Niš, and Bahovec from the Pedagogy Institute of Ljubljana).

These works represent the very beginning of such research, but the work of Dimitrijević and Đošić (1984) has done a lot to popularize this discipline. Such examples indicate that new generations will research new issues and expand the sphere of applied psycholinguistics. Here one should also mention works on speech analysis by Polovina (Belgrade), and different types of textual analyses by Velčić (Zagreb).

New tendencies and fields of interest within the area of psycholinguistics are being advanced by young researchers in the same manner as by earlier generations by getting specialized professional training at some of the big centres for psycholinguistics, or by the less efficient method of self-education. This is so if one considers the future physiognomy of psycholinguistics in Yugoslavia will not alter without change in some of the main conditions in interdisciplinary language education. But, the fact is that linguistics everywhere has taken on a holistic orientation, and psychology is turning towards the cognitive, i.e. towards language problems. This has caused new changes in the monodisciplines, and if these are reflected in Yugoslavia then the situation for psycholinguistics will be changed.

Instead of a conclusion

It could be concluded for now that psycholinguistics in Yugoslavia has quite a long tradition, its own specific path of development and that some researchers are recognized abroad.

Research carried out abroad during the past thirty-five years has only been partly reflected in Yugoslavia. Here, psycholinguistics depended on what was happening in psychology or linguistics within the country during that time.

The theoretical emphasis in Yugoslavia then was a matter of setting out to inform the general public about the relevance of psycholinguistics to this particular country. Selective adoption and translation of original texts written in other languages was highly significant in the course of this development.

Psycholinguistics is still not yet a coherently organized scientific discipline, taught as a separate course at universities within psychology and linguistics. Research projects, with few exceptions, are not long-term and they are not sufficiently financed. Most research is still conducted individually.

The discipline is not yet sufficiently organized to set up an association, journal, etc. From that point of view, its situation is similar to that of minor

European languages.

But, since the early 80s, a lot of interest has been shown in Yugoslavia in the interdisciplinary approach to science in general, and this includes languages too. This general interest has made society pay more attention to psycholinguistics which, differing from sociolinguistics, has never had such strong social support.

If we were to foresee the development of psycholinguistics in the late 90s, it could be presumed that its influence might be quite remarkable, and so it will probably continue to actively participate in the development of global language research. Interdisciplinarity will enable psycholinguistics to flourish just as this broadening of interest has enabled other subjects within the social sciences to develop worldwide.

Notes

1. This is an effort to review research in Yugoslav psycholinguistics in a situation where there is no detailed review of psychology or linguistics developments as separate disciplines (there is a partial review of linguistics in the work of M. Ivić 1976). Therefore, this review of the interdisciplinary interaction of the two mentioned disciplines will be incomplete. The list of psycholinguistic works on the problems of bilingualism in Vojvodina has been deliberately omitted here (there is very little research of this kind in other areas) because it is a subject of a separate project by Lajos Göncz. Publications on the sociolinguistics of bilingualism are also omitted since they are listed in the book by M. Mikes, which touches on psycholinguistics. Only the work on the issues of bilingualism among children whose parents work in Western Europe is explained here in more detail.

2. This is no longer a subject of discussion as psycholinguistics is regarded as an independent discipline. This is not only because of its subject, theories and methods, but also because of its professional organization at the international, European, and regional (in this case Yugoslav) levels. There is an International Society for Applied Psycholinguistics (founded in June 1985 in Barcelona) and The European Society of Psycholinguistics (founded in Nijmegen in 1979) which publishes a journal called *Newsletter*, issued twice a year. There is also The International Association for Child Language Research (founded in Florence in 1972 with congresses every three years) which publishes the *Journal of Child Language* (Cambridge University Press). Furthermore, there are different commissions for psycholinguistics such as the AILA Commission for Psycholinguistics with its *Newsletter* issued twice a year since 1981. There are other journals specialized in psycholinguistics such as: the *Journal of Psycholinguistic Research*, the *Journal of Applied Psycholinguistics* and the *International Journal of Psycholinguistics* (Mouton, discontinued publishing in 1981). Together with all this, there are various series of books on psycholinguistics from publishing companies.

3. There are a few reviews of psycholinguistics at different stages of its development in the Yugoslav literature (M. Ivić 1963, 1970; Bugarski 1976, 1980; Fulgosi 1976; Opačić 1976, 1981; Škiljan 1980; only in the review S. Vasić are there some details about Yugoslav research, mainly by the author and her colleagues).

4. Ivić writes of M. Pavlović (1891-1974): "[he is] the only linguist in Yugoslavia, except [for] Belić, who was seriously concerned with [the] theoretical problems [in the inter-war period]" (1976: 222) and she adds that he is best known for his enthusiasm for the psychology of language.

5. About A. Belić (1876-1960), one of the leading theorists of language at that time, M. Ivić (1976: 218) says: "Belić's attitude towards language was basically mentalistic. He always emphasized the complexity of language itself viewing it as a unity 'function', 'meaning' and 'form'. In his ranking of these three aspects of language, the first place was given to 'function', the second to 'meaning'. The distinction between these two notions was never precisely defined by Belić."

6. M. Mikeš defended her dissertation in 1965 under the supervision of Pavlović also on the problems of the bilingual (Serbo-Croatian/Hungarian) child's acquisition of phonology, and since 1971 has been at the Institute for Linguistics (founded 1968). She supervises a project called Syntax of Child Speech, and S. Savić, M. Jocić and later V. Vasić, have been her assistants. She cooperates with other colleagues and with P. Vlahović (and L. Göncz, most of them Serbo-Croatists who have remained the nucleus of psycholinguistics at the Novi Sad centre until today.

7. G. Opačić (1975: 165) stated that "the main concern of psycholinguistics — theoretical and empirical — is the question of how language is acquired by children and how it is created and understood by adults; the issue of the psychological mechanisms that underlie our use of language."

8. There is no special study of theoretical linguistics (the only Department for General Linguistics exists at the Faculty of Philosophy in Zagreb). There are no specialized journals dealing with questions of theoretical language problems, but *Suvremena lingvistika* (published in Zagreb since 1972) and *Zbornik za filologiju i lingvistiku* (published in Novi Sad since 1957). They are the only ones concentrating on general linguistic issues. There is no specialized journal for psycholinguistics. Psycholinguistic works are published in psychology or linguistic journals, reducing their accessibility, and they rarely reach the people for whom they are intended.

9. After special training at Osgood's centre Opačić started teaching at the University of Niš, where she continued to work using Osgood's theory. While she was testng the validity of this theory, other researchers remained at an earlier stage, using only the measuring instruments — semantic differential or the ITPLA — without knowing enough about Osgood's theory. The second test was rejected in Yugoslav works (Savić 1980: 10) and it is now being modified at the Faculty of Defectology with the intention of applying it in work with children suffering from damaged speech and sight.

338 SVENKA SAVIĆ

References**

Bronckart, Jean-Paul, et al. (eds). 1977. *La gènese de la parole*. Paris: PUF.
Brown, Roger. 1973. *A First Language: The Early Stage*. Cambridge, Mass.: Harvard University Press.
Bugarski, Ranko. 1976. "Položaj psiholingvistike u krugu lingvističkih disciplina" [The position of psycholinguistics among the linguistic disciplines]. Strani jezici 5.4: 262-267.
-----. 1980. "Šta je psiholingvistika?" [What is psycholinguistics?]. *Treći program Radio Beograda* 44: 251-260.
Carlson, N. Greg & Michael K. Tannenhaus. 1982. "Some preliminaries to psycholinguistics". *Chicago Linguistic Society* 18: 48-59.
Chafe, L. Wallace (ed.). 1980. *The Pear Stories: Cognitive, Cultural and Linguistic Aspects of Narrative Production*. Norwood, New Jersey: Ablex Publishing Corporation.
Chomsky, Noam. 1957. *Syntactic Structures*. The Hague: Mouton.
-----. 1965. *Aspects of the Theory of Syntax*. Cambridge, Mass.: MIT Press.
Dimitrijević, R. Naum. 1969. *Lexical Availability: A New Aspect of the Lexical Availability of Secondary School Children*. Heidelberg: Julius Groos Verlag.
----- and Slobodanka Djošić. 1984. *A Bibliography on Neurolinguistics II*. (= *Studii Italiani de linguistica teoretica ed applicata* 13.1). 67-142. (Part I in 1980. 9.1).
Drachman, Gaberell (ed.). 1978. *Salzburger Beiträge zur Linguistik 5*. Salzburg: Verlagsbuchhandlung Wolfgang Neugebauer.
Dressler, U. Wolfgang, O.E. Pfiefer, and Thomas Herok (eds). 1978. *Proceedings of the International Congress of Linguists*. (= *Innsbruck Beiträge zur Sprachwissenschaft*). Innsbruck.
Filipović, Rudolf. 1976. "Psiholingvistički aspekti kontrastivne analize" [Psycholinguistic aspects of contrastive analysis]. *Strani jezici* 5.4: 267-272.
Fulgosi, Ante. 1976. "Novija istraživanja na području eksperimentalne psiholingvistike" [The latest research in the field of experimental psycholinguistics]. *Strani jezici* 5.4: 249-263.

** As this work is intended for readers outside Yugoslavia, the publications selected are mainly those published in foreign languages.

----- and Slobodanka Marković. 1976. "Faktorska struktura psiholingvističkih sposobnosti i intelektualna retardiranost" [The factor structure of psycholinguistic capacities and intellectual retardation]. Revija za psihologiju 6.1-2: 3-12.

Girke, Wolfgang and Helmut Jachnow (eds). 1976. *Theoretische Linguistik in Osteuropa*. Tübingen: Max Niemeyer Verlag.

Heilmann, Luigi (ed.). 1974. *Proceedings of the Eleventh International Congress of Linguists*. Bologna: Societa editrice il Mulino Bologna.

Hjelmquist, Erland. 1978. "Psycholinguistics as scientific encounters." *Folia Linguistica* 13. 3-4: 215-227.

Ivić, Milka. 1963. *Pravci u lingvistici* [Trends in linguistics]. Ljubljana: Državna založba Slovenije.

-----. 1970. *Trends in Linguistics*. The Hague: Mouton (= *Janua Linguarum. Series Minor* 42).

-----. 1976. "Linguistic Theory in Yugoslavia." In: Girke and Jachnow (eds). 1976: 217-233.

Jocić, Mirjana. 1977. "Influence du milieu sur la development de la communication verbale." In: J-P. Bronckart, et al. (eds). 1977: 241-247.

-----. 1977. "Some psycholinguistic aspects of the acquisition of reading in early childhood." In: G. Nickel (ed.). 1977. 3: 369-378.

-----. 1978. "Adaptation in adult speech during communication with children." In: N. Waterson, and C. Snow (eds). 1978: 217-225.

Kay, Bruce, A. Kostić, and R. Leonard Katz. 1982. "Decomposition and grammatical priming in lexical decision." *Proceedings of 53rd Annual Meeting of the Eastern Psychological Association*.

Kess, F. Joseph. 1976. *Psycholinguistics: Introductory Perspectives*. London/San Francisco: Academic Press.

Kostić, Aleksandar. 1983. "Verb valence and lexical decision." Unpublished dissertation, University of Connecticut.

Kostić, Dragan, S. Vasić, and Prvoslav S. Plavšić. 1975. "Analysis of wrong answers at vocabulary test: Contribution to the study of semantic space." *4 AILA Congress. Stuttgart, August 25-30 1975*.

Kunst, Gnamuš, Olga. 1979. *Vloga jezika v spoznavnem razvoju školskega otroka* [The role of language in the cognitive development of school children]. Ljubljana: Pedagoški inštitut.

-----. 1981. *Pomenska sestava povedi* [The meaning structure of narratives]. Ljubljana: Pedagoški inštitut.

-----. 1984. *Govorno dejanje — družbeno dejanje: komunikacijski model jezikovne vzgoje* [Speech activity — social activity: a communication model of language education]. Ljubljana: Pedagoški inštitut.

Lenneberg, Eric H. 1967. *Biological Foundations of Language*. New York: John Wiley and Sons.

Linell, Per. 1978. "Notes on the relation between linguistics and psycholinguistics." In: G. Drachman (ed.). 1978.

Lukatela, G., Z. Mandić, B. Gligorijević, A. Kostić, M. Savić, and M.T. Turvey. 1978. "Lexical decision for inflected nouns." *Language and Speech* 17: 61-71.

-----, M. Savić, P. Ognjenović, and M.T. Turvey. 1978. "On the relation between processing the Roman and the Cyrillic alphabets: A preliminary analysis with bi-alphabetical readers." *Language and Speech* 21.2: 113-141.

-----, M. Savić, B. Gligorijević, P. Ognjenović, and M.T. Turvey. 1978. "Bi-alphabetical lexical decision." *Language and Speech* 21.2: 142-165.

-----, B. Gligorijević, A. Kostić, and M.T. Turvey. 1980. "Representation of inflected nouns in the internal lexicon." *Memory and Cognition* 8.5: 415-423.

-----, D. Popović, P. Ognjenović, and M.T. Turvey. 1980. "Lexical decision in a phonologically shallow orthography." *Memory and Cognition* 8.2: 214-132.

-----, A. Kostić, L.B. Feldman, and M.T. Turvey. 1983. "Grammatical priming of inflected nouns." *Memory and Cognition* 11.1: 59-63.

Lukić, Vera. 1982. *Dečja leksika* [Child lexis]. Beograd: Institut za pedagoška istraživanja.

Lund, Horace. 1963. "Yugoslavia." In: T.A. Sebeok (ed.). 1963: 563-564.

Marjanović, Ana. 1984. *Razvoj značenja reči* [The development of word meaning]. Beograd: Institut za pedagoška istraživanja.

Mikeš, Melanija. 1967. "Acquisition des catégories grammaticales dans le language de l'enfant." *Enfance* 20: 289-298.

----- (ed.). 1983. *Kontrastivna jezička istraživanja: Simpozijum, Novi Sad, 10-11 - XII 1982* [Contrastive linguistic studies: Symposium, Novi Sad, 10-11th December 1982]. Novi Sad: Filozofski fakultet.

----- and Plemenka Vlahović. 1968. "Acquisition du système associatif des sons." *Bulletin de la Société de Linguistique de Paris*. 1: 236-261.

----- and Plemenka Vlahović. 1970. "Approche méthodologique aux recherches de l'apprentissage du langage par l'enfant." *Actes du Xe Congrès International de Linguists*. Bucarest: Acadèmia. 137-143.

-----, L. Dezső, and Plemenka Vlahović. 1972. "Sentence programming span in child language". In: K. Ohnesorg (ed.). 1972: 166-178.

----- and László Dezső. 1974. "Diachronic syntax and the ontogenesis of language." In: L. Heilmann (ed.). 1974: 911-916.

Miller, George, A. 1964. "The psycholinguists." *Encounter* 23: 29-37.

Newmeyer, Frederick J. 1980. *Linguistic Theory in America: The First Quarter-century of Transformational Generative Grammar.* London/San Francisco: Academic Press.

Nickel, Gerchard (ed.). 1977. *Proceedings from IV AILA Congress.* Vols. I-IV. Stuttgart: Hochschule Verlag.

Ochs, Elinor and Bambi B. Schieffelin (eds). 1979. *Developmental Pragmatics.* London/New York: Academic Press.

----- and Bambi B. Schieffelin (eds). 1983. *Acquiring Conversational Competence.* London/Boston: Routledge and Kegan Paul.

Ohnesorg, Karel (ed.). 1972. *Colloquium paedolinguisticum: Proceedings of the First International Symposium of Paedolinguistics held at Brno, 14-16 October 1970.* The Hague: Mouton (= *Janua Linguarum. Series Minor* 133).

Opačić, Gordana. 1973. "Natural ordering in cognizing and clause order in the sentencing of conjoined expressions." Unpublished dissertation. University of Illinois, Champaign - Urbana.

-----. 1975. "On psycholinguistics and its assumed relevance to contrastive analysis." *Studies* 6 (= *The Yugoslav Serbo-Croatian English Contrastive Project*). Zagreb: Institute of Linguistics, Faculty of Philosophy. 165-172.

-----. 1976. "Psiholingvistika u SAD" [Psycholinguistics in the USA]. *Suvremena lingvistika* 13-14: 69-72.

-----. 1977. "Natural order in cognizing and clause order in the sentencing of conjoined expressions." *Salzburger Beiträge zur Linguistik* 4: 367-377.

-----. 1979. "O prethodnicama S-a" [On the 'antecedents' of S]. *Suvremena lingvistika* 19-20: 59-63.

-----. 1980. "On the nature and origin of conjunction." *Zbornik radova Odeljenja za anglistiku Filozofskog fakulteta u Nišu* 1: 69-87.

-----. 1981. "A look at early experimental psycholinguistics." *Zbornik radova Odeljenja za anglistiku Filozofskog fakulteta u Nišu* 2: 301-306.

----- and Vid Pečjak. 1977. "Psihološka funkcija rečenice" [The psychological function of the sentence]. *Stručni skup psihologa "Dani Ramira Bujasa 1976."* Zagreb: Društvo psihologa SR Hrvatske. 57-70.

-----, V. Pečjak, and Polona Matjan. 1979. "Redosled klauza u složenim rečenicama kao odraz kognitivnih determinatora" [The order of clauses in compound sentences as a reflection of cognitive determiners]. *Stručni skup psihologa "Dani Ramira Bujasa 1978."* Zagreb: Društvo psihologa SR Hrvatske. 291-305.

----- and Vid Pečjak. 1980. "Kognitivna pripadnost direktnog objekta u bitranzitivnim rečenicama" [The cognitive origin of the direct object in bitransitive sentences]. *Zagrebačka psihološka škola 1920-1980.* Zagreb: Društvo psihologa ASR Hrvatske.

Osgood, Charles E. and Thomas A. Sebeok (eds). 1954. *Psycholinguistics: A Survey of Theory and Research Problems.* Bloomington: Indiana University Press.

-----, W.H. May, and Murray S. Miron. 1975. *Cross-cultural Universals of Affective Meaning.* Urbana: University of Illinois Press.

-----, G.J. Suci, and Percy H. Tannenbaum. 1957. *The Measurement of Meaning.* Urbana: University of Illinois Press.

Pavlovitch, Milivoie. 1920. *Le langage enfantin: Acquisition du Serbe et du Français par un enfant Serbe.* Paris: Champion.

Pečjak, Vid. 1970. "Semantičke zavisnosti među pojmovima" [Semantic dependence between notions]. *Psihologija* 3.1: 5-13.

Savić, Svenka. 1975. "Aspects of adult-child communication: The problem of question acquisition." *Journal of Child Language* 2.2: 251-260.

-----. 1976. "The functioning of twin language in adult-child communication." *Salzburger Beiträge zur Linguistik* 2. Tübingen: Verlag Gunter Narr. 303-314.

-----. 1977. "Quelque fonction des question posées les adultes jeunes enfants." In: J-P. Bronckart, et al. (eds). 1977: 231-240.

-----. 1978. "Children's strategies in answering adults' questions." In: Waterson and C. Snow (eds). 1978: 217-225.

-----. 1978. "Do grammatical and communicative competence develop in parallel fashion during the process of language acquisition by children?" In: W. Dressler, et al. (eds). 1978: 716-720.

-----. 1979. "Mother-child verbal interaction: The functioning of completion in the twin situation." *Journal of Child Language* 6: 153-158.

-----. 1980. *How Twins Learn to Talk.* London/San Francisco: Academic Press.

Savić, Svenka. 1983. "Terminološki problemi u jugoslovenskoj psiholingvistici" [Terminological problems in Yugoslav psycholinguistics]. In: M. Mikeš (ed.). 1983: 139-144.

-----. 1985. "Pragmatic aspects of the gender of occupation terms in Serbo-Croatian". Arbejdspapirer Slavisk Instituts: Aarhus Universitet.

-----. 1985. Narativi kod dece [Narratives in children]. Novi Sad: Institut za južnoslovenske jezike, Filozofski fakultet.

----- and Mirjana Jocić. 1975. "Some features of dialogue between twins." International Journal of Psycholinguistics 4.34-51.

----- and Melanija Mikeš. 1974. "Noun phrase expansion in child language." Journal of Child Language 1.1: 107-110.

Sebeok, Thomas A. (ed.). 1963. Current Trends in Linguistics. Vol. I: Soviet and East European linguistics. The Hague: Mouton.

Škiljan, Dubravko. 1980. Pogled u lingvistiku [An insight into linguistics]. Zagreb: Školska knjiga.

Slama-Cazacu, Tatiana. 1973. Introduction to Psycholinguistics. The Hague: Mouton (= Janua Linguarum. Series Major 60).

-----. 1973. "Is a socio-psycholinguistics necessary?" International Journal of Psycholinguistics 1.2: 93-104.

-----. 1976. "Psycholinguistics and applied linguistics." International Journal of Psycholinguistics 3: 79-94.

-----. 1979. Psicolinguistica applicata ao ensico de linguas. Sao Paulo: Pioncira.

Todorović, Dragan. 1985. "Hemispheric differences and syntactic processing." Unpublished dissertation. University of Connecticut.

Vasić, Smiljka. 1979. "Osnovi psiholingvistike" [The basics of psycholinguistics]. Dikcijse teme [Diction topics]. Beograd: Univerzitet umetnosti.

Vasić, Vera. 1980. "Linguistische Aspekte der Sprachadaptation in der Kindersprache." Folia Linguistica 14.3-4: 427-431.

-----. 1984. Razgovor sestre sa bratom [Conversations of a sister with a brother]. Novi Sad: Institut za južnoslovenske jezike, Filozofski fakultet.

Vidanović, Đorđe. 1985. "Psiholingvistika ili psihopragmatika?" [Psycholinguistics or psychopragmatics?]. Unpublished MS. Filozofski fakultet u Nišu.

-----. 1986. "An attempt at the experimentum crucis in modern linguistic theory." Studi Italiani di linguistica teorica ed applicata. 2-3: 235-256.

Vilke, Mirjana. 1979. "English as a foreign language at the age of eight." *Studia Romanica et Anglica Zagrebiensia* 24.1-2: 297-336.

Vlahović, Plemenka, M. Mikeš, and László Dezső. 1972. "Développement des constructions de complément d'object et du lieu dans le langage des enfants Serbocroates et Hongrois." In: K. Ohnesorg (ed.). 1972: 260-269.

Waterson, Natalie and Chaterine Snow (eds). 1978. *The Development of Communication*. New York/London: John Wiley and Sons.

On linguistic autonomy[1]

Dubravko Škiljan
Faculty of Philosophy, University of Zagreb

Virtually the whole history of modern linguistics, especially its structuralist trends, could doubtless take as its motto the famous, though probably apocryphal, final sentence of de Saussure's *Cours de linguistique générale*: "*...la linguistique a pour unique et véritable objet la langue envisagée en elle-même et pour elle-même*".[2] In other words, the history of modern linguistics has also been the history of the struggle for the autonomy of linguistics, and it is not accidental that it began with the great Swiss teacher who believed that linguistics must be clearly set apart from the group of other sciences which do indeed deal with various aspects of speech, but for which language is only a means toward some other end and not the primary object of study.

But if we take a closer look at the reason for seeking autonomy for linguistics, we will see that there are, in fact, two closely connected but mutually distinct elements. The first is the establishment of linguistics as a separate science, different, for example, from philology or psychology (in de Saussure's conception). The second is the rigid delimitation of its object of study: language, which must be distinguished not only from the totality of speech itself, but also from all other phenomena in man's life which are bound up with speech. It must be emphasized at once that de Saussure and his followers, and later — explicitly or implicitly — the great majority of structuralist-oriented linguists believed that the independence of linguistics could be attained only by the unequivocal isolation of the linguistic system, which would itself be the focal point of linguistic analyses.

This ambition is not characteristic only of linguistics; it arose at least partially from the spirit of positivism which carried over from, again, the natural to the social sciences at the beginning of the 20th century. Thanks to de Saussure, the science of language was among the first to feel this influence, characterized by the conviction that the scientific approach requires mathematical exactness of description and complete independence of the object of study from all parameters over which the investigator cannot have total control. However, this desired exactness of description is not achieved only by isolating the object, but also by supposing the identity of that object with itself in time and space. Since this identity, especially in the case of such an obviously mutable phenomenon as language, cannot be achieved on the material level, in the use of language in concrete situations, nor even on the level of the entities comprising the phenomenon, the focus of the study was shifted from the units of the linguistic system to the mutual relations into which these units enter. Thus the ancient definition of structure as a whole made up of interconnected parts gave way to a new definition according to which structure is a set of relevant relations between the units of a system. This change in the conception of structure was a precondition for the appearance of structuralism, first as a methodology and then as a specific world view and philosophical orientation.

There is no doubt that Saussurian linguistics represents not only the beginning of the modern structuralist science of language, but also a clear anticipation of structuralism in general. De Saussure's aim to (1) point out the necessary (in his view) autonomy of language and (2) define the latter as form and not substance, as a system of pure values, essentially determined the direction of development of modern linguistics, even in those theoretical trends which are not considered to be directly derived from the ideas of the Swiss scholar. Moreover, the autonomy of the object of study accordingly represents both a definition of the scope of modern linguistics and a series of unavoidable limitations which the structuralist science of language had to impose upon itself. I believe that it can be shown with little difficulty that all the important structuralist schools in linguistics after de Saussure have remained, in virtually all essential points, within the framework indicated by the Genevese, teacher with his famous dichotomies, the latter being, of course, directly dependent on the choice of a point of departure.

Remaining in Saussurian terms and separating, within the totality of speech, language as an abstract system of signs defined by the interrelations of its units from speaking as a concretization of that system in matter, de Saussure had to view his linguistics exclusively as a linguistics of language, since speaking, with its material mutability and its potential and actual deviations from the rules of the system, seemed too inexact to be an object of scientific analysis. It must be pointed out that, from today's perspective, de Saussure's assertion of the abstract nature of the linguistic system as opposed to the concrete and material nature of speaking was much more important for the establishment of structuralist linguistics than the distinction which he actually emphasized more: the differentiation of the social dimension of language and the individual aspect of speaking. Sociolinguistics long ago pointed out the "Saussurian paradox", according to which the linguistic system is necessarily also individual, because in its abstractness it is a presupposition of the individual's speech, while speaking is an eminently social phenomenon because it serves primarily to establish interpersonal relations. Therefore, it would be better to say that speaking and language possess both a social and an individual dimension in roughly equal measure. In addition, the invariability of structure, which in the structuralist view is a precondition for the identity of the object with itself, can ensure not the social, but rather the abstract nature of the system.

In any case, linguistics is today for the most part a linguistics of language. Not one of the great linguists — with the partial exception of the members of the Prague Linguistic Circle — studies the specific characteristics of speaking in relation to language, either because they do not recognize the existence of such characteristics, or because they do not consider them relevant. Noam Chomsky is one of the few theorists who, despite certain terminological and conceptual differences, at least open up the possibility of a linguistics of speaking; but even his research, certainly not surprisingly, is limited exclusively to linguistic competence and does not include performance. Therefore, structuralists will usually maintain, implicitly or explicitly, that nothing appears in speaking which is not already contained in language, in the inventory of its units and the rules governing their mutual relations.

Just as the act of speaking is closely bound up with non-linguistic and changeable phenomena, even partially determined by them, and thus cannot be sufficiently autonomous to become a suitable object for the science of language (in contrast to language defined by structuralist linguistics), so did the diachronic dimension of the linguistic system seem to de Saussure to be inappropriate for his structuralist approach *ante litteram*. The Swiss scholar's arguments are very clear: if a system is defined by the relations between its units — that is, by its structure — every change in these relations represents a change in both the structure and the system itself, and that excludes the possibility of their exact study. Since diachrony consists of changes, it cannot be described in structuralist terms. Thus de Saussure's diachronic linguistics, although it contains some hints of structuralist elements, shows the characteristics of the neogrammarian approach and so, in this second dichotomy, clearly differs from synchronic linguistics in both methodology and epistemology. Subsequent researchers, first Jakobson and most successfully Martinet (and later many others), included the diachronic dimension of the linguistic system in structuralist theory (and practice), but only with regard to its internal evolution, that is, to the extent that this evolution is conditioned by determinants inherent in the system itself. This ultimately means that changes in the structure of the linguistic system can be included in some superordinate structure, and thus the postulate of immutability is simple shifted from one level to another. It must be pointed out that this shift in linguists' attitude occurred at the moment when structuralism was beginning to develop from a very useful methodology (as it appears in de Saussure's work, though not without certain reservations) into a world view (to which, as is known, Claude Lévi-Strauss made a large contribution under Jakobson's influence). This form of structuralism, in its most rigid formulations, characteristically asserts that mutable phenomena are generally determined by static structures; these also represent the ultimate goal of human knowledge in the teleological version of structuralism. It is interesting to note that this standpoint, aside from the distinction between diachrony and synchrony, is clearly reflected in the theory of Noam Chomsky. But in spite of the "digressions" toward diachronic studies, it can be said that modern linguistics, in its most important theoretical directions, is still primarily synchronic. Again, this is without doubt due to the choice of an autonomous point of departure, the more so since every diachrony in man's world is necessarily also history, or a set of closely connected changes which determine each other. In other words, no matter how much we may wish it, we will find it difficult to understand changes in language outside of their social, historical, cultural, political and, in the widest sense, civilizational contexts.

De Saussure's theory of the linguistic sign, which includes the dichotomy between the signifier (*signifiant*) and the signified (*signifié*), incorporates the fundamental concept of value (*valeur*), and deals with the essential characteristics of the sign (arbitrariness, conventionality, and linearity) has from the beginning stimulated numerous interpretations, as well as opposition. But the part relating to the duality of the linguistic sign has remained virtually axiomatic in linguistic and semiological theory. In de Saussure's model, both supposed parts of the sign are equal (Hjelmslev, in contrast to Martinet, for example, was to interpret this equality as the isomorphism of the two planes). This is the basic precondition for the description of the linguistic system: signifiers — or the plane of expression, in more modern terminology — can be described only on the assumption that they are clearly distinguished from the signified, or plane of content; and the reverse relation holds as well. These theoretical assumptions, however, have had different fates in linguistic practice; a great part of modern linguistics deals exclusively or almost exclusively with the plane of linguistic expression.

This, of course, is not at all accidental. The division of the sign into the planes of expression and content has, from the time of Aristotle and antiquity, occasioned the need to distinguish within the model that part of the sign which can be realized in matter (expression) from the part which is in some way connected with the signified phenomenon (content): a sign is a sign only because it signifies something else, something which it itself is not. Therefore, the place of content is always necessarily bound up with the extralinguistic universe and is too dependent on its mutability and on the complex dynamics of its structures to be described exactly enough in a structuralist sense. Bloomfield's attitude toward semantic problems shows this very well: a true semantic description will not be possible until the entire extralinguistic universe has been described. In contrast, the plane of expression has a sufficiently autonomous linguistic organization and can thus be much more exactly described without reference to extralinguistic phenomena. Therefore, it is not surprising that semantics was long ignored, to a certain extent, by linguistics; and when semantics began to develop, the rules for the structuring of the plane of linguistic content were usually identified with the logical rules of thinking. In our Western civilizations, one of the more or less tacit assumptions is that these rules (formulated on Aristotelian principles) are constant and immutable. One consequence of such a view is that linguistic semantics is usually quite powerless to deal with illogical, irrational, or even poetic utterances, and so for the most part its results are ultimately not very interesting.

Finally, the last of de Saussure's four dichotomies, which describes the relation between the units in a system as either syntagmatic or associative, underwent perhaps the most changes in later interpretations. Hjelmslev had already reduced the manifold breadth of Saussurian associations to a single paradigmatic vertical encompassing all units which could occupy a particular position in a string in place of the units actually there. Thus modified, the dichotomy between syntagmatic and paradigmatic relations in fact determines the rules of a system; and since this dichotomy can, in principle, be applied to any system and its structure, regardless of whether our conception of this structure is static or dynamic, it least restricts the field of structuralist research.

In other words, if we wish to define in rough schematism the basic scope of the structuralist orientation in the science of language, leaving aside the specifies of particular trends within the structuralist framework, we could say that structuralists primarily study the plane of expression of the abstract linguistic system in its synchronic or, possible, achronic aspect. This means, of course, that within the Saussurian assumptions themselves, speaking, the plane of content, and the diachronic aspect of speech have been partially or completely ignored (with allowance made for particular exceptions which confirm the rule). To this narrowing of the scope of linguistics we must add the fact that structuralism in the science of language, although it does include an assertion of the primacy of the communicative function of language in its basic theorems, has nevertheless reduced the communication act mainly to a system of signs, and more or less excluded concrete speakers and hearers from its analyses. All these restrictions, which are generally manifested as an attempt to delimit rigidly the autonomous object of study — language *"in and for itself"* — have ultimately arisen from the postulate of the necessarily static nature of structure and its *a priori* existence.

Yet, with regard to structuralism, it is, I think, necessary to distinguish its methodological level (which is chronologically earlier) from structuralism as a philosophy. "Methodological" structuralism has certainly advanced linguistics in many ways, and, within the boundaries set by its own assumptions and set of instruments, has contributed tremendously to the more efficient and exact description of many linguistic phenomena. The restrictions imposed by "philosophical" structuralism also represent the outer limits to which linguistics can spread; structuralist methodology has in great measure exhausted that limited scope, outside of which remain many problems with special relevance to human speech. The point at which methodology becomes a world view could be identified, again schematically, with the moment when structuralists are no longer satisfied with constructing a particular model, and begin to assume that the characteristics of the model are also essential characteristics of the real object under analysis, that is, of language itself. As long as a model is only an instrument of scientific study, it can, at least in theory, be changed and adapted to the reality being investigated; once we assume that it contains the essential features of the reality, the model is changeable only when we construct it as such. Since linguistic (and not only linguistic) structuralism has postulated the immutability of the basic structures of the model, structuralism in its orthodox version necessarily projects this static quality onto reality itself.

Structuralism, with its claim of complete autonomy for the object of study, as well as for the science dealing with this object, did not, of course, appear in a vacuum. Both the tradition of European thought and the concrete social context of the time when structuralism was formed can be clearly seen in its origin and development. Without closely examining the general determinants in the birth of the structuralist world view, I would only point out that the assertion of the ultimate basic immutability of structures is an essential part of the foundation of every developed bourgeois ideology, as well as of every totalitarian regime and every doctrine which strives to preserve the social status quo. From the perspective of linguistics, then, it is not at all surprising that the first articulated resistance to structuralism in the science of language appeared within the framework of sociolinguistics and psycholinguistics, disciplines which had observed, on a descriptive level, the constant disturbances of the equilibrium of linguistic structures both in their collective and individual aspects.

However, over approximately the last fifteen years, explicit opposition to the structuralist view of language and of speech as a whole has begun to appear in various parts of the world, especially in Western Europe. The leaders of this opposition, in contrast to previous critics of structuralism, were for the most part themselves educated within the framework of structuralist linguistics, and thus their arguments have been based on a knowledge of its theoretical assumptions from the "inside", instead of from the "outside". In the first phase, critically disposed linguists directed most of their attention toward the ideological and philosophical component of structuralism, while in the second, more recent phase, they have turned toward the construction of new theories of speech which are fundamentally different from structuralism. All these studies which have arisen in direct opposition to structuralist axioms could be given the common name of post-structuralism. Of course, we must be aware that investigations which are sometimes very different and even mutually contradictory, in both their theory and practice, are thus counted as post-structuralist trends. But their common denominator is their opposition to the structuralist world view. Thus, we could include among post-structuralists the representatives of expression theory, which arose from the work of Jean Dubois; Italian and German Marxist-oriented critics of the philosophy of structuralism; certain representatives of modern sociolinguistics and psycholinguistics; and the founders and representatives of certain trends in text grammar and pragmalinguistics. They all attempt, in one way or another, to reject the absolute autonomy of the object which is characteristic of structural linguistics, and to link the abstract linguistic system with some concrete circumstances of its use — either with the speaker, the hearer, the context in which the communication act takes place, the extralinguistic phenomena to which it relates, or some combination of these elements.

It could be said that the traditional boundaries of the scope of linguistics are today being crossed, with varying success, on all sides. Speaking, or at least the act of speaking, is becoming as important as the linguistic system itself; the plane of content and, especially, its connection with phenomena denoted by signs, are being placed at the center of interest; the diachronic dimension (perhaps in shorter time segments than is usual in comparative-historical studies) is again becoming a subject of investigation; and the abstractly conceived communicative function of language is yielding to the concretely observed communicative act. In addition, sociolinguistics, psycholinguistics and pragmalinguistics are pointing out that the use of language in speaking should not be viewed exclusively as communication and transmission of information, as structuralism under the influence of information theory and cybernetics would sometimes have it, but that speech has a number of other functions. Some of these are not even included in the six functions of the Jakobsonian model: for example, language and speaking as an expression of membership in some social grouping or as an affirmation of the speaker's social status; or language in speaking as an expression of man's irrational dimension. In other words, the autonomy of the object of linguistic investigation is weakening on all sides, but it is interesting that this process is not being accompanied by a simultaneous weakening of the autonomy of linguistics itself.

This fact can be explained in various ways, but no doubt one reason is that the methodology of linguistic work has not essentially changed, despite the epistemological differences. Post-structuralists, then, have usually continued using structuralist instruments. This in itself would not necessarily be bad if these instruments did not, because of their connection with the theory from which they originated, to some extent determine the scope of the results of investigations. I believe that it is therefore not surprising that the results of post-structuralist analyses, in spite of a huge and often inspired theoretical apparatus, are often virtually trivial, and ultimately less useful than those of structuralist linguistics. This does not at all mean that I am advocating either a return to "integral" structuralism or a total rejection of its methods and achievements (these are a permanent part of the science of language, however linguistics develops in the future). Rather, I wish only to point out the partial incompatibility of post-structuralist theoretical though with its own practice.

But the linguistic studies which we have here tentatively grouped under the name post-structuralism have rendered probably their greatest service (at this point, while they are still developing) by clearly showing that the framework of structuralist linguistics is too narrow for the efficient description of the various facets of human speech. It seems obvious to me that the relative narrowness of the structuralist approach is due primarily to the assumption of the necessity of a non-dynamic conception of linguistic structures. (Perhaps it should be mentioned here that the dynamics of structures are considered neither in transformational generative grammar nor in the applicational generative theory of S.K. Šaumjan. In "classical" Chomsky, dynamics appears only in surface structures, and in the recent development of his theory the generalized α-transformation no longer introduces any essential changes into sentence structure. But all this is, of course, a potential topic for special study.) Before the post-structuralists in linguistics, one of the harshest critics of structuralism as a world view, the French philosopher and sociologist Henri Lefebvre, had already argued that the static conceptions of orthodox structuralism were totally inadequate for the explanation of any given phenomenon in man's world, and that structure should be understood not as a set of constant relations, assigned once and for all, but rather as the continually changing product of structuring and destructuring processes. In Lefebvre's philosophical metaphor, the difference between the advocates of the static nature of structures and those who wish to define structures as processes harks back to the ancient opposition between the adherents of Zeno's Eleatic school and Heraclitus' philosophy.

Since speech as a whole, however defined and however analyzed within itself, is indisputably bound up with and intimately connected to the other forms of man's practical activity, and since it necessarily stands in some relation to the universe in which people live and act (otherwise it could not have the nature of sign system nor fulfill even its communicative function), it is realistic to assume in a scientific model that speech itself is a dynamic phenomenon (and this assumption is continually confirmed in everyday practice), and that its description in terms of dynamic structures would be more appropriate. But before we enter into the arguments for this assertion and an analysis of its consequences, it should perhaps be mentioned that it assumes the rejection of the absolute autonomy of the object of linguistics. For if we consider linguistic structures in the widest sense of the word to be dynamic categories, and if we wish to thus transcend the self-imposed limitations of structuralism, then we must admit that the sources of this dynamics are partially external; considering them to be exclusively internal and inherent to the structures themselves would ultimately mean (1) referring to some other superposed structure, static in itself, and (2) remaining powerless to deal with the real contacts of language as a system of signs with the extralinguistic universe. Since these actual contacts are, of course, always a result of human actions, a linguistic theory which desired to rise above the structuralist delimitations would have to explicitly take into account man and his world, and thus historical and social determinants as well.

If we attempted to apply these very general assertions in the construction of a framework for a possible linguistic theory, I think it would be most useful to examine the basic assumptions of Saussurian and structuralist linguistics in general, and to see to what extent these assumptions would, accordingly, have to be redefined or transformed. Since linguistics, like every other science and every other form of human cognition, develops on the basis of its own experience and tradition, it would certainly be wrong to reject *a priori* the achievements of structuralism, especially its methodological aspect, and ignore the enormity of its influence on both the theory and practice of linguistics.

Distinguishing between language, defined on the abstract level of system, and speaking as the realization of language in matter has proved to be useful and effective in linguistics, but this distinction largely loses its meaning if we assume that speaking only occurs within the boundaries of language. It seems to me that between these two aspects of speech there exists a relation of mutual confirmation and disruption. Language does not exist without speaking (and is in fact extracted from speaking's material aspect as a construct), and we recognize speaking as speaking only if we can discern linguistic organization within it. But speakers, consciously or unconsciously, introduce numerous deviations from the linguistic system into their speaking either because they simply make mistakes, or because they find that, in the widest sense, the existing inventory and rules of the linguistic system are simply inadequate to express the constant changes in the extralinguistic world. Thus speaking, by destructuring and restructuring (because some changes originating in speaking are in time incorporated into language) disrupts the linguistic system. But language, by striving toward the constant and static state necessary for the maintenance of communication in space and time, disrupts speaking, which must, at least from time to time, express what has not yet been expressed, what is new and as yet outside the linguistic system. Thus we can think of speaking as containing elements unstructured by language, elements which will perhaps at some time enter the linguistic system and modify its structure; while in language there are elements which virtually no longer appear in speaking and whose loss from the system will again cause a change in its structure. These continual processes of structuring, destructuring and restructuring can be observed on various linguistic levels; on some levels, such as the phonological or morphological, they are slower, while on others, such as the semantic, they are faster. But perhaps more interesting is the fact that these processes can be studied as the interaction of various sociolinguistic (and geolinguistic) levels. Since the act of speaking is really always individual, innovations in speaking naturally appear first in the idiolect and can enter the idiolectal linguistic system without yet necessarily belonging to the system of some group of speakers; for them, the innovations represent only unstructured phenomena in speaking. The same situation recurs on every higher level: that which is already (or still) a part of the linguistic system of one group of speakers represents only a phenomenon of speaking for some other group. In each individual case, the criterion for distinguishing what is an element of the abstract linguistic structure from what is an unstructured element of speaking is whether the element enters into close relations with other elements. The linguist must determine in advance in which social or geographic groupings of speakers he will study the relation between language and speaking and whether he will compare this relation to that within some other larger or smaller grouping. The researcher may, of course, decide to completely ignore the dynamics of structures and the processes of destructuring and restructuring in some concrete analysis, but if he wishes to come to grips with speech in its totality, he must take them into account.

If we attempted to describe the relation between language and speaking in this way, in their constant mutual tension, we could probably see the dichotomy between synchrony and diachrony in a different light. Structuralist linguistics, in the Saussurian version, describes diachrony as a succession of static synchronic cross-sections which follow one another, and it is unclear (as with the philosophers from Elea) how one gets from synchronic statics to diachronic dynamics. In contrast, a theory holding that language changes continuously under the influence of speaking (although such a theory would allow those changes to be ignored, as until now, for the purposes of some analyses) clearly would be able to explain the evolution of the linguistic system over time, an evolution resulting precisely from the tension we have outlined between language and speaking. It is perhaps necessary to emphasize that in such a view neither language nor speaking is given primacy, either in a hierarchical or chronological sense. This is because first, they are considered equally important and practically inseparable aspects of speech; and second, precisely because language and speaking condition each other, they cannot be separated in a temporal sequence such that we can assert that speaking precedes language or vice versa. In other words, the diachronic and synchronic aspects of speech are in this view two dimensions of the same phenomenon — the dynamics of linguistic structures; except that in diachrony more attention is given to processes, in synchrony to the relations themselves. Elements of such a view were already hinted at in some parts of de Saussure's *Cours*.

A certain kind of tension and mutual conditioning undoubtedly also exists between the plane of expression and the place of content, and this tension is especially evident — as shown long ago by both linguistics and literary theory, for example, and more recently by semiology — in the use of language in art, where the elements of the plane of expression themselves often receive a semantic dimension. But, in contrast to structuralist linguistics, which has paid more attention to the plane of expression than to the plane of content of linguistic signs (and which has more or less avoided serious consideration of language in art), an approach which aspired to deal with the dynamism of linguistic structures would have to be more interested in the plane of content itself and develop a specific semantic theory. We have attempted to show that the relation of mutual confirmation and disruption between language and speaking results from the act of speaking — the point at which language and speaking necessarily meet and transcend their ontological difference. In other words, language and speaking meet within speech, but speech truly conceived of as a specific form of man's practical activity. Here we mean practical activity with its Marxist connotation: human action conditioned by the social and historical determinants both of man's phylogenetic and ontogenetic existence, but action through which man actively participates in his own world, changing it and at the same time transforming himself, thus creating social and historical scope for his existence. During the course of his development, man has engaged in very diverse forms of practical activity, but in a certain sense linguistic activity holds a special place among them, because through it we act on the universe (and on man within it), transferring information and ideas about all forms of practical activity, their processes, objects and relations, using a special system of signs — language. In addition, speech is a total social phenomenon, which means that it is one of the evolving multidimensional totalities whose continuous dynamics is found in all social groupings. And since society be definition cannot exist without mutual communication between its members, and since man is a social creature, we must assume that speech is as old as man and that it is the *differentia specifica* by which the human race differs from the animals.

Since linguistic activity, then, is bound up with all forms of man's practical activity, and since it is the most general form of communication between people, it is clear that linguistic signs stand in a definite relation to man's total universe. The dynamics of linguistic structures results from precisely this relation, the relation of practical activity; this dynamics is projected on language and speaking through the act of speaking. Not only are linguistic signs connected with the universe, which changes both according to its own laws and under the influence of all forms of human activity, but the use of these signs — in fact, speech as a whole — is itself practical action in the universe: they transform the world as reflected in signs, and man who uses signs, and signs and their systems themselves. Therefore, both between signs and the phenomena they denote and between language and the extralinguistic universe as the totality of all denoted phenomena, a relation of mutual conditioning is again established, affecting both its correlates. This relation is most clearly manifested, of course, on the plane of linguistic content, because the latter is introduced into a linguistic model in order to be able to examine that aspect of linguistic system which is connected to extralinguistic phenomena, in contrast to the plane of expression which represent that aspect of signs capable of being realized in matter. Therefore, semantic research, if it does not wish to remain sterile, must not restrict itself to the examination of the structures of the linguistic system; as soon as it brings speaking and the act of speaking within the scope of its interest, semantic research in a way includes extralinguistic phenomena. Of course, as long as the instruments of semantics come only from structural theory, it is not very easy to imagine by what paths one could approach these extremely complex problems, but one of them is perhaps hinted at by the ideas of modern semiology in its form known as the semiology of meaning.

All of the relations mentioned here and outlined only very roughly — both those between language and speaking and those between the linguistic and extralinguistic universe — are in essence dialectical relations based on the interaction of their elements and on their mutual connection which simultaneously confirms and disrupts them; and the very activity of their operation always results ultimately from man's practical action, inasmuch as man is a creature of socially and historically determined practical activity. In this perspective, linguistics could no longer be established as only a linguistics of language or as only a linguistics of speaking, but rather as primarily a linguistics of speech. In this case, the problem of the autonomy of the object of linguistic study appears in an entirely new light.

If we accept the assertion that in man's reality (and for man there is no reality other than his own) both speech as a whole and its two aspects, language and speaking, are intimately bound up with nonlinguistic phenomena in the widest sense of the word, then linguistics must take this into account; however, it cannot, of course, be expected to explain the entire universe in its totality while dealing with language and speaking. Linguistics is itself one of the forms of practical activity (or meta-activity); it is necessarily connected with the other forms and should, I believe, be more open to their results than it has been until now. At the same time, dealing with speech and the intimate link between language and speaking and man's world, linguistics subjects the results of its own practice to continual re-examination, not only in its own domain but also in other domains of human activity. Therefore, the autonomy of language and speaking, and even more so the autonomy of speech, is only relative and illusory. In certain stages and on certain levels of investigation it can be temporarily justified, if it makes possible a better — if incomplete — understanding; but in the end the autonomy is always destroyed by placing linguistic phenomena in the context of man's world in which they appear. For, since speech is a form of human existence, linguistics should strive to be ultimately nothing but one of the sciences of man. And today that means a great deal.

Notes

1. This article was translated into English by Nancy Trotić-Wilson.

2. Since this article discusses some basic linguistic concepts, it seemed to me unnecessary to give footnotes for quotes and paraphrases from the works of the great linguists which are generally known. However, a bibliography is given at the end of the text.

References

Bloomfield, Leonard. 1933. *Language*. New York: Holt, Rinehart and Winston.

Calvet, Louis-Jean. 1975. *Pour et contre Saussure*. Paris: Payot.

Chomsky, Noam. 1965. *Aspects of the Theory of Syntax*. Cambridge: M.I.T.

-----. 1966. *Cartesian Linguistics*. New York: Harper and Row.

-----. 1968. *Language and Mind*. New York: Harcourt, Brace and World.

-----. 1981. *Lectures on Government and Binding*. Dordrecht: Foris.

De Mauro, Tullio. 1971. *Senso e significato*. Bari: Adriatica.

Hjelmslev, Louis. 1943. *Omkring sprogteoriens grundlaeggelse*. København: Akademisk Forlag.

Hjemlslev, Louis. 1971. *Essais linguistiques*. Paris: Les Éditions de Minuit.

Jakobson, Roman. 1963. *Essais de linguistique générale*. Paris: Les Éditions de Minuit.

Lafont, Robert. 1978. *Le travail et la langue*. Paris: Flammarion.

Lefebvre, Henri. 1971. *Au de-là du structuralisme*. Paris: Anthropos.

Martinent, André. 1955. *Économie des changements phonétiques*. Berne: Francke.

-----. 1965. *La linguistique synchronique*. Paris: P.U.F.

Ponzio, Augusto. 1973. *Produzione linguistica e ideologia sociale*. Bari: De Donato.

Rossi-Landi, Ferruccio. 1972. *Semiotica e ideologia*. Milano: Bompiani.

Sapir, Edward. 1921. *Language*. New York: Harcourt, Brace and World.

Saussure, Ferdinand de. 1916. *Cours de linguistique générale*. Paris — Genève: Payot.

360   DUBRAVKO ŠKILJAN

Shaff, Adam. 1964. *Język a poznanie* [Language and thought]. Warszawa: Państwowe naukowe.

Šaumjan, Sebastijan K. 1965. *Strukturnaja lingvistika* [Structural linguistics]. Moscow: Nauka.

Škiljan, Dubravko. 1976. *Dinamika jezičnih struktura* [The dynamics of language structures]. Zagreb: Studentski centar.

-----. 1980. *Pogled u lingvistiku* [An insight into linguistics]. Zagreb: Školska knjiga.

Language contact, language system and language code

Olga Mišeska Tomić
Faculty of Philology, University of Skopje

With reference to a given language community, the notion 'language' can be observed on two levels of abstraction. On one level it refers to the set of speech codes used by the members of that community, on the other it implies its "institutionalized socially acknowledged collective" speech code (Bugarski 1984: 25), its standard as an antipode of its dialects.[1] In areas of intensive contacts among languages of different families, the dichotomy language/dialect and, consequently, the differential reference of the term 'language' are not so perspicuous. As linguistics influences do not spread uniformly over a given language area, there are perpetual variations in the degree of contact-conditioned grammaticization of given conceptual categories. Though by and large coextensive with dialect boundaries, these variations do not exist only between dialect codes. The use of standardized structures being highly influenced by the dialectal heritage of the respective users of the language standard, the inter-language contact-conditioned grammaticizations are sanctioned differentially even after they are standardized. We shall examine these grammaticizations and their intralanguage sanctions on the example of the Balkan Slavonic verbal systems.

The movement of the Indo-European Perfect

The central reference point in the verbal systems of the Indo-European languages is the fundamental point in every speech situation — the moment of speaking. The forms referring to the future are former present forms that denote not actions but rather obligations, desires or intentions of actions, which suggest that the actions themselves will take place after the moment

of speaking, i.e. in the future. The past tense, in its turn, is perpetually
nourished by forms which originaly had denoted a present state resulting
from a previous action.

Through internal reconstruction, one is led to deduce that Proto-Indo-
European had only two sets of verbal forms: Present and Aorist. Very
likely, the original distinction between them was a distinction of aspect,
similar to that now obtaining in a number of West African language. Time
reference has actually developed as a consequence of aspectual distinctions.
At an interim stage, the same set of forms probably incorporated both past
tense and perfective aspect functions, as do the forms of present-day written Arabic, referred to by Cormie (1976). When the Imperfect came into
existence[2], the Aorist was established as a Past Definite Tense, aspectually
distinguished from the Imperfect, which referred to a past action lasting
over a period of time.

Subsequently, the Indo-European verbal system was enriched with
another set of forms — those of the Perfect. According to Kuryłowicz
(1971), the Perfect has been going through four stages of development: 1.
present state resulting from previous actions; 2. action occurring prior to
the moment of speaking, with effects in the present; 3. past action referring
to the moment of speaking; 4. past action. Most Indo-European languages
have gone through stages 1. to 3. but only some have reached stage 4. As I
have argued elsewhere (Tomić 1983b), whether and to what extent a language reaches this stage depends significantly on contacts with genetically
remote or totally alien languages.

In French and Italian, at least in their colloquial registers, the Perfect
is very close to stage 4. Spoken French, for example, does not maintain the
difference between the Past Definite — the Indo-European Aorist — and
the Past Composite — the Indo-European Perfect — which in written
French is made through regular morphonologically signalled oppositions,
such as those between the respective forms *lut* 'read' and *a lu* 'has read' in:

(1)   a. *Jean   lut   le   livre.*
          John   read   the   book
          'John read the book.'
       b. *Jean   a   lu   le   livre.*
          John   has   read   the   book
          'John (has) read the book.'

In Spanish, Portuguese and Romanian, however, the distinction Aorist/
Perfect has persisted in the colloquial language as well. And these are the

Romance languages which have been in very intensive contact with geneti-cally remote or unrelated languages.

In German, the Preterite — a simple past tense in which the functions of the (Slavonic or Romance) Aorist and Imperfect are combined — is gradually becoming obsolete; in the South German and Swiss German dialects it has been completely lost and replaced by the Perfect, which, in its turn, has lost its aspectual features. But in English — a Germanic language extensively exposed to alien influences — the Perfect has become firmly established as an aspectual category whose exponents combine with expo-nents of other verbal categories (tense being only one of them) to produce a well-balanced, symmetric system.

The origin of the English Perfect is to be found in the changes of the word order of the so-called causative constructions, such as:

(2)   *She has the dress made.*

When word order became fixed, former communicative variants acquired differential semantic values. So, while in (2) *has* is a full verb and *made* reflects a state resulting from a previous action, in its word order variant:

(3)   *She has made the dress.*

has is an auxiliary and *made* refers to a previous action, inherent in the result. Subsequently, *have* + past participle constructions became gram-maticized and began to be used not only where change of previous state was assumed but also where the event had no pre-existing state. Thus, alongside (3) we have:

(4)   *She has suffered great pain.*[3]

In the early stages of its existence, the English Perfect followed the pattern of the present-day German or French Perfect — it was formed with the forms of the equivalents of *have* or *be*, depending chiefly upon the transitive or intransitive character of the respective verb. Subsequently, *have* came to be the only auxiliary and the English Perfect became a com-pletely developed aspectual category, which spread over the whole English verb system with remarkable regularity. This development — unique in the German languages — was most probably influenced by the contacts of Eng-lish with the Celtic languages, which embody pronounced aspectual distinc-tions.

To wit, in Irish, Scots Gaelic and Welsh, these distinctions are not completely grammaticized. Perfective aspect is marked in these languages through periphrastic expressions containing temporal prepositions, just as progressive aspect is signalled by periphrastic expressions including locative prepositions.[4] The only pure grammatical aspectual signal in Celtic is the North Welsh Imperfect, denoting habitual aspect. Nevertheless, the notational meanings of the aspectual categories are, in the Celtic languages, very distinct, and the oppositions with non-aspectual constructions are regular enough to have helped the English Perfect become established as a fully-fledged aspectual category, denoting relevance of a preceding action at a given point of time, as well as to sponsor the development of the category of progressive aspect, reflecting the duration of an action over a time span[5] and that of habitual aspect, signalling the usual occurrence of a past action.

The category of perfective aspect in Macedonian is as distinctly grammaticized as in English. This is worth noting (and discussing!) since Macedonian belongs to the Slavonic family of languages, in many members of which the Perfect has gone through all Kuryłowicz's stages of development and beyond. So, in Russian, a Slavonic language which has been developing relatively independently of alien influences, the Aorist has completely vanished, and past actions are denoted by remnants of the Perfect signals — the active participle constituents of the former auxiliary *byt* 'be' + active participle constructions, which have lost their aspectual values. Compare the following Russian and Serbo-Croatian sentences, respectively:

(5)   R. *Ana   napisala   pis'mo.*[6]
          Ana   wrote (3rd f.   letter
          sg.non-dur.past)[7]
          'Ana wrote a/the letter.'
      SC. Ana   je napisala   pismo.
          Ana   is write (act. letter
          part.f.s.)
          'Ana wrote a/the letter.'

While in Serbo-Croatian the past tense is denoted by auxiliary + active participle construction, in Russian it is signalled through one single lexeme, which is formally equivalent to the Serbo-Croatian active participle. In Russian, as a matter of fact, not only the Perfect, but also the Imperfect has disappeared, and the contrast between the former Aorist and Imperfect is expressed by the presence or absence of the affixal markers of the durative aspect, the aspectual category *par excellence*, so characteristic of all modern Slavonic languages.

The West Slavonic languages, whose contacts with 'aliens' have been moderate, have also lost their respective Aorists and Imperfects and use their former Perfect forms to refer to past actions — though not without the auxiliary, except in the third person. In the Slavonic languages which take part in the Balkan Sprachbund, however, the Aorist and the Imperfect are still thriving; not equally well in all of them, it must be admitted.

Though all Serbo-Croatian grammars list the complete paradigms of the Aorist and the Imperfect, not all speakers of Serbo-Croatian use them. In fact, usage of these 'past tenses' is restricted to specific dialectal areas. Most educated speakers born since the Second World War would be able to tell you what *videh* 'see' 1st sg. Aorist and *vidah* 'see' 1st sg. Imperfect are. (They learnt it at school!) Neverteless, not only in their conversations but also in their writing, they would use *video sam* 'see' 1st m.sg.non-dur. Perfect and *vidao sam* 'see' 1st m.sg.dur. Perfect. The Perfect is very rapidly becoming the only past tense, *the* past tense, which assimilates the markers of the former Aorist/Imperfect distinction and transforms them into markers of Durative Aspect.

In Bulgarian, at least for the time being, no bell has tolled finally for either the Aorist or the Imperfect; they are still there. Yet, because of the interplay with an abundance of affixes marking the durative aspect, their functions are twisted. Both the Aorist and the Imperfect, and well as the Perfect, can combine with both Durative and Non-Durative Aorist, Durative or Non-Durative Imperfect and Durative and Non-Durative Perfect. The verb *hodi*[8] 'go', for example, has the following past forms:

(6)   *hodi* – Durative Aorist
        nahodi (se) – Non-Durative (Reflexive) Aorist
        hodeše – Durative Imperfect
        hodil sǝm – Durative Perfect
        nahodil sǝm (se) – Non-Durative (Reflexive) Perfect

Under the influence of Turkish, the exponents of the Perfect — various forms of *sǝm* 'be' + active participle — have in addition acquired the function of denoting reported actions and/or states. Thus, contact with an 'alien' language has constrained the movement of the Perfect through the four stages mentioned, its signals acquiring a wide scope of reference, in relation to which the forms of the Aorist, with their restricted function of denoting an action or a state that takes place at a certain past point of time, are marked.

In Macedonian, the Imperfect has become the past tense *par excellence*. The Aorist here appears only in certain set expressions, while the exponents of the Perfect — various forms of the verb *sum* 'be' + active participle — are being transformed into exponents of reporting modality, which combine with exponents of all other verbal categories. In this language, the contact with Turkish has completely turned the Perfect off the path it had been following in the other Slavonic languages; instead of developing into a past tense, it provides formal devices for expressing a modal category. The category of perfective aspect is not lost, however. Through intensive contacts with Albanian, Aromanian and Greek, the Macedonian Perfect is being reactivated with new exponents — forms of the verb *ima* 'have' + deverbative adverb, and forms of the verb *sum* 'be' + passive participle. The distribution of these exponents is not even. *Ima* + deverbative adverb, both with transitive and intransitive verbs, represents the Perfect of Experience, which denotes that the given event happened at least once up to the moment to which it refers. Examples:

(7)　a. *Dosega　　nemam　　　　jadeno*
　　　　until now　not have(1st sg.)　eaten(deverb.adv.)
　　　　vakva　　　riba.
　　　　such (f.prox.)　fish
　　　　'So far, I haven't eaten such a fish.'

　　　b. *Vo ovaa　　　　kuḱa　imam*
　　　　in　this(f.prox.sg.) house　have(1st sg.)
　　　　dojdeno　　　　　poveḱe pati.
　　　　come(deverb.adv.)　more　times
　　　　'In this house, I have been more than once.'

With transitive verbs only, the same signals also represent the Perfect of Result, which indicates that the given state is a result of a previous event. For example:

(8)　　*Knigata　veḱe　　ja　imam*
　　　　book the　already　her　have(1st sg.)
　　　　pročitano.
　　　　read(non-durat.deverb.adv.)
　　　　'The book, I have read it already.'

Sum + passive participle has a much more restricted usage — it signals the Perfect of Result with intransitive verbs. For example:

(9)   *Jadena*   *sum.*[9]
        eaten (pass.part.f.)   am
        'I have eaten.'

The Balkan Reporting Modality

In both Macedonian and Bulgarian the signals of the Perfect functions as signals of reported actions or states. Since in Bulgarian the latter function prompts the omission of the auxiliary *səm* 'be' in third person singular and plural number, grammarians of that language have been setting up two distinct paradigms of Past Indefinite and Past Reporting "tenses", respectively, which differ only in the presence or absence of auxiliary in only one person. For the verb *piše* 'write' one would thus have the following two paradigms:

(10)   Past Indefinite   Past Reporting

1st sg.	*pisal səm*	*pisal səm*
2nd sg.	*pisal si*	*pisal si*
3rd sg.	*pisa e*	*pisal*
1st pl.	*pisali sme*	*pisali sme*
2nd pl.	*pisali ste*	*pisali ste*
3rd pl.	*pisale sə*	*pisali*

Pairs of paradigms such as these have been paralleled with the Turkish sets of forms with *miş* + *dir* and only with *miş*, respectively. For the verb *yazmak* 'write' the latter sets would be as follows:

(11)   *miş* + *dir* forms   *miş* forms

1st sg.	*yazmişimdir*	*yazmişim*
2nd sg.	*yazmişindir*	*yazmişin*
3rd sg.	yazmiştir[10]	yazmiş
1st pl.	yazmişiktir	*yazmişik*
2nd pl.	*yazmişinizdir*	*yazmişiniz*
3rd pl.	yazmişlardir	*yazmişlar*

It has been argued (*cf.* Friedman 1978) that the presence of the (third person) auxiliary in the Bulgarian paradigm cancels the reporting function of the active participle, just as the presence of *dir* in the Turkish paradigm cancels the reporting function of *miş*. As I have pointed out (Tomić 1983a), this argument does not hold. Turkish being an agglutinative language, each suffix in its verb expression carries its own meaning and contributes to the meaning of the unit to which it is added. Thus, the suffix *dir* does not cancel the meaning of *miş* but enriches the verb expression with an additional meaning, that of assurance. Verb expressions containing both *miş* and *dir* have the value 'reported but very probable'. The speaker marks an event as reported but at the same time expresses a belief that it has taken or will take place.[11] Compare the following sentences:

(12) a. *Yarin   böyle   şeyler görecegiz.*
      tomorrow   such(prox.) things see(fut.1st pl.)
      'Tomorrow we shall see such things.'

   b. Yarin   böyle   *şeyler görecekmişiz.*
      tomorrow   such(prox.) things see fut. report. 1st pl.)
      'Tomorrow we shall, as reported, see such things.'

   c. Yarin   böyle   *şeyler görecekmişizdir.*
      tomorrow   such(prox.) things see(fut. reporting reassuring
                                            1st pl.)
      'Tomorrow we shall, as reported, for sure see such things.'

As we move from (12a) to (12b) and (12c) the verbal expressions are being enriched with an additional notional feature, which is represented by an additional morpheme. Just as reporting is representing by *miş*, assurance is signalled by *dir*. The occurrence of the latter morpheme is not contingent on the occurrence of the former. Compare (12) to:

(13) a. *Biliyorsunuz.*
      know (pres. 2nd pl.)
      'You know.'

   b. *Biliyorsunuzdur.*
      know (pres. reassuring 2nd pl.)
      'You surely know.'

The morpheme *miş* is lacking from both expressions; they differ, however, in having or not having the morpheme *dir*.

As for the alternation of verb expressions with and without the auxiliary *sem* 'be' in Bulgarian, it is in line with the general tendency in the Balkan Slavonic languages to leave out the auxiliaries in contexts in which reference is made to more than one point in time (cf. Tomić 1983a, 1984d). This tendency is observed even in Serbo-Croatian, a Balkan language in which reportedness is not grammaticized (cf. Grickat 1954). Compare:

(14) a. *Bio*   *je u žurbi*
       be(act.part.m.sg.) is in haste(loc.sg.)
       'He was in a hurry.'

      b. *Bio,*   *veli, u žurbi*
       be(act.part.m.sg.) says in haste(loc.sg.)
       'He was in a hurry, he says.'

In (14a), where we have just one verb expression, the active participle is followed by an auxiliary; in (14b), where reference is made to two points in time (one coextensive with the moment of speaking, the other prior to it), the auxiliary is left out.

In Bulgarian, the signals of the former Perfect have evolved into signals of a past tense which contrasts with Past Definite but has a very large range of functions, including the function of reporting. The omission of the auxiliary in third person is not *a priori* contingent on reporting and the delineation of two distinct paradigms, which differ only in the presence or absence of the auxiliary in only one person, is not warranted. As a matter of fact, the auxiliary often appears in reporting contexts, as well. Compare:

(15) a. *Ošte li*   *ne sə*
       still (inter.part.) not are(3rd pl.)
       došli?
       come(act.part.pl.)
       'Haven't they come yet?'

      b. *Čuh*   *če*   *ošte ne*
       heard(1st sg.) that(conj.) still not
       sə   *došli.*
       are(3rd pl.) come(act.part.pl.)
       'I heard that they haven't yet come.'

While in (15a) the predicate *sə došli* is indefinite, in (15b) it is reporting; formally, however, there is no distinction.

In Macedonian, there is no formal variation in the signals of the former Perfect, now used to denote reported actions and states. Yet, the overall functioning of these signals makes characterization difficult. Koneski (1967) points out that the Macedonian *sum* 'be' + active participle forms can refer not only to reported actions and states but also to events that happened at some time prior to the moment of speaking, or to events that took place at a certain time in the past. In the former case they overlap with the signals of the recently developed Perfective Aspect, in the latter — with those of the Past Indefinite, the Indo-European Aorist. Examine the following sets of sentences:

(16) a. *Go   nemam   odamna*
        him not have(1st sg.)   for a long time
        videno.
        see(deverb.adv.)
    b. Ne sum go videl   odamna.
        not am him see(act.part.m.sg.) for a long time.
        'I haven't seen him for a long time.'

(17) a. Se iznaprikašuvavme.
        (refl.part.) have a long chat(1st pl.non-dur.)
    b. *Sme   se   iznaprikažuvale*.
        are(1st pl.)   (refl.part.)   have a long chat(act.part.pl.)
        'We had a long chat.'

Both (16a) and (16b) denote an action that occurred some time before the moment of speaking, but the signals are forms of *ima* 'have' + deverbative adverb and *sum* 'be' + active participle, respectively. Both (17a) and (17b) refer to an action that took place at a certain time in the past, but whereas in the former sentence reference is made through a past definite tense in the latter — a *sum* 'be' + active participle form is used. These bothersome overlaps can be accounted for by the following respective facts:

A. The *sum* 'be' + active participle verb forms were for a long time functioning as signals of actions and/or states that occurred at an indefinite time prior to the moment of speaking. This function has subsequently been taken over by the *ima* 'have' + deverbative adverb forms. The takeover is, however, not complete.

B. One can treat as reported events that the speaker has witnessed but wants to emphasize. He does so by bringing into the scene another self of his, whose story he is telling.

Linguistic changes should not be treated as distinct phenomena which begin and end at definite points of time. They develop and disappear gradually. At a given span of time there are many changes under way, but they are never parallel — when one change is at its peak another may begin and a third one may be in its post-initial phase. The signals of the Indo-European Perfect, worn out and looking for a change of function throughout Europe, have in the Balkan Slavonic languages been shaping up into markers of reportedness, a grammatical category developed through contacts with Turkish. In Bulgarian, the traditional function of denoting indefinite time still prevails; there, reportedness has only widened the functional scope of the Past Indefinite — the former Perfect.[12] In Macedonian, however, while the exponents of the former Perfect were still in the process of extending the scope of their functions to cover reportedness, a new set of exponents for reference to past actions which refer to the moment of speaking appeared. As a consequence, the former exponents could develop into exponents of the modal category of reportedness, analogous to that in Turkish.

The explicit marking of categories not realized in other Slavonic languages, brought about through contacts with genetically remote or unrelated languages, has broken the old (present, past, perfect, future) tense-based verbal system of the language and has led to a system in which the exponents of only two tenses, present and past, interact with exponents of aspect (resultative in addition to, and not instead of, the typically Slavonic durative one) and modality (conditional as well as reporting). So, we have expressions which contain marked exponents of as many as seven grammatical categcries, tense being only one of them. Examine the following sentence:

(18)   *Do sega ke   si   go*
       till now (fut.part.) are(2nd sg.) him
       imal   naučeno
       have(act. part.m.sg.) learn (deverb.adv.non-dur.)
       da   pliva.
       to   swim(3rd sg.)
       'By now you would have, reportedly, taught him to swim.'

Here *ké* is an exponent of conditional modality, *si* contains features of person, number, tense and reporting modality, *imal* — of resultative aspect and reporting modality, *naučeno* — of durative and resultative aspects. The exponents of the former Perfect thus appear in a sentence that has no reference to the past. They have, as a matter of fact, lost their temporal function and occur in present, future and ex-temporal contexts as much as in past ones. Examine the following sentences:

(19) a. *Vo Teksas imale   po   dve*
        in Texas   have(act.part. each two
                   3rd pl.)

žetvi   *godišno.*
harvests   annually
'In Texas, they reportedly have two harvests annually.'

     b. *Ti*   *si*   *bila*   *posilna*   *od*   *nego*!
       you   are(2nd   be (act.part. stronger   than   him
            sg.)   3rd f.sg.)
       'You surprise me in being stronger than him!'

(19a) and (19b) do not make reference to any definite time.

It is interesting to note that the *sum* 'be' + active participle signals combine with other forms of the verb *sum* 'be', which in the Balkan Sprachbund have developed other specific functions. For example, they combine with a form equivalent to the second person singular past tense form of the verb *sum* 'be', *beše*, which imparts the meaning 'unlikely', 'hardly':

     (20)   a. *Na*   *vakov*   *den beše*   *si*
              on   such(prox.m.sg.) day   hardly   are(2nd sg.)
              me   *našla*   *doma.*
              me(acc.)   find(act.   at home
                         part.f.sg.)
              'On a day like this you would hardly find me at home.'

       b. *Beše*   *sme*   *im*   *go*
           hardly   are(1st pl.)   them(dat.)   it(acc.)
           videle   *liceto*!
           see(act.part.pl.) face the
           'We'll never see their face again!'

In (20a) *beše* refers to second person singular, in (20b) — to first person plural. While *sum* 'be' + active participle has lost its temporal function, *beše* (in the above context) has detached itself from all the functions it usually performs, the function of denoting second person singular, in that number.

The Macedonian dual standard

Verb expressions such as those in (16) through (20) are fully in accord with the Macedonian standard, which sanctions all the exponents they illustrate, though referring to reporting modality and resultative aspects as "the reporting function of the indefinite tense" and "the function of the *ima* + -

no forms", respectively (*cf.* for example Koneski 1967: 459-481, 502-506). Yet, not all speakers of the standard code of Macedonian use all these expressions. As a matter of fact, within the Macedonian standard code itself, two verb subsystems coexist. One of them has two past tenses: a Simple Past Tense (the former Imperfect) and a Composite Past Tense (the former Perfect); the latter, in addition to its traditional functions, signalling reported actions and states. The other system has only one past tense, whose exponents are in interaction with distinct exponents of more than one aspectual and modal category. Hence the overlaps illustrated in (16) and discussed in connection with it.

The two subsystems of the standard code are tightly connected with and lavishly nourished by the verb systems in individual dialects or rather groups of dialects. Whereas the need to grammaticize reportedness was felt throughout the territory of the Macedonian language community, the necessity to establish distinct formal exponents for an aspectual category which denote resultativeness of a past action in the moment of speaking appeared only in the Western and South-Western Macedonian dialect areas. Consequently, in Eastern and Northern Macedonia, the Indo-European Perfect evolved into a Past Indefinite Tense, with extended scope to cover the function of reportedness; in the West and South West, in its turn, we witness a complete restructuring of the verbal system.

When the Macedonian standard was codified (by and large in the late forties and in the fifties) the formal exponents and functional loads of both systems were sanctioned. This might have been done inadvertently, in which case no justification is in order; yet, looking carefully into the overall linguistic situation in synchrony and diachrony, one comes to think that, at least subconsciously, the codifiers might have been reasoning along the following lines: The *ima* + deverbative adverb forms have restricted scope of usage but they are built into the verbal systems of the Western dialects, which constitute the core of the Macedonian standard code.[13] In accordance with the tradition of standardization obtaining throughout the Slavonic world, the decision to base the standard on these dialects has been substantially influenced by the fact that they exhibit features that distinguish Macedonian from the neighbouring Slavonic language. As the *ima* + deverbative adverb forms count among those features, one couldn't keep them out of the standard code. Even less so, since they were assumed to belong to it in Misirkov's manifesto of Macedonian linguistic policy (Misirkov 1903),[14] to which the Macedonian linguists refer with reverence. On the other hand, the Macedonian speakers of the Eastern and Northern dialects, who outnumber those of the Western and South Western ones, express resultativeness through the signals of the old Perfect, which are also used to denote reported actions and states. So, one has to take into consideration those signals with that functional load. Even more, since the capital of Macedonia, Skopje, is in a Northern dialect area.

The use of the *ima* + deverbative adverb signals in the standard code is highly conditioned by the dialectal heritage of the respective speaker(s), and so is the functional load of the *sum* + active participle ones. Typically, a Macedonian develops in a specific local dialect atmosphere. If he lives in one of the provincial towns, he grows up with a specific local dialect — distinct from the one in the next town even when the latter is no more than ten to fifteen kilometers off — and with a version of the Macedonian standard, which includes all the elements that the dialect shares with the standard code, as well as a varying number of nonstandardized elements characteristic of the language of the area, but definitely excludes all optional standardized features which have their roots in another area. An average speaker of Macedonian who was born and lives in the captial would follow the same pattern; if he is well educated and involved in activities that require official communication, however, he would grow up with: (a) a local dialect, (b) a broader regional code in which the local dialect and the standard are interwoven[15] and (c) a version of the standard code excludes the optional standardized features rooted in an 'alien' dialect. Most complicated is the language situation of speakers who have moved into the capital — and these constitute a major factor, the city having more than tripled in population within the forty post-war years, largely through immigration from other parts of the republic. Adult immigrants usually keep the two codes with which they have grown up, though brushing up their versions of the standard code by getting rid of nonstandardized elements. Their children, however, grow up with three code: (a) the dialect of the parents, (b) a broader regional code in which the local Skopje dialect and the standard interweave, but which is to some extent influenced by the dialect of their parents as well, and (c) a version of the standard code in which the standard codes of the Macedonian speakers in one's environment intersect. Things being as they are, the *ima* + deverbative adverb forms are part of the standard codes of the Western dialect speakers and of those of their immediate descendants; all other speakers of Macedonian develop standard codes in which the *sum* + active participle signals have a very wide scope of functions, including resultativeness and reportedness.

Lunt (1984:126) benevolently contends that "standard Macedonian has the same sort of problems in maintaining consistency and uniformity that every European language has — the differences are matters of specific detail". I find it difficult to go along with this contention. The dual verbal system is not a 'matter of specific detail', nor are the factors that have brought it about: (a) the discrepancy between the verbal system of the dialect area of the capital and those of the dialect areas which had served as a basis for the standard code, (b) the persistent prestige of (at least some of) the Western dialects over the Eastern and Northern ones[16] and (c) the very intensive immigration into the capital. If these factors were not in constant operation[17], one would have expected the system used in the dialect area of the capital to prevail. As it is, not only do both systems continue to be used, but usage of one or the other has secondary symbolic effects.[18] The *ima* + deverbative adverb, along with another very distinct feature of the Western dialect which has entered the standard, the triple definite article, symbolises superiority of linguistic manners. The use of *sum* + active participle has the opposite effect of imparting solidarity with the broader regional code of Skopje, which shows signals of developing into a colloquial register. In spite of their prestige effect, the use of Western features for which the standard allows an alternative do not spread among Macedonian speakers with Eastern and Northern dialectal heritage, who (one must remember) outnumber those with Western and South Western one. What's more, especially in the capital, the influence of Serbo-Croatian, a language spoken by the majority of the inhabitants of four out of the six Yugoslav republics[19], exerts standing influence and even shifts linguistic choice in a direction opposite to the one it would be expected to follow if the prestige factor were left to operate undisturbed. Thus, the *sum* + active participle construction not only intersects with the *ima* + deverbative adverb one but also shows signs of joining its Serbo-Croatian formal counterpart in its successful efforts to function as a general past tnese. I have heard the Skopje born Macedonian speakers use the *sum* + active participle forms when speaking of events which had occurred in their presence and whose occurrence they do not question. Examine this sentence:

(20) *Kako možeš   toa da go*
      how   can(2nd sg.) it   to it(acc.m.)
      tvrdiš   koga jas sum bila
      contend(2nd sg.)   when I   am   be(act.part.f.sg.)

tamo   i   sve sum videla.
there and   all   am   see(act.part.f.sg.)
'How can you contend that when I was there and saw everything?!'

An event which was witnessed by the speaker is here referred to by the
forms of the old Perfect. Thus, while contacts with genetically remote languages divert linguistic development off the course typically taken by the
members of its linguistic family, reintensified contacts with genetically close
languages pull it back and try to fit it into the general current of evolution.

The meaning/form relationship in any language is in a permanent state
of flux. In areas where contacts with genetically remote languages are
intensive this flux is specifically observable. There it penetrates deeply into
the systems of the standard code itself, thus breaking the dichotomy lan-
guage/dialect and transforming it into a continuum with the dialects of the
inhabitants of remote places whose mobility is restricted, at one end, and
an idealized standard code, at the other.

Notes

1.   This duality is historically conditioned. As Bugarski (1984) points out, the notions "lan-
      guage" and "dialect" abstract over the notion "idiolect". These abstractions are, however,
      of different orders and the scale idiolect-dialect-language cannot be regulated only quan-
      titatively.

2.   Not all Indo-European languages developed the Imperfect. The Germanic languages lack
      it altogether.

3.   Note that sentences such as (3) do not have "causative" counterparts.

4.   Initially, the English Progressive also included a locative preposition. Consider the some-
      what obsolete:

          He is a-coming.

5.   Examples such as:

          a. *He is come.*
          b. *He is gone.*

      are residuals from those stages.

6.   All items are rendered in Latin script.

7.   The grammatical features of individual items are denoted only when they do not transpire
      through the translation.

8.   Since the Bulgarian and Macedonian verbs have no infinitive forms we shall be represent-
      ing them through their third person, singular number, present tense forms, which are

morphologically least complicated and can be treated as unmarked. The only exception will be the equivalents of the auxiliary *be*, whose third person, singular number, present tense forms cannot be morphonologically related to the other forms; they will be represented through their first person, singular number, present tense forms — B. *səm*; M. *sum*.

9.   Note that intensive contacts with genetically relatively remote languages have kept the Greek, Albanian and Aromenian Perfect in the third of Kuryłowicz's four stages of development, with equivalents of *have* as uniform exponents. The introduction of the auxiliary *ima* 'have' as a signal for the new Macedonian Perfect is actually analogous to the auxiliaries in the perfects of these languages. Compare:

M.	*Vakva*	*riba*		*nemam*	*jadeno.*
Al.	*Ksi*	*peshku*	*nuc kam*		*ngrana.*
Gr.	*Tetio*	*psari*	*en*	*eho*	*fai.*
Ar.	*Ahtarä*	*pesku*	*nu*	*am*	*mäkatä.*
	such	fish		not have	eaten.

'I haven't eaten such a fish.'

The correspondence of the sentence constituents is remarkable.

10. The morphonological variation (*dir* versus *tir* in this case) is the result of consonant and vowel harmony.

11. The cumulative meaning 'reporting-reassuring' is not restricted to Turkish; we also find it in Macedonian, where it is signalled by combination of exponents of the modal *ke*, used for denoting futurity, plus the particle *da* 'to' and the auxiliary *sum* 'be' + active participle:

Ke   *da sum zaspal.*
(fut.part.) to   am   fall asleep(act. part. non-dur.m.)
'I have, to be sure, fallen asleep (though I am not aware of it).'

Note that the Bulgarian verb *šte* 'will/want', which comes from the same Common Slavonic root as the Macedonian *ke*, is a fully inflected verb which in combination with the particle *da* 'to' imparts the meaning 'be about to'.

12. Note that the functioning of *səm* + active participle forms as signals of reportedness in non past verb expressions indicates that a core for the establishment of a new category is being established. Examine the following sentences:

   a. *Trjabva   da nauča   frenski.*
       have(pres. to   learn(1st   French
       impers.)   sg.pres.)
       'I have to learn French.'

   b. *Trjabva   da səem naučel   frenski.*
       have(pres. to   am   learn(act. French
       impers.)   part.m.)
       'They save I have to learn French.'

   c. *Pijva   edno   kafe   ako   ima.*
       drink(3rd   one/a(neutr.) coffee if   have(pres.
       sg.pres.)   impers.)
       'He would take a cup of coffee if there is any.'

   d. *Pijval*   *edno*   *kafe* *ako* *ima.*
     drink(act. one/a(neutr.) coffee if   have(pres.
     part.3rd
     m.sg.)
     'He would, reportedly, take a cup of coffee if there is any.'

Sentences b. and d. have reporting verbs which are used in imperative and conditional contexts, respectively. Each of them contrasts with a sentence in the Present Simple Tense.

13.   The choice of the Western dialects was not made after Macedonia became part of the Yugoslav federation; the Macedonian grammarians of the late forties, fifties and sixties only described explicitly and sanctioned a code which had begun developing in the 19th century and whose basic distinctive features were shaped in the first half of this century.

14.   Misirkov calls for the establishment of a Macedonian literary language based on the Prilep-Bitola Western dialects. As Friedman (1985) points out, his book *Za Makedonckite raboti* [On Macedonian Matters] (Misirkov 1903) is a valuable document for the fact that the concept of a Macedonian nationality and literary language was already clearly defined by the beginning of the century, and not created *ex nihilo* by Yugoslav fiat in 1944.

15.   This regional code moves in the direction of becoming a regional register.

16.   The prestige follows not only from the choice of these dialects as the core for the standard code, but also from the fact that throughout history it was in the Western dialect area that the cultural centers were situated. Anyhow, these two phenomena are interdependent.

17.   Lencek (1981:42) points out that every language has unifying, separating and prestige functions. They are charged with symbolism "which in the Slavic societies has served and still serves as a peculiarly potent image of the social solidarity of those who speak the language".

18.   Kalogjera (1985:99) is specifically concerned with secondary, symbolic effects off language. Discussing the attitude toward Serbo-Croatian language varieties he says that the process of standardization of Serbo-Croatian has given rise to "specific attitudes toward dialects, particularly in the educated sector of the population and among men of letters". He stresses that such attitudes occur "in situations where one of the existing dialects obtains favourite treatment and becomes selected as the basis for the standard language".

19.   Serbo-Croatian penetrates through the mass media. It is also the language Macedonians use when speaking to Yugoslavs who do not speak Macedonian. One should, however, note that the dialects of Serbo-Croatian and Macedonian form a continuum. There are substantial differences between Western Serbo-Croatian and Southern Macedonian, but the differences between Southern Serbo-Croatian and Northern Macedonian are very small. This is one more reason why Macedonian speakers of the Northern Macedonian dialect of Skopje should be so receptive to Serbo-Croatian influence.

References

Andrejčin, L. 1938. *Kategorie znaczeniowe koniugacji bułgarskej* [The meaning categories of the Bulgarian conjugations]. Kraków: Polska akademie umiejętności.

Aronson, H.I. 1977. "Interrelationships between Aspect and Mood in Bulgarian". *Folia Slavica*.1: 9-32.

Belan, A.T. 1958. *Nova bəlgarska gramatika za vsjakogo*. Djal I: *Za dumite*. Sveska treta: *Glagol* [New Bulgarian Grammar for Everybody. Part I: For the Words. Book 3: The Verb]. Sofija.

Bugarski, R. 1984a. "Jezik i dijalekt" [Language and dialect]. In: Tomić. 1984b: 25-32.

-----. 1984b. Jezik i nacija" [Language and nation]. *Sveske Institute za proučavanje nacionalnih odnosa* 5-6: 23-27.

Comrie, G. 1977. *Aspect*. Cambridge: Cambridge University Press.

Friedman, V.A. 1977. *The Grammatical Categories of the Macedonian Indicative*. Columbus: Slavica.

-----. 1978. *"On the semantic and morphological influence of Turkish on Balkan Slavic." Papers from the Fourteenth Regional Meeting*. Chicago: Chicago Linguistic Society. 108-118.

-----. 1985. "The sociolinguistics of literary Macedonian". *International Journal of the Sociology of Language* 52: 31-57.

Gołąb, Z. 1960. "The influence of Turkish upon the Macedonian Slavonic dialects". *Folia Orientalia*. 1: 26-45.

Grickat, I. 1954. *O perfektu bez pomoćnog glagola u srpsko-hrvatskom jeziku i srodnim sintaktičkim pojavama* [On the Perfect without an Auxiliary Verb in Serbocroatian, and Related Syntactic Phenomena]. Beograd: Srpska akademija nauka.

Jakobson, R. 1932. "Zur Struktur des russischen Verbums". *Charisteria G. Mathesio*. Prague: Cercle Linguistique de Prague. 74-84.

Jespersen, O. 1924. *The Philosophy of Grammar*. London: George, Allen and Unwin.

Kalogjera, D. 1985. "Attitudes toward Serbo-Croatian language varieties". *International Journal of the Sociology of Language* 52: 93-109.

Klein, H.G. 1974. *Tempus, Aspekt, Aktionsart*. Tübingen: Niemeyer.

Koneski, B. 1967. *Gramatika na makedonskiot literaturen jazik* [A grammar of Standard Macedonian]. Skopje: Kultura.

Kucarov, I. 1976. "Izrazjavane na preizkaznost v slavjanskite ezici črez vmjatane na modificirašti dumi, izrazi i izrečenija" [The expression of reportedness in the Slavonic languages through insertion of modifying words, phrases and sentences]. *Godišnik na Sofijskija univerzitet. Fakultet po slavjanski filologii* 69: 3.

Kuryłowicz, J. 1964. *The inflectional categories of Indo-European.* Heidelberg: Carl Winter.

-----. 1971a. "The evolution of grammatical categories". In: Kuryłowiecz. 1971b: 38-54.

-----. 1971b. *Esquisses linguistiques* 2. München: Wilhelm Fink.

Lencek, R. 1981. "On sociolinguistic determinants in the evolution of Slavic literary languages." In: D. Stone and G. Worth (eds). 1981: 39-51.

Lunt, H. 1984. "Some sociolinguistic aspects of Macedonian and Bulgarian". In: B.A. Stolz, *et al.* (eds). 1984: 83-132.

Mac Mathúna, L. and D. Singleton (eds). 1983. *Language Across Cultures.* Dublin: Irish Association for Applied Linguistics.

Misirkov, K.P. 1903. *Za makedonckite raboti* [For the Macedonian Matters]. Sofija: Liberalni klub. (Reprinted 1974. Skopje: Institut za makedonski jazik.)

Palmer, F.R. 1965. *A Linguistic Study of the English Verb.* London: Longman.

Panevoná, J., E. Benešová, and P. Sgall. 1971. *Čas a modalité v češčině* [Tense and Modality in Czech]. Praha: Universita Karlova.

Stolz, B.A., *et al.* (eds). 1984. *Language and Literary Theory. In Honor of Ladislav Matejka.* Ann Arbor, MI: Department of Slavic Languages and Literatures.

Stone, G. and D. Worth (eds). 1981. *The Formation of the Slavonic Literary Languages.* Columbus: Slavica.

Tomić, O. Mišeska. 1981. "Typological features of Balkan languages and their pedagogical consequences". *Studia Linguistica* 35.1-2: 183-205.

-----. 1983a. "Linguistic Features and Grammatical Categories". *Folia Linguistica* 17. 1-4: 387-401.

-----. 1983b. "Grammatical categories across cultures". In: L. Mac Mathúna and D. Singleton (eds). 1983: 31-39.

-----. 1984a. "Jazičnite kontakti i gramatičkite kategorii" [Language contacts and grammatical categories]. In: O.M. Tomić (ed.). 1984b: 11-17.

----- (ed.). 1984b. *Jazičnite kontakti vo jugoslovenskata zaednica* [Language contacts within the Yugoslav community]. Skopje: Sojuz na društvata za primeneta lingvistika na Jugoslavija.

-----. 1984c. "Jezički kontakt i jezički kod" [Language contact and language code]. *Sveske Institute za proučavanje nacionalnih odnosa* 5-6: 23-27.

-----. 1984d. "Prekažanosta kako modalna kategorija" [Reportedness as a modal category]. *Zbornik vo čest na Blaže Koneski*. Skopje: Univerzitet Kiril i Metodij. 161-170.

In the series LINGUISTIC AND LITERARY STUDIES IN EASTERN EUROPE the following volumes have been published and will be published during 1989:

1. ODMARK, John (ed.): *LANGUAGE, LITERATURE & MEANING. I: Problems of Literary Theory.* Amsterdam, 1979.
2. ibid. *II: Current Trends in Literary Research.* Amsterdam, 1980.
3. BAUR, Rupprecht S., et al.: *RESÜMIERENDE AUSWAHLBIBLIOGRAPHIE ZUR NEUEREN SOWJETISCHEN SPRACHLEHRFORSCHUNG (gesteuerter Fremdsprachenerwerb).* Amsterdam, 1980.
4. KIEFER, Férenc (ed.): *HUNGARIAN GENERAL LINGUISTICS.* Amsterdam, 1982.
5. ZIMA, Peter V. (ed.): *SEMIOTICS AND DIALECTICS: Ideology and the Text.* Amsterdam, 1981.
6. FIZER, John: *Psychologism and Psychoaesthetics: A Historical and Critical View of Their Relations.* Amsterdam, 1981.
7. SMITH, Barry (ed.): *STRUCTURE AND GESTALT: Philosophy and literature in Austria-Hungary and her successor states.* Amsterdam, 1981.
8. STEINER, P., M. ČERVENKA & R. VROON (eds): *THE STRUCTURE OF THE LITERARY PROCESS: Studies dedicated to the Memory of Felix Vodička.* Amsterdam, 1982.
9. *PRAGUE STUDIES IN MATHEMATICAL LINGUISTICS,* vol. 7. Amsterdam, 1981.
10. SCHMID, Herta & Aloysius Van KESTEREN (eds): *SEMIOTICS OF DRAMA AND THEATRE.* Amsterdam, 1985.
11. BOJTÁR, Endre: *Slavic Structuralism in Literary Science.* Transl. from the Hungarian. Amsterdam, 1985.
12. VACHEK, J. (ed.): *PRAGUIANA: Some Basic and Less Known Aspects of the Prague Linguistic School.* Amsterdam, 1983.
13. MEL'ČUK, Igor A. & Nikolaj V. PERTSOV: *Surface Syntax of English: a Formal Model within the Meaning-Text Framework.* Amsterdam, 1987.
14. ŠVEJCER, A.D.: *Contemporary Sociolinguistics.* Amsterdam, 1986.
15. ŠVEJCER, A.D. & L.B. NIKOL'SKIJ: *Introduction to Sociolinguistics.* Amsterdam, 1986.
16. SGALL, Petr (ed.): *CONTRIBUTIONS TO FUNCTIONAL SYNTAX, SEMANTICS, AND LANGUAGE COMPREHENSION.* Amsterdam, 1984.
17. *PRAGUE STUDIES IN MATHEMATICAL LINGUISTICS.* Volume 8. Amsterdam, 1983.
18. SHCHEGLOV, Yu & A. ZHOLKOVSKY: *Poetics of Expressiveness: A Theory and Application.* Amsterdam, 1987.
19. COMPENDIUM OF RUSSIAN AVANT-GARDE TERMINOLOGY. Taken from the program. Instead: MEY, Jacob (ed.): *LANGUAGE AND DISCOURSE: TEST AND PROTEST. A Festschrift for Petr Sgall.* Amsterdam, 1986.
20. DIRVEN, R. & W. FRIED (eds): *FUNCTIONALISM IN LINGUISTICS.* Amsterdam, 1987.
21. ANDRÁS, Lászlo & Zoltán KOVECSES (comps): *HUNGARIAN-ENGLISH SLANG DICTIONARY.* Amsterdam, 1988. n.y.p.

22. *PRAGUE STUDIES IN MATHEMATICAL LINGUISTICS*. Volume 9. Amsterdam, 1987.
23. CHLOUPEK, Jan and Jiří NEKVAPIL (eds): *READER IN CZECH SOCIOLINGUISTICS*. Amsterdam, 1987.
24. VOLEK, Bronislava: *Emotive Signs in Language and Semantic Functioning of Derived Nouns in Russian*. Amsterdam, 1987.
25. BUSZKOWSKI, W., W. MARCISZEWSKI & J. van BENTHEM (eds): *CATEGORIAL GRAMMAR*. Amsterdam/Philadelphia, 1988.
26. RADOVANOVIĆ, Milorad (ed.): *YUGOSLAV GENERAL LINGUISTICS*. Amsterdam/Philadelphia, 1989.
27. TOBIN, Yishai (ed.): *THE PRAGUE SCHOOL AND ITS LEGACY*. Amsterdam/Philadelphia, 1988.
28. TOMASZCYCK, Jerzy (ed.): *METALINGUISTIC BEHAVIOUR AND LANGUAGE STUDY*. Amsterdam/Philadelphia, 1989. n.y.p.
29. PETERSON, Ronald E.: *A History of Russian Symbolism*. Amsterdam/Philadelphia, 1989. n.y.p.
30. FISIAK, Jacek (ed.): *FURTHER INSIGHTS INTO CONTRASTIVE ANALYSIS*. Amsterdam/Philadelphia, 1989. n.y.p.
31. RANCOUR-LAFERRIERE, Daniel (ed.): *RUSSIAN LITERATURE AND PSYCHOANALYSIS*. Amsterdam/Philadelphia, 1989. n.y.p.
32. MILOSAVLJEVIC, Petar (ed.): *YUGOSLAV LITERARY-THEORETICAL THOUGHT*. Amsterdam/Philadelphia, 1989. n.y.p.